THE MATHEMATICAL THEORY
OF
RELATIVITY

BY

A. S. EDDINGTON, M.A., M.Sc., F.R.S.

PLUMIAN PROFESSOR OF ASTRONOMY AND EXPERIMENTAL
PHILOSOPHY IN THE UNIVERSITY OF CAMBRIDGE

CAMBRIDGE
AT THE UNIVERSITY PRESS
1923

PREFACE

A FIRST draft of this book was published in 1921 as a mathematical supplement to the French Edition of *Space, Time and Gravitation*. During the ensuing eighteen months I have pursued my intention of developing it into a more systematic and comprehensive treatise on the mathematical theory of Relativity. The matter has been rewritten, the sequence of the argument rearranged in many places, and numerous additions made throughout; so that the work is now expanded to three times its former size. It is hoped that, as now enlarged, it may meet the needs of those who wish to enter fully into these problems of reconstruction of theoretical physics.

The reader is expected to have a general acquaintance with the less technical discussion of the theory given in *Space, Time and Gravitation*, although there is not often occasion to make direct reference to it. But it is eminently desirable to have a general grasp of the revolution of thought associated with the theory of Relativity before approaching it along the narrow lines of strict mathematical deduction. In the former work we explained how the older conceptions of physics had become untenable, and traced the gradual ascent to the ideas which must supplant them. Here our task is to formulate mathematically this new conception of the world and to follow out the consequences to the fullest extent.

The present widespread interest in the theory arose from the verification of certain minute deviations from Newtonian laws. To those who are still hesitating and reluctant to leave the old faith, these deviations will remain the chief centre of interest; but for those who have caught the spirit of the new ideas the observational predictions form only a minor part of the subject. It is claimed for the theory that it leads to an understanding of the world of physics clearer and more penetrating than that previously attained, and it has been my aim to develop the theory in a form which throws most light on the origin and significance of the great laws of physics.

It is hoped that difficulties which are merely analytical have been minimised by giving rather fully the intermediate steps in all the proofs with abundant cross-references to the auxiliary formulae used.

For those who do not read the book consecutively attention may be called to the following points in the notation. The summation convention (p. 50) is used. German letters always denote the product of the corresponding English letter by $\sqrt{-g}$ (p. 111). $\mathfrak{H}$ is the symbol for "Hamiltonian differentiation" introduced on p. 139. An asterisk is prefixed to symbols generalised so as to be independent of or covariant with the gauge (p. 203).

A selected list of original papers on the subject is given in the Bibliography at the end, and many of these are sources (either directly or at second-hand) of the developments here set forth. To fit these into a continuous chain of deduction has involved considerable modifications from their original form, so that it has not generally been found practicable to indicate the sources of the separate sections. A frequent cause of deviation in treatment is the fact that in the view of most contemporary writers the Principle of Stationary Action is the final governing law of the world; for reasons explained in the text I am unwilling to accord it so exalted a position. After the original papers of Einstein, and those of de Sitter from which I first acquired an interest in the theory, I am most indebted to Weyl's *Raum, Zeit, Materie*. Weyl's influence will be especially traced in §§ 49, 58, 59, 61, 63, as well as in the sections referring to his own theory.

I am under great obligations to the officers and staff of the University Press for their help and care in the intricate printing.

A. S. E.

10 *August* 1922.

CONTENTS

PAGE

INTRODUCTION 1

CHAPTER I

ELEMENTARY PRINCIPLES

SECTION

1. Indeterminateness of the space-time frame 8
2. The fundamental quadratic form 10
3. Measurement of intervals 11
4. Rectangular coordinates and time 13
5. The Lorentz transformation 17
6. The velocity of light 18
7. Timelike and spacelike intervals 22
8. Immediate consciousness of time 23
9. The "3+1 dimensional" world 25
10. The FitzGerald contraction 25
11. Simultaneity at different places 27
12. Momentum and Mass 29
13. Energy 32
14. Density and temperature 33
15. General transformations of coordinates 34
16. Fields of force 37
17. The Principle of Equivalence 39
18. Retrospect. 41

CHAPTER II

THE TENSOR CALCULUS

19. Contravariant and covariant vectors. 43
20. The mathematical notion of a vector 44
21. The physical notion of a vector 47
22. The summation convention 50
23. Tensors 51
24. Inner multiplication and contraction. The quotient law 52
25. The fundamental tensors 55
26. Associated tensors 56
27. Christoffel's 3-index symbols 58
28. Equations of a geodesic 59
29. Covariant derivative of a vector 60
30. Covariant derivative of a tensor 62
31. Alternative discussion of the covariant derivative 65
32. Surface-elements and Stokes's theorem 66
33. Significance of covariant differentiation 68
34. The Riemann-Christoffel tensor 71
35. Miscellaneous formulae 74

CHAPTER III

THE LAW OF GRAVITATION

SECTION		PAGE
36	The condition for flat space-time. Natural coordinates	76
37	Einstein's law of gravitation	81
38.	The gravitational field of an isolated particle	82
39.	Planetary orbits	85
40	The advance of perihelion	88
41	The deflection of light	90
42.	Displacement of the Fraunhofer lines	91
43.	Isotropic coordinates	93
44	Problem of two bodies—Motion of the moon	95
45.	Solution for a particle in a curved world	100
46	Transition to continuous matter	101
47.	Experiment and deductive theory	104

CHAPTER IV

RELATIVITY MECHANICS

48	The antisymmetrical tensor of the fourth rank	107
49	Element of volume. Tensor-density	109
50	The problem of the rotating disc	112
51.	The divergence of a tensor	113
52.	The four identities	115
53.	The material energy-tensor	116
54.	New derivation of Einstein's law of gravitation	119
55	The force	122
56.	Dynamics of a particle	125
57.	Equality of gravitational and inertial mass. Gravitational waves	128
58	Lagrangian form of the gravitational equations	131
59	Pseudo-energy-tensor of the gravitational field	134
60.	Action	137
61.	A property of invariants	140
62.	Alternative energy-tensors	141
63	Gravitational flux from a particle	144
64.	Retrospect	146

CHAPTER V

CURVATURE OF SPACE AND TIME

65	Curvature of a four-dimensional manifold	149
66	Interpretation of Einstein's law of gravitation	152
67	Cylindrical and spherical space-time	155
68.	Elliptical space	157
69.	Law of gravitation for curved space-time	159
70.	Properties of de Sitter's spherical world	161
71.	Properties of Einstein's cylindrical world	166
72.	The problem of the homogeneous sphere	168

CHAPTER VI

ELECTRICITY

SECTION PAGE
73. The electromagnetic equations 171
74. Electromagnetic waves 175
75. The Lorentz transformation of electromagnetic force . . 179
76. Mechanical effects of the electromagnetic field 180
77. The electromagnetic energy-tensor 182
78. The gravitational field of an electron 185
79. Electromagnetic action 187
80. Explanation of the mechanical force 189
81. Electromagnetic volume 193
82. Macroscopic equations 194

CHAPTER VII

WORLD GEOMETRY

PART I. WEYL'S THEORY

83. Natural geometry and world geometry 196
84. Non-integrability of length 198
85. Transformation of gauge-systems 200
86. Gauge-invariance 202
87 The generalised Riemann-Christoffel tensor 204
88. The in-invariants of a region 205
89. The natural gauge 206
90. Weyl's action-principle 209

PART II. GENERALISED THEORY

91. Parallel displacement 213
92. Displacement round an infinitesimal circuit 214
93. Introduction of a metric 216
94 Evaluation of the fundamental in-tensors 218
95. The natural gauge of the world 219
96 The principle of identification 222
97. The bifurcation of geometry and electrodynamics 223
98. General relation-structure 224
99. The tensor $*B^{\epsilon}_{\mu\nu\sigma}$ 226
100. Dynamical consequences of the general properties of world-invariants . 228
101. The generalised volume 232
102. Numerical values 235
103. Conclusion 237
BIBLIOGRAPHY 241
INDEX 244

INTRODUCTION

THE subject of this mathematical treatise is not pure mathematics but physics. The vocabulary of the physicist comprises a number of words such as length, angle, velocity, force, work, potential, current, etc., which we shall call briefly "physical quantities" Some of these terms occur in pure mathematics also; in that subject they may have a generalised meaning which does not concern us here. The pure mathematician deals with ideal quantities defined as having the properties which he deliberately assigns to them. But in an experimental science we have to discover properties not to assign them; and physical quantities are defined primarily according to the way in which we recognise them when confronted by them in our observation of the world around us.

Consider, for example, a length or distance between two points. It is a numerical quantity associated with the two points; and we all know the procedure followed in practice in assigning this numerical quantity to two points in nature. A definition of distance will be obtained by stating the exact procedure; that clearly must be the primary definition if we are to make sure of using the word in the sense familiar to everybody. The pure mathematician proceeds differently, he defines distance as an attribute of the two points which obeys certain laws—the axioms of the geometry which he happens to have chosen—and he is not concerned with the question how this "distance" would exhibit itself in practical observation. So far as his own investigations are concerned, he takes care to use the word self-consistently; but it does not necessarily denote the thing which the rest of mankind are accustomed to recognise as the distance of the two points

To find out any physical quantity we perform certain practical operations followed by calculations, the operations are called experiments or observations according as the conditions are more or less closely under our control. The physical quantity so discovered is primarily the result of the operations and calculations, it is, so to speak, *a manufactured article*—manufactured by our operations But the physicist is not generally content to believe that the quantity he arrives at is something whose nature is inseparable from the kind of operations which led to it; he has an idea that if he could become a god contemplating the external world, he would see his manufactured physical quantity forming a distinct feature of the picture. By finding that he can lay x unit measuring-rods in a line between two points, he has manufactured the quantity x which he calls the distance between the points, but he believes that that distance x is something already existing in the picture of the world—a gulf which would be apprehended by a superior intelligence as existing in itself without reference to the notion of operations with measuring-rods.

Yet he makes curious and apparently illogical discriminations. The parallax of a star is found by a well-known series of operations and calculations; the distance across the room is found by operations with a tape-measure. Both parallax and distance are quantities manufactured by our operations, but for some reason we do not expect parallax to appear as a distinct element in the true picture of nature in the same way that distance does. Or again, instead of cutting short the astronomical calculations when we reach the parallax, we might go on to take the cube of the result, and so obtain another manufactured quantity, a "cubic parallax." For some obscure reason we expect to see distance appearing plainly as a gulf in the true world-picture; parallax does not appear directly, though it can be exhibited as an angle by a comparatively simple construction, and cubic parallax is not in the picture at all. The physicist would say that he *finds* a length, and *manufactures* a cubic parallax; but it is only because he has inherited a preconceived theory of the world that he makes the distinction. We shall venture to challenge this distinction.

Distance, parallax and cubic parallax have the same kind of potential existence even when the operations of measurement are not actually made—*if* you will move sideways you will be able to determine the angular shift, *if* you will lay measuring-rods in a line to the object you will be able to count their number. Any one of the three is an indication to us of some existent condition or relation in the world outside us—a condition not created by our operations. But there seems no reason to conclude that this world-condition *resembles* distance any more closely than it resembles parallax or cubic parallax. Indeed any notion of "resemblance" between physical quantities and the world-conditions underlying them seems to be inappropriate. If the length AB is double the length CD, the parallax of B from A is half the parallax of D from C; there is undoubtedly some world-relation which is different for AB and CD, but there is no reason to regard the world-relation of AB as being better represented by double than by half the world-relation of CD.

The connection of manufactured physical quantities with the existent world-condition can be expressed by saying that the physical quantities are *measure-numbers* of the world-condition. Measure-numbers may be assigned according to any code, the only requirement being that the same measure-number always indicates the same world-condition and that different world-conditions receive different measure-numbers. Two or more physical quantities may thus be measure-numbers of the same world-condition, *but in different codes*, e.g. parallax and distance; mass and energy; stellar magnitude and luminosity. The constant formulae connecting these pairs of physical quantities give the relation between the respective codes. But in admitting that physical quantities can be used as measure-numbers of world-conditions existing independently of our operations, we do not alter their status as manufactured quantities. The same series of operations will naturally manufacture the same result when world-conditions are the same, and different results when they are different. (Differences of world-conditions which do not influence the results of experiment and observation are *ipso facto* excluded from the domain of physical knowledge.) The size to which a crystal grows may be a measure-number of the temperature of the mother-liquor, but it is none the less a manufactured size, and we do not conclude that the true nature of size is caloric.

The study of physical quantities, although they are the results of our own operations (actual or potential), gives us some kind of knowledge of the world-conditions, since the same operations will give different results in different world-conditions. It seems that this indirect knowledge is all that we can ever attain, and that it is only through its influences on such operations that we can represent to ourselves a "condition of the world." Any attempt to describe a condition of the world otherwise is either mathematical symbolism or meaningless jargon. To grasp a condition of the world as completely as it is in our power to grasp it, we must have in our minds a symbol which comprehends at the same time its influence on the results of all possible kinds of operations. Or, what comes to the same thing, we must contemplate its measures according to all possible measure-codes—of course, without confusing the different codes. It might well seem impossible to realise so comprehensive an outlook, but we shall find that the mathematical calculus of tensors does represent and deal with world-conditions precisely in this way. A tensor expresses simultaneously the whole group of measure-numbers associated with any world-condition; and machinery is provided for keeping the various codes distinct. For this reason the somewhat difficult tensor calculus is not to be regarded as an evil necessity in this subject, which ought if possible to be replaced by simpler analytical devices; our knowledge of conditions in the external world, as it comes to us through observation and experiment, is precisely of the kind which can be expressed by a tensor and not otherwise. And, just as in arithmetic we can deal freely with a billion objects without trying to visualise the enormous collection; so the tensor calculus enables us to deal with the world-condition in the totality of its aspects without attempting to picture it.

Having regard to this distinction between physical quantities and world-conditions, we shall not define a physical quantity as though it were a feature in the world-picture which had to be sought out. *A physical quantity is defined by the series of operations and calculations of which it is the result.* The tendency to this kind of definition had progressed far even in pre-relativity physics. Force had become "mass × acceleration," and was no longer an invisible agent in the world-picture, at least so far as its definition was concerned. Mass is defined by experiments on inertial properties, no longer as "quantity of matter." But for some terms the older kind of definition (or lack of definition) has been obstinately adhered to; and for these the relativity theory must find new definitions. In most cases there is no great difficulty in framing them We do not need to ask the physicist what conception he attaches to "length"; we watch him measuring length, and frame our definition according to the operations he performs There may sometimes be cases in which theory outruns experiment and requires us to decide between two definitions, either of which would be consistent with present experimental practice, but usually we can foresee which of them corresponds to the ideal which the experimentalist has set before himself For example, until recently the practical man was never confronted with problems of non-Euclidean space, and it might be suggested that he would be uncertain how to construct a straight line when so confronted, but as a matter of fact he showed no hesitation, and the eclipse observers measured without ambiguity the bending of light from the "straight line" The appropriate practical definition was so obvious that there was never any danger of different people meaning different loci by this term. Our guiding rule will be that a physical quantity must be defined by prescribing operations and calculations which will lead to an unambiguous result, and that due heed must be paid to existing practice; the last clause should secure that everyone uses the term to denote the same *quantity*, however much disagreement there may be as to the *conception* attached to it.

When defined in this way, there can be no question as to whether the operations give us the real physical quantity or whether some theoretical correction (not mentioned in the definition) is needed The physical quantity is the measure-number of a world-condition in some code; we cannot assert that a code is right or wrong, or that a measure-number is real or unreal, what we require is that the code should be the accepted code, and the measure-number the number in current use For example, what is the real difference of time between two events at distant places? The operation of determining time has been entrusted to astronomers, who (perhaps for mistaken reasons) have elaborated a regular procedure If the times of the two events are found in accordance with this procedure, the difference must be the real difference of time; the phrase has no other meaning. But there is a certain generalisation to be noticed. In cataloguing the operations of the astronomers, so as to obtain a definition of time, we remark that one condition is adhered to in practice evidently from necessity and not from design—the observer and his apparatus are placed on the earth and move with the earth This condition is so accidental and parochial that we are reluctant to insist on it in our definition of time; yet it so happens that the motion of the apparatus makes an important difference in the measurement, and without this restriction the operations lead to no definite result and cannot define anything. We adopt what seems to be the commonsense solution of the difficulty. We decide that time is *relative to an observer*, that is to say, we admit that an observer on another star, who carries out all the rest of the operations and calculations as specified in our definition, is also measuring time—not our time, but a time relative to himself. The same relativity affects the great majority of elementary physical quantities*; the description of the operations is insufficient to lead to a unique answer unless we arbitrarily prescribe a particular motion of the observer and his apparatus.

In this example we have had a typical illustration of "relativity," the recognition of which has had far-reaching results revolutionising the outlook of physics. Any operation of measurement involves a comparison between a measuring-appliance and the thing measured. Both play an equal part in the comparison and are theoretically, and indeed often practically, interchangeable; for example, the result of an observation with the meridian circle gives the right ascension of the star or the error of the clock indifferently, and we can regard either the clock or the star as the instrument or the object of measurement. Remembering that physical quantities are results of comparisons of this kind, it is clear that they cannot be considered to belong solely to one partner in the comparison. It is true that we standardise the measuring appliance as far as possible (the method of standardisation being explained or implied in the definition of the physical quantity) so that in general the variability of the measurement can only indicate a variability of the object measured. To that extent there is no great practical harm in regarding the measurement as belonging solely to the second partner in the relation. But even so we have often puzzled ourselves needlessly over paradoxes, which disappear when we realise that the physical quantities are not properties of certain external objects but are relations between these objects and something else. Moreover, we have seen that the standardisation of the measuring-appliance is usually left incomplete, as regards the specification of its motion; and rather than complete it in a way which would be arbitrary and pernicious, we prefer to recognise explicitly that our physical quantities belong not solely to the objects measured but have reference also to the particular frame of motion that we choose.

The principle of relativity goes still further. Even if the measuring-appliances were standardised completely, the physical quantities would still involve the properties of the constant standard. We have seen that the world-condition or object which is surveyed can only be apprehended in our knowledge as the sum total of all the measurements in which it can be concerned; any *intrinsic* property of the object must appear as a uniformity or law in these measures. When one partner in the comparison is fixed and the other partner varied widely, whatever is common to all the measurements may be ascribed exclusively to the first partner and regarded as an intrinsic property of it. Let us apply this to the converse comparison; that is to say, keep the measuring-appliance constant or standardised, and vary as widely as possible the objects measured—or, in simpler terms, make a particular

* The most important exceptions are number (of discrete entities), action, and entropy.

kind of measurement in all parts of the field. Intrinsic properties of the measuring-appliance should appear as uniformities or laws in these measures. We are familiar with several such uniformities; but we have not generally recognised them as properties of the measuring-appliance. We have called them *laws of nature*!

The development of physics is progressive, and as the theories of the external world become crystallised, we often tend to replace the elementary physical quantities defined through operations of measurement by theoretical quantities believed to have a more fundamental significance in the external world. Thus the *vis viva* mv^2, which is immediately determinable by experiment, becomes replaced by a generalised energy, virtually defined by having the property of conservation; and our problem becomes inverted—we have not to discover the properties of a thing which we have recognised in nature, but to discover how to recognise in nature a thing whose properties we have assigned. This development seems to be inevitable; but it has grave drawbacks especially when theories have to be reconstructed. Fuller knowledge may show that there is nothing in nature having precisely the properties assigned; or it may turn out that the thing having these properties has entirely lost its importance when the new theoretical standpoint is adopted*. When we decide to throw the older theories into the melting-pot and make a clean start, it is best to relegate to the background terminology associated with special hypotheses of physics. Physical quantities defined by operations of measurement are independent of theory, and form the proper starting-point for any new theoretical development.

Now that we have explained how physical quantities are to be defined, the reader may be surprised that we do not proceed to give the definitions of the leading physical quantities. But to catalogue all the precautions and provisos in the operation of determining even so simple a thing as length, is a task which we shirk. We might take refuge in the statement that the task though laborious is straightforward, and that the practical physicist knows the whole procedure without our writing it down for him. But it is better to be more cautious. I should be puzzled to say off-hand what is the series of operations and calculations involved in measuring a length of 10^{-15} cm.; nevertheless I shall refer to such a length when necessary as though it were a quantity of which the definition is obvious. We cannot be forever examining our foundations; we look particularly to those places where it is reported to us that they are insecure. I may be laying myself open to the charge that I am doing the very thing I criticise in the older physics—using terms that

* We shall see in § 59 that this has happened in the case of energy. The dead-hand of a superseded theory continues to embarrass us, because in this case the recognised terminology still has implicit reference to it. This, however, is only a slight drawback to set off against the many advantages obtained from the classical generalisation of energy as a step towards the more complete theory.

have no definite observational meaning, and mingling with my physical quantities things which are not the results of any conceivable experimental operation. I would reply—

By all means explore this criticism if you regard it as a promising field of inquiry. I here assume that you will probably find me a justification for my 10^{-15} cm., but you may find that there is an insurmountable ambiguity in defining it. In the latter event you may be on the track of something which will give a new insight into the fundamental nature of the world. Indeed it has been suspected that the perplexities of quantum phenomena may arise from the tacit assumption that the notions of length and duration, acquired primarily from experiences in which the average effects of large numbers of quanta are involved, are applicable in the study of individual quanta. There may need to be much more excavation before we have brought to light all that is of value in this critical consideration of experimental knowledge. Meanwhile I want to set before you the treasure which has already been unearthed in this field.

CHAPTER I

ELEMENTARY PRINCIPLES

1. Indeterminateness of the space-time frame.

It has been explained in the early chapters of *Space, Time and Gravitation* that observers with different motions use different reckonings of space and time, and that no one of these reckonings is more fundamental than another. Our problem is to construct a method of description of the world in which this indeterminateness of the space-time frame of reference is formally recognised.

Prior to Einstein's researches no doubt was entertained that there existed a "true even-flowing time" which was unique and universal. The moving observer, who adopts a time-reckoning different from the unique true time, must have been deluded into accepting a fictitious time with a fictitious space-reckoning modified to correspond. The compensating behaviour of electromagnetic forces and of matter is so perfect that, so far as present knowledge extends, there is no test which will distinguish the true time from the fictitious. But since there are many fictitious times and, according to this view, only one true time, some kind of distinction is implied although its nature is not indicated.

Those who still insist on the existence of a unique "true time" generally rely on the possibility that the resources of experiment are not yet exhausted and that some day a discriminating test may be found. But the off-chance that a future generation may discover a significance in our utterances is scarcely an excuse for making meaningless noises.

Thus in the phrase *true time*, "true" is an epithet whose meaning has yet to be discovered. It is a blank label. We do not know what is to be written on the label, nor to which of the apparently indistinguishable time-reckonings it ought to be attached. There is no way of progress here. We return to firmer ground, and note that in the mass of experimental knowledge which has accumulated, the words *time* and *space* refer to one of the "fictitious" times and spaces—primarily that adopted by an observer travelling with the earth, or with the sun—and our theory will deal directly with these space-time frames of reference, which are admittedly fictitious or, in the more usual phrase, *relative to an observer with particular motion.*

The observers are studying the same external events, notwithstanding their different space-time frames. The space-time frame is therefore something overlaid by the observer on the external world; the partitions representing his space and time reckonings are imaginary surfaces drawn in the world like the lines of latitude and longitude drawn on the earth. They do not follow the natural lines of structure of the world, any more than the meridians follow the lines of geological structure of the earth. Such a mesh-system is of great utility and convenience in describing phenomena, and we shall continue to employ it; but we must endeavour not to lose sight of its fictitious and arbitrary nature.

It is evident from experience that a four-fold mesh-system must be used; and accordingly an event is located by four coordinates, generally taken as x, y, z, t. To understand the significance of this location, we first consider the simple case of two dimensions. If we describe the points of a plane figure by their rectangular coordinates x, y, the description of the figure is complete and would enable anyone to construct it; but it is also more than complete, because it specifies an arbitrary element, the orientation, which is irrelevant to the intrinsic properties of the figure and ought to be cast aside from a description of those properties. Alternatively we can describe the figure by stating the distances between the various pairs of points in it; this description is also complete, and it has the merit that it does not prescribe the orientation or contain anything else irrelevant to the intrinsic properties of the figure. The drawback is that it is usually too cumbersome to use in practice for any but the simplest figures.

Similarly our four coordinates x, y, z, t may be expected to contain an arbitrary element, analogous to an orientation, which has nothing to do with the properties of the configuration of events. A different set of values of x, y, z, t may be chosen in which this arbitrary element of the description is altered, but the configuration of events remains unchanged. It is this arbitrariness in coordinate specification which appears as the indeterminateness of the space-time frame. The other method of description, by giving the distances between every pair of events (or rather certain relations between pairs of events which are analogous to distance), contains all that is relevant to the configuration of events and nothing that is irrelevant. By adopting this latter method we can strip away the arbitrary part of the description, leaving only that which has an exact counterpart in the configuration of the external world.

To put the contrast in another form, in our common outlook the idea of position or *location* seems to be fundamental. From it we derive distance or *extension* as a subsidiary notion, which covers part but not all of the conceptions which we associate with location. Position is looked upon as the physical fact—a coincidence with what is vaguely conceived of as an identifiable point of space—whereas distance is looked upon as an abstraction or a computational result calculable when the positions are known. The view which we are going to adopt reverses this. Extension (distance, interval) is now fundamental; and the location of an object is a computational result summarising the physical fact that it is at certain intervals from the other objects in the world. Any idea contained in the concept location which is not expressible by reference to distances from other objects, must be dismissed from our minds. Our ultimate analysis of space leads us not to a "here" and a "there," but to an extension such as that which relates "here" and "there." To put the conclusion rather crudely—space is not a lot of points close together; it is a lot of distances interlocked.

Accordingly our fundamental hypothesis is that—

Everything connected with location which enters into observational knowledge—everything we can know about the configuration of events—is contained in a relation of extension between pairs of events.

This relation is called the *interval*, and its measure is denoted by ds.

If we have a system S consisting of events $A, B, C, D, \ldots$, and a system S' consisting of events $A', B', C', D', \ldots$, then the fundamental hypothesis implies that the two systems will be exactly alike observationally if, and only if, all pairs of corresponding intervals in the two systems are equal, $AB = A'B'$, $AC = A'C', \ldots$. In that case if S and S' are material systems they will appear to us as precisely similar bodies or mechanisms, or if S and S' correspond to the same material body at different times, it will appear that the body has not undergone any change detectable by observation. But the position, motion, or orientation of the body may be different; that is a change detectable by observation, not of the system S, but of a wider system comprising S and surrounding bodies.

Again let the systems S and S' be abstract coordinate-frames of reference, the events being the corners of the meshes; if all corresponding intervals in the two systems are equal, we shall recognise that the coordinate-frames are of precisely the same kind—rectangular, polar, unaccelerated, rotating, etc.

2. The fundamental quadratic form.

We have to keep side by side the two methods of describing the configurations of events by coordinates and by the mutual intervals, respectively—the first for its conciseness, and the second for its immediate absolute significance. It is therefore necessary to connect the two modes of description by a formula which will enable us to pass readily from one to the other. The particular formula will depend on the coordinates chosen as well as on the absolute properties of the region of the world considered, but it appears that in all cases the formula is included in the following general form—

The interval ds between two neighbouring events with coordinates (x_1, x_2, x_3, x_4) and $(x_1 + dx_1, x_2 + dx_2, x_3 + dx_3, x_4 + dx_4)$ in any coordinate-system is given by

$$ds^2 = g_{11}dx_1^2 + g_{22}dx_2^2 + g_{33}dx_3^2 + g_{44}dx_4^2 + 2g_{12}dx_1dx_2 + 2g_{13}dx_1dx_3 + 2g_{14}dx_1dx_4 + 2g_{23}dx_2dx_3 + 2g_{24}dx_2dx_4 + 2g_{34}dx_3dx_4 \quad \ldots\ldots (2\cdot1),$$

where the coefficients g_{11}, etc. are functions of x_1, x_2, x_3, x_4. That is to say, ds^2 is some quadratic function of the differences of coordinates.

This is, of course, not the most general case conceivable, for example, we might have a world in which the interval depended on a general quartic function of the dx's. But, as we shall presently see, the quadratic form (2·1) is definitely indicated by observation as applying to the actual world. Moreover near the end of our task (§ 97) we shall find in the general theory of relation-structure a precise reason why a quadratic function of the coordinate-differences should have this paramount importance.

Whilst the form of the right-hand side of (2·1) is that required by observation, the insertion of ds^2 on the left, rather than some other function of ds, is merely a convention. The quantity ds is a measure of the interval. It is necessary to consider carefully how measure-numbers are to be affixed to the different intervals occurring in nature. We have seen in the last section that equality of intervals can be tested observationally, but so far as we have yet gone, intervals are merely either equal or unequal, and their differences have not been further particularised. Just as wind-strength may be measured by velocity, or by pressure, or by a number on the Beaufort scale, so the relation of extension between two events could be expressed numerically according to many different plans. To conform to (2·1) a particular code of measure-numbers must be adopted; the nature and advantages of this code will be explained in the next section.

The pure geometry associated with the general formula (2·1) was studied by Riemann, and is generally called Riemannian geometry. It includes Euclidean geometry as a special case.

3. Measurement of intervals.

Consider the operation of proving by measurement that a distance AB is equal to a distance CD. We take a configuration of events $LMNOP$..., viz. a measuring-scale, and lay it over AB, and observe that A and B coincide with two particular events P, Q (scale-divisions) of the configuration. We find that the same configuration* can also be arranged so that C and D coincide with P and Q respectively. Further we apply all possible tests to the measuring-scale to see if it has "changed" between the two measurements, and we are only satisfied that the measures are correct if no observable difference can be detected. According to our fundamental axiom, the absence of any observable difference between the two configurations (the structure of the measuring-scale in its two positions) signifies that the intervals are unchanged; in particular the interval between P and Q is unchanged. It follows that the interval A to B is equal to the interval C to D. We consider that the experiment proves equality of distance; but it is primarily a test of equality of interval.

* The logical point may be noticed that the measuring-scale in two positions (necessarily at different times) represents the same *configuration* of events, not the same events.

In this experiment time is not involved, and we conclude that in space considered apart from time the test of equality of distance is equality of interval. There is thus a one-to-one correspondence of distances and intervals. We may therefore adopt the same measure-number for the interval as is in general use for the distance, thus settling our plan of affixing measure-numbers to intervals. It follows that, when time is not involved, the interval reduces to the distance.

It is for this reason that the quadratic form (2·1) is needed in order to agree with observation, for it is well known that in three dimensions the square of the distance between two neighbouring points is a quadratic function of their infinitesimal coordinate-differences—a result depending ultimately on the experimental law expressed by Euclid I, 47.

When time is involved other appliances are used for measuring intervals. If we have a mechanism capable of cyclic motion, its cycles will measure equal intervals provided the mechanism, its laws of behaviour, and all relevant surrounding circumstances, remain precisely similar. For the phrase "precisely similar" means that no observable differences can be detected in the mechanism or its behaviour; and that, as we have seen, requires that all corresponding intervals should be equal. In particular the interval between the events marking the beginning and end of the cycle is unaltered. Thus a clock primarily measures equal intervals; it is only under more restricted conditions that it also measures the time-coordinate t.

In general any repetition of an operation under similar conditions, but for a different time, place, orientation and velocity (attendant circumstances which have a relative but not an absolute significance*), tests equality of interval.

It is obvious from common experience that intervals which can be measured with a clock cannot be measured with a scale, and *vice versa*. We have thus two varieties of intervals, which are provided for in the formula (2·1), since ds^2 may be positive or negative and the measure of the interval will accordingly be expressed by a real or an imaginary number. The abbreviated phrase "imaginary interval" must not be allowed to mislead; there is nothing imaginary in the corresponding relation, it is merely that in our arbitrary code an imaginary number is assigned as its measure-number. We might have adopted a different code, and have taken, for example, the antilogarithm of ds^2 as the measure of the interval; in that case space-intervals would have received code-numbers from 1 to ∞, and time-interva numbers from 0 to 1. When we encounter $\sqrt{-1}$ in our investigations, w must remember that it has been introduced by our choice of measure-cod and must not think of it as occurring with some mystical significance in th external world.

* They express relations to events which are not concerned in the test, e.g. to the sun an stars

4. Rectangular coordinates and time.

Suppose that we have a small region of the world throughout which the g's can be treated as constants*. In that case the right-hand side of (2·1) can be broken up into the sum of four squares, admitting imaginary coefficients if necessary. Thus writing

$$y_1 = a_1x_1 + a_2x_2 + a_3x_3 + a_4x_4,$$
$$y_2 = b_1x_1 + b_2x_2 + b_3x_3 + b_4x_4, \text{ etc.},$$

so that $$dy_1 = a_1dx_1 + a_2dx_2 + a_3dx_3 + a_4dx_4; \text{ etc.},$$

we can choose the constants a_1, b_1, ... so that (2·1) becomes

$$ds^2 = dy_1^2 + dy_2^2 + dy_3^2 + dy_4^2 \quad \text{.....................(4·1).}$$

For, substituting for the dy's and comparing coefficients with (2·1), we have only 10 equations to be satisfied by the 16 constants. There are thus many ways of making the reduction. Note, however, that the reduction to the sum of four squares of complete differentials is not in general possible for a *large* region, where the g's have to be treated as functions, not constants.

Consider all the events for which y_4 has some specified value. These will form a three-dimensional world. Since dy_4 is zero for every pair of these events, their mutual intervals are given by

$$ds^2 = dy_1^2 + dy_2^2 + dy_3^2 \quad \text{.....................(4·2).}$$

But this is exactly like familiar space in which the interval (which we have shown to be the same as the distance for space without time) is given by

$$ds^2 = dx^2 + dy^2 + dz^2 \quad \text{.....................(4·3),}$$

where x, y, z are rectangular coordinates.

Hence a section of the world by $y_4 = \text{const.}$ will appear to us as space, and y_1, y_2, y_3 will appear to us as rectangular coordinates. The coordinate-frames y_1, y_2, y_3, and x, y, z, are examples of the systems S and S' of § 1, for which the intervals between corresponding pairs of mesh-corners are equal. The two systems are therefore exactly alike observationally, and if one appears to us to be a rectangular frame in space, so also must the other. One proviso must be noted; the coordinates y_1, y_2, y_3 for real events must be real, as in familiar space, otherwise the resemblance would be only formal.

Granting this proviso, we have reduced the general expression to

$$ds^2 = dx^2 + dy^2 + dz^2 + dy_4^2 \quad \text{.....................(4·4),}$$

where x, y, z will be recognised by us as rectangular coordinates in space. Clearly y_4 must involve the time, otherwise our location of events by the four coordinates would be incomplete, but we must not too hastily identify it with the time t.

* It will be shown in § 36 that it is always possible to transform the coordinates so that the first derivatives of the g's vanish at a selected point. We shall suppose that this preliminary transformation has already been made, in order that the constancy of the g's may be a valid approximation through as large a region as possible round the selected point.

I suppose that the following would be generally accepted as a satisfactory (pre-relativity) definition of equal time-intervals:—if we have a mechanism capable of cyclic motion, its cycles will measure equal durations of time *anywhere* and *anywhen*, provided the mechanism, its laws of behaviour, and all outside influences remain precisely similar. To this the relativist would add the condition that the mechanism (as a whole) must be at rest in the space-time frame considered, because it is now known that a clock in motion goes slow in comparison with a fixed clock. The non-relativist does not disagree in fact, though he takes a slightly different view; he regards the proviso that the mechanism must be at rest as already included in his enunciation, because for him motion involves progress through the aether, which (he considers) directly affects the behaviour of the clock, and is one of those "outside influences" which have to be kept "precisely similar."

Since then it is agreed that the mechanism as a whole is to be at rest, and the moving parts return to the same positions after a complete cycle, we shall have for the two events marking the beginning and end of the cycle

$$dx,\ dy,\ dz = 0.$$

Accordingly (4·4) gives for this case

$$ds^2 = dy_4^2.$$

We have seen in § 3 that the cycles of the mechanism in all cases correspond to equal intervals ds; hence they correspond to equal values of dy_4. But by the above definition of time they also correspond to equal lapses of time dt; hence we must have dy_4 proportional to dt, and we express this proportionality by writing

$$dy_4 = icdt \qquad\qquad (4·5),$$

where $i = \sqrt{-1}$, and c is a constant. It is, of course, possible that c may be an imaginary number, but provisionally we shall suppose it real. Then (4·4) becomes

$$ds^2 = dx^2 + dy^2 + dz^2 - c^2dt^2 \qquad\qquad (4·6)$$

A further discussion is necessary before it is permissible to conclude that (4·6) is the most general possible form for ds^2 in terms of ordinary space and time coordinates. If we had reduced (2·1) to the rather more general form

$$ds^2 = dx^2 + dy^2 + dz^2 - c^2dt^2 - 2c\alpha\, dx\, dt - 2c\beta\, dy\, dt - 2c\gamma\, dz\, dt \quad ...(4·7),$$

this would have agreed with (4·6) in the only two cases yet discussed, viz. (1) when $dt = 0$, and (2) when $dx, dy, dz = 0$. To show that this more general form is inadmissible we must examine pairs of events which differ both in time and place.

In the preceding pre-relativity definition of t our clocks had to remain stationary and were therefore of no use for comparing time at different places. What did the pre-relativity physicist mean by the difference of time dt between two events at different places? I do not think that we can attach any meaning to his hazy conception of what dt signified; but we know one or two ways in which he was accustomed to determine it. One method which he used was that of transport of chronometers. Let us examine then what happens when we move a clock from $(x_1, 0, 0)$ at the time t_1 to another place $(x_2, 0, 0)$ at the time t_2.

We have seen that the clock, whether at rest or in motion, provided it remains a precisely similar mechanism, records equal *intervals*; hence the difference of the clock-readings at the beginning and end of the journey will be proportional to the integrated interval

$$\int_1^2 ds \quad \text{.................................}(4\cdot81).$$

If the transport is made in the direct line ($dy = 0$, $dz = 0$), we shall have according to (4·7)

$$\begin{aligned} -ds^2 &= c^2dt^2 + 2c\alpha dxdt - dx^2 \\ &= c^2dt^2\left\{1 + \frac{2\alpha}{c}\frac{dx}{dt} - \frac{1}{c^2}\left(\frac{dx}{dt}\right)^2\right\}. \end{aligned}$$

Hence the difference of the clock-readings (4·81) is proportional to

$$\int_{t_1}^{t_2} dt\left(1 + \frac{2\alpha u}{c} - \frac{u^2}{c^2}\right)^{\frac{1}{2}} \quad \text{......................}(4\cdot82),$$

where $u = dx/dt$, i.e the velocity of the clock. The integral will not in general reduce to $t_2 - t_1$; so that the difference of time at the two places is not given correctly by the reading of the clock. Even when $\alpha = 0$, the moving clock does not record correct time.

Now introduce the condition that the velocity u is very small, remembering that $t_2 - t_1$ will then become very large. Neglecting u^2/c^2, (4·82) becomes

$$\begin{aligned} &\int_{t_1}^{t_2} dt\left(1 + \frac{\alpha}{c}\frac{dx}{dt}\right) \quad \text{approximately} \\ &= (t_2 - t_1) + \frac{\alpha}{c}(x_2 - x_1). \end{aligned}$$

The clock, if moved sufficiently slowly, will record the correct time-difference if, and only if, $\alpha = 0$. Moving it in other directions, we must have, similarly, $\beta = 0$, $\gamma = 0$. Thus (4·6) is the most general formula for the interval, when the time at different places is compared by slow transport of clocks from one place to another.

I do not know how far the reader will be prepared to accept the condition that it must be possible to correlate the times at different places by moving a clock from one to the other with infinitesimal velocity. The method employed in accurate work is to send an electromagnetic signal from one to the other, and we shall see in § 11 that this leads to the same formulae. We can scarcely consider that either of these methods of comparing time at different places is an essential part of our primitive notion of time in the same way that measurement at one place by a cyclic mechanism is; therefore they are best regarded as conventional. Let it be understood, however, that although the relativity theory has formulated the convention explicitly, the usage of the word *time-difference* for the quantity fixed by this convention is in accordance with the long established practice in experimental physics and astronomy.

Setting $\alpha = 0$ in (4·82), we see that the accurate formula for the clock-reading will be

$$\int_{t_1}^{t_2} dt\,(1 - u^2/c^2)^{\frac{1}{2}}$$

$$= (1 - u^2/c^2)^{\frac{1}{2}}\,(t_2 - t_1) \qquad (4{\cdot}9)$$

for a uniform velocity u. Thus a clock travelling with finite velocity gives too small a reading—the clock goes slow compared with the time-reckoning conventionally adopted.

To sum up the results of this section, if we choose coordinates such that the general quadratic form reduces to

$$ds^2 = dy_1^2 + dy_2^2 + dy_3^2 + dy_4^2 \qquad (4{\cdot}95),$$

then y_1, y_2, y_3 and $y_4\sqrt{-1}$ will represent ordinary rectangular coordinates and time. If we choose coordinates for which

$$ds^2 = dy_1^2 + dy_2^2 + dy_3^2 + dy_4^2 + 2\alpha dy_1 dy_4 + 2\beta dy_2 dy_4 + 2\gamma dy_3 dy_4 \ldots (4{\cdot}96),$$

these coordinates also will agree with rectangular coordinates and time so far as the more primitive notions of time are concerned; but the reckoning by this formula of differences of time at different places will not agree with the reckoning adopted in physics and astronomy according to long established practice. For this reason it would only introduce confusion to admit these coordinates as a permissible space and time system.

We who regard all coordinate-frames as equally fictitious structures have no special interest in ruling out the more general form (4·96). It is not a question of ascribing greater significance to one frame than to another, but of discovering which frame corresponds to the space and time reckoning generally accepted and used in standard works such as the Nautical Almanac.

As far as § 14 our work will be subject to the condition that we are dealing with a region of the world in which the g's are constant, or approximately constant. A region having this property is called *flat*. The theory of this case is called the "special" theory of relativity; it was discussed by Einstein in 1905—some ten years before the general theory. But it becomes much simpler when regarded as a special case of the general theory, because it is no longer necessary to defend the conditions for its validity as being essential properties of space-time. For a given region these conditions may hold, or they may not. The special theory applies only if they hold; other cases must be referred to the general theory.

5. The Lorentz transformation.

Make the following transformation of coordinates

$$x = \beta(x' - ut'), \quad y = y', \quad z = z', \quad t = \beta(t' - ux'/c^2) \quad \text{......(5·1)},$$
$$\beta = (1 - u^2/c^2)^{-\frac{1}{2}},$$

where u is any real constant not greater than c.

We have by (5·1)

$$dx^2 - c^2dt^2 = \beta^2\{(dx' - u\,dt')^2 - c^2(dt' - u\,dx'/c^2)^2\}$$
$$= \beta^2\left\{\left(1 - \frac{u^2}{c^2}\right)dx'^2 - (c^2 - u^2)\,dt'^2\right\}$$
$$= dx'^2 - c^2dt'^2.$$

Hence from (4·6)

$$ds^2 = dx^2 + dy^2 + dz^2 - c^2dt^2 = dx'^2 + dy'^2 + dz'^2 - c^2dt'^2 \quad \text{......(5·2)}.$$

The accented and unaccented coordinates give the same formula for the interval, so that the intervals between corresponding pairs of mesh-corners will be equal, and therefore in all observable respects they will be alike. We shall recognise x', y', z' as rectangular coordinates in space, and t' as the associated time. We have thus arrived at another possible way of reckoning space and time—another fictitious space-time frame, equivalent in all its properties to the original one For convenience we say that the first reckoning is that of an observer S and the second that of an observer S', both observers being at rest in their respective spaces*.

The constant u is easily interpreted. Since S is at rest in his own space, his location is given by x = const. By (5·1) this becomes, in S''s coordinates, $x' - ut'$ = const.; that is to say, S is travelling in the x'-direction with velocity u. Accordingly the constant u is interpreted as the velocity of S relative to S'.

It does not follow immediately that the velocity of S' relative to S is $-u$; but this can be proved by algebraical solution of the equations (5·1) to determine x', y', z', t' We find

$$x' = \beta(x + ut), \quad y' = y, \quad z' = z, \quad t' = \beta(t + ux/c^2) \quad \text{.....(5·3)},$$

showing that an interchange of S and S' merely reverses the sign of u

The essential property of the foregoing transformation is that it leaves the formula for ds^2 unaltered (5·2), so that the coordinate-systems which it connects are alike in their properties. Looking at the matter more generally, we have already noted that the reduction to the sum of four squares can be made in many ways, so that we can have

$$ds^2 = dy_1^2 + dy_2^2 + dy_3^2 + dy_4^2 = dy_1'^2 + dy_2'^2 + dy_3'^2 + dy_4'^2 \qquad (5·4)$$

* This is partly a matter of nomenclature. A sentient observer can force himself to "recollect that he is moving" and so adopt a space in which he is not at rest; but he does not so readily adopt the time which properly corresponds, unless he uses the space time frame in which he is at rest, he is likely to adopt a hybrid space-time which leads to inconsistencies. There is no ambiguity if the "observer" is regarded as merely an involuntary measuring apparatus, which by the principles of § 4 naturally partitions a space and time with respect to which it is at rest

The determination of the necessary connection between any two sets of coordinates satisfying this equation is a problem of pure mathematics; we can use freely the conceptions of four-dimensional geometry and imaginary rotations to find this connection, whether the conceptions have any physical significance or not. We see from (5·4) that ds is the distance between two points in four-dimensional Euclidean space, the coordinates (y_1, y_2, y_3, y_4) and (y_1', y_2', y_3', y_4') being rectangular systems (real or imaginary) in that space. Accordingly these coordinates are related by the general transformations from one set of rectangular axes to another in four dimensions, viz translations and rotations. Translation, or change of origin, need not detain us; nor need a rotation of the space-axes (y_1, y_2, y_3) leaving time unaffected. The interesting case is a rotation in which y_4 is involved, typified by

$$y_1 = y_1' \cos\theta - y_4' \sin\theta, \quad y_4 = y_1' \sin\theta + y_4' \cos\theta.$$

Writing $u = ic \tan\theta$, so that $\beta = \cos\theta$, this leads to the Lorentz transformation (5·1).

Thus, apart from obvious trivial changes of axes, the Lorentz transformations are the only ones which leave the form (4·6) unaltered.

Historically this transformation was first obtained for the particular case of electromagnetic equations. Its more general character was pointed out by Einstein in 1905.

6. The velocity of light.

Consider a point moving along the x-axis whose velocity measured by S' is v', so that

$$v' = \frac{dx'}{dt'} \quad \text{.................................(6·1).}$$

Then by (5·1) its velocity measured by S is

$$v = \frac{dx}{dt} = \frac{\beta(dx' - u\,dt')}{\beta(dt' - u\,dx'/c^2)}$$

$$= \frac{v' - u}{1 - uv'/c^2} \quad \text{by (6·1) ....(6·2).}$$

In non-relativity kinematics we should have taken it as axiomatic that $v = v' - u$.

If two points move relatively to S' with equal velocities in opposite directions $+v'$ and $-v'$, their velocities relative to S are

$$\frac{v' - u}{1 - uv'/c^2} \quad \text{and} \quad -\frac{v' + u}{1 + uv'/c^2}.$$

As we should expect, these speeds are usually unequal; but there is an exceptional case when $v' = c$. The speeds relative to S are then also equal, both in fact being equal to c.

Again it follows from (5·2) that when

$$\left(\frac{dx'}{dt'}\right)^2 + \left(\frac{dy'}{dt'}\right)^2 + \left(\frac{dz'}{dt'}\right)^2 = c^2,$$

$ds = 0$, and hence

$$\left(\frac{dx}{dt}\right)^2 + \left(\frac{dy}{dt}\right)^2 + \left(\frac{dz}{dt}\right)^2 = c^2.$$

Thus when the resultant velocity relative to S' is c, the velocity relative to S is also c, whatever the direction. We see that the velocity c has a unique and very remarkable property.

According to the older views of absolute time this result appears incredible. Moreover we have not yet shown that the formulae have practical significance, since c might be imaginary But experiment has revealed a real velocity with this remarkable property, viz. 299,860 km. per sec. We shall call this the *fundamental velocity*.

By good fortune there is an entity—light—which travels with the fundamental velocity. It would be a mistake to suppose that the existence of such an entity is responsible for the prominence accorded to the fundamental velocity c in our scheme; but it is helpful in rendering it more directly accessible to experiment. The Michelson-Morley experiment detected no difference in the velocity of light in two directions at right angles. Six months later the earth's orbital motion had altered the observer's velocity by 60 km. per sec., corresponding to the change from S' to S, and there was still no difference. Hence the velocity of light has the distinctive property of the fundamental velocity.

Strictly speaking the Michelson-Morley experiment did not prove directly that the velocity of light was constant in all directions, but that the average to-and-fro velocity was constant in all directions. The experiment compared the times of a journey "there-and-back" If $v(\theta)$ is the velocity of light in the direction θ, the experimental result is

$$\left.\begin{aligned}\frac{1}{v(\theta)} + \frac{1}{v(\theta+\pi)} &= \text{const.} = C\\ \frac{1}{v'(\theta)} + \frac{1}{v'(\theta+\pi)} &= \text{const.} = C'\end{aligned}\right\} \qquad (6\cdot3)$$

for all values of θ. The constancy has been established to about 1 part in 10^{10}.

It is exceedingly unlikely that the first equation could hold unless

$$v(\theta) = v(\theta+\pi) = \text{const.},$$

and it is fairly obvious that the existence of the second equation excludes the possibility altogether. However, on account of the great importance of the identification of the fundamental velocity with the velocity of light, we give a formal proof.

Let a ray travelling with velocity v traverse a distance R in a direction θ, so that

$$dt = R/v, \quad dx = R\cos\theta, \quad dy = R\sin\theta.$$

Let the relative velocity of S and S' be small so that u^2/c^2 is neglected. Then by (5·3)

$$dt' = dt + u\,dx/c^2, \quad dx' = dx + u\,dt, \quad dy' = dy.$$

Writing δR, $\delta\theta$, δv for the change in R, θ, v when a transformation is made to S''s system, we obtain

$$\delta(R/v) = dt' - dt = uR\cos\theta/c^2,$$
$$\delta(R\cos\theta) = dx' - dx = uR/v,$$
$$\delta(R\sin\theta) = dy' - dy = 0.$$

Whence the values of δR, $\delta\theta$, $\delta(1/v)$ are found as follows:

$$\delta R = uR\cos\theta/v,$$
$$\delta\theta = -u\sin\theta/v,$$
$$\delta\left(\frac{1}{v}\right) = u\cos\theta\left(\frac{1}{c^2} - \frac{1}{v^2}\right).$$

Here $\delta(1/v)$ refers to a comparison of velocities in the directions θ in S's system and θ' in S''s system. Writing $\Delta(1/v)$ for a comparison when the direction is θ in both systems

$$\Delta\left(\frac{1}{v}\right) = \delta\left(\frac{1}{v}\right) - \frac{\partial}{\partial\theta}\left(\frac{1}{v}\right).\delta\theta$$
$$= \frac{u}{c^2}\cos\theta - \frac{u}{v^2}\cos\theta + \frac{u\sin\theta}{v}\frac{\partial}{\partial\theta}\left(\frac{1}{v}\right)$$
$$= \frac{u}{c^2}\cos\theta + \tfrac{1}{2}u\sin^3\theta\frac{\partial}{\partial\theta}\left(\frac{1}{v^2\sin^2\theta}\right).$$

Hence

$$\Delta\left(\frac{1}{v(\theta)} + \frac{1}{v(\theta+\pi)}\right) = \tfrac{1}{2}u\sin^3\theta\frac{\partial}{\partial\theta}\left\{\frac{1}{\sin^3\theta}\left(\frac{1}{v^2(\theta)} - \frac{1}{v^2(\theta+\pi)}\right)\right\}.$$

By (6·3) the left-hand side is independent of θ, and equal to the constant $C' - C$. We obtain on integration

$$\frac{1}{v^2(\theta)} - \frac{1}{v^2(\theta+\pi)} = \frac{C'-C}{u}(\sin^2\theta \,.\, \log\tan\tfrac{1}{2}\theta - \cos\theta),$$

or

$$\frac{1}{v(\theta)} - \frac{1}{v(\theta+\pi)} = \frac{C'-C}{C}\,.\,\frac{1}{u}(\sin^2\theta\ \log\tan\tfrac{1}{2}\theta - \cos\theta).$$

It is clearly impossible that the difference of $1/v$ in opposite directions should be a function of θ of this form; because the origin of θ is merely the direction of relative motion of S and S', which may be changed at will in different experiments, and has nothing to do with the propagation of light relative to S. Hence $C' - C = 0$, and $v(\theta) = v(\theta+\pi)$. Accordingly by (6·3) $v(\theta)$ is independent of θ; and similarly $v'(\theta)$ is independent of θ. Thus the velocity of light is uniform in all directions for both observers and is therefore to be identified with the fundamental velocity.

When this proof is compared with the statement commonly (and correctly) made that the equality of the forward and backward velocity of light cannot be deduced from experiment, regard must be paid to the context. The use of the Michelson-Morley experiment to fill a particular gap in a generally deductive argument must not be confused with its use (e.g. in *Space, Time and Gravitation*) as the basis of a pure induction from experiment. Here we have not even used the fact that it is a second-order experiment. We have deduced the Lorentz transformation from the fundamental hypothesis of § 1, and have already introduced a conventional system of time-reckoning explained in § 4. The present argument shows that the convention that time is defined by the slow transport of chronometers is equivalent to the convention that the forward velocity of light is equal to the backward velocity. The proof of this equivalence is mainly deductive except for one hiatus—the connection of the propagation of light and the fundamental velocity—and for that step appeal is made to the Michelson-Morley experiment.

The law of composition of velocities (6·2) is well illustrated by Fizeau's experiment on the propagation of light along a moving stream of water. Let the observer S' travel with the stream of water, and let S be a fixed observer. The water is at rest relatively to S' and the velocity of the light relative to him will thus be the ordinary velocity of propagation in still water, viz. $v' = c/\mu$, where μ is the refractive index. The velocity of the stream being w, $-w$ is the velocity of S relative to S'; hence by (6·2) the velocity v of the light relative to S is

$$v = \frac{v' + w}{1 + wv'/c^2} = \frac{c/\mu + w}{1 + w/\mu c}$$

$$= c/\mu + w(1 - 1/\mu^2) \text{ approximately,}$$

neglecting the square of w/c.

Accordingly the velocity of the light is not increased by the full velocity of the stream in which it is propagated, but by the fraction $(1 - 1/\mu^2)\,w$. For water this is about $0{\cdot}44\,w$. The effect can be measured by dividing a beam of light into two parts which are sent in opposite directions round a circulating stream of water. The factor $(1 - 1/\mu^2)$ is known as Fresnel's convection-coefficient; it was confirmed experimentally by Fizeau in 1851.

If the velocity of light *in vacuo* were a constant c' differing from the fundamental velocity c, the foregoing calculation would give for Fresnel's convection-coefficient

$$1 - \frac{c'^2}{c^2} \cdot \frac{1}{\mu^2}.$$

Thus Fizeau's experiment provides independent evidence that the fundamental velocity is at least approximately the same as the velocity of light. In the most recent repetitions of this experiment made by Zeeman* the agreement between theory and observation is such that c' cannot differ from c by more than 1 part in 500.

* *Amsterdam Proceedings*, vol. XVIII, pp. 398 and 1240.

7. Timelike and spacelike intervals.

We make a slight change of notation, the quantity hitherto denoted by ds^2 being in all subsequent formulae replaced by $-ds^2$, so that (4·6) becomes

$$ds^2 = c^2dt^2 - dx^2 - dy^2 - dz^2 \quad \text{.....................(7·1).}$$

There is no particular advantage in this change of sign; it is made in order to conform to the customary notation.

The formula may give either positive or negative values of ds^2, so that the interval between real events may be a real or an imaginary number. We call real intervals timelike, and imaginary intervals spacelike.

From (7·1)
$$\left(\frac{ds}{dt}\right)^2 = c^2 - \left(\frac{dx}{dt}\right)^2 - \left(\frac{dy}{dt}\right)^2 - \left(\frac{dz}{dt}\right)^2$$
$$= c^2 - v^2 \quad \text{.......................................(7·2),}$$

where v is the velocity of a point describing the track along which the interval lies. The interval is thus real or imaginary according as v is less than or greater than c. Assuming that a material particle cannot travel faster than light, the intervals along its track must be timelike. We ourselves are limited by material bodies and therefore can only have direct experience of timelike intervals. We are immediately aware of the passage of time without the use of our external senses; but we have to infer from our sense perceptions the existence of spacelike intervals outside us.

From any event x, y, z, t, intervals radiate in all directions to other events, and the real and imaginary intervals are separated by the cone

$$0 = c^2dt^2 - dx^2 - dy^2 - dz^2,$$

which is called the *null-cone*. Since light travels with velocity c, the track of any light-pulse proceeding from the event lies on the null-cone. When the g's are not constants and the fundamental quadratic form is not reducible to (7·1), there is still a null-surface, given by $ds = 0$ in (2·1), which separates the timelike and spacelike intervals. There can be little doubt that in this case also the light-tracks lie on the null-surface, but the property is perhaps scarcely self-evident, and we shall have to justify it in more detail later.

The formula (6·2) for the composition of velocities in the same straight line may be written

$$\tanh^{-1} v/c = \tanh^{-1} v'/c - \tanh^{-1} u/c \quad \text{..............(7·3).}$$

The quantity $\tanh^{-1} v/c$ has been called by Robb the *rapidity* corresponding to the velocity v. Thus (7·3) shows that relative rapidities in the same direction compound according to the simple addition-law. Since $\tanh^{-1} 1 = \infty$, the velocity of light corresponds to infinite rapidity. We cannot reach infinite rapidity by adding any finite number of finite rapidities; therefore we cannot reach the velocity of light by compounding any finite number of relative velocities less than that of light.

There is an essential discontinuity between speeds greater than and less than that of light which is illustrated by the following example. If two points move in the same direction with velocities

$$v_1 = c + \epsilon, \quad v_2 = c - \epsilon$$

respectively, their relative velocity is by (6 2)

$$\frac{v_1 - v_2}{1 - v_1 v_2/c^2} = \frac{2\epsilon}{1 - (c^2 - \epsilon^2)/c^2} = \frac{2c^2}{\epsilon},$$

which tends to infinity as ϵ is made infinitely small! If the fundamental velocity is exactly 300,000 km. per sec., and two points move in the same direction with speeds of 300,001 and 299,999 km. per sec., the speed of one relative to the other is 180,000,000,000 km per sec. The barrier at 300,000 km. per sec. is not to be crossed by approaching it A particle which is aiming to reach a speed of 300,001 km. per sec. might naturally hope to attain its object by continually increasing its speed; but when it has reached 299,999 km. per sec., and takes stock of the position, it sees its goal very much farther off than when it started.

A particle of matter is a structure whose linear extension is timelike. We might perhaps imagine an analogous structure ranged along a spacelike track. That would be an attempt to picture a particle travelling with a velocity greater than that of light, but since the structure would differ fundamentally from matter as known to us, there seems no reason to think that it would be recognised by us as a particle of matter, even if its existence were possible. For a suitably chosen observer a spacelike track can lie wholly in an instantaneous space. The structure would exist along a line in space at one moment; at preceding and succeeding moments it would be non-existent. Such instantaneous intrusions must profoundly modify the continuity of evolution from past to future. In default of any evidence of the existence of these spacelike particles we shall assume that they are impossible structures.

8. Immediate consciousness of time.

Our minds are immediately aware of a "flight of time" without the intervention of external senses. Presumably there are more or less cyclic processes occurring in the brain, which play the part of a material clock, whose indications the mind can read. The rough measures of duration made by the internal time-sense are of little use for scientific purposes, and physics is accustomed to base time-reckoning on more precise external mechanisms. It is, however, desirable to examine the relation of this more primitive notion of time to the scheme developed in physics.

Much confusion has arisen from a failure to realise that time as currently used in physics and astronomy deviates widely from the time recognised by the primitive time-sense. In fact the time of which we are immediately conscious is not in general physical time, but the more fundamental quantity which we have called interval (confined, however, to timelike intervals).

Our time-sense is not concerned with events outside our brains; it relates only to the linear chain of events along our own track through the world. We may learn from another observer similar information as to the time-succession of events along his track. Further we have inanimate observers—clocks—from which we may obtain similar information as to their local time-successions. The combination of these linear successions along different tracks into a complete ordering of the events in relation to one another is a problem that requires careful analysis, and is not correctly solved by the haphazard intuitions of pre-relativity physics. Recognising that both clocks and time-sense measure *ds* between pairs of events along their respective tracks, we see that the problem reduces to that which we have already been studying, viz. to pass from a description in terms of intervals between pairs of events to a description in terms of coordinates.

The external events which we see appear to fall into our own local time-succession; but in reality it is not the events themselves, but the sense-impressions to which they indirectly give rise, which take place in the time-succession of our consciousness. The popular outlook does not trouble to discriminate between the external events themselves and the events constituted by their light-impressions on our brains; and hence events throughout the universe are crudely located in our private time-sequence. Through this confusion the idea has arisen that the instants of which we are conscious extend so as to include external events, and are world-wide, and the enduring universe is supposed to consist of a succession of instantaneous states. This crude view was disproved in 1675 by Römer's celebrated discussion of the eclipses of Jupiter's satellites; and we are no longer permitted to locate external events in the instant of our visual perception of them. The whole foundation of the idea of world-wide instants was destroyed 250 years ago, and it seems strange that it should still survive in current physics. But, as so often happens, the theory was patched up although its original *raison d'être* had vanished. Obsessed with the idea that the external events had to be put somehow into the instants of our private consciousness, the physicist succeeded in removing the pressing difficulties by placing them not in the instant of visual perception but in a suitable preceding instant. Physics borrowed the idea of world-wide instants from the rejected theory, and constructed mathematical continuations of the instants in the consciousness of the observer, making in this way time-partitions throughout the four-dimensional world. We need have no quarrel with this very useful construction which gives physical time. We only insist that its artificial nature should be recognised, and that the original demand for a *world-wide* time arose through a mistake. We should probably have had to invent universal time-partitions in any case in order to obtain a complete mesh-system; but it might have saved confusion if we had arrived at it as a deliberate invention instead of an inherited misconception. If it is found that physical time has properties which would ordinarily be regarded as contrary to common sense, no surprise need be felt; this highly technical construct of physics is not to be confounded with the time of common sense. It is important for us to discover the exact properties of physical time, but those properties were put into it by the astronomers who invented it.

9. The "3 + 1 dimensional" world.

The constant c^2 in (7·1) is positive according to experiments made in regions of the world accessible to us. The 3 minus signs with 1 plus sign particularise the world in a way which we could scarcely have predicted from first principles. H. Weyl expresses this specialisation by saying that the world is 3 + 1 dimensional. Some entertainment may be derived by considering the properties of a 2 + 2 or a 4 + 0 dimensional world. A more serious question is, Can the world change its type? Is it possible that in making the reduction of (2·1) to the sum or difference of squares for some region remote in space or time, we might have 4 minus signs? I think not; because if the region exists it must be separated from our 3 + 1 dimensional region by some boundary. On one side of the boundary we have

$$ds^2 = -dx^2 - dy^2 - dz^2 + c_1^2 dt^2,$$

and on the other side

$$ds^2 = -dx^2 - dy^2 - dz^2 - c_2^2 dt^2.$$

The transition can only occur through a boundary where

$$ds^2 = -dx^2 - dy^2 - dz^2 + 0\,dt^2,$$

so that the fundamental velocity is zero. Nothing can move at the boundary, and no influence can pass from one side to another. The supposed region beyond is thus not in any spatio-temporal relation to our own universe—which is a somewhat pedantic way of saying that it does not exist.

This barrier is more formidable than that which stops the passage of light round the world in de Sitter's spherical space-time (*Space, Time and Gravitation*, p. 160). The latter stoppage was relative to the space and time of a distant observer; but everything went on normally with respect to the space and time of an observer at the region itself. But here we are contemplating a barrier which does not recede as it is approached.

The passage to a 2 + 2 dimensional world would occur through a transition region where

$$ds^2 = -dx^2 - dy^2 + 0\,dz^2 + c^2 dt^2.$$

Space here reduces to two dimensions, but there does not appear to be any barrier. The conditions on the far side, where time becomes two-dimensional, defy imagination.

10. The FitzGerald contraction.

We shall now consider some of the consequences deducible from the Lorentz transformation.

The first equation of (5·3) may be written

$$x'/\beta = x + ut,$$

which shows that S, besides making the allowance ut for the motion of his origin, divides by β all lengths in the x-direction measured by S'. On the other hand the equation $y'=y$ shows that S accepts S''s measures in directions transverse to their relative motion. Let S' take his standard metre (at rest relative to him, and therefore moving relative to S) and point it first in the transverse direction y' and then in the longitudinal direction x'. For S' its length is 1 metre in each position, since it is his standard, for S the length is 1 metre in the transverse position and $1/\beta$ metres in the longitudinal position. Thus S finds that a moving rod contracts when turned from the transverse to the longitudinal position.

The question remains, How does the length of this moving rod compare with the length of a similarly constituted rod at rest relative to S? The answer is that the transverse dimensions are the same whilst the longitudinal dimensions are contracted. We can prove this by a *reductio ad absurdum*. For suppose that a rod moving transversely were longer than a similar rod at rest. Take two similar transverse rods A and A' at rest relatively to S and S' respectively. Then S must regard A' as the longer, since it is moving relatively to him; and S' must regard A as the longer, since it is moving relatively to him. But this is impossible since, according to the equation $y=y'$, S and S' agree as to transverse measures.

We see that the Lorentz transformation (5·1) requires that (x, y, z, t) and (x', y', z', t') should be measured with standards of identical material constitution, but moving respectively with S and S'. This was really implicit in our deduction of the transformation, because the property of the two systems is that they give the same formula (5·2) for the interval; and the test of complete similarity of the standards is equality of all corresponding intervals occurring in them.

The fourth equation of (5·1) is

$$t=\beta(t'-ux'/c^2).$$

Consider a clock recording the time t', which accordingly is at rest in S''s system ($x'=$ const.). Then for any time-lapse by this clock, we have

$$\delta t=\beta\,\delta t',$$

since $\delta x'=0$. That is to say, S does not accept the time as recorded by this moving clock, but multiplies its readings by β, as though the clock were going slow. This agrees with the result already found in (4·9).

It may seem strange that we should be able to deduce the contraction of a material rod and the retardation of a material clock from the general geometry of space and time. But it must be remembered that the contraction and retardation do not imply any absolute change in the rod and clock. The "configuration of events" constituting the four-dimensional structure which we call a rod is unaltered, all that happens is that the observer's space and time partitions cross it in a different direction.

Further we make no prediction as to what would happen to the rod set in motion in an actual experiment. There may or may not be an absolute change of the configuration according to the circumstances by which it is set in motion. Our results apply to the case in which the rod after being set in motion is (according to all experimental tests) found to be similar to the rod in its original state of rest*.

When a number of phenomena are connected together it becomes somewhat arbitrary to decide which is to be regarded as the explanation of the others. To many it will seem easier to regard the strange property of the fundamental velocity as *explained* by these differences of behaviour of the observers' clocks and scales. They would say that the observers arrive at the same value of the velocity of light because they omit the corrections which would allow for the different behaviour of their measuring-appliances. That is the relative point of view, in which the relative quantities, length, time, etc., are taken as fundamental. From the absolute point of view, which has regard to intervals only, the standards of the two observers are equal and behave similarly; the so-called *explanations* of the invariance of the velocity of light only lead us away from the root of the matter.

Moreover the recognition of the FitzGerald contraction does not enable us to avoid paradox. From (5·3) we found that S''s longitudinal measuring-rods were contracted relatively to those of S. From (5·1) we can show similarly that S's rods are contracted relatively to those of S'. There is complete reciprocity between S and S'. This paradox is discussed more fully in *Space, Time and Gravitation*, p. 55.

11. Simultaneity at different places.

It will be seen from the fourth equation of (5·1), viz.

$$t = \beta (t' - ux'/c^2),$$

that events at different places which are simultaneous for S' are not in general simultaneous for S. In fact, if $dt' = 0$,

$$dt = -\beta u dx'/c^2 \qquad (11·1)$$

It is of some interest to examine in detail how this difference of reckoning of simultaneity arises. It has been explained in § 4 that by convention the time at two places is compared by transporting a clock from one to the other with infinitesimal velocity. Our formulae are based on this convention; and, of course, (11·1) will only be true if the convention is adhered to. The fact that infinitesimal velocity relative to S' is not the same as infinitesimal velocity relative to S, leaves room for the discrepancy of reckoning of simultaneity to creep in. Consider two points A and B at rest relative to S', and distant x' apart. Take a clock at A and move it gently to B by giving it an

* It may be impossible to change the motion of a rod without causing a rise of temperature. Our conclusions will then not apply until the temperature has fallen again, i.e. until the temperature-test shows that the rod is precisely similar to the rod before the change of motion.

infinitesimal velocity du' for a time x'/du'. Owing to the motion, the clock will by (4·9) be retarded in the ratio $(1 - du'^2/c^2)^{-\frac{1}{2}}$, this continues for a time x'/du' and the total loss is thus

$$\{1 - (1 - du'^2/c^2)^{\frac{1}{2}}\}\, x'/du',$$

which tends to zero when du' is infinitely small. S' may accordingly accept the result of the comparison without applying any correction for the motion of the clock.

Now consider S's view of this experiment. For him the clock had already a velocity u, and accordingly the time indicated by the clock is only $(1 - u^2/c^2)^{\frac{1}{2}}$ of the true time for S. By differentiation, an additional velocity du* causes a supplementary loss

$$(1 - u^2/c^2)^{-\frac{1}{2}}\, u\, du/c^2 \text{ clock seconds} \quad \ldots\ldots\ldots\ldots \quad (11{\cdot}2)$$

per true second. Owing to the FitzGerald contraction of the length AB, the distance to be travelled is x'/β, and the journey will occupy a time

$$x'/\beta du \text{ true seconds} \quad \ldots\ldots\ldots\ldots\ldots\ldots\ldots\ldots \quad (11{\cdot}3).$$

Multiplying (11·2) and (11·3), the total loss due to the journey is

$$ux'/c^2 \text{ clock seconds},$$

or

$$\beta u x'/c^2 \text{ true seconds for } S \quad \ldots\ldots\ldots\ldots\ldots\ldots \quad (11{\cdot}4).$$

Thus, whilst S' accepts the uncorrected result of the comparison, S has to apply a correction $\beta u x'/c^2$ for the disturbance of the chronometer through transport. This is precisely the difference of their reckonings of simultaneity given by (11·1).

In practice an accurate comparison of time at different places is made, not by transporting chronometers, but by electromagnetic signals—usually wireless time-signals for places on the earth, and light-signals for places in the solar system or stellar universe. Take two clocks at A and B, respectively. Let a signal leave A at clock-time t_1, reach B at time t_B by the clock at B, and be reflected to reach A again at time t_2. The observer S', who is at rest relatively to the clocks, will conclude that the instant t_B at B was simultaneous with the instant $\frac{1}{2}(t_1 + t_2)$ at A, because he assumes that the forward velocity of light is equal to the backward velocity. But for S the two clocks are moving with velocity u, therefore he calculates that the outward journey will occupy a time $x/(c - u)$ and the homeward journey a time $x/(c + u)$. Now

$$\frac{x}{c-u} = \frac{x(c+u)}{c^2 - u^2} = \frac{\beta^2 x}{c^2}(c+u),$$

$$\frac{x}{c+u} = \frac{x(c-u)}{c^2 - u^2} = \frac{\beta^2 x}{c^2}(c-u).$$

Thus the instant t_B of arrival at B must be taken as $\beta^2 x u/c^2$ later than the half-way instant $\frac{1}{2}(t_1 + t_2)$. This correction applied by S, but not by S', agrees with (11·4) when we remember that owing to the FitzGerald contraction $x = x'/\beta$.

* Note that du will not be equal to du'.

Thus the same difference in the reckoning of simultaneity by S and S' appears whether we use the method of transport of clocks or of light-signals. In either case a convention is introduced as to the reckoning of time-differences at different places; this convention takes in the two methods the alternative forms—

(1) A clock moved with infinitesimal velocity from one place to another continues to read the correct time at its new station, *or*

(2) The forward velocity of light along any line is equal to the backward velocity*.

Neither statement is by itself a statement of observable fact, nor does it refer to any intrinsic property of clocks or of light; it is simply an announcement of the rule by which we propose to extend fictitious time-partitions through the world. But the mutual agreement of the two statements is a fact which could be tested by observation, though owing to the obvious practical difficulties it has not been possible to verify it directly. We have here given a theoretical proof of the agreement, depending on the truth of the fundamental axiom of § 1.

The two alternative forms of the convention are closely connected. In general, in any system of time-reckoning, a change du in the velocity of a clock involves a change of rate proportional to du, but there is a certain turning-point for which the change of rate is proportional to du^2. In adopting a time-reckoning such that this stationary point corresponds to his own motion, the observer is imposing a symmetry on space and time with respect to himself, which may be compared with the symmetry imposed in assuming a constant velocity of light in all directions. Analytically we imposed the same general symmetry by adopting (4·6) instead of (4·7) as the form for ds^2, making our space-time reckoning symmetrical with respect to the interval and therefore with respect to all observational criteria.

12. Momentum and mass.

Besides possessing extension in space and time, matter possesses inertia. We shall show in due course that *inertia, like extension, is expressible in terms of the interval relation*, but that is a development belonging to a later stage of our theory. Meanwhile we give an elementary treatment based on the empirical laws of conservation of momentum and energy rather than on any deep-seated theory of the nature of inertia.

For the discussion of space and time we have made use of certain ideal apparatus which can only be imperfectly realised in practice—rigid scales and

* The chief case in which we require for practical purposes an accurate convention as to the reckoning of time at places distant from the earth, is in calculating the elements and mean places of planets and comets. In these computations the velocity of light in any direction is taken to be 300,000 km. per sec., an assumption which rests on the convention (2). All experimental methods of measuring the velocity of light determine only an average to-and-fro velocity.

perfect cyclic mechanisms or clocks, which always remain similar configurations from the absolute point of view. Similarly for the discussion of inertia we require some ideal material object, say a perfectly elastic billiard ball, whose condition as regards inertial properties remains constant from an absolute point of view. The difficulty that actual billiard balls are not perfectly elastic must be surmounted in the same way as the difficulty that actual scales are not rigid. To the ideal billiard ball we can affix a constant number, called the *invariant mass**, which will denote its absolute inertial properties; and this number is supposed to remain unaltered throughout the vicissitudes of its history, or, if temporarily disturbed during a collision, is restored at the times when we have to examine the state of the body.

With the customary definition of momentum, the components

$$M\frac{dx}{dt}, \quad M\frac{dy}{dt}, \quad M\frac{dz}{dt} \qquad \text{.....................(12·1)}$$

cannot satisfy a general law of conservation of momentum unless the mass M is allowed to vary with the velocity. But with the slightly modified definition

$$m\frac{dx}{ds}, \quad m\frac{dy}{ds}, \quad m\frac{dz}{ds} \qquad \text{.....................(12·2)}$$

the law of conservation can be satisfied simultaneously in all space-time systems, m being an invariant number. This was shown in *Space, Time and Gravitation*, p. 142.

Comparing (12·1) and (12·2), we have

$$M = m\frac{dt}{ds} \qquad \text{.....................(12·3)}.$$

We call m the *invariant mass*, and M the *relative mass*, or simply the *mass*.

The term "invariant" signifies unchanged for any transformation of coordinates, and, in particular, the same for all observers, constancy during the life-history of the body is an additional property of m attributed to our ideal billiard balls, but not assumed to be true for matter in general.

Choosing units of length and time so that the velocity of light is unity, we have by (7·2)

$$\frac{ds}{dt} = (1 - v^2)^{\frac{1}{2}}.$$

Hence by (12·3)

$$M = m(1 - v^2)^{-\frac{1}{2}} \qquad \text{.....................(12·4)}.$$

The mass increases with the velocity by the same factor as that which gives the FitzGerald contraction, and when $v = 0$, $M = m$. The invariant mass is thus equal to the mass at rest.

It is natural to extend (12·2) by adding a fourth component, thus

$$m\frac{dx}{ds}, \quad m\frac{dy}{ds}, \quad m\frac{dz}{ds}, \quad m\frac{dt}{ds} \qquad \text{.....................(12·5)}.$$

* Or proper-mass.

By (12·3) the fourth component is equal to M. Thus the momenta and mass (relative mass) form together a symmetrical expression, the momenta being space-components, and the mass the time-component. We shall see later that the expression (12·5) constitutes a vector, and the laws of conservation of momentum and mass assert the conservation of this vector.

The following is an analytical proof of the law of variation of mass with velocity directly from the principle of conservation of mass and momentum. Let M_1, M_1' be the mass of a body as measured by S and S' respectively, v_1, v_1' being its velocity in the x-direction. Writing

$$\beta_1 = (1 - v_1^2/c^2)^{-\frac{1}{2}}, \quad \beta_1' = (1 - v_1'^2/c^2)^{-\frac{1}{2}}, \quad \beta = (1 - u^2/c^2)^{-\frac{1}{2}},$$

we can easily verify from (6·2) that

$$\beta_1 v_1 = \beta\beta_1'(v_1' - u) \quad \text{.................. ......} \quad (12·6).$$

Let a number of such particles be moving in a straight line subject to the conservation of mass and momentum as measured by S', viz.

$$\Sigma M_1' \text{ and } \Sigma M_1' v_1' \text{ are conserved}$$

Since β and u are constants it follows that

$$\Sigma M_1' \beta (v_1' - u) \text{ is conserved.}$$

Therefore by (12·6)

$$\Sigma M_1' \beta_1 v_1/\beta_1' \text{ is conserved} \quad \text{.........................} (12·71).$$

But since momentum must also be conserved for the observer S

$$\Sigma M_1 v_1 \text{ is conserved} \quad \text{.........................} (12·72)$$

The results (12·71) and (12·72) will agree if

$$M_1/\beta_1 = M_1'/\beta_1',$$

and it is easy to see that there can be no other general solution. Hence for different values of v_1, M_1 is proportional to β_1, or

$$M = m(1 - v^2/c^2)^{-\frac{1}{2}},$$

where m is a constant for the body.

It requires a greater impulse to produce a given change of velocity δv in the original direction of motion than to produce an equal change δw at right angles to it. For the momenta in the two directions are initially

$$mv(1 - v^2/c^2)^{-\frac{1}{2}}, \quad 0,$$

and after a change δv, δw, they become

$$m(v + \delta v)[1 - \{(v + \delta v)^2 + (\delta w)^2\}/c^2]^{-\frac{1}{2}}, \quad m\delta w[1 - \{(v + \delta v)^2 + (\delta w)^2\}/c^2]^{-\frac{1}{2}}.$$

Hence to the first order in δv, δw the changes of momentum are

$$m(1 - v^2/c^2)^{-\frac{3}{2}}\delta v, \quad m(1 - v^2/c^2)^{-\frac{1}{2}}\delta w,$$

or

$$M\beta^2\delta v, \quad M\delta w,$$

where β is the FitzGerald factor for velocity v. The coefficient $M\beta^2$ was formerly called the *longitudinal mass*, M being the *transverse mass*; but the longitudinal mass is of no particular importance in the general theory, and the term is dropping out of use.

13. Energy.

When the units are such that $c = 1$, we have

$$M = m(1 - v^2)^{-\frac{1}{2}}$$
$$= m + \tfrac{1}{2}mv^2 \text{ approximately} \quad \text{(13·1)},$$

if the speed is small compared with the velocity of light. The second term is the kinetic energy, so that the change of mass is the same as the change of energy, when the velocity alters. This suggests the identification of mass with energy. It may be recalled that in mechanics the total energy of a system is left vague to the extent of an arbitrary additive constant, since only changes of energy are defined. In identifying energy with mass we fix the additive constant m for each body, and m may be regarded as the internal energy of constitution of the body.

The approximation used in (13·1) does not invalidate the argument. Consider two ideal billiard balls colliding. The conservation of mass (relative mass) states that

$$\Sigma m(1 - v^2)^{-\frac{1}{2}} \text{ is unaltered.}$$

The conservation of energy states that

$$\Sigma m(1 + \tfrac{1}{2}v^2) \text{ is unaltered.}$$

But if both statements were exactly true we should have two equations determining unique values of the speeds of the two balls; so that these speeds could not be altered by the collision. The two laws are not independent, but one is an approximation to the other. The first is the accurate law since it is independent of the space-time frame of reference. Accordingly the expression $\frac{1}{2}mv^2$ for the kinetic energy in elementary mechanics is only an approximation in which terms in v^4, etc. are neglected.

When the units of length and time are not restricted by the condition $c = 1$, the relation between the mass M and the energy E is

$$M = E/c^2 \quad \text{(13·2)}.$$

Thus the energy corresponding to a gram is $9 . 10^{20}$ ergs. This does not affect the identity of mass and energy—that both are measures of the same world-condition. A world-condition can be examined by different kinds of experimental tests, and the units gram and erg are associated with different tests of the mass-energy condition. But when once the measure has been made it is of no consequence to us which of the experimental methods was chosen, and grams or ergs can be used indiscriminately as the unit of mass. In fact, measures made by energy-tests and by mass-tests are convertible like measures made with a yard-rule and a metre-rule.

The principle of conservation of mass has thus become merged in the principle of conservation of energy. But there is another independent phenomenon which perhaps corresponds more nearly to the original idea of Lavoisier when he enunciated the law of conservation of matter. I refer to the permanence of *invariant mass* attributed to our ideal billiard balls but not supposed to be a general property of matter. The conservation of m is an accidental property like rigidity; the conservation of M is an invariable law of nature.

When radiant heat falls on a billiard ball so that its temperature rises, the increased energy of motion of the molecules causes an increase of mass M. The invariant mass m also increases since it is equal to M for a body at rest. There is no violation of the conservation of M, because the radiant heat has mass M which it transfers to the ball; but we shall show later that the electromagnetic waves have no invariant mass, and the addition to m is created out of nothing. Thus invariant mass is not conserved in general.

To some extent we can avoid this failure by taking the microscopic point of view. The billiard ball can be analysed into a very large number of constituents—electrons and protons—each of which is believed to preserve the same invariant mass for life. But the invariant mass of the billiard ball is not exactly equal to the sum of the invariant masses of its constituents*. The permanence and permanent similarity of all electrons seems to be the modern equivalent of Lavoisier's "conservation of matter." It is still uncertain whether it expresses a universal law of nature; and we are willing to contemplate the possibility that occasionally a positive and negative electron may coalesce and annul one another. In that case the mass M would pass into the electromagnetic waves generated by the catastrophe, whereas the invariant mass m would disappear altogether. Again if ever we are able to synthesise helium out of hydrogen, 0·8 per cent of the invariant mass will be annihilated, whilst the corresponding proportion of relative mass will be liberated as radiant energy.

It will thus be seen that although in the special problems considered the quantity m is usually supposed to be permanent, its conservation belongs to an altogether different order of ideas from the universal conservation of M.

14. Density and temperature.

Consider a volume of space delimited in some invariant way, e.g. the content of a material box. The counting of a number of discrete particles continually within (i.e. moving with) the box is an absolute operation; let the absolute number be N. The volume V of the box will depend on the space-reckoning, being decreased in the ratio β for an observer moving relatively to the box and particles, owing to the FitzGerald contraction of one of the dimensions of the box. Accordingly the particle-density $\sigma = N/V$ satisfies

$$\sigma' = \sigma\beta \qquad\qquad (14\cdot1),$$

* This is because the invariant mass of each electron is its relative mass referred to axes moving with it; the invariant mass of the billiard ball is the relative mass referred to axes at rest in the billiard ball as a whole.

where σ' is the particle-density for an observer in relative motion, and σ the particle-density for an observer at rest relative to the particles.

It follows that the mass-density ρ obeys the equation

$$\rho' = \rho\beta^2 \qquad (14{\cdot}2),$$

since the mass of each particle is increased for the moving observer in the ratio β.

Quantities referred to the space-time system of an observer moving with the body considered are often distinguished by the prefix *proper-* (German, *Eigen-*), e.g. proper-length, proper-volume, proper-density, proper-mass = invariant mass.

The transformation of temperature for a moving observer does not often concern us. In general the word obviously means proper-temperature, and the motion of the observer does not enter into consideration. In thermometry and in the theory of gases it is essential to take a standard with respect to which the matter is at rest on the average, since the indication of a thermometer moving rapidly through a fluid is of no practical interest. But thermodynamical temperature is defined by

$$dS = dM/T \qquad (14{\cdot}3),$$

where dS is the change of entropy for a change of energy dM. The temperature T defined by this equation will depend on the observer's frame of reference. Entropy is clearly meant to be an invariant, since it depends on the probability of the statistical state of the system compared with other states which might exist. Hence T must be altered by motion in the same way as dM, that is to say

$$T' = \beta T \qquad (14{\cdot}4).$$

But it would be useless to apply such a transformation to the adiabatic gas-equation

$$T = k\rho^{\gamma-1},$$

for, in that case, T is evidently intended to signify the proper-temperature and ρ the proper-density.

In general it is unprofitable to apply the Lorentz transformation to the *constitutive equations* of a material medium and to coefficients occurring in them (permeability, specific inductive capacity, elasticity, velocity of sound). Such equations naturally take a simpler and more significant form for axes moving with the matter. The transformation to moving axes introduces great complications without any evident advantages, and is of little interest except as an analytical exercise

15. General transformations of coordinates.

We obtain a transformation of coordinates by taking new coordinates x_1', x_2', x_3', x_4' which are any four functions of the old coordinates x_1, x_2, x_3, x_4. Conversely, x_1, x_2, x_3, x_4 are functions of x_1', x_2', x_3', x_4'. It is assumed that multiple values are excluded, at least in the region considered, so that values of (x_1, x_2, x_3, x_4) and (x_1', x_2', x_3', x_4') correspond one to one.

If $\quad x_1 = f_1(x_1', x_2', x_3', x_4')$; $x_2 = f_2(x_1', x_2', x_3', x_4')$; etc.,

$$dx_1 = \frac{\partial f_1}{\partial x_1'} dx_1' + \frac{\partial f_1}{\partial x_2'} dx_2' + \frac{\partial f_1}{\partial x_3'} dx_3' + \frac{\partial f_1}{\partial x_4'} dx_4', \text{ etc.} \quad \ldots\ldots(15\cdot1),$$

or it may be written simply,

$$dx_1 = \frac{\partial x_1}{\partial x_1'} dx_1' + \frac{\partial x_1}{\partial x_2'} dx_2' + \frac{\partial x_1}{\partial x_3'} dx_3' + \frac{\partial x_1}{\partial x_4'} dx_4'; \text{ etc} \quad \ldots\ldots(15\cdot2)$$

Substituting from (15·2) in (2·1) we see that ds^2 will be a homogeneous quadratic function of the differentials of the new coordinates, and the new coefficients g_{11}', g_{22}', etc could be written down in terms of the old, if desired

For an example consider the usual transformation to axes revolving with constant angular velocity ω, viz.

$$\left.\begin{aligned} x &= x_1' \cos \omega x_4' - x_2' \sin \omega x_4' \\ y &= x_1' \sin \omega x_4' + x_2' \cos \omega x_4' \\ z &= x_3' \\ t &= x_4' \end{aligned}\right\} \quad \ldots\ldots\ldots\ldots\ldots\ldots(15\cdot3)$$

Hence

$$dx = dx_1' \cos \omega x_4' - dx_2' \sin \omega x_4' + \omega(-x_1' \sin \omega x_4' - x_2' \cos \omega x_4') dx_4',$$

$$dy = dx_1' \sin \omega x_4' + dx_2' \cos \omega x_4' + \omega(x_1' \cos \omega x_4' - x_2' \sin \omega x_4') dx_4',$$

$$dz = dx_3',$$

$$dt = dx_4'$$

Taking units of space and time so that $c = 1$, we have for our original fixed coordinates by (7·1)

$$ds^2 = -dx^2 - dy^2 - dz^2 + dt^2.$$

Hence, substituting the values found above,

$$ds^2 = -dx_1'^2 - dx_2'^2 - dx_3'^2 + \{1 - \omega^2(x_1'^2 + x_2'^2)\} dx_4'^2 + 2\omega x_2' dx_1' dx_4' - 2\omega x_1' dx_2' dx_4' \quad \ldots\ldots(15\cdot4).$$

Remembering that all observational differences of coordinate-systems must arise *via* the interval, this formula must comprise everything which distinguishes the rotating system from a fixed system of coordinates.

In the transformation (15·3) we have paid no attention to any contraction of the standards of length or retardation of clocks due to motion with the rotating axes. The formulae of transformation are those of elementary kinematics, so that x_1', x_2', x_3', x_4' are quite strictly the coordinates used in the ordinary theory of rotating axes But it may be suggested that elementary kinematics is now seen to be rather crude, and that it would be worth while to touch up the formulae (15·3) so as to take account of these small changes of the standards. A little consideration shows that the suggestion is impracticable It was shown in § 4 that if x_1', x_2', x_3', x_4' represent rectangular coordinates and time as partitioned by direct readings of scales and clocks, then

$$ds^2 = -dx_1'^2 - dx_2'^2 - dx_3'^2 + c^2dx_4'^2 \qquad\qquad (15\cdot45),$$

so that coordinates which give any other formula for the interval cannot represent the immediate indications of scales and clocks. As shown at the end of § 5, the only transformations which give (15·45) are Lorentz transformations If we wish to make a transformation of a more general kind, such as that of (15 3), we must necessarily abandon the association of the coordinate-system with uncorrected scale and clock readings. It is useless to try to "improve" the transformation to rotating axes, because the supposed improvement could only lead us back to a coordinate-system similar to the fixed axes with which we started.

The inappropriateness of rotating axes to scale and clock measurements can be regarded from a physical point of view. We cannot keep a scale or clock at rest in the rotating system unless we constrain it, i.e. subject it to molecular bombardment—an "outside influence" whose effect on the measurements must not be ignored.

In the x, y, z, t system of coordinates the scale and clock are the natural equipment for exploration. In other systems they will, if unconstrained, continue to measure ds; but the reading of ds is no longer related in a simple way to the differences of coordinates which we wish to determine; it depends on the more complicated calculations involved in (2 1). The scale and clock to some extent lose their pre-eminence, and since they are rather elaborate appliances it may be better to refer to some simpler means of exploration. We consider then two simpler test-objects—the moving particle and the light-pulse.

In ordinary rectangular coordinates and time x, y, z, t an undisturbed particle moves with uniform velocity, so that its track is given by the equations

$$x = a + bt, \qquad y = c + dt, \qquad z = e + ft \qquad\qquad (15\cdot5),$$

i.e. the equations of a straight line in four dimensions. By substituting from (15·3) we could find the equations of the track in rotating coordinates; or by substituting from (15·2) we could obtain the differential equations for any desired coordinates. But there is another way of proceeding. The differential equations of the track may be written

$$\frac{d^2x}{ds^2}, \frac{d^2y}{ds^2}, \frac{d^2z}{ds^2}, \frac{d^2t}{ds^2} = 0 \qquad\qquad (15\cdot6),$$

which on integration, having regard to the condition (7·1), give equations (15·5).

The equations (15·6) are comprised in the single statement

$$\int ds \text{ is stationary} \qquad\qquad (15\cdot7)$$

for all arbitrary small variations of the track which vanish at the initial and final limits—a well-known property of the straight line.

In arriving at (15·7) we use freely the geometry of the x, y, z, t system given by (7·1); but the final result does not allude to coordinates at all, and must be unaltered whatever system of coordinates we are using. To obtain explicit equations for the track in any desired system of coordinates, we substitute in (15·7) the appropriate expression (2·1) for ds and apply the calculus of variations. The actual analysis will be given in § 28.

The track of a light-pulse, being a straight line in four dimensions, will also satisfy (15·7), but the light-pulse has the special velocity c which gives the additional condition obtained in § 7, viz

$$ds = 0 \qquad \text{.........................(15·8)}.$$

Here again there is no reference to any coordinates in the final result.

We have thus obtained equations (15·7) and (15·8) for the behaviour of the moving particle and light-pulse which must hold good whatever the coordinate-system chosen. The indications of our two new test-bodies are connected with the interval, just as in § 3 the indications of the scale and clock were connected with the interval. It should be noticed however that whereas the use of the older test-bodies depends only on the truth of the fundamental axiom, the use of the new test-bodies depends on the truth of the empirical laws of motion and of light-propagation. In a deductive theory this appeal to empirical laws is a blemish which we must seek to remove later.

16. Fields of force.

Suppose that an observer has chosen a definite system of space-coordinates and of time-reckoning (x_1, x_2, x_3, x_4) and that the geometry of these is given by

$$ds^2 = g_{11}dx_1^2 + g_{22}dx_2^2 + \ldots + 2g_{12}dx_1dx_2 + \ldots \qquad \text{.....(16·1)}$$

Let him be under the mistaken impression that the geometry is

$$ds_0^2 = - dx_1^2 - dx_2^2 - dx_3^2 + dx_4^2 \qquad \text{..............(16·2)},$$

that being the geometry with which he is most familiar in pure mathematics. We use ds_0 to distinguish his mistaken value of the interval. Since intervals can be compared by experimental methods, he ought soon to discover that his ds_0 cannot be reconciled with observational results, and so realise his mistake. But the mind does not so readily get rid of an obsession. It is more likely that our observer will continue in his opinion, and attribute the discrepancy of the observations to some influence which is present and affects the behaviour of his test-bodies. He will, so to speak, introduce a supernatural agency which he can blame for the consequences of his mistake. Let us examine what name he would apply to this agency.

Of the four test-bodies considered the moving particle is in general the most sensitive to small changes of geometry, and it would be by this test that the observer would first discover discrepancies. The path laid down for it by our observer is

$$\int ds_0 \text{ is stationary,}$$

i.e. a straight line in the coordinates (x_1, x_2, x_3, x_4). The particle, of course, pays no heed to this, and moves in the different track

$$\int ds \text{ is stationary.}$$

Although apparently undisturbed it deviates from "uniform motion in a straight line." The name given to any agency which causes deviation from uniform motion in a straight line is *force* according to the Newtonian definition of force. Hence the agency invoked through our observer's mistake is described as a "field of force."

The field of force is not always introduced by inadvertence as in the foregoing illustration. It is sometimes introduced deliberately by the mathematician, e.g. when he introduces the centrifugal force. There would be little advantage and many disadvantages in banishing the phrase "field of force" from our vocabulary. We shall therefore regularise the procedure which our observer has adopted. We call (16·2) the *abstract geometry* of the system of coordinates (x_1, x_2, x_3, x_4), it may be chosen arbitrarily by the observer. The *natural geometry* is (16·1).

A field of force represents the discrepancy between the natural geometry of a coordinate-system and the abstract geometry arbitrarily ascribed to it.

A field of force thus arises from an attitude of mind. If we do not take our coordinate-system to be something different from that which it really is, there is no field of force. If we do not regard our rotating axes as though they were non-rotating, there is no centrifugal force.

Coordinates for which the natural geometry is

$$ds^2 = -dx_1^2 - dx_2^2 - dx_3^2 + dx_4^2$$

are called Galilean coordinates. They are the same as those we have hitherto called ordinary rectangular coordinates and time (the velocity of light being unity). Since this geometry is familiar to us, and enters largely into current conceptions of space, time and mechanics, we usually choose Galilean geometry when we have to ascribe an abstract geometry. Or we may use slight modifications of it, e.g. substitute polar for rectangular coordinates.

It has been shown in § 4 that when the g's are constants, coordinates can be chosen so that Galilean geometry is actually the natural geometry. There is then no need to introduce a field of force in order to enjoy our accustomed outlook; and if we deliberately choose non-Galilean coordinates and attribute to them abstract Galilean geometry, we recognise the artificial character of the field of force introduced to compensate the discrepancy. But in the more general case it is not possible to make the reduction of § 4 accurately throughout the region explored by our experiments; and no Galilean coordinates exist. In that case it has been usual to select some system (preferably an approximation to a Galilean system) and ascribe to it the abstract geometry of the Galilean system. The field of force so introduced is called "Gravitation."

It should be noticed that the rectangular coordinates and time in current use can scarcely be regarded as a close approximation to the Galilean system, since the powerful force of terrestrial gravitation is needed to compensate the error.

The naming of coordinates (e.g. time) usually follows the *abstract geometry* attributed to the system. In general the natural geometry is of some complicated kind for which no detailed nomenclature is recognised. Thus when we call a coordinate t the "time," we may either mean that it fulfils the observational conditions discussed in § 4, or we may mean that any departure from those conditions will be ascribed to the interference of a field of force. In the latter case "time" is an arbitrary name, useful because it fixes a consequential nomenclature of velocity, acceleration, etc.

To take a special example, an observer at a station on the earth has found a particular set of coordinates x_1, x_2, x_3, x_4 best suited to his needs. He calls them x, y, z, t in the belief that they are actually rectangular coordinates and time, and his terminology—straight line, circle, density, uniform velocity, etc.—follows from this identification. But, as shown in § 4, this nomenclature can only agree with the measures made by clocks and scales provided (16·2) is satisfied; and if (16·2) is satisfied, the tracks of undisturbed particles must be straight lines. Experiment immediately shows that this is not the case; the tracks of undisturbed particles are parabolas. But instead of accepting the verdict of experiment and admitting that x_1, x_2, x_3, x_4 are not what he supposed they were, our observer introduces a field of force to explain why his test is not fulfilled. A certain part of this field of force might have been avoided if he had taken originally a different set of coordinates (not rotating with the earth), and in so far as the field of force arises on this account it is generally recognised that it is a mathematical fiction—the centrifugal force. But there is a residuum which cannot be got rid of by any choice of coordinates; there exists no extensive coordinate-system having the simple properties which were ascribed to x, y, z, t. The intrinsic nature of space-time near the earth is not of the kind which admits coordinates with Galilean geometry. This irreducible field of force constitutes the field of terrestrial gravitation. The statement that space-time round the earth is "curved"—that is to say, that it is not of the kind which admits Galilean coordinates—is not an hypothesis; it is an equivalent expression of the observed fact that an irreducible field of force is present, having regard to the Newtonian definition of force. It is this fact of observation which demands the introduction of non-Galilean space-time and non-Euclidean space into the theory.

17. The Principle of Equivalence.

In § 15 we have stated the laws of motion of undisturbed material particles and of light-pulses in a form independent of the coordinates chosen. Since a great deal will depend upon the truth of these laws it is desirable to consider what justification there is for believing them to be both accurate and universal. Three courses are open:

(*a*) It will be shown in Chapters IV and VI that these laws follow rigorously from a more fundamental discussion of the nature of matter and of electromagnetic fields, that is to say, the hypotheses underlying them may be pushed a stage further back.

(*b*) The track of a moving particle or light-pulse under specified initial conditions is unique, and it does not seem to be possible to specify any unique tracks in terms of intervals only other than those given by equations (15·7) and (15·8).

(*c*) We may arrive at these laws by induction from experiment.

If we rely solely on experimental evidence we cannot claim exactness for the laws. It goes without saying that there always remains a possibility of small amendments of the laws too slight to affect any observational tests yet tried. Belief in the perfect accuracy of (15·7) and (15·8) can only be justified on the theoretical grounds (*a*) or (*b*). But the more important consideration is the universality, rather than the accuracy, of the experimental laws; we have to guard against a spurious generalisation extended to conditions intrinsically dissimilar from those for which the laws have been established observationally.

We derived (15·7) from the equations (15·5) which describe the observed behaviour of a particle moving under no field of force. We assume that the result holds in all circumstances. The risky point in the generalisation is not in introducing a field of force, because that may be due to an attitude of mind of which the particle has no cognizance. The risk is in passing from regions of the world where Galilean coordinates (x, y, z, t) are possible to intrinsically dissimilar regions where no such coordinates exist—from flat space-time to space-time which is not flat.

The *Principle of Equivalence* asserts the legitimacy of this generalisation. It is essentially an hypothesis to be tested by experiment as opportunity offers. Moreover it is to be regarded as a suggestion, rather than a dogma admitting of no exceptions. It is likely that some of the phenomena will be determined by comparatively simple equations in which the components of curvature of the world do not appear; such equations will be the same for a curved region as for a flat region. It is to these that the Principle of Equivalence applies. It is a plausible suggestion that the undisturbed motion of a particle and the propagation of light are governed by laws of this specially simple type; and accordingly (15·7) and (15·8) will apply in all circumstances. But there are more complex phenomena governed by equations in which the curvatures of the world are involved; terms containing these curvatures will vanish in the equations summarising experiments made in a flat region, and would have to be reinstated in passing to the general equations. Clearly there must be some phenomena of this kind which discriminate between a flat world and a curved world; otherwise we could have no knowledge of world-curvature. For these the Principle of Equivalence breaks down.

The Principle of Equivalence thus asserts that *some* of the chief differential equations of physics are the same for a curved region of the world as for an osculating flat region*. There can be no infallible rule for generalising experimental laws; but the Principle of Equivalence offers a suggestion for trial, which may be expected to succeed sometimes, and fail sometimes.

The Principle of Equivalence has played a great part as a guide in the original building up of the generalised relativity theory; but now that we have reached the new view of the nature of the world it has become less necessary. Our present exposition is in the main deductive. We start with a general theory of world-structure and work down to the experimental consequences, so that our progress is from the general to the special laws, instead of *vice versa*.

18. Retrospect.

The investigation of the external world in physics is a quest for *structure* rather than *substance*. A structure can best be represented as a complex of relations and relata; and in conformity with this we endeavour to reduce the phenomena to their expressions in terms of the relations which we call intervals and the relata which we call events.

If two bodies are of identical structure as regards the complex of interval relations, they will be exactly similar as regards observational properties†, if our fundamental hypothesis is true. By this we show that experimental measurements of lengths and duration are equivalent to measurements of the interval relation.

To the events we assign four identification-numbers or coordinates according to a plan which is arbitrary within wide limits. The connection between our physical measurements of interval and the system of identification-numbers is expressed by the general quadratic form (2.1). In the particular case when these identification-numbers can be so assigned that the product terms in the quadratic form disappear leaving only the four squares, the coordinates have the metrical properties belonging to rectangular coordinates and time, and are accordingly so identified. If any such system exists an infinite number of others exist connected with it by the Lorentz transformation, so that there is no unique space-time frame. The relations of these different space-time reckonings have been considered in detail. It is

* The correct equations for a curved world will necessarily include as a special case those already obtained for a flat world. The practical point on which we seek the guidance of the Principle of Equivalence is whether the equations already obtained for a flat world will serve as they stand or will require generalisation.

† At present this is limited to extensional properties (in both space and time). It will be shown later that all mechanical properties are also included. Electromagnetic properties require separate consideration.

shown that there must be a particular speed which has the remarkable property that its value is the same for all these systems; and by appeal to the Michelson-Morley experiment or to Fizeau's experiment it is found that this is a distinctive property of the speed of light.

But it is not possible throughout the world to choose coordinates fulfilling the current definitions of rectangular coordinates and time. In such cases we usually relax the definitions, and attribute the failure of fulfilment to a field of force pervading the region. We have now no definite guide in selecting what coordinates to take as rectangular coordinates and time; for whatever the discrepancy, it can always be ascribed to a suitable field of force. The field of force will vary according to the system of coordinates selected; but in the general case it is not possible to get rid of it altogether (in a large region) by any choice of coordinates. This irreducible field of force is ascribed to gravitation. It should be noticed that the gravitational influence of a massive body is not properly expressed by a definite field of force, but by the property of irreducibility of the field of force. We shall find later that the irreducibility of the field of force is equivalent to what in geometrical nomenclature is called a curvature of the continuum of space-time.

For the fuller study of these problems we require a special mathematical calculus which will now be developed *ab initio.*

CHAPTER II

THE TENSOR CALCULUS

19. Contravariant and covariant vectors.

We consider the transformation from one system of coordinates x_1, x_2, x_3, x_4 to another system x_1', x_2', x_3', x_4'

The differentials (dx_1, dx_2, dx_3, dx_4) are transformed according to the equations (15·2), viz.

$$dx_1' = \frac{\partial x_1'}{\partial x_1} dx_1 + \frac{\partial x_1'}{\partial x_2} dx_2 + \frac{\partial x_1'}{\partial x_3} dx_3 + \frac{\partial x_1'}{\partial x_4} dx_4, \text{ etc.}$$

which may be written shortly

$$dx_\mu' = \sum_{\alpha=1}^{4} \frac{\partial x_\mu'}{\partial x_\alpha} dx_\alpha,$$

four equations being obtained by taking $\mu = 1, 2, 3, 4$, successively.

Any set of four quantities transformed according to this law is called a *contravariant vector*. Thus if (A^1, A^2, A^3, A^4) becomes (A'^1, A'^2, A'^3, A'^4) in the new coordinate-system, where

$$A'^\mu = \sum_{\alpha=1}^{4} \frac{\partial x_\mu'}{\partial x_\alpha} A^\alpha \quad \ldots\ldots\ldots\ldots\ldots\ldots(19\cdot1),$$

then (A^1, A^2, A^3, A^4), denoted briefly as A^μ, is a contravariant vector. The upper position of the suffix (which is, of course, not an exponent) is reserved to indicate contravariant vectors.

If ϕ is an invariant function of position, i.e. if it has a fixed value at each point independent of the coordinate-system employed, the four quantities

$$\left(\frac{\partial \phi}{\partial x_1}, \frac{\partial \phi}{\partial x_2}, \frac{\partial \phi}{\partial x_3}, \frac{\partial \phi}{\partial x_4}\right)$$

are transformed according to the equations

$$\frac{\partial \phi}{\partial x_1'} = \frac{\partial x_1}{\partial x_1'}\frac{\partial \phi}{\partial x_1} + \frac{\partial x_2}{\partial x_1'}\frac{\partial \phi}{\partial x_2} + \frac{\partial x_3}{\partial x_1'}\frac{\partial \phi}{\partial x_3} + \frac{\partial x_4}{\partial x_1'}\frac{\partial \phi}{\partial x_4}, \text{ etc.}$$

which may be written shortly

$$\frac{\partial \phi}{\partial x_\mu'} = \sum_{\alpha=1}^{4} \frac{\partial x_\alpha}{\partial x_\mu'}\frac{\partial \phi}{\partial x_\alpha}.$$

Any set of four quantities transformed according to this law is called a *covariant vector*. Thus if A_μ is a covariant vector, its transformation law is

$$A_\mu' = \sum_{\alpha=1}^{4} \frac{\partial x_\alpha}{\partial x_\mu'} A_\alpha \quad \ldots\ldots\ldots\ldots\ldots(19\cdot2).$$

We have thus two varieties of vectors which we distinguish by the upper or lower position of the suffix. The first illustration of a contravariant vector, dx_μ, forms rather an awkward exception to the rule that a lower suffix indicates covariance and an upper suffix contravariance. There is no other exception likely to mislead the reader, so that it is not difficult to keep in mind this peculiarity of dx_μ; but we shall sometimes find it convenient to indicate its contravariance explicitly by writing

$$dx_\mu \equiv (dx)^\mu \quad \text{..............................} \quad (19\cdot3)$$

A vector may either be a single set of four quantities associated with a special point in space-time, or it may be a set of four functions varying continuously with position. Thus we can have an "isolated vector" or a "vector-field."

For an illustration of a covariant vector we considered the gradient of an invariant, $\partial\phi/\partial x_\mu$; but a covariant vector is not necessarily the gradient of an invariant.

The reader will probably be already familiar with the term vector, but the distinction of covariant and contravariant vectors will be new to him. This is because in the elementary analysis only rectangular coordinates are contemplated, and for transformations from one rectangular system to another the laws (19·1) and (19·2) are equivalent to one another. From the geometrical point of view, the *contravariant vector* is the vector with which everyone is familiar, this is because a displacement, or directed distance between two points, is regarded as representing (dx_1, dx_2, dx_3)* which, as we have seen, is contravariant. The covariant vector is a new conception which does not so easily lend itself to graphical illustration.

20. The mathematical notion of a vector.

The formal definitions in the preceding section do not help much to an understanding of what the notion of a vector really is. We shall try to explain this more fully, taking first the mathematical notion of a vector (with which we are most directly concerned) and leaving the more difficult physical notion to follow.

We have a set of four numbers (A_1, A_2, A_3, A_4) which we associate with some point (x_1, x_2, x_3, x_4) and with a certain system of coordinates. We make a change of the coordinate-system, and we ask, What will these numbers become in the new coordinates? The question is meaningless, they do not automatically "become" anything. Unless we interfere with them they stay as they were. But the mathematician may say "When I am using the coordinates x_1, x_2, x_3, x_4, I want to talk about the numbers A_1, A_2, A_3, A_4, and when I am using x_1', x_2', x_3', x_4' I find that at the corresponding stage of my work I shall want to talk about four different numbers A_1', A_2', A_3', A_4'.

* The customary resolution of a displacement into components in oblique directions assumes this.

So for brevity I propose to call both sets of numbers by the same symbol $\mathfrak{A}$." We reply "That will be all right, provided that you tell us just what numbers will be denoted by $\mathfrak{A}$ for *each* of the coordinate-systems you intend to use. Unless you do this we shall not know what you are talking about."

Accordingly the mathematician begins by giving us a list of the numbers that $\mathfrak{A}$ will signify in the different coordinate-systems. We here denote these numbers by letters. $\mathfrak{A}$ will mean*

X, Y, Z for certain rectangular coordinates x, y, z,

R, Θ, Φ for certain polar coordinates r, θ, ϕ,

Λ, M, N for certain ellipsoidal coordinates λ, μ, ν.

"But," says the mathematician, "I shall never finish at this rate. There are an infinite number of coordinate-systems which I want to use. I see that I must alter my plan. I will give you a general rule to find the new values of $\mathfrak{A}$ when you pass from one coordinate-system to another; so that it is only necessary for me to give you one set of values and you can find all the others for yourselves."

In mentioning a *rule* the mathematician gives up his arbitrary power of making $\mathfrak{A}$ mean anything according to his fancy at the moment. He binds himself down to some kind of regularity. Indeed we might have suspected that our orderly-minded friend would have some principle in his assignment of different meanings to $\mathfrak{A}$. But even so, can we make any guess at the rule he is likely to adopt unless we have some idea of the problem he is working at in which $\mathfrak{A}$ occurs? I think we can; it is not necessary to know anything about the nature of his problem, whether it relates to the world of physics or to something purely conceptual; it is sufficient that we know a little about the nature of a mathematician.

What kind of rule could he adopt? Let us examine the quantities which can enter into it. There are first the two sets of numbers to be connected, say, X, Y, Z and R, Θ, Φ. Nothing has been said as to these being analytical functions of any kind; so far as we know they are isolated numbers. Therefore there can be no question of introducing their derivatives. They are regarded as located at some point of space (x, y, z) and (r, θ, ϕ), otherwise the question of coordinates could scarcely arise. They are changed because the coordinate-system has changed *at this point*, and that change is defined by quantities like $\frac{\partial r}{\partial x}, \frac{\partial^2\theta}{\partial x \partial y}$, and so on. The integral coordinates themselves, x, y, z, r, θ, ϕ, cannot be involved; because they express relations to a distant origin, whereas we are concerned only with changes at the spot where (X, Y, Z) is located. Thus the rule must involve only the numbers X, Y, Z, R, Θ, Φ combined with the mutual derivatives of x, y, z, r, θ, ϕ.

* For convenience I take a three-dimensional illustration.

One such rule would be

$$\left.\begin{aligned} R &= \frac{\partial r}{\partial x} X + \frac{\partial r}{\partial y} Y + \frac{\partial r}{\partial z} Z \\ \Theta &= \frac{\partial \theta}{\partial x} X + \frac{\partial \theta}{\partial y} Y + \frac{\partial \theta}{\partial z} Z \\ \Phi &= \frac{\partial \phi}{\partial x} X + \frac{\partial \phi}{\partial y} Y + \frac{\partial \phi}{\partial z} Z \end{aligned}\right\} \quad \ldots\ldots\ldots\ldots(20{\cdot}1).$$

Applying the same rule to the transformation from (r, θ, ϕ) to (λ, μ, ν) we have

$$\Lambda = \frac{\partial \lambda}{\partial r} R + \frac{\partial \lambda}{\partial \theta} \Theta + \frac{\partial \lambda}{\partial \phi} \Phi \quad \ldots\ldots\ldots\ldots(20{\cdot}2),$$

whence, substituting for R, Θ, Φ from (20·1) and collecting terms,

$$\begin{aligned} \Lambda &= \left(\frac{\partial \lambda}{\partial r}\frac{\partial r}{\partial x} + \frac{\partial \lambda}{\partial \theta}\frac{\partial \theta}{\partial x} + \frac{\partial \lambda}{\partial \phi}\frac{\partial \phi}{\partial x}\right) X + \left(\frac{\partial \lambda}{\partial r}\frac{\partial r}{\partial y} + \frac{\partial \lambda}{\partial \theta}\frac{\partial \theta}{\partial y} + \frac{\partial \lambda}{\partial \phi}\frac{\partial \phi}{\partial y}\right) Y \\ &\quad + \left(\frac{\partial \lambda}{\partial r}\frac{\partial r}{\partial z} + \frac{\partial \lambda}{\partial \theta}\frac{\partial \theta}{\partial z} + \frac{\partial \lambda}{\partial \phi}\frac{\partial \phi}{\partial z}\right) Z \\ &= \frac{\partial \lambda}{\partial x} X + \frac{\partial \lambda}{\partial y} Y + \frac{\partial \lambda}{\partial z} Z \quad \ldots\ldots\ldots\ldots(20{\cdot}3), \end{aligned}$$

which is the same formula as we should have obtained by applying the rule to the direct transformation from (x, y, z) to (λ, μ, ν). The rule is thus self-consistent. But this is a happy accident, pertaining to this particular rule, and depending on the formula

$$\frac{\partial \lambda}{\partial x} = \frac{\partial \lambda}{\partial r}\frac{\partial r}{\partial x} + \frac{\partial \lambda}{\partial \theta}\frac{\partial \theta}{\partial x} + \frac{\partial \lambda}{\partial \phi}\frac{\partial \phi}{\partial x},$$

and amid the apparently infinite choice of formulae it will not be easy to find others which have this self-consistency.

The above rule is that already given for the contravariant vector (19·1) The rule for the covariant vector is also self-consistent. There do not appear to be any other self-consistent rules for the transformation of a set of three numbers (or four numbers for four coordinates) *.

We see then that unless the mathematician disregards the need for self-consistency in his rule, he must inevitably make his quantity $\mathfrak{A}$ either a contravariant or a covariant vector. The choice between these is entirely at his discretion. He might obtain a wider choice by disregarding the property of self-consistency—by selecting a particular coordinate-system, x, y, z, and insisting that values in other coordinate-systems must always be obtained by

* Except that we may in addition multiply by any power of the Jacobian of the transformation. This is self-consistent because

$$\frac{\partial (x, y, z)}{\partial (r, \theta, \phi)} \frac{\partial (r, \theta, \phi)}{\partial (\lambda, \mu, \nu)} = \frac{\partial (x, y, z)}{\partial (\lambda, \mu, \nu)}.$$

Sets of numbers transformed with this additional multiplication are degenerate cases of tensors of higher rank considered later. See §§ 48, 49.

applying the rule immediately to X, Y, Z, and not permitting intermediate transformations. In practice he does not do this, perhaps because he can never make up his mind that any particular coordinates are deserving of this special distinction.

We see now that a mathematical vector is a common name for an infinite number of sets of quantities, each set being associated with one of an infinite number of systems of coordinates. The arbitrariness in the association is removed by postulating that some method is followed, and that no one system of coordinates is singled out for special distinction. In technical language the transformations must form a *Group*. *The quantity* (R, Θ, Φ) *is in no sense the same quantity as* (X, Y, Z); they have a common name and a certain analytical connection, but the idea of anything like identity is entirely excluded from the mathematical notion of a vector.

21. The physical notion of a vector.

The components of a force (X, Y, Z), (X', Y', Z'), etc. in different systems of Cartesian coordinates, rectangular or oblique, form a contravariant vector. This is evident because in elementary mechanics a force is resolved into components according to the parallelogram law just as a displacement dx_μ is resolved, and we have seen that dx_μ is a contravariant vector. So far as the mathematical notion of the vector is concerned, the quantities (X, Y, Z) and (X', Y', Z') are not to be regarded as in any way identical; but in physics we conceive that both quantities express some kind of condition or relation of the world, and this condition is the same whether expressed by (X, Y, Z) or by (X', Y', Z'). The physical vector is this vaguely conceived entity, which is independent of the coordinate-system, and is at the back of our measurements of force.

A world-condition cannot appear directly in a mathematical equation; only the *measure* of the world-condition can appear. Any number or set of numbers which can serve to specify uniquely a condition of the world may be called a measure of it. In using the phrase "condition of the world" I intend to be as non-committal as possible, whatever in the external world determines the values of the physical quantities which we observe, will be included in the phrase.

The simplest case is when the condition of the world under consideration can be indicated by a single measure-number. Take two such conditions underlying respectively the wave-length λ and period T of a light-wave. We have the equation

$$\lambda = 3 \,.\, 10^{10} T \quad \text{.........................(21·1)}.$$

This equation holds only for one particular plan of assigning measure-numbers (the C.G.S. system). But it may be written in the more general form

$$\lambda = cT \quad \text{.................................(21·2)},$$

where c is a velocity having the value $3 \,.\, 10^{10}$ in the C.G.S. system. This comprises any number of particular equations of the form (21·1). For each measure-plan, or system of units, c has a different numerical value. The method of determining the necessary change of c when a new measure-plan is adopted, is well known, we assign to it the *dimensions* length ÷ time, and by a simple rule we know how it must be changed when the units of λ and T are changed. For any general equation the total dimensions of every term ought to be the same.

The tensor calculus extends this *principle of dimensions* to changes of measure-code much more general than mere changes of units. There are conditions of the world which cannot be specified by a single measure-number; some require 4, some 16, some 64, etc., measure-numbers. Their variety is such that they cannot be arranged in a single serial order. Consider then an equation between the measure-numbers of two conditions of the world which require 4 measure-numbers. The equation, if it is of the necessary general type, must hold for every possible measure-code; this will be the case if, when we transform the measure-code, both sides of the equation are transformed in the same way, i.e. if we have to perform the same series of mathematical operations on both sides.

We can here make use of the mathematical vector of § 20. Let our equation in some measure-code be

$$A_1, A_2, A_3, A_4 = B_1, B_2, B_3, B_4 \qquad (21·3).$$

Now let us change the code so that the left-hand side becomes *any* four numbers A_1', A_2', A_3', A_4'. We identify this with the transformation of a covariant vector by associating with the change of measure-code the corresponding transformation of coordinates from x_μ to x_μ' as in (19·2). But since (21·3) is to hold in all measure-codes, the transformation of the right-hand side must involve the same set of operations, and the change from B_1, B_2, B_3, B_4 to B_1', B_2', B_3', B_4' will also be the transformation of a covariant vector associated with the *same* transformation of coordinates from x_μ to x_μ'.

We thus arrive at the result that in an equation which is independent of the measure-plan both sides must be covariant or both contravariant vectors. We shall extend this later to conditions expressed by 16, 64, ..., measure-numbers; the general rule is that both sides of the equation must have the same elements of covariance and contravariance. Covariance and contravariance are a kind of generalised dimension, showing how the measure of one condition of the world is changed when the measure of another condition is changed. The ordinary theory of change of units is merely an elementary case of this.

Coordinates are the identification-numbers of the points of space-time. There is no fundamental distinction between measure-numbers and identification-numbers, so that we may regard the change of coordinates as part of the general change applied to all measure-numbers. The change of coordinates no longer leads the way, as it did in § 20; it is placed on the same level with the other changes of measure.

When we applied a change of measure-code to (21·3) we associated with it a change of coordinates; but it is to be noted that the change of coordinates was then ambiguous, since the two sides of the equation might have been taken as both contravariant instead of both covariant; and further the change did not refer explicitly to coordinates *in* the world—it was a mere entry in the mathematician's note-book in order that he might have the satisfaction of calling A_μ and B_μ vectors consistently with his definition. Now if the measure-plan of a condition A_μ is changed the measures of other conditions and relations associated with it will be changed. Among these is a certain relation of two events which we may call the *aspect** of one from the other; and this relation requires four measure-numbers to specify it. Somewhat arbitrarily we decide to make the aspect a contravariant vector, and the measure-numbers assigned to it are denoted by $(dx)^\mu$. That settles the ambiguity once for all. For obscure psychological reasons the mind has singled out this transcendental relation of aspect for graphical representation, so that it is conceived by us as a *displacement* or difference of location in a frame of space-time. Its measure-numbers $(dx)^\mu$ are represented graphically as coordinate-differences dx_μ, and so for each measure-code of aspect we get a corresponding coordinate-frame of location. This "real" coordinate-frame can now replace the abstract frame in the mathematician's note-book, because as we have seen in (19·1) the actual transformation of coordinates *resulting* in a change of dx_μ is the same as the transformation *associated* with the change of dx_μ according to the law of a contravariant vector.

I do not think it is too extravagant to claim that the method of the tensor calculus, which presents all physical equations in a form independent of the choice of measure-code, is the only possible means of studying the conditions of the world which are at the basis of physical phenomena. The physicist is accustomed to insist (sometimes quite unnecessarily) that all equations should be stated in a form independent of the units employed. Whether this is desirable depends on the purpose of the formulae. But whatever additional insight into underlying causes is gained by stating equations in a form independent of units, must be gained to a far greater degree by stating them in a form altogether independent of the measure-code. An equation of this general form is called a *tensor equation*.

When the physicist is attacking the everyday problems of his subject, he may use any form of the equations—any specialised measure-plan—which will shorten the labour of calculation; for in these problems he is concerned with the outward significance rather than the inward significance of his

* The relation of *aspect* (or in its graphical conception *displacement*) with four measure-numbers seems to be derived from the relation of *interval* with one measure-number, by taking account not only of the mutual interval between the two events but also of their intervals from all surrounding events.

formulae. But once in a while he turns to consider their inward significance —to consider that relation of things in the world-structure which is the origin of his formulae The only intelligible idea we can form of such a structural relation is that it exists between the world-conditions themselves and not between the measure-numbers of a particular code A law of nature resolves itself into a constant relation, or even an identity, of the two world-conditions to which the different classes of observed quantities forming the two sides of the equation are traceable Such a constant relation independent of measure-code is only to be expressed by a tensor equation.

It may be remarked that if we take a force (X, Y, Z) and transform it to polar coordinates, whether as a covariant or a contravariant vector, in neither case do we obtain the quantities called polar components in elementary mechanics The latter are not in our view the true polar components, they are merely rectangular components in three new directions, viz. radial and transverse. In general the elementary definitions of physical quantities do not contemplate other than rectangular components, and they may need to be supplemented before we can decide whether the physical vector is covariant or contravariant. Thus if we define force as "mass × acceleration," the force turns out to be contravariant, but if we define it by "work = force × displacement," the force is covariant With the latter definition, however, we have to abandon the method of resolution into *oblique* components adopted in elementary mechanics.

In what follows it is generally sufficient to confine attention to the mathematical notion of a vector Some idea of the physical notion will probably give greater insight, but is not necessary for the formal proofs.

22. The summation convention.

We shall adopt the convention that whenever a literal suffix appears twice in a term that term is to be summed for values of the suffix 1, 2, 3, 4. For example, (2·1) will be written

$$ds^2 = g_{\mu\nu}\, dx_\mu\, dx_\nu \qquad (g_{\nu\mu} = g_{\mu\nu}) \quad \ldots\ldots\ldots\ldots\ldots\ldots(22·1).$$

Here, since μ and ν each appear twice, the summation

$$\sum_{\mu=1}^{4} \sum_{\nu=1}^{4}$$

is indicated; and the result written out in full gives (2·1).

Again, in the equation

$$A_\mu' = \frac{\partial x_\alpha}{\partial x_\mu'} A_\alpha,$$

the summation on the right is with respect to α only (μ appearing only once). The equation is equivalent to (19·2)

The convention is not merely an abbreviation but an immense aid to the analysis, giving it an impetus which is nearly always in a profitable direction. Summations occur in our investigations without waiting for our tardy approval.

A useful rule may be noted—

Any literal suffix appearing twice in a term is a dummy suffix, which may be changed freely to any other letter not already appropriated in that term. Two or more dummy suffixes can be interchanged*. For example

$$g_{\alpha\beta}\frac{\partial^2 x_\alpha}{\partial x_\mu'\partial x_\nu'}\frac{\partial x_\beta}{\partial x_\lambda'}=g_{\alpha\beta}\frac{\partial^2 x_\beta}{\partial x_\mu'\partial x_\nu'}\frac{\partial x_\alpha}{\partial x_\lambda'}\qquad(22\cdot2)$$

by interchanging the dummy suffixes α and β, remembering that $g_{\beta\alpha}=g_{\alpha\beta}$.

For a further illustration we shall prove that

$$\left.\begin{aligned}\frac{\partial x_\mu}{\partial x_\alpha'}\frac{\partial x_\alpha'}{\partial x_\nu}=\frac{dx_\mu}{dx_\nu}&=0,\quad \text{if } \mu\neq\nu\\ &=1,\quad \text{if } \mu=\nu\end{aligned}\right\}\qquad(22\cdot3).$$

The left-hand side written in full is

$$\frac{\partial x_\mu}{\partial x_1'}\frac{\partial x_1'}{\partial x_\nu}+\frac{\partial x_\mu}{\partial x_2'}\frac{\partial x_2'}{\partial x_\nu}+\frac{\partial x_\mu}{\partial x_3'}\frac{\partial x_3'}{\partial x_\nu}+\frac{\partial x_\mu}{\partial x_4'}\frac{\partial x_4'}{\partial x_\nu},$$

which by the usual theory gives the change dx_μ consequent on a change dx_ν. But x_μ and x_ν are coordinates of the same system, so that their variations are independent; hence dx_μ is zero unless x_μ and x_ν are the same coordinate, in which case, of course, $dx_\mu=dx_\nu$. Thus the theorem is proved.

The multiplier $\frac{\partial x_\mu}{\partial x_\alpha'}\frac{\partial x_\alpha'}{\partial x_\nu}$ acts as a *substitution-operator*. That is to say if $A(\mu)$ is any expression involving the suffix μ

$$\frac{\partial x_\mu}{\partial x_\alpha'}\frac{\partial x_\alpha'}{\partial x_\nu}A(\mu)=A(\nu)\qquad(22\cdot4).$$

For on the left the summation with respect to μ gives four terms corresponding to the values 1, 2, 3, 4 of μ. One of these values will agree with ν. Denote the other three values by σ, τ, ρ. Then by (22·3) the result is

$$1\,.\,A(\nu)+0\,.\,A(\sigma)+0\,.\,A(\tau)+0\,.\,A(\rho)$$
$$A(\nu).$$

The multiplier accordingly has the effect of substituting ν for μ in the multiplicand.

23. Tensors.

The two laws of transformation given in § 19 are now written—

Contravariant vectors $$A'^\mu=\frac{\partial x_\mu'}{\partial x_\alpha}A^\alpha\qquad(23\cdot11).$$

Covariant vectors $$A_\mu'=\frac{\partial x_\alpha}{\partial x_\mu'}A_\alpha\qquad(23\cdot12).$$

We can denote by $A_{\mu\nu}$ a quantity with 16 components obtained by giving μ and ν the values from 1 to 4 independently. Similarly $A_{\mu\nu\sigma}$ has 64 com-

* At first we shall call attention to such changes when we employ them; but the reader will be expected gradually to become familiar with the device as a common process of manipulation.

ponents. By a generalisation of the foregoing transformation laws we classify quantities of this kind as follows—

Contravariant tensors $$A'^{\mu\nu} = \frac{\partial x_\mu'}{\partial x_\alpha}\frac{\partial x_\nu'}{\partial x_\beta} A^{\alpha\beta} \quad\text{.....................}\quad (23\cdot21)$$

Covariant tensors $$A'_{\mu\nu} = \frac{\partial x_\alpha}{\partial x_\mu'}\frac{\partial x_\beta}{\partial x_\nu'} A_{\alpha\beta} \quad\text{.....................}\quad (23\cdot22)$$

Mixed tensors $$A'^{\nu}_{\mu} = \frac{\partial x_\alpha}{\partial x_\mu'}\frac{\partial x_\nu'}{\partial x_\beta} A^{\beta}_{\alpha} \quad\text{.....................}\quad (23\cdot23)$$

The above are called tensors of the second rank. We have similar laws for tensors of higher ranks. E.g.

$$A'^{\tau}_{\mu\nu\sigma} = \frac{\partial x_\alpha}{\partial x_\mu'}\frac{\partial x_\beta}{\partial x_\nu'}\frac{\partial x_\gamma}{\partial x_\sigma'}\frac{\partial x_\tau'}{\partial x_\delta} A^{\delta}_{\alpha\beta\gamma} \quad\text{.....................}\quad (23\cdot3).$$

It may be worth while to remind the reader that (23·3) typifies 256 distinct equations each with a sum of 256 terms on the right-hand side.

It is easily shown that these transformation laws fulfil the condition of self-consistency explained in § 20, and it is for this reason that quantities governed by them are selected for special nomenclature.

If a tensor vanishes, i.e. if all its components vanish, in one system of coordinates, it will continue to vanish when any other system of coordinates is substituted. This is clear from the linearity of the above transformation laws.

Evidently the sum of two tensors of the same covariant or contravariant character is a tensor. Hence a law expressed by the vanishing of the sum of a number of tensors, or by the equality of two tensors of the same kind, will be independent of the coordinate-system used.

The product of two tensors such as $A_{\mu\nu}$ and B^{τ}_{σ} is a tensor of the character indicated by $A^{\tau}_{\mu\nu\sigma}$. This is proved by showing that the transformation law of the product is the same as (23·3).

The general term *tensor* includes vectors (tensors of the first rank) and invariants or scalars* (tensors of zero rank).

A tensor of the second or higher rank need not be expressible as a product of two tensors of lower rank.

A simple example of an expression of the second rank is afforded by the stresses in a solid or viscous fluid. The component of stress denoted by p_{xy} is the traction in the y-direction across an interface perpendicular to the x-direction. Each component is thus associated with two directions.

24. Inner multiplication and contraction. The quotient law.

If we multiply A_μ by B^ν we obtain sixteen quantities $A_1B^1, A_1B^2, A_2B^1, \ldots$ constituting a mixed tensor. Suppose that we wish to consider the four

* Scalar is a synonym for invariant. I generally use the latter word as the more self-explanatory.

"diagonal" terms A_1B^1, A_2B^2, A_3B^3, A_4B^4; we naturally try to abbreviate these by writing them $A_\mu B^\mu$. But by the summation convention $A_\mu B^\mu$ stands for the sum of the four quantities. The convention is right. We have no use for them individually since they do not form a vector; but the sum is of great importance.

$A_\mu B^\mu$ is called the *inner product* of the two vectors, in contrast to the ordinary or *outer product* $A_\mu B^\nu$.

In rectangular coordinates the inner product coincides with the *scalar-product* defined in the well-known elementary theory of vectors; but the outer product is not the so-called *vector-product* of the elementary theory.

By a similar process we can form from any mixed tensor $A^\tau_{\mu\nu\sigma}$ a "contracted*" tensor $A^\sigma_{\mu\nu\sigma}$, which is two ranks lower since σ has now become a dummy suffix. To prove that $A^\sigma_{\mu\nu\sigma}$ is a tensor, we set $\tau=\sigma$ in (23·3),

$$A'^\sigma_{\mu\nu\sigma}=\frac{\partial x_\alpha}{\partial x_\mu'}\frac{\partial x_\beta}{\partial x_\nu'}\frac{\partial x_\gamma}{\partial x_\sigma'}\frac{\partial x_\sigma'}{\partial x_\delta}A^\delta_{\alpha\beta\gamma}.$$

The substitution operator $\frac{\partial x_\gamma}{\partial x_\sigma'}\frac{\partial x_\sigma'}{\partial x_\delta}$ changes δ to γ in $A^\delta_{\alpha\beta\gamma}$ by (22·4). Hence

$$A'^\sigma_{\mu\nu\sigma}=\frac{\partial x_\alpha}{\partial x_\mu'}\frac{\partial x_\beta}{\partial x_\nu'}A^\gamma_{\alpha\beta\gamma}.$$

Comparing with the transformation law (23·22) we see that $A^\sigma_{\mu\nu\sigma}$ is a covariant tensor of the second rank. Of course, the dummy suffixes γ and σ are equivalent.

Similarly, setting $\nu=\mu$ in (23·23),

$$A'^\mu_\mu=\frac{\partial x_\alpha}{\partial x_\mu'}\frac{\partial x_\mu'}{\partial x_\beta}A^\beta_\alpha=A^\alpha_\alpha=A^\mu_\mu,$$

that is to say A^μ_μ is unaltered by a transformation of coordinates. Hence it is an invariant.

By the same method we can show that $A_\mu B^\mu$, $A^{\mu\nu}_{\mu\nu}$, $A^\nu_\mu B^\mu_\nu$ are invariants. In general when an upper and lower suffix are the same the corresponding covariant and contravariant qualities cancel out. If all suffixes cancel out in this way, the expression must be invariant. The identified suffixes must be of opposite characters; the expression $A^\tau_{\mu\sigma\sigma}$ is not a tensor, and no interest is attached to it.

We see that the suffixes keep a tally of what we have called the generalised dimensions of the terms in our equations. After cancelling out any suffixes which appear in both upper and lower positions, the remaining suffixes must appear in the same position in each term of an equation. When that is satisfied each term will undergo the same set of operations when a transformation of coordinates is made, and the equation will continue to hold in all

* German, *verjüngt*.

systems of coordinates. This may be compared with the well-known condition that each term must have the same physical dimensions, so that it undergoes multiplication by the same factor when a change of units is made and the equation continues to hold in all systems of units.

Just as we can infer the physical dimensions of some novel entity entering into a physical equation, so we can infer the contravariant and covariant dimensions of an expression whose character was hitherto unknown. For example, if the equation is

$$A(\mu\nu) B_{\nu\sigma} = C_{\mu\sigma} \quad \text{.........................(24·1)},$$

where the nature of $A(\mu\nu)$ is not known initially, we see that $A(\mu\nu)$ must be a tensor of the character A_μ^ν, so as to give

$$A_\mu^\nu B_{\nu\sigma} = C_{\mu\sigma},$$

which makes the covariant dimensions on both sides consistent.

The equation (24·1) may be written symbolically

$$A(\mu\nu) = C_{\mu\sigma}/B_{\nu\sigma},$$

and the conclusion is that not only the product but also the (symbolic) quotient of two tensors is a tensor. Of course, the operation here indicated is not that of ordinary division.

This quotient law is a useful aid in detecting the tensor-character of expressions. It is not claimed that the general argument here given amounts to a strict mathematical proof. In most cases we can supply the proof required by one or more applications of the following rigorous theorem—

A quantity which on inner multiplication by *any* covariant (alternatively, by *any* contravariant) vector always gives a tensor, is itself a tensor.

For suppose that $\qquad A(\mu\nu) B^\nu$

is always a covariant vector for any choice of the contravariant vector B^ν. Then by (23·12)

$$\{A'(\mu\nu) B'^\nu\} = \frac{\partial x_\alpha}{\partial x_\mu'} \{A(\alpha\beta) B^\beta\} \quad \text{.................(24·2)}.$$

But by (23·11) applied to the reverse transformation from accented to unaccented coordinates

$$B^\beta = \frac{\partial x_\beta}{\partial x_\nu'} B'^\nu.$$

Hence, substituting for B^β in (24·2),

$$B'^\nu \left(A'(\mu\nu) - \frac{\partial x_\alpha}{\partial x_\mu'} \frac{\partial x_\beta}{\partial x_\nu'} A(\alpha\beta) \right) = 0.$$

Since B'^ν is arbitrary the quantity in the bracket must vanish. This shows that $A(\mu\nu)$ is a covariant tensor obeying the transformation law (23·22).

We shall cite this theorem as the "rigorous quotient theorem."

25. The fundamental tensors.

It is convenient to write (22·1) as

$$ds^2 = g_{\mu\nu}(dx)^\mu (dx)^\nu$$

in order to show explicitly the contravariant character of $dx_\mu = (dx)^\mu$. Since ds^2 is independent of the coordinate-system it is an invariant or tensor of zero rank. The equation shows that $g_{\mu\nu}(dx)^\mu$ multiplied by an arbitrarily chosen contravariant vector $(dx)^\nu$ always gives a tensor of zero rank, hence $g_{\mu\nu}(dx)^\mu$ is a vector. Again, we see that $g_{\mu\nu}$ multiplied by an arbitrary contravariant vector $(dx)^\mu$ always gives a vector; hence $g_{\mu\nu}$ is a tensor. This double application of the rigorous quotient theorem shows that $g_{\mu\nu}$ is a tensor, and it is evidently covariant as the notation has anticipated.

Let g stand for the determinant

$$\begin{vmatrix} g_{11} & g_{12} & g_{13} & g_{14} \\ g_{21} & g_{22} & g_{23} & g_{24} \\ g_{31} & g_{32} & g_{33} & g_{34} \\ g_{41} & g_{42} & g_{43} & g_{44} \end{vmatrix}$$

Let $g^{\mu\nu}$ be defined as the minor of $g_{\mu\nu}$ in this determinant, divided by g*.

Consider the inner product $g_{\mu\sigma}g^{\nu\sigma}$. We see that μ and ν select two rows in the determinant; we have to take each element in turn from the μ row, multiply by the minor of the corresponding element of the ν row, add together, and divide the result by g. This is equivalent to substituting the μ row for the ν row and dividing the resulting determinant by g. If μ is not the same as ν this gives a determinant with two rows identical, and the result is 0. If μ is the same as ν we reproduce the determinant g divided by itself, and the result is 1. We write

$$\left.\begin{aligned} g_\mu^\nu &= g_{\mu\sigma}g^{\nu\sigma} \\ &= 0 \quad \text{if } \mu \neq \nu \\ &= 1 \quad \text{if } \mu = \nu \end{aligned}\right\} \qquad (25 \cdot 1)$$

Thus g_μ^ν has the same property of a substitution-operator that we found for $\frac{\partial x_\mu}{\partial x_\alpha'}\frac{\partial x_\alpha'}{\partial x_\nu}$ in (22·4). For example†,

$$g_\mu^\nu A^\mu = A^\nu + 0 + 0 + 0 \qquad (25 \cdot 2).$$

Note that g_ν^ν has not the same meaning as g_μ^ν with $\mu = \nu$, because a summation is implied. Evidently

$$g_\nu^\nu = 1 + 1 + 1 + 1 = 4 \qquad (25 \cdot 3)$$

The equation (25·2) shows that g_μ^ν multiplied by any contravariant vector always gives a vector. Hence g_μ^ν is a tensor. It is a very exceptional tensor since its components are the same in all coordinate-systems.

* The notation anticipates the result proved later that $g^{\mu\nu}$ is a contravariant tensor.

† Note that g_μ^ν will act as a substitution-operator on *any* expression and is not restricted to operating on tensors.

Again since $g_{\mu\sigma}g^{\nu\sigma}$ is a tensor we can infer that $g^{\nu\sigma}$ is a tensor. This is proved rigorously by remarking that $g_{\mu\sigma}A^{\mu}$ is a covariant vector, arbitrary on account of the free choice of A^{μ}. Multiplying this vector by $g^{\nu\sigma}$ we have

$$g_{\mu\sigma}g^{\nu\sigma}A^{\mu} = g^{\nu}_{\mu}A^{\mu} = A^{\nu},$$

so that the product is always a vector. Hence the rigorous quotient theorem applies.

The tensor character of $g^{\mu\nu}$ may also be demonstrated by a method which shows more clearly the reason for its definition as the minor of $g_{\mu\nu}$ divided by g. Since $g_{\mu\nu}A^{\nu}$ is a covariant vector, we can denote it by B_{μ}. Thus

$$g_{11}A^1 + g_{12}A^2 + g_{13}A^3 + g_{14}A^4 = B_1; \text{ etc.}$$

Solving these four linear equations for A^1, A^2, A^3, A^4 by the usual method of determinants, the result is

$$A^1 = g^{11}B_1 + g^{12}B_2 + g^{13}B_3 + g^{14}B_4; \text{ etc.},$$

so that $$A^{\mu} = g^{\mu\nu}B_{\nu}.$$

Whence by the rigorous quotient theorem $g^{\mu\nu}$ is a tensor.

We have thus defined three fundamental tensors

$$g_{\mu\nu},\ g^{\nu}_{\mu},\ g^{\mu\nu}$$

of covariant, mixed, and contravariant characters respectively.

26. Associated tensors.

We now define the operation of raising or lowering a suffix. Raising the suffix of a vector is defined by the equation

$$A^{\mu} = g^{\mu\nu}A_{\nu},$$

and lowering by the equation

$$A_{\mu} = g_{\mu\nu}A^{\nu}.$$

For a more general tensor such as $A^{\gamma\delta}_{\alpha\beta\mu}$, the operation of raising μ is defined in the same way, viz.

$$A^{\gamma\delta\mu}_{\alpha\beta} = g^{\mu\nu}A^{\gamma\delta}_{\alpha\beta\nu} \quad \text{......................... (26·1)},$$

and for lowering

$$A^{\gamma\delta}_{\alpha\beta\mu} = g_{\mu\nu}A^{\gamma\delta\nu}_{\alpha\beta} \quad \text{.........................(26·2)}.$$

These definitions are consistent, since if we raise a suffix and then lower it we reproduce the original tensor. Thus if in (26·1) we multiply by $g_{\mu\sigma}$ in order to lower the suffix on the left, we have

$$\begin{aligned} g_{\mu\sigma}A^{\gamma\delta\mu}_{\alpha\beta} &= g_{\mu\sigma}g^{\mu\nu}A^{\gamma\delta}_{\alpha\beta\nu} \\ &= g^{\nu}_{\sigma}A^{\gamma\delta}_{\alpha\beta\nu} \\ &= A^{\gamma\delta}_{\alpha\beta\sigma} \qquad \text{by (25·2)}, \end{aligned}$$

which is the rule expressed by (26·2).

It will be noticed that the raising of a suffix ν by means of $g^{\mu\nu}$ is accompanied by the substitution of μ for ν. The whole operation is closely akin to the plain substitution of μ for ν by means of g_μ^ν. Thus

multiplication by $g^{\mu\nu}$ gives substitution with raising,
multiplication by g_μ^ν gives plain substitution,
multiplication by $g_{\mu\nu}$ gives substitution with lowering.

In the case of non-symmetrical tensors it may be necessary to distinguish the place from which the raised suffix has been brought, e.g. to distinguish between $A_\mu{}^\nu$ and $A^\nu{}_\mu$.

It is easily seen that this rule of association between tensors with suffixes in different positions is fulfilled in the case of $g^{\mu\nu}$, g_μ^ν, $g_{\mu\nu}$, in fact the definition of g_μ^ν in (25·1) is a special case of (26·1).

For rectangular coordinates the raising or lowering of a suffix leaves the components unaltered in three-dimensional space*; and it merely reverses the signs of some of the components for Galilean coordinates in four-dimensional space-time. Since the elementary definitions of physical quantities refer to rectangular axes and time, we can generally use any one of the associated tensors to represent a physical entity without infringing pre-relativity definitions. This leads to a somewhat enlarged view of a tensor as having in itself no particular covariant or contravariant character, but having *components* of various degrees of covariance or contravariance represented by the whole system of associated tensors. That is to say, the raising or lowering of suffixes will not be regarded as altering the individuality of the tensor; and reference to a tensor $A_{\mu\nu}$ may (if the context permits) be taken to include the associated tensors A_μ^ν and $A^{\mu\nu}$.

It is useful to notice that dummy suffixes have a certain freedom of movement between the tensor-factors of an expression. Thus

$$A_{\alpha\beta}B^{\alpha\beta} = A^{\alpha\beta}B_{\alpha\beta}, \quad A_{\mu\alpha}B^{\nu\alpha} = A_\mu{}^\alpha B^\nu{}_\alpha \quad \text{.............} (26·3).$$

The suffix may be raised in one term provided it is lowered in the other. The proof follows easily from (26·1) and (26·2).

In the elementary vector theory two vectors are said to be *perpendicular* if their scalar-product vanishes, and the square of the *length* of the vector is its scalar-product into itself. Corresponding definitions are adopted in the tensor calculus.

The vectors A_μ and B_μ are said to be *perpendicular* if

$$A_\mu B^\mu = 0 \quad \text{.........................} (26·4).$$

If l is the *length* of A_μ (or A^μ)

$$l^2 = A_\mu A^\mu \quad \text{.........................} (26·5)$$

A vector is self-perpendicular if its length vanishes.

* If $ds^2 = dx_1^2 + dx_2^2 + dx_3^2$, $g_{\mu\nu} = g^{\mu\nu} = g_\mu^\nu$ so that all three tensors are merely substitution-operators.

The interval is the length of the corresponding displacement dx_μ because

$$ds^2 = g_{\mu\nu}(dx)^\mu (dx)^\nu$$
$$= (dx)_\nu (dx)^\nu$$

by (26·2). A displacement is thus self-perpendicular when it is along a light-track, $ds = 0$.

If a vector A_μ receives an infinitesimal increment dA_μ perpendicular to itself, its length is unaltered to the first order; for by (26·5)

$$(l + dl)^2 = (A_\mu + dA_\mu)(A^\mu + dA^\mu)$$
$$= A_\mu A^\mu + A^\mu dA_\mu + A_\mu dA^\mu \quad \text{to the first order}$$
$$= l^2 + 2A_\mu dA^\mu \quad \text{by (26·3)},$$

and $A_\mu dA^\mu = 0$ by the condition of perpendicularity (26·4).

In the elementary vector theory, the scalar-product of two vectors is equal to the product of their lengths multiplied by the cosine of the angle between them. Accordingly in the general theory the angle θ between two vectors A_μ and B_μ is defined by

$$\cos\theta = \frac{A_\mu B^\mu}{\sqrt{(A_\alpha A^\alpha)(B_\beta B^\beta)}} \qquad \text{.................(26·6).}$$

Clearly the angle so defined is an invariant, and agrees with the usual definition when the coordinates are rectangular. In determining the angle between two intersecting lines it makes no difference whether the world is curved or flat, since only the initial directions are concerned and these in any case lie in the tangent plane. The angle θ (if it is real) has thus the usual geometrical meaning even in non-Euclidean space. It must not, however, be inferred that ordinary angles are invariant for the Lorentz transformation; naturally an angle in three dimensions is invariant only for transformations in three dimensions, and the angle which is invariant for Lorentz transformations is a four-dimensional angle.

From a tensor of even rank we can construct an invariant by bringing half the suffixes to the upper and half to the lower position and contracting. Thus from $A_{\mu\nu\sigma\tau}$ we form $A_{\mu\nu}^{\sigma\tau}$ and contract, obtaining $A = A_{\mu\nu}^{\mu\nu}$. This invariant will be called the *spur**. Another invariant is the square of the length $A_{\mu\nu\sigma\tau}A^{\mu\nu\sigma\tau}$. There may also be intermediate invariants such as $A_{\mu\nu\alpha}^{\alpha}A_{\beta}^{\mu\nu\beta}$.

27. Christoffel's 3-index symbols.

We introduce two expressions (not tensors) of great importance throughout our subsequent work, namely

$$[\mu\nu, \sigma] = \tfrac{1}{2}\left(\frac{\partial g_{\mu\sigma}}{\partial x_\nu} + \frac{\partial g_{\nu\sigma}}{\partial x_\mu} - \frac{\partial g_{\mu\nu}}{\partial x_\sigma}\right) \qquad \text{.....................(27·1),}$$

$$\{\mu\nu, \sigma\} = \tfrac{1}{2}g^{\sigma\lambda}\left(\frac{\partial g_{\mu\lambda}}{\partial x_\nu} + \frac{\partial g_{\nu\lambda}}{\partial x_\mu} - \frac{\partial g_{\mu\nu}}{\partial x_\lambda}\right) \qquad \text{.......(27·2)}$$

* Originally the German word *Spur*.

We have

$$\{\mu\nu, \sigma\} = g^{\sigma\lambda}[\mu\nu, \lambda] \quad \ldots\ldots\ldots\ldots\ldots\ldots(27\cdot3),$$

$$[\mu\nu, \sigma] = g_{\sigma\lambda}\{\mu\nu, \lambda\} \quad \ldots\ldots\ldots\ldots\ldots\ldots(27\cdot4).$$

The result (27·3) is obvious from the definitions. To prove (27·4), multiply (27·3) by $g_{\sigma\alpha}$; then

$$g_{\sigma\alpha}\{\mu\nu, \sigma\} = g_{\sigma\alpha}g^{\sigma\lambda}[\mu\nu, \lambda]$$
$$= g_\alpha^\lambda[\mu\nu, \lambda]$$
$$= [\mu\nu, \alpha],$$

which is equivalent to (27·4).

Comparing with (26·1) and (26·2) we see that the passage from the "square" to the "curly" symbol, and *vice versa*, is the same process as raising and lowering a suffix. It might be convenient to use a notation in which this was made evident, e.g.

$$\Gamma_{\mu\nu,\sigma} = [\mu\nu, \sigma], \quad \Gamma^\sigma_{\mu\nu} = \{\mu\nu, \sigma\},$$

but we shall adhere to the more usual notation.

From (27·1) it is found that

$$[\mu\nu, \sigma] + [\sigma\nu, \mu] = \frac{\partial g_{\mu\sigma}}{\partial x_\nu} \quad \ldots\ldots\ldots\ldots\ldots\ldots(27\cdot5)$$

There are 40 different 3-index symbols of each kind. It may here be explained that the $g_{\mu\nu}$ are components of a generalised *potential*, and the 3-index symbols components of a generalised *force* in the gravitational theory (see § 55).

28. Equations of a geodesic.

We shall now determine the equations of a geodesic or path between two points for which

$$\int ds \text{ is stationary.}$$

This absolute track is of fundamental importance in dynamics, but at the moment we are concerned with it only as an aid in the development of the tensor calculus*.

Keeping the beginning and end of the path fixed, we give every intermediate point an arbitrary infinitesimal displacement δx_σ so as to deform the path. Since

$$ds^2 = g_{\mu\nu}dx_\mu dx_\nu,$$

$$2ds\,\delta(ds) = dx_\mu dx_\nu \delta g_{\mu\nu} + g_{\mu\nu}dx_\mu \delta(dx_\nu) + g_{\mu\nu}dx_\nu \delta(dx_\mu)$$

$$= dx_\mu dx_\nu \frac{\partial g_{\mu\nu}}{\partial x_\sigma}\delta x_\sigma + g_{\mu\nu}dx_\mu d(\delta x_\nu) + g_{\mu\nu}dx_\nu d(\delta x_\mu) \quad \ldots(28\cdot1).$$

The stationary condition is

$$\int \delta(ds) = 0 \quad \ldots\ldots\ldots\ldots\ldots\ldots(28\cdot2),$$

* Our ultimate goal is equation (29·3). An alternative proof (which does not introduce the calculus of variations) is given in § 31.

which becomes by (28·1)

$$\frac{1}{2}\int\left\{\frac{dx_\mu}{ds}\frac{dx_\nu}{ds}\frac{\partial g_{\mu\nu}}{\partial x_\sigma}\delta x_\sigma + g_{\mu\nu}\frac{dx_\mu}{ds}\frac{d}{ds}(\delta x_\nu) + g_{\mu\nu}\frac{dx_\nu}{ds}\frac{d}{ds}(\delta x_\mu)\right\} ds = 0,$$

or, changing dummy suffixes in the last two terms,

$$\frac{1}{2}\int\left\{\frac{dx_\mu}{ds}\frac{dx_\nu}{ds}\frac{\partial g_{\mu\nu}}{\partial x_\sigma}\delta x_\sigma + \left(g_{\mu\sigma}\frac{dx_\mu}{ds} + g_{\sigma\nu}\frac{dx_\nu}{ds}\right)\frac{d}{ds}(\delta x_\sigma)\right\} ds = 0.$$

Applying the usual method of partial integration, and rejecting the integrated part since δx_σ vanishes at both limits,

$$\frac{1}{2}\int\left\{\frac{dx_\mu}{ds}\frac{dx_\nu}{ds}\frac{\partial g_{\mu\nu}}{\partial x_\sigma} - \frac{d}{ds}\left(g_{\mu\sigma}\frac{dx_\mu}{ds} + g_{\sigma\nu}\frac{dx_\nu}{ds}\right)\right\}\delta x_\sigma ds = 0.$$

This must hold for all values of the arbitrary displacements δx_σ at all points, hence the coefficient in the integrand must vanish at all points on the path. Thus

$$\frac{1}{2}\frac{dx_\mu}{ds}\frac{dx_\nu}{ds}\frac{\partial g_{\mu\nu}}{\partial x_\sigma} - \frac{1}{2}\frac{dg_{\mu\sigma}}{ds}\frac{dx_\mu}{ds} - \frac{1}{2}\frac{dg_{\sigma\nu}}{ds}\frac{dx_\nu}{ds} - \frac{1}{2}g_{\mu\sigma}\frac{d^2x_\mu}{ds^2} - \frac{1}{2}g_{\sigma\nu}\frac{d^2x_\nu}{ds^2} = 0$$

Now* $$\frac{dg_{\mu\sigma}}{ds} = \frac{\partial g_{\mu\sigma}}{\partial x_\nu}\frac{dx_\nu}{ds} \text{ and } \frac{dg_{\sigma\nu}}{ds} = \frac{\partial g_{\sigma\nu}}{\partial x_\mu}\frac{dx_\mu}{ds}.$$

Also in the last two terms we replace the dummy suffixes μ and ν by ϵ. The equation then becomes

$$\frac{1}{2}\frac{dx_\mu}{ds}\frac{dx_\nu}{ds}\left(\frac{\partial g_{\mu\nu}}{\partial x_\sigma} - \frac{\partial g_{\mu\sigma}}{\partial x_\nu} - \frac{\partial g_{\nu\sigma}}{\partial x_\mu}\right) - g_{\epsilon\sigma}\frac{d^2x_\epsilon}{ds^2} = 0 \quad \text{..........(28·3).}$$

We can get rid of the factor $g_{\epsilon\sigma}$ by multiplying through by $g^{\sigma\alpha}$ so as to form the substitution operator g_ϵ^α. Thus

$$\frac{1}{2}\frac{dx_\mu}{ds}\frac{dx_\nu}{ds}g^{\sigma\alpha}\left(\frac{\partial g_{\mu\sigma}}{\partial x_\nu} + \frac{\partial g_{\nu\sigma}}{\partial x_\mu} - \frac{\partial g_{\mu\nu}}{\partial x_\sigma}\right) + \frac{d^2x_\alpha}{ds^2} = 0 \quad \text{........(28·4),}$$

or, by (27·2) $$\frac{d^2x_\alpha}{ds^2} + \{\mu\nu, \alpha\}\frac{dx_\mu}{ds}\frac{dx_\nu}{ds} = 0 \quad \text{........ .... (28·5).}$$

For $\alpha = 1, 2, 3, 4$ this gives the four equations determining a geodesic.

29. Covariant derivative of a vector.

The derivative of an invariant is a covariant vector (§ 19), but the derivative of a vector is not a tensor. We proceed to find certain tensors which are used in this calculus in place of the ordinary derivatives of vectors.

Since dx_μ is contravariant and ds invariant, a "velocity" dx_μ/ds is a contravariant vector. Hence if A_μ is any covariant vector the inner product

$$A_\mu\frac{dx_\mu}{ds} \text{ is invariant.}$$

* These simple formulae are noteworthy as illustrating the great value of the summation convention. The law of total differentiation for four coordinates becomes *formally* the same as for one coordinate.

The rate of change of this expression per unit interval along any assigned curve must also be independent of the coordinate-system, i.e.

$$\frac{d}{ds}\left(A_\mu \frac{dx_\mu}{ds}\right) \text{ is invariant} \quad \ldots\ldots(29\cdot1).$$

This assumes that we keep to the same absolute curve however the coordinate-system is varied. The result (29·1) is therefore only of practical use if it is applied to a curve which is defined independently of the coordinate-system. We shall accordingly apply it to a geodesic. Performing the differentiation,

$$\frac{\partial A_\mu}{\partial x_\nu}\frac{dx_\nu}{ds}\cdot\frac{dx_\mu}{ds} + A_\mu \frac{d^2x_\mu}{ds^2} \text{ is invariant along a geodesic} \quad \ldots\ldots(29\cdot2).$$

From (28·5) we have that along a geodesic

$$A_\mu \frac{d^2x_\mu}{ds^2} = A_\alpha \frac{d^2x_\alpha}{ds^2} = -A_\alpha \{\mu\nu, \alpha\} \frac{dx_\mu}{ds}\frac{dx_\nu}{ds}.$$

Hence (29·2) gives

$$\frac{dx_\mu}{ds}\frac{dx_\nu}{ds}\left(\frac{\partial A_\mu}{\partial x_\nu} - A_\alpha \{\mu\nu, \alpha\}\right) \text{ is invariant.}$$

The result is now general since the curvature (which distinguishes the geodesic) has been eliminated by using the equations (28·5) and only the gradient of the curve (dx_μ/ds and dx_ν/ds) has been left in the expression.

Since dx_μ/ds and dx_ν/ds are contravariant vectors, their co-factor is a covariant tensor of the second rank. We therefore write

$$A_{\mu\nu} = \frac{\partial A_\mu}{\partial x_\nu} - \{\mu\nu, \alpha\} A_\alpha, \quad \ldots\ldots(29\cdot3),$$

and the tensor $A_{\mu\nu}$ is called the *covariant derivative* of A_μ.

By raising a suffix we obtain two associated tensors $A^\mu{}_\nu$ and $A_\mu{}^\nu$ which must be distinguished since the two suffixes are not symmetrical. The first of these is the most important, and is to be understood when the tensor is written simply as A_ν^μ without distinction of original position.

Since $$A_\sigma = g_{\sigma\epsilon} A^\epsilon,$$

we have by (29·3)

$$\begin{aligned} A_{\sigma\nu} &= \frac{\partial}{\partial x_\nu}(g_{\sigma\epsilon}A^\epsilon) - \{\sigma\nu, \alpha\}(g_{\alpha\epsilon}A^\epsilon) \\ &= g_{\sigma\epsilon}\frac{\partial A^\epsilon}{\partial x_\nu} + A^\epsilon \frac{\partial g_{\sigma\epsilon}}{\partial x_\nu} - [\sigma\nu, \epsilon] A^\epsilon \quad \text{by (27·4)} \\ &= g_{\sigma\epsilon}\frac{\partial A^\epsilon}{\partial x_\nu} + [\epsilon\nu, \sigma] A^\epsilon \quad \text{by (27·5)}. \end{aligned}$$

Hence multiplying through by $g^{\mu\sigma}$, and remembering that $g^{\mu\sigma}g_{\sigma\epsilon}$ is a substitution-operator, we have

$$A^\mu{}_\nu = \frac{\partial A^\mu}{\partial x_\nu} + \{\epsilon\nu, \mu\} A^\epsilon \quad \ldots\ldots(29\cdot4).$$

This is called the covariant derivative of A^μ. The considerable differences between the formulae (29·3) and (29·4) should be carefully noted.

The tensors $A_\mu{}^\nu$ and $A^{\mu\nu}$, obtained from (29·3) and (29·4) by raising the second suffix, are called the *contravariant derivatives* of A_μ and A^μ. We shall not have much occasion to refer to contravariant derivatives.

30. Covariant derivative of a tensor.

The covariant derivatives of tensors of the second rank are formed as follows—

$$A^{\mu\nu}_\sigma = \frac{\partial A^{\mu\nu}}{\partial x_\sigma} + \{\alpha\sigma, \mu\} A^{\alpha\nu} + \{\alpha\sigma, \nu\} A^{\mu\alpha} \quad \text{............(30·1)},$$

$$A^\nu_{\mu\sigma} = \frac{\partial A^\nu_\mu}{\partial x_\sigma} - \{\mu\sigma, \alpha\} A^\nu_\alpha + \{\alpha\sigma, \nu\} A^\alpha_\mu \quad \text{............(30·2)},$$

$$A_{\mu\nu\sigma} = \frac{\partial A_{\mu\nu}}{\partial x_\sigma} - \{\mu\sigma, \alpha\} A_{\alpha\nu} - \{\nu\sigma, \alpha\} A_{\mu\alpha} \quad \text{............(30·3)}.$$

And the general rule for covariant differentiation with respect to x_σ is illustrated by the example

$$A^\rho_{\lambda\mu\nu\sigma} = \frac{\partial}{\partial x_\sigma} A^\rho_{\lambda\mu\nu} - \{\lambda\sigma, \alpha\} A^\rho_{\alpha\mu\nu} - \{\mu\sigma, \alpha\} A^\rho_{\lambda\alpha\nu} - \{\nu\sigma, \alpha\} A^\rho_{\lambda\mu\alpha} + \{\alpha\sigma, \rho\} A^\alpha_{\lambda\mu\nu} \quad \text{.........(30·4)}$$

The above formulae are primarily definitions; but we have to prove that the quantities on the right are actually tensors. This is done by an obvious generalisation of the method of the preceding section. Thus if in place of (29·1) we use

$$\frac{d}{ds}\left(A_{\mu\nu} \frac{dx_\mu}{ds} \frac{dx_\nu}{ds}\right) \text{ is invariant along a geodesic,}$$

we obtain

$$\frac{\partial A_{\mu\nu}}{\partial x_\sigma} \frac{dx_\sigma}{ds} \frac{dx_\mu}{ds} \frac{dx_\nu}{ds} + A_{\mu\nu} \frac{dx_\nu}{ds} \frac{d^2x_\mu}{ds^2} + A_{\mu\nu} \frac{dx_\mu}{ds} \frac{d^2x_\nu}{ds^2}.$$

Then substituting for the second derivatives from (28·5) the expression reduces to

$$A_{\mu\nu\sigma} \frac{dx_\mu}{ds} \frac{dx_\nu}{ds} \frac{dx_\sigma}{ds} \text{ is invariant,}$$

showing that $A_{\mu\nu\sigma}$ is a tensor.

The formulae (30·1) and (30·2) are obtained by raising the suffixes ν and μ, the details of the work being the same as in deducing (29·4) from (29·3).

Consider the expression

$$B_{\mu\sigma} C_\nu + B_\mu C_{\nu\sigma},$$

the σ denoting covariant differentiation. By (29·3) this is equal to

$$\left(\frac{\partial B_\mu}{\partial x_\sigma} - \{\mu\sigma, \alpha\} B_\alpha\right) C_\nu + B_\mu \left(\frac{\partial C_\nu}{\partial x_\sigma} - \{\nu\sigma, \alpha\} C_\alpha\right)$$

$$= \frac{\partial}{\partial x_\sigma}(B_\mu C_\nu) - \{\mu\sigma, \alpha\}(B_\alpha C_\nu) - \{\nu\sigma, \alpha\}(B_\mu C_\alpha).$$

But comparing with (30·3) we see that this is the covariant derivative of the tensor of the second rank $(B_\mu C_\nu)$. Hence

$$(B_\mu C_\nu)_\sigma = B_{\mu\sigma} C_\nu + B_\mu C_{\nu\sigma} \quad \ldots\ldots\ldots\ldots\ldots\ldots \quad (30\cdot5).$$

Thus in covariant differentiation of a product the distributive rule used in ordinary differentiation holds good.

Applying (30·3) to the fundamental tensor, we have

$$\begin{aligned} g_{\mu\nu\sigma} &= \frac{\partial g_{\mu\nu}}{\partial x_\sigma} - \{\mu\sigma, \alpha\} g_{\alpha\nu} - \{\nu\sigma, \alpha\} g_{\mu\alpha} \\ &= \frac{\partial g_{\mu\nu}}{\partial x_\sigma} - [\mu\sigma, \nu] - [\nu\sigma, \mu] \\ &= 0 \quad \text{by } (27\cdot5). \end{aligned}$$

Hence the covariant derivatives of the fundamental tensors vanish identically, and the fundamental tensors can be treated as *constants* in covariant differentiation. It is thus immaterial whether a suffix is raised before or after the differentiation, as our definitions have already postulated.

If I is an invariant, IA_μ is a covariant vector; hence its covariant derivative is

$$\begin{aligned} (IA_\mu)_\nu &= \frac{\partial}{\partial x_\nu}(IA_\mu) - \{\mu\nu, \alpha\} IA_\alpha \\ &= A_\mu \frac{\partial I}{\partial x_\nu} + IA_{\mu\nu}. \end{aligned}$$

But by the rule for differentiating a product (30·5)

$$(IA_\mu)_\nu = I_\nu A_\mu + IA_{\mu\nu},$$

so that

$$I_\nu = \frac{\partial I}{\partial x_\nu}.$$

Hence the covariant derivative of an invariant is the same as its ordinary derivative.

It is, of course, impossible to reserve the notation $A_{\mu\nu}$ exclusively for the covariant derivative of A_μ, and the concluding suffix does not denote differentiation unless expressly stated. In case of doubt we may indicate the covariant and contravariant derivatives by $(A_\mu)_\nu$ and $(A_\mu)^\nu$.

The utility of the covariant derivative arises largely from the fact that, when the $g_{\mu\nu}$ are constants, the 3-index symbols vanish and the covariant derivative reduces to the ordinary derivative. Now in general our physical equations have been stated for the case of Galilean coordinates in which the $g_{\mu\nu}$ are constants; and we may in Galilean equations replace the ordinary derivative by the covariant derivative without altering anything. This is a necessary step in reducing such equations to the general tensor form which holds true for all coordinate-systems.

As an illustration suppose we wish to find the general equation of propagation of a potential with the velocity of light. In Galilean coordinates the equation is of the well-known form

$$\Box\phi \equiv \frac{\partial^2\phi}{\partial t^2} - \frac{\partial^2\phi}{\partial x^2} - \frac{\partial^2\phi}{\partial y^2} - \frac{\partial^2\phi}{\partial z^2} = 0 \qquad (30\cdot 6).$$

The Galilean values of $g^{\mu\nu}$ are $g^{44} = 1$, $g^{11} = g^{22} = g^{33} = -1$, and the other components vanish. Hence (30·6) can be written

$$g^{\mu\nu}\frac{\partial^2\phi}{\partial x_\mu \partial x_\nu} = 0 \qquad (30\cdot 65).$$

The potential ϕ being an invariant, its ordinary derivative is a covariant vector $\phi_\mu = \partial\phi/\partial x_\mu$, and since the coordinates are Galilean we may insert the covariant derivative $\phi_{\mu\nu}$ instead of $\partial\phi_\mu/\partial x_\nu$. Hence the equation becomes

$$g^{\mu\nu}\phi_{\mu\nu} = 0 \qquad (30\cdot 7).$$

Up to this point Galilean coordinates are essential; but now, by examining the covariant dimensions of (30·7), we notice that the left-hand side is an invariant, and therefore its value is unchanged by any transformation of coordinates. Hence (30·7) holds for all coordinate-systems, if it holds for any. Using (29·3) we can write it more fully

$$g^{\mu\nu}\left(\frac{\partial^2\phi}{\partial x_\mu \partial x_\nu} - \{\mu\nu, \alpha\}\frac{\partial\phi}{\partial x_\alpha}\right) = 0 \qquad (30\cdot 8).$$

This formula may be used for transforming Laplace's equation into curvilinear coordinates, etc.

It must be remembered that a transformation of coordinates does not alter the kind of space. Thus if we know by experiment that a potential ϕ is propagated according to the law (30·6) in Galilean coordinates, it follows rigorously that it is propagated according to the law (30·8) in any system of coordinates in flat space-time; but it does not follow rigorously that it will be propagated according to (30·8) when an irreducible gravitational field is present which alters the kind of space-time. It is, however, a plausible suggestion that (30·8) may be the general law of propagation of ϕ in any kind of space-time; that is the suggestion which the principle of equivalence makes. Like all generalisations which are only tested experimentally in a particular case, it must be received with caution.

The operator $\Box$ will frequently be referred to. In general coordinates it is to be taken as defined by

$$\Box A_{\mu\nu} = g^{\alpha\beta}(A_{\mu\nu})_{\alpha\beta} \qquad (30\cdot 9).$$

Or we may write it in the form

$$\Box = ((\ \ )_\alpha)^\alpha,$$

i.e. we perform a covariant and contravariant differentiation and contract them.

SUMMARY OF RULES FOR COVARIANT DIFFERENTIATION

1. To obtain the covariant derivative of any tensor $A_{\cdot\cdot}^{\cdot\cdot\cdot}$ with respect to x_σ, we take first the ordinary derivative

$$\frac{\partial}{\partial x_\sigma} A^{\cdots};$$

and for *each* covariant suffix $A^{\cdot\cdot}_{\cdot\mu\cdot}$, we add a term

$$-\{\mu\sigma, \alpha\} A^{\cdot\cdot}_{\cdot\alpha\cdot},$$

and for *each* contravariant suffix $A^{\cdot\cdot\mu\cdot}_{\cdot\cdot\cdot}$, we add a term

$$+\{\alpha\sigma, \mu\} A^{\cdot\cdot\alpha\cdot}_{\cdot\cdot\cdot}.$$

2. The covariant derivative of a product is formed by covariant differentiation of each factor in turn, by the same rule as in ordinary differentiation.

3. The fundamental tensor $g_{\mu\nu}$ or $g^{\mu\nu}$ behaves as though it were a constant in covariant differentiation

4. The covariant derivative of an invariant is its ordinary derivative.

5. In taking second, third or higher derivatives, the order of differentiation is not interchangeable*.

31. Alternative discussion of the covariant derivative.

By (23·22)
$$g'_{\mu\nu} = \frac{\partial x_\alpha}{\partial x_\mu'} \frac{\partial x_\beta}{\partial x_\nu'} g_{\alpha\beta}.$$

Hence differentiating

$$\frac{\partial g'_{\mu\nu}}{\partial x_\lambda'} = g_{\alpha\beta} \left\{ \frac{\partial^2 x_\alpha}{\partial x_\lambda' \partial x_\mu'} \frac{\partial x_\beta}{\partial x_\nu'} + \frac{\partial^2 x_\alpha}{\partial x_\lambda' \partial x_\nu'} \frac{\partial x_\beta}{\partial x_\mu'} \right\} + \frac{\partial x_\alpha}{\partial x_\mu'} \frac{\partial x_\beta}{\partial x_\nu'} \frac{\partial x_\gamma}{\partial x_\lambda'} \frac{\partial g_{\alpha\beta}}{\partial x_\gamma} \quad \text{...(31·11)}$$

Here we have used

$$\frac{\partial g_{\alpha\beta}}{\partial x_\lambda'} = \frac{\partial g_{\alpha\beta}}{\partial x_\gamma} \frac{\partial x_\gamma}{\partial x_\lambda'},$$

and further we have interchanged the dummy suffixes α and β in the second term in the bracket. Similarly

$$\frac{\partial g'_{\nu\lambda}}{\partial x_\mu'} = g_{\alpha\beta} \left\{ \frac{\partial^2 x_\alpha}{\partial x_\mu' \partial x_\nu'} \frac{\partial x_\beta}{\partial x_\lambda'} + \frac{\partial^2 x_\alpha}{\partial x_\mu' \partial x_\lambda'} \frac{\partial x_\beta}{\partial x_\nu'} \right\} + \frac{\partial x_\alpha}{\partial x_\mu'} \frac{\partial x_\beta}{\partial x_\nu'} \frac{\partial x_\gamma}{\partial x_\lambda'} \frac{\partial g_{\beta\gamma}}{\partial x_\alpha} \quad \text{... (31·12)},$$

$$\frac{\partial g'_{\mu\lambda}}{\partial x_\nu'} = g_{\alpha\beta} \left\{ \frac{\partial^2 x_\alpha}{\partial x_\nu' \partial x_\mu'} \frac{\partial x_\beta}{\partial x_\lambda'} + \frac{\partial^2 x_\alpha}{\partial x_\nu' \partial x_\lambda'} \frac{\partial x_\beta}{\partial x_\mu'} \right\} + \frac{\partial x_\alpha}{\partial x_\mu'} \frac{\partial x_\beta}{\partial x_\nu'} \frac{\partial x_\gamma}{\partial x_\lambda'} \frac{\partial g_{\alpha\gamma}}{\partial x_\beta} \quad \text{... (31·13)}.$$

Add (31·12) and (31·13) and subtract (31·11), we obtain by (27·1)

$$[\mu\nu, \lambda]' = g_{\alpha\beta} \frac{\partial^2 x_\alpha}{\partial x_\mu' \partial x_\nu'} \frac{\partial x_\beta}{\partial x_\lambda'} + \frac{\partial x_\alpha}{\partial x_\mu'} \frac{\partial x_\beta}{\partial x_\nu'} \frac{\partial x_\gamma}{\partial x_\lambda'} [\alpha\beta, \gamma] \quad \text{......(31·2)}.$$

* This is inserted here for completeness; it is discussed later.

Multiply through by $g'^{\lambda\rho}\frac{\partial x_\epsilon}{\partial x_\rho'}$, we have by (27·3)

$$\{\mu\nu, \rho\}'\frac{\partial x_\epsilon}{\partial x_\rho'} = g_{\alpha\beta}\frac{\partial^2 x_\alpha}{\partial x_\mu'\partial x_\nu'}\cdot g'^{\lambda\rho}\frac{\partial x_\beta}{\partial x_\lambda'}\frac{\partial x_\epsilon}{\partial x_\rho'} + g'^{\lambda\rho}\frac{\partial x_\gamma}{\partial x_\lambda'}\frac{\partial x_\epsilon}{\partial x_\rho'}\cdot\frac{\partial x_\alpha}{\partial x_\mu'}\frac{\partial x_\beta}{\partial x_\nu'}[\alpha\beta, \gamma]$$

$$= g_{\alpha\beta}g^{\beta\epsilon}\frac{\partial^2 x_\alpha}{\partial x_\mu'\partial x_\nu'} + \frac{\partial x_\alpha}{\partial x_\mu'}\frac{\partial x_\beta}{\partial x_\nu'}g^{\gamma\epsilon}[\alpha\beta, \gamma] \qquad \text{by (23·21)}$$

$$= \frac{\partial^2 x_\epsilon}{\partial x_\mu'\partial x_\nu'} + \frac{\partial x_\alpha}{\partial x_\mu'}\frac{\partial x_\beta}{\partial x_\nu'}\{\alpha\beta, \epsilon\} \quad \text{..............................(31·3)},$$

a formula which determines the second derivative $\partial^2 x_\epsilon/\partial x_\mu'\partial x_\nu'$ in terms of the first derivatives.

By (23·12)
$$A_\mu' = \frac{\partial x_\epsilon}{\partial x_\mu'}A_\epsilon \quad \text{...........................(31·4)}.$$

Hence differentiating

$$\frac{\partial A_\mu'}{\partial x_\nu'} = \frac{\partial^2 x_\epsilon}{\partial x_\mu'\partial x_\nu'}A_\epsilon + \frac{\partial x_\epsilon}{\partial x_\mu'}\cdot\frac{\partial x_\delta}{\partial x_\nu'}\frac{\partial A_\epsilon}{\partial x_\delta}$$

$$= \left(\{\mu\nu, \rho\}'\frac{\partial x_\epsilon}{\partial x_\rho'} - \frac{\partial x_\alpha}{\partial x_\mu'}\frac{\partial x_\beta}{\partial x_\nu'}\{\alpha\beta, \epsilon\}\right)A_\epsilon + \frac{\partial x_\alpha}{\partial x_\mu'}\frac{\partial x_\beta}{\partial x_\nu'}\frac{\partial A_\alpha}{\partial x_\beta} \quad \text{......(31·5)}$$

by (31·3) and changing the dummy suffixes in the last term.

Also by (23·12)
$$A_\epsilon\frac{\partial x_\epsilon}{\partial x_\rho'} = A_\rho'.$$

Hence (31·5) becomes

$$\frac{\partial A_\mu'}{\partial x_\nu'} - \{\mu\nu, \rho\}'A_\rho' = \frac{\partial x_\alpha}{\partial x_\mu'}\frac{\partial x_\beta}{\partial x_\nu'}\left(\frac{\partial A_\alpha}{\partial x_\beta} - \{\alpha\beta, \epsilon\}A_\epsilon\right) \quad \text{.........(31·6)},$$

showing that
$$\frac{\partial A_\mu}{\partial x_\nu} - \{\mu\nu, \rho\}A_\rho$$

obeys the law of transformation of a covariant tensor. We thus reach the result (29·3) by an alternative method.

A tensor of the second or higher rank may be taken instead of A_μ in (31·4), and its covariant derivative will be found by the same method.

32. Surface-elements and Stokes's theorem.

Consider the outer product $\Sigma^{\mu\nu}$ of two different displacements dx_μ and δx_ν. The tensor $\Sigma^{\mu\nu}$ will be unsymmetrical in μ and ν. We can decompose any such tensor into the sum of a symmetrical part $\frac{1}{2}(\Sigma^{\mu\nu} + \Sigma^{\nu\mu})$ and an antisymmetrical part $\frac{1}{2}(\Sigma^{\mu\nu} - \Sigma^{\nu\mu})$.

Double* the antisymmetrical part of the product $dx_\mu\delta x_\nu$ is called the *surface-element* contained by the two displacements, and is denoted by $dS^{\mu\nu}$. We have accordingly

$$dS^{\mu\nu} = dx_\mu\delta x_\nu - dx_\nu\delta x_\mu \quad \text{.......................(32·1)}$$

$$= \begin{vmatrix} dx_\mu & dx_\nu \\ \delta x_\mu & \delta x_\nu \end{vmatrix}.$$

* The doubling of the natural expression is avenged by the appearance of the factor $\frac{1}{2}$ in most formulae containing $dS^{\mu\nu}$.

In rectangular coordinates this determinant represents the area of the projection on the $\mu\nu$ plane of the parallelogram contained by the two displacements; thus the components of the tensor are the projections of the parallelogram on the six coordinate planes. In the tensor $dS^{\mu\nu}$ these are repeated twice, once with positive and once with negative sign (corresponding perhaps to the two sides of the surface). The four components dS^{11}, dS^{22}, etc. vanish, as must happen in every antisymmetrical tensor The appropriateness of the name "surface-element" is evident in rectangular coordinates, the geometrical meaning becomes more obscure in other systems.

The surface-element is always a tensor of the second rank whatever the number of dimensions of space; but in *three* dimensions there is an alternative representation of a surface area by a simple *vector* at right angles to the surface and of length proportional to the area, indeed it is customary in three dimensions to represent any antisymmetrical tensor by an adjoint vector Happily in four dimensions it is not possible to introduce this source of confusion.

The invariant $\frac{1}{2} A_{\mu\nu} dS^{\mu\nu}$

is called the *flux* of the tensor $A_{\mu\nu}$ through the surface-element. The flux involves only the antisymmetrical part of $A_{\mu\nu}$, since the inner product of a symmetrical and an antisymmetrical tensor evidently vanishes.

Some of the chief antisymmetrical tensors arise from the operation of *curling*. If $K_{\mu\nu}$ is the covariant derivative of K_μ, we find from (29·3) that

$$K_{\mu\nu} - K_{\nu\mu} = \frac{\partial K_\mu}{\partial x_\nu} - \frac{\partial K_\nu}{\partial x_\mu} \quad \text{.....................(32·2)}$$

since the 3-index symbols cancel out. Since the left-hand side is a tensor, the right-hand side is also a tensor. The right-hand side will be recognised as the "curl" of elementary vector theory, except that we have apparently reversed the sign. Strictly speaking, however, we should note that the curl in the elementary three-dimensional theory is a vector, whereas our curl is a tensor; and comparison of the sign attributed is impossible.

The result that the covariant curl is the same as the ordinary curl does not apply to contravariant vectors or to tensors of higher rank:

$$K^\mu{}_\nu - K^\nu{}_\mu \neq \frac{\partial K^\mu}{\partial x_\nu} - \frac{\partial K^\nu}{\partial x_\mu}.$$

In tensor notation the famous theorem of Stokes becomes

$$\int K_\mu dx_\mu = -\frac{1}{2}\iint \left(\frac{\partial K_\mu}{\partial x_\nu} - \frac{\partial K_\nu}{\partial x_\mu}\right) dS^{\mu\nu} \quad \text{............(32·3)},$$

the double integral being taken over any surface bounded by the path of the single integral. The factor $\frac{1}{2}$ is needed because each surface-element occurs twice, e.g. as dS^{12} and $-dS^{21}$. The theorem can be proved as follows—

Since both sides of the equation are invariants it is sufficient to prove the equation for any one system of coordinates. Choose coordinates so that the surface is on one of the fundamental partitions $x_3 = \text{const.}$, $x_4 = \text{const.}$, and so that the contour consists of four parts given successively by $x_1 = \alpha$, $x_2 = \beta$, $x_1 = \gamma$, $x_2 = \delta$; the rest of the mesh-system may be filled up arbitrarily. For an elementary mesh the containing vectors are $(dx_1, 0, 0, 0)$ and $(0, dx_2, 0, 0)$, so that by (32·1)

$$dS^{12} = dx_1 dx_2 = -dS^{21}.$$

Hence the right-hand side of (32·3) becomes

$$-\int_\alpha^\gamma \int_\beta^\delta \left(\frac{\partial K_1}{\partial x_2} - \frac{\partial K_2}{\partial x_1}\right) dx_1 dx_2$$

$$= -\int_\alpha^\gamma \{[K_1]^\delta - [K_1]^\beta\} \, dx_1 + \int_\beta^\delta \{[K_2]^\gamma - [K_2]^\alpha\} \, dx_2,$$

which consists of four terms giving $\int K_\mu dx_\mu$ for the four parts of the contour.

This proof affords a good illustration of the methods of the tensor calculus. The relation to be established is between two quantities which (by examination of their covariant dimensions) are seen to be invariants, viz. $K_\mu (dx)^\mu$ and $(K_{\mu\nu} - K_{\nu\mu}) dS^{\mu\nu}$, the latter having been simplified by (32·2). Accordingly it is a relation which does not depend on any particular choice of coordinates, although in (32·3) it is expressed as it would appear when referred to a coordinate-system. In proving the relation of the two invariants once for all, we naturally choose for the occasion coordinates which simplify the analysis, and the work is greatly shortened by drawing our curved meshes so that four partition-lines make up the contour.

33. Significance of covariant differentiation.

Suppose that we wish to discuss from the physical point of view how a field of force varies from point to point. If polar coordinates are being used, a change of the r-component does not necessarily indicate a want of uniformity in the field of force; it is at least partly attributable to the inclination between the r-directions at different points. Similarly when rotating axes are used, the rate of change of momentum h is given not by dh_1/dt, etc., but by

$$dh_1/dt - \omega_3 h_2 + \omega_2 h_3, \text{ etc.} \quad \text{.....................(33·1).}$$

The momentum may be constant even when the time-derivatives of its components are not zero.

We must recognise then that the change of a physical entity is usually regarded as something distinct from the change of the mathematical components into which we resolve it. In the elementary theory a definition of the former change is obtained by identifying it with the change of the components in unaccelerated rectangular coordinates; but this is of no avail in the general case because space-time may be of a kind for which no such coordinates exist. Can we still preserve this notion of a *physical* rate of change in the general case?

Our attention is directed to the rate of change of a physical entity because of its importance in the laws of physics, e.g. force is the time-rate of change of momentum, or the space-rate of change of potential; therefore the rate of change should be expressed by a tensor of some kind in order that it may enter into the general physical laws. Further in order to agree with the customary definition in elementary cases, it must reduce to the rate of change of the rectangular components when the coordinates are Galilean. Both conditions are fulfilled if we define the physical rate of change of the tensor by its covariant derivative.

The covariant derivative $A_{\mu\nu}$ consists of the term $\partial A_\mu/\partial x_\nu$, giving the apparent gradient, from which is subtracted the "spurious change" $\{\mu\nu, \alpha\} A_\alpha$ attributable to the curvilinearity of the coordinate-system. When Cartesian coordinates (rectangular or oblique) are used, the 3-index symbols vanish and there is, as we should expect, no spurious change. For the present we shall call $A_{\mu\nu}$ the rate of *absolute change* of the vector A_μ.

Consider an elementary mesh in the plane of $x_\nu x_\sigma$, the corners being at

$$A\,(x_\nu,\, x_\sigma),\quad B\,(x_\nu + dx_\nu,\, x_\sigma),\quad C\,(x_\nu + dx_\nu,\, x_\sigma + dx_\sigma),\quad D\,(x_\nu,\, x_\sigma + dx_\sigma).$$

Let us calculate the whole absolute change of the vector-field A_μ as we pass round the circuit $ABCDA$.

(1) From A to B, the absolute change is $A_{\mu\nu} dx_\nu$, calculated for x_σ*.

(2) From B to C, the absolute change is $A_{\mu\sigma} dx_\sigma$, calculated for $x_\nu + dx_\nu$.

(3) From C to D, the absolute change is $-A_{\mu\nu} dx_\nu$, calculated for $x_\sigma + dx_\sigma$.

(4) From D to A, the absolute change is $-A_{\mu\sigma} dx_\sigma$, calculated for x_ν.

Combining (2) and (4) the net result is the difference of the changes $A_{\mu\sigma} dx_\sigma$ at $x_\nu + dx_\nu$ and at x_ν respectively. We might be tempted to set this difference down as

$$\frac{\partial}{\partial x_\nu}(A_{\mu\sigma} dx_\sigma)\, dx_\nu.$$

But as already explained that would give only the difference of the mathematical components and not the "absolute difference." We must take the covariant derivative instead, obtaining (since dx_σ is the same for (2) and (4))

$$A_{\mu\sigma\nu} dx_\sigma dx_\nu.$$

Similarly (3) and (1) give

$$-A_{\mu\nu\sigma} dx_\nu dx_\sigma,$$

so that the total absolute change round the circuit is

$$(A_{\mu\sigma\nu} - A_{\mu\nu\sigma})\, dx_\nu dx_\sigma \quad \text{.......................(33·2)}.$$

We should naturally expect that on returning to our starting point the absolute change would vanish. How could there have been any absolute change on balance, seeing that the vector is now the same A_μ that we started with? Nevertheless in general $A_{\mu\nu\sigma} \neq A_{\mu\sigma\nu}$, that is to say the order of covariant differentiation is not permutable, and (33·2) does not vanish.

* We suspend the summation convention since dx_ν and dx_σ are edges of a particular mesh. The convention would give correct results; but it goes too fast, and we cannot keep pace with it.

That this result is not unreasonable may be seen by considering a two-dimensional space, the surface of the ocean. If a ship's head is kept straight on the line of its wake, the course is a great circle. Now suppose that the ship sails round a circuit so that the final position and course are the same as at the start. If account is kept of all the successive changes of course, and the angles are added up, these will not give a change zero (or 2π) on balance. For a triangular course the difference is the well-known "spherical excess." Similarly the changes of velocity do not cancel out on balance. Here we have an illustration that the absolute changes of a vector do not cancel out on bringing it back to its initial position.

If the present result sounds self-contradictory, the fault lies with the name "absolute change" which we have tentatively applied to the thing under discussion. The name is illuminating in some respects, because it shows the continuity of covariant differentiation with the conceptions of elementary physics. For instance, no one would hesitate to call (33·1) the absolute rate of change of momentum in contrast to the apparent rate of change dh_1/dt. But having shown the continuity, we find it better to avoid the term in the more general case of non-Euclidean space.

Following Levi-Civita and Weyl we use the term *parallel displacement* for what we have hitherto called displacement without "absolute change." The condition for parallel displacement is that the covariant derivative vanishes.

We have hitherto considered the absolute change necessary in order that the vector may return to its original value, and so be a single-valued function of position. If we do not permit any change *en route*, i.e. if we move the vector by parallel displacement, the same quantity will appear (with reversed sign) as a discrepancy δA_μ between the final and initial vectors. Since these are at the same point the difference of the initial and final vectors can be measured immediately. We have then by (33·2)

$$\delta A_\mu = (A_{\mu\nu\sigma} - A_{\mu\sigma\nu})\, dx_\nu dx_\sigma,$$

which may also be written

$$\delta A_\mu = \tfrac{1}{2} \iint (A_{\mu\nu\sigma} - A_{\mu\sigma\nu})\, dS^{\nu\sigma} \quad \text{.................} \quad (33\cdot 3),$$

where the summation convention is now restored. We have only proved this for an infinitesimal circuit occupying a coordinate-mesh, for which $dS^{\nu\sigma}$ has only two non-vanishing components $dx_\nu dx_\sigma$ and $-dx_\nu dx_\sigma$. But the equation is seen to be a tensor-equation, and therefore holds independently of the coordinate-system; thus it applies to circuits of any shape, since we can always choose coordinates for which the circuit becomes a coordinate-mesh. But (33·3) is still restricted to infinitesimal circuits and there is no way of extending it to finite circuits—unlike Stokes's theorem. The reason for this restriction is as follows—

An *isolated vector* A_μ may be taken at the starting point and carried by parallel displacement round the circuit, leading to a determinate value of δA_μ.

In (33·3) this is expressed in terms of derivatives of a *vector-field* A_μ extending throughout the region of integration. For a large circuit this would involve values of A_μ remote from the initial vector, which are obviously irrelevant to the calculation of δA_μ. It is rather remarkable that there should exist such a formula even for an infinitesimal circuit; the fact is that although $A_{\mu\nu\sigma} - A_{\mu\sigma\nu}$ at a point formally refers to a vector-field, its value turns out to depend solely on the isolated vector A_μ (see equation (34·3)).

The contravariant vector dx_μ/ds gives a direction in the four-dimensional world which is interpreted as a velocity from the ordinary point of view which separates space and time. We shall usually call it a "velocity"; its connection with the usual three-dimensional vector (u, v, w) is given by

$$\frac{dx_\mu}{ds} = \beta\,(u, v, w, 1),$$

where β is the FitzGerald factor dt/ds. The length (26·5) of a velocity is always unity.

If we transfer dx_μ/ds continually along itself by parallel displacement we obtain a geodesic. For by (29·4) the condition for parallel displacement is

$$\frac{\partial}{\partial x_\nu}\left(\frac{dx_\mu}{ds}\right) + \{\alpha\nu, \mu\}\frac{dx_\alpha}{ds} = 0.$$

Hence multiplying by dx_ν/ds

$$\frac{d^2 x_\mu}{ds^2} + \{\alpha\nu, \mu\}\frac{dx_\alpha}{ds}\frac{dx_\nu}{ds} = 0 \quad \text{.................}(33·4),$$

which is the condition for a geodesic (28·5). Thus in the language used at the beginning of this section, a geodesic is a line in four dimensions whose direction undergoes no absolute change.

34. The Riemann-Christoffel tensor.

The second covariant derivative of A_μ is found by inserting in (30·3) the value of $A_{\mu\nu}$ from (29·3). This gives

$$A_{\mu\nu\sigma} = \frac{\partial}{\partial x_\sigma}\left(\frac{\partial A_\mu}{\partial x_\nu} - \{\mu\nu, \alpha\}A_\alpha\right) - \{\mu\sigma, \alpha\}\left(\frac{\partial A_\alpha}{\partial x_\nu} - \{\alpha\nu, \epsilon\}A_\epsilon\right)$$
$$- \{\nu\sigma, \alpha\}\left(\frac{\partial A_\mu}{\partial x_\alpha} - \{\mu\alpha, \epsilon\}A_\epsilon\right)$$
$$= \frac{\partial^2 A_\mu}{\partial x_\sigma \partial x_\nu} - \{\mu\nu, \alpha\}\frac{\partial A_\alpha}{\partial x_\sigma} - \{\mu\sigma, \alpha\}\frac{\partial A_\alpha}{\partial x_\nu} - \{\nu\sigma, \alpha\}\frac{\partial A_\mu}{\partial x_\alpha} + \{\nu\sigma, \alpha\}\{\mu\alpha, \epsilon\}A_\epsilon$$
$$+ \{\mu\sigma, \alpha\}\{\alpha\nu, \epsilon\}A_\epsilon - A_\alpha\frac{\partial}{\partial x_\sigma}\{\mu\nu, \alpha\} \quad \text{.................}(34·1)$$

The first five terms are unaltered when ν and σ are interchanged. The last two terms may be written, by changing the dummy suffix α to ϵ in the last term,

$$A_\epsilon\left(\{\mu\sigma, \alpha\}\{\alpha\nu, \epsilon\} - \frac{\partial}{\partial x_\sigma}\{\mu\nu, \epsilon\}\right).$$

Hence

$$A_{\mu\nu\sigma} - A_{\mu\sigma\nu} = A_\epsilon \left(\{\mu\sigma, \alpha\} \{\alpha\nu, \epsilon\} - \frac{\partial}{\partial x_\sigma} \{\mu\nu, \epsilon\} - \{\mu\nu, \alpha\} \{\alpha\sigma, \epsilon\} + \frac{\partial}{\partial x_\nu} \{\mu\sigma, \epsilon\} \right) \quad \text{.....(34·2).}$$

The rigorous quotient theorem shows that the co-factor of A_ϵ must be a tensor. Accordingly we write

$$A_{\mu\nu\sigma} - A_{\mu\sigma\nu} = A_\epsilon B^\epsilon_{\mu\nu\sigma} \quad \text{.....................(34·3),}$$

where

$$B^\epsilon_{\mu\nu\sigma} = \{\mu\sigma, \alpha\} \{\alpha\nu, \epsilon\} - \{\mu\nu, \alpha\} \{\alpha\sigma, \epsilon\} + \frac{\partial}{\partial x_\nu} \{\mu\sigma, \epsilon\} - \frac{\partial}{\partial x_\sigma} \{\mu\nu, \epsilon\} \text{...(34·4)}$$

This is called the Riemann-Christoffel tensor. It is only when this tensor vanishes that the order of covariant differentiation is permutable.

The suffix ϵ may be lowered. Thus

$$B_{\mu\nu\sigma\rho} = g_{\rho\epsilon} B^\epsilon_{\mu\nu\sigma}$$

$$= \{\mu\sigma, \alpha\} [\alpha\nu, \rho] - \{\mu\nu, \alpha\} [\alpha\sigma, \rho] + \frac{\partial}{\partial x_\nu} [\mu\sigma, \rho] - \frac{\partial}{\partial x_\sigma} [\mu\nu, \rho]$$

$$- \{\mu\sigma, \alpha\} \frac{\partial g_{\rho\alpha}}{\partial x_\nu} + \{\mu\nu, \alpha\} \frac{\partial g_{\rho\alpha}}{\partial x_\sigma} \quad \text{..............................(34·45),}$$

where ϵ has been replaced by α in the last two terms,

$$= - \{\mu\sigma, \alpha\} [\rho\nu, \alpha] + \{\mu\nu, \alpha\} [\rho\sigma, \alpha]$$

$$+ \tfrac{1}{2} \left(\frac{\partial^2 g_{\rho\sigma}}{\partial x_\mu \partial x_\nu} + \frac{\partial^2 g_{\mu\nu}}{\partial x_\rho \partial x_\sigma} - \frac{\partial^2 g_{\mu\sigma}}{\partial x_\rho \partial x_\nu} - \frac{\partial^2 g_{\rho\nu}}{\partial x_\mu \partial x_\sigma} \right) \quad \text{...........(34·5),}$$

by (27·5) and (27·1).

It will be seen from (34·5) that $B_{\mu\nu\sigma\rho}$, besides being antisymmetrical in ν and σ, is also antisymmetrical in μ and ρ. Also it is symmetrical for the double interchange μ and ν, ρ and σ. It has the further cyclic property

$$B_{\mu\nu\sigma\rho} + B_{\mu\sigma\rho\nu} + B_{\mu\rho\nu\sigma} = 0 \quad \text{...................(34·6),}$$

as is easily verified from (34·5).

The general tensor of the fourth rank has 256 different components. Here the double antisymmetry reduces the number (apart from differences of sign) to 6×6. 30 of these are paired because μ, ρ can be interchanged with ν, σ; but the remaining 6 components, in which μ, ρ is the same pair of numbers as ν, σ, are without partners. This leaves 21 different components, between which (34·6) gives only one further relation. We conclude that the Riemann-Christoffel tensor has 20 *independent* components*.

The Riemann-Christoffel tensor is derived solely from the $g_{\mu\nu}$ and therefore belongs to the class of fundamental tensors. Usually we can form from any tensor a series of tensors of continually increasing rank by covariant

* Writing the suffixes in the order $\mu\rho\sigma\nu$ the following scheme gives 21 different components:

1212	1223	1313	1324	1423	2323	2424
1213	1224	1314	1334	1424	2324	2434
1214	1234	1323	1414	1434	2334	3434

with the relation 1234 − 1324 + 1423 = 0.

If we omit those containing the suffix 4, we are left with 6 components in three-dimensional space. In two dimensions there is only the one component 1212.

differentiation. But this process is frustrated in the case of the fundamental tensors because $g_{\mu\nu\sigma}$ vanishes identically. We have got round the gap and reached a fundamental tensor of the fourth rank. The series can now be continued indefinitely by covariant differentiation

When the Riemann-Christoffel tensor vanishes, the differential equations

$$A_{\mu\nu} \equiv \frac{\partial A_\mu}{\partial x_\nu} - \{\mu\nu, \alpha\} A_\alpha = 0 \quad \dots \quad (34\cdot7)$$

are integrable. For the integration will be possible if (34·7) makes dA_μ or

$$\frac{\partial A_\mu}{\partial x_\nu} dx_\nu$$

a complete differential, i.e. if

$$\{\mu\nu, \alpha\} A_\alpha dx_\nu$$

is a complete differential. By the usual theory the condition for this is

$$\frac{\partial}{\partial x_\sigma}(\{\mu\nu, \alpha\} A_\alpha) - \frac{\partial}{\partial x_\nu}(\{\mu\sigma, \alpha\} A_\alpha) = 0,$$

or

$$A_\alpha \left(\frac{\partial}{\partial x_\sigma}\{\mu\nu, \alpha\} - \frac{\partial}{\partial x_\nu}\{\mu\sigma, \alpha\}\right) + \{\mu\nu, \alpha\}\frac{\partial A_\alpha}{\partial x_\sigma} - \{\mu\sigma, \alpha\}\frac{\partial A_\alpha}{\partial x_\nu} = 0.$$

Substituting for $\partial A_\alpha/\partial x_\sigma$, $\partial A_\alpha/\partial x_\nu$ from (34·7)

$$A_\alpha \left(\frac{\partial}{\partial x_\sigma}\{\mu\nu, \alpha\} - \frac{\partial}{\partial x_\nu}\{\mu\sigma, \alpha\}\right) + (\{\mu\nu, \alpha\}\{\alpha\sigma, \epsilon\} - \{\mu\sigma, \alpha\}\{\alpha\nu, \epsilon\}) A_\epsilon = 0.$$

Changing the suffix α to ϵ in the first term, the condition becomes

$$A_\epsilon B^\epsilon_{\mu\sigma\nu} = 0.$$

Accordingly when $B^\epsilon_{\mu\sigma\nu}$ vanishes, the differential dA_μ determined by (34·7) will be a complete differential, and

$$\int dA_\mu$$

between any two points will be independent of the path of integration. We can then carry the vector A_μ by parallel displacement to any point obtaining a unique result independent of the route of transfer. If a vector is displaced in this way all over the field, we obtain a *uniform vector-field*.

This construction of a uniform vector-field is only possible when the Riemann-Christoffel tensor vanishes throughout. In other cases the equations have no complete integral, and can only be integrated along a particular route. E.g., we can prescribe a *uniform direction* at all points of a plane, but there is nothing analogous to a uniform direction over the surface of a sphere.

Formulae analogous to (34·3) can be obtained for the second derivatives of a tensor $A_{\dots\mu\dots}$ instead of for a vector A_μ. The result is easily found to be

$$A_{\dots\mu\dots\nu\sigma} - A_{\dots\mu\dots\sigma\nu} = \Sigma B^\epsilon_{\mu\nu\sigma} A_{\dots\epsilon\dots} \quad \dots \quad (34\cdot8),$$

the summation being taken over all the suffixes μ of the original tensor.

The corresponding formulae for contravariant tensors follow at once, since the $g^{\mu\nu}$ behave as constants in covariant differentiation, and suffixes may be raised on both sides of (34·8).

35. Miscellaneous formulae.

The following are needed for subsequent use—

Since $$g_{\mu\nu}g^{\mu\alpha} = 0 \text{ or } 1,$$
$$g^{\mu\alpha}dg_{\mu\nu} + g_{\mu\nu}dg^{\mu\alpha} = 0.$$

Hence $$g^{\mu\alpha}g^{\nu\beta}dg_{\mu\nu} = -g_{\mu\nu}g^{\nu\beta}dg^{\mu\alpha} = -g^{\beta}_{\mu}dg^{\mu\alpha}$$
$$= -dg^{\alpha\beta} \qquad \text{.................................(35·11).}$$

Similarly $$dg_{\alpha\beta} = -g_{\mu\alpha}g_{\nu\beta}dg^{\mu\nu} \qquad \text{............................(35·12).}$$

Multiplying by $A^{\alpha\beta}$, we have by the rule for lowering suffixes
$$A^{\alpha\beta}dg_{\alpha\beta} = -(g_{\mu\alpha}g_{\nu\beta}A^{\alpha\beta})\,dg^{\mu\nu}$$
$$= -A_{\mu\nu}dg^{\mu\nu} = -A_{\alpha\beta}dg^{\alpha\beta} \qquad \text{..............(35·2).}$$

For any tensor $B_{\alpha\beta}$ other than the fundamental tensor the corresponding formula would be
$$A^{\alpha\beta}dB_{\alpha\beta} = A_{\alpha\beta}dB^{\alpha\beta}$$
by (26·3). The exception for $B_{\alpha\beta} = g_{\alpha\beta}$ arises because a change $dg_{\alpha\beta}$ has an additional indirect effect through altering the operation of raising and lowering suffixes.

Again dg is formed by taking the differential of each $g_{\mu\nu}$ and multiplying by its co-factor $g\,.\,g^{\mu\nu}$ in the determinant. Thus
$$\frac{dg}{g} = g^{\mu\nu}dg_{\mu\nu} = -g_{\mu\nu}dg^{\mu\nu} \qquad \text{.....................(35·3).}$$

The contracted 3-index symbol
$$\{\mu\sigma, \sigma\} = \tfrac{1}{2}g^{\sigma\lambda}\left\{\frac{\partial g_{\mu\lambda}}{\partial x_\sigma} + \frac{\partial g_{\sigma\lambda}}{\partial x_\mu} - \frac{\partial g_{\mu\sigma}}{\partial x_\lambda}\right\}$$
$$= \tfrac{1}{2}g^{\sigma\lambda}\frac{\partial g_{\sigma\lambda}}{\partial x_\mu}.$$

The other two terms cancel by interchange of the dummy suffixes σ and λ. Hence by (35·3)
$$\{\mu\sigma, \sigma\} = \frac{1}{2g}\frac{\partial g}{\partial x_\mu}$$
$$= \frac{\partial}{\partial x_\mu}\log\sqrt{-g} \qquad \text{....................... (35·4).}$$

We use $\sqrt{-g}$ because g is always negative for real coordinates.

A possible pitfall in differentiating a summed expression should be noticed. The result of differentiating $a_{\mu\nu}x_\mu x_\nu$ with respect to x_ν is not $a_{\mu\nu}x_\mu$ but $(a_{\mu\nu} + a_{\nu\mu})\,x_\mu$. The method of performing such differentiations may be illustrated by the following example. Let
$$h_{\nu\tau} = a_{\mu\nu}a_{\sigma\tau}x_\mu x_\sigma,$$
where $a_{\mu\nu}$ represents constant coefficients. Then
$$\frac{\partial h_{\nu\tau}}{\partial x_\alpha} = a_{\mu\nu}a_{\sigma\tau}\left(\frac{\partial x_\mu}{\partial x_\alpha}x_\sigma + \frac{\partial x_\sigma}{\partial x_\alpha}x_\mu\right)$$
$$= a_{\mu\nu}a_{\sigma\tau}(g^{\mu}_{\alpha}x_\sigma + g^{\sigma}_{\alpha}x_\mu) \quad \text{by (22·3).}$$

Repeating the process,

$$\frac{\partial^2 h_{\nu\tau}}{\partial x_\alpha \partial x_\beta} = a_{\mu\nu} a_{\sigma\tau} (g^\mu_\alpha g^\sigma_\beta + g^\sigma_\alpha g^\mu_\beta)$$

$$= a_{\alpha\nu} a_{\beta\tau} + a_{\beta\nu} a_{\alpha\tau}.$$

Hence changing dummy suffixes

$$\frac{\partial^2}{\partial x_\mu \partial x_\sigma} (a_{\mu\nu} a_{\sigma\tau} x_\mu x_\sigma) = a_{\mu\nu} a_{\sigma\tau} + a_{\sigma\nu} a_{\mu\tau} \quad \ldots\ldots\ldots\ldots (35 \cdot 5).$$

Similarly if $a_{\mu\nu\sigma}$ is symmetrical in its suffixes

$$\frac{\partial^3}{\partial x_\mu \partial x_\nu \partial x_\sigma} (a_{\mu\nu\sigma} x_\mu x_\nu x_\sigma) = 6 a_{\mu\nu\sigma} \quad \ldots\ldots\ldots\ldots (35 \cdot 6)$$

The pitfall arises from repeating a suffix three times in one term. In these formulae the summation applies to the repetition within the bracket, and not to the differentiation.

Summary.

Tensors are quantities obeying certain transformation laws. Their importance lies in the fact that if a tensor equation is found to hold for one system of coordinates, it continues to hold when any transformation of coordinates is made. New tensors are recognised either by investigating their transformation laws directly or by the property that the sum, difference, product or quotient of tensors is a tensor. This is a generalisation of the method of dimensions in physics.

The principal operations of the tensor calculus are addition, multiplication (outer and inner), summation (§ 22), contraction (§ 24), substitution (§ 25), raising and lowering suffixes (§ 26), covariant differentiation (§§ 29, 30). There is no operation of division; but an inconvenient factor $g_{\mu\nu}$ or $g^{\mu\nu}$ can be removed by multiplying through by $g^{\mu\sigma}$ or $g_{\mu\sigma}$ so as to form the substitution-operator. The operation of summation is practically outside our control and always presents itself as a *fait accompli*. The most characteristic process of manipulation in this calculus is the free alteration of dummy suffixes (those appearing twice in a term); it is probably this process which presents most difficulty to the beginner.

Of special interest are the fundamental tensors or world-tensors, of which we have discovered two, viz. $g_{\mu\nu}$ and $B_{\mu\nu\sigma\rho}$. The latter has been expressed in terms of the former and its first and second derivatives. It is through these that the gap between pure geometry and physics is bridged; in particular $g_{\mu\nu}$ relates the observed quantity ds to the mathematical coordinate specification dx_μ.

Since in our work we generally deal with tensors, the reader may be led to overlook the rarity of this property. The juggling tricks which we seem to perform in our manipulations are only possible because the material used is of quite exceptional character.

The further development of the tensor calculus will be resumed in § 48; but a stage has now been reached at which we may begin to apply it to the theory of gravitation.

CHAPTER III

THE LAW OF GRAVITATION

36. The condition for flat space-time. Natural coordinates.

A region of the world is called *flat* or *homaloidal* if it is possible to construct in it a Galilean frame of reference.

It was shown in § 4 that when the $g_{\mu\nu}$ are constants, ds^2 can be reduced to the sum of four squares, and Galilean coordinates can be constructed. Thus an equivalent definition of flat space-time is that it is such that coordinates can be found for which the $g_{\mu\nu}$ are constants.

When the $g_{\mu\nu}$ are constants the 3-index symbols all vanish; but since the 3-index symbols do not form a tensor, they will not in general continue to vanish when other coordinates are substituted in the same flat region. Again, when the $g_{\mu\nu}$ are constants, the Riemann-Christoffel tensor, being composed of products and derivatives of the 3-index symbols, will vanish; and since it is a tensor, it will continue to vanish when any other coordinate-system is substituted in the same region.

Hence the vanishing of the Riemann-Christoffel tensor is a necessary condition for flat space-time.

This condition is also *sufficient*—if the Riemann-Christoffel tensor vanishes space-time must be flat. This can be proved as follows—

We have found (§ 34) that if

$$B^{\epsilon}_{\mu\nu\sigma} = 0 \quad \text{.........................(36·1)},$$

it is possible to construct a uniform vector-field by parallel displacement of a vector all over the region. Let $A^{\mu}_{(\alpha)}$ be four uniform vector-fields given by $\alpha = 1, 2, 3, 4$, so that

$$(A^{\mu}_{(\alpha)})_{\sigma} = 0$$

or by (29·4)

$$\frac{\partial A^{\mu}_{(\alpha)}}{\partial x_{\sigma}} = -\{\epsilon\sigma, \mu\} A^{\epsilon}_{(\alpha)} \quad \text{.........................(36·2)}.$$

Note that α is not a tensor-suffix, but merely distinguishes the four independent vectors.

We shall use these four uniform vector-fields to define a new coordinate-system distinguished by accents. Our unit mesh will be the hyperparallelopiped contained by the four vectors at any point, and the complete mesh-system will be formed by successive parallel displacements of this unit mesh until the whole region is filled. One edge of the unit mesh, given in the old coordinates by

$$dx_{\mu} = A^{\mu}_{(1)},$$

has to become in the new coordinates

$$dx_{\alpha}' = (1, 0, 0, 0).$$

Similarly the second edge, $dx_\mu = A^\mu_{(2)}$, must become $dx_\alpha' = (0, 1, 0, 0)$, etc. This requires the law of transformation

$$dx_\mu = A^\mu_{(\alpha)} dx_\alpha' \qquad \text{......(36·3).}$$

Of course, the construction of the accented coordinate-system depends on the possibility of constructing uniform vector-fields, and this depends on (36·1) being satisfied.

Since ds^2 is an invariant

$$g'_{\alpha\beta} dx_\alpha' dx_\beta' = g_{\mu\nu} dx_\mu dx_\nu$$
$$= g_{\mu\nu} A^\mu_{(\alpha)} A^\nu_{(\beta)} dx_\alpha' dx_\beta' \quad \text{by (36·3)}$$

Hence $$g'_{\alpha\beta} = g_{\mu\nu} A^\mu_{(\alpha)} A^\nu_{(\beta)}.$$

Accordingly, by differentiation,

$$\frac{\partial g'_{\alpha\beta}}{\partial x_\sigma} = g_{\mu\nu} A^\mu_{(\alpha)} \frac{\partial A^\nu_{(\beta)}}{\partial x_\sigma} + g_{\mu\nu} A^\nu_{(\beta)} \frac{\partial A^\mu_{(\alpha)}}{\partial x_\sigma} + A^\mu_{(\alpha)} A^\nu_{(\beta)} \frac{\partial g_{\mu\nu}}{\partial x_\sigma}$$

$$= -g_{\mu\nu} A^\mu_{(\alpha)} A^\epsilon_{(\beta)} \{\epsilon\sigma, \nu\} - g_{\mu\nu} A^\nu_{(\beta)} A^\epsilon_{(\alpha)} \{\epsilon\sigma, \mu\} + A^\mu_{(\alpha)} A^\nu_{(\beta)} \frac{\partial g_{\mu\nu}}{\partial x_\sigma}$$

by (36·2). By changing dummy suffixes, this becomes

$$\frac{\partial g'_{\alpha\beta}}{\partial x_\sigma} = A^\mu_{(\alpha)} A^\nu_{(\beta)} \left[-g_{\mu\epsilon} \{\nu\sigma, \epsilon\} - g_{\epsilon\nu} \{\mu\sigma, \epsilon\} + \frac{\partial g_{\mu\nu}}{\partial x_\sigma} \right]$$

$$= A^\mu_{(\alpha)} A^\nu_{(\beta)} \left[-[\nu\sigma, \mu] - [\mu\sigma, \nu] + \frac{\partial g_{\mu\nu}}{\partial x_\sigma} \right]$$

$$= 0 \quad \text{by (27·5).}$$

Hence the $g'_{\alpha\beta}$ are constant throughout the region. We have thus constructed a coordinate-system fulfilling the condition that the g's are constant, and it follows that the space-time is flat.

It will be seen that a *uniform* mesh-system, i.e. one in which the unit meshes are connected with one another by parallel displacement, is necessarily a Cartesian system (rectangular or oblique). Uniformity in this sense is impossible in space-time for which the Riemann-Christoffel tensor does not vanish, e.g. there can be no uniform mesh-system on a sphere.

When space-time is not flat we can introduce coordinates which will be approximately Galilean in a small region round a selected point, the $g_{\mu\nu}$ being not constant but stationary there; this amounts to identifying the curved space-time with the osculating flat space-time for a small distance round the point. Expressing the procedure analytically, we choose coordinates such that the 40 derivatives $\partial g_{\mu\nu}/\partial x_\sigma$ vanish *at the selected point*. It is fairly obvious from general considerations that this will always be possible, but the following is a formal proof. Having transferred the origin to the selected point, make the following transformation of coordinates

$$x_\epsilon = g^\mu_\epsilon x_\mu' - \tfrac{1}{2} \{\alpha\beta, \epsilon\}_0 \, g^\mu_\alpha g^\nu_\beta x_\mu' x_\nu' \qquad \text{......(36·4),}$$

where the value of the 3-index symbol at the origin is to be taken. Then at the origin

$$\frac{\partial x_\epsilon}{\partial x_\mu'} = g_\epsilon^\mu \qquad \text{.........................(36·45)},$$

$$\frac{\partial^2 x_\epsilon}{\partial x_\mu' \partial x_\nu'} = -\{\alpha\beta, \epsilon\} g_\alpha^\mu g_\beta^\nu$$

$$= -\{\alpha\beta, \epsilon\} \frac{\partial x_\alpha}{\partial x_\mu'} \frac{\partial x_\beta}{\partial x_\nu'} \qquad \text{by (36·45)}.$$

Hence by (31·3) $$\{\mu\nu, \rho\}' \frac{\partial x_\epsilon}{\partial x_\rho'} = 0.$$

But $$\{\mu\nu, \rho\}' \frac{\partial x_\epsilon}{\partial x_\rho'} = \{\mu\nu, \rho\}' g_\epsilon^\rho = \{\mu\nu, \epsilon\}'.$$

Hence in the new coordinates the 3-index symbols vanish at the origin; and it follows by (27·4) and (27·5) that the first derivatives of the $g'_{\mu\nu}$ vanish. This is the preliminary transformation presupposed in § 4.

We pass on to a somewhat more difficult transformation which is important as contributing an insight into the significance of $B^\epsilon_{\mu\nu\sigma}$.

It is not possible to make the second derivatives of the $g_{\mu\nu}$ vanish at the selected point (as well as the first derivatives) unless the Riemann-Christoffel tensor vanishes there; but a great number of other special conditions can be imposed on the 100 second derivatives by choosing the coordinates suitably. Make an additional transformation of the form

$$x_\epsilon = g_\mu^\epsilon x_\mu' + \tfrac{1}{6} a^\epsilon_{\mu\nu\sigma} x_\mu' x_\nu' x_\sigma' \qquad \text{.....................(36·5)},$$

where $a^\epsilon_{\mu\nu\sigma}$ represents arbitrary coefficients symmetrical in μ, ν, σ. This new transformation will not affect the first derivatives of the $g_{\mu\nu}$ at the origin, which have already been made to vanish by the previous transformation, but it alters the second derivatives. By differentiating (31·3), viz.

$$\{\mu\nu, \rho\}' \frac{\partial x_\epsilon}{\partial x_\rho'} - \frac{\partial x_\alpha}{\partial x_\mu'} \frac{\partial x_\beta}{\partial x_\nu'} \{\alpha\beta, \epsilon\} = \frac{\partial^2 x_\epsilon}{\partial x_\mu' \partial x_\nu'},$$

we obtain at the origin

$$\frac{\partial}{\partial x_\sigma'} \{\mu\nu, \rho\}' \frac{\partial x_\epsilon}{\partial x_\rho'} - \frac{\partial x_\alpha}{\partial x_\mu'} \frac{\partial x_\beta}{\partial x_\nu'} \frac{\partial x_\gamma}{\partial x_\sigma'} \frac{\partial}{\partial x_\gamma} \{\alpha\beta, \epsilon\} = \frac{\partial^3 x_\epsilon}{\partial x_\mu' \partial x_\nu' \partial x_\sigma'},$$

since the 3-index symbols themselves vanish. Hence by (36·5)*

$$\frac{\partial}{\partial x_\sigma} \{\mu\nu, \rho\}' . g_\rho^\epsilon - g_\mu^\alpha g_\nu^\beta g_\sigma^\gamma \frac{\partial}{\partial x_\gamma} \{\alpha\beta, \epsilon\} = a^\epsilon_{\mu\nu\sigma},$$

which reduces to $$\frac{\partial}{\partial x_\sigma'} \{\mu\nu, \epsilon\}' - \frac{\partial}{\partial x_\sigma} \{\mu\nu, \epsilon\} = a^\epsilon_{\mu\nu\sigma} \qquad \text{............. (36·55)}.$$

The transformation (36·5) accordingly increases $\partial \{\mu\nu, \epsilon\}/\partial x_\sigma$ by $a^\epsilon_{\mu\nu\sigma}$.

Owing to the symmetry of $a^\epsilon_{\mu\nu\sigma}$, all three quantities

$$\frac{\partial}{\partial x_\sigma} \{\mu\nu, \epsilon\}, \quad \frac{\partial}{\partial x_\nu} \{\mu\sigma, \epsilon\}, \quad \frac{\partial}{\partial x_\mu} \{\nu\sigma, \epsilon\}$$

* For the disappearance of the factor $\frac{1}{6}$, see (35·6).

are necessarily increased by the same amount. Now the unaltered difference

$$\frac{\partial}{\partial x_\nu}\{\mu\sigma, \epsilon\} - \frac{\partial}{\partial x_\sigma}\{\mu\nu, \epsilon\} = B^\epsilon_{\mu\nu\sigma} \quad \text{.................}(36\cdot6),$$

since the remaining terms of (34·4) vanish in the coordinates here used. We cannot alter any of the components of the Riemann-Christoffel tensor; but, subject to this limitation, the alterations of the derivatives of the 3-index symbols are arbitrary.

The most symmetrical way of imposing further conditions is to make a transformation such that

$$\frac{\partial}{\partial x_\sigma}\{\mu\nu, \epsilon\} + \frac{\partial}{\partial x_\nu}\{\mu\sigma, \epsilon\} + \frac{\partial}{\partial x_\mu}\{\nu\sigma, \epsilon\} = 0 \quad \text{...........}(36\cdot7).$$

There are 80 different equations of this type, each of which fixes one of the 80 arbitrary coefficients $a^\epsilon_{\mu\nu\sigma}$. In addition there are 20 independent equations of type (36·6) corresponding to the 20 independent components of the Riemann-Christoffel tensor. Thus we have just sufficient equations to determine uniquely the 100 second derivatives of the $g_{\mu\nu}$. Coordinates such that $\partial g_{\mu\nu}/\partial x_\sigma$ is zero and $\partial^2 g_{\mu\nu}/\partial x_\sigma \partial x_\tau$ satisfies (36·7) may be called *canonical coordinates*.

By solving the 100 equations we obtain all the $\partial^2 g_{\mu\nu}/\partial x_\sigma \partial x_\tau$ for canonical coordinates expressed as linear functions of the $B^\epsilon_{\mu\nu\sigma}$.

The two successive transformations which lead to canonical coordinates are combined in the formula

$$x_\epsilon = g^\epsilon_\mu x_\mu' - \tfrac{1}{2}\{\mu\nu, \epsilon\}_0 x_\mu' x_\nu'$$
$$- \frac{1}{18}\left[\frac{\partial}{\partial x_\mu}\{\nu\sigma, \epsilon\} + \frac{\partial}{\partial x_\nu}\{\mu\sigma, \epsilon\} + \frac{\partial}{\partial x_\sigma}\{\mu\nu, \epsilon\}\right]_0 x_\mu' x_\nu' x_\sigma' \quad \text{...}(36\cdot8).$$

At the origin $\partial x_\epsilon/\partial x_\mu' = g^\epsilon_\mu$, so that the transformation does not alter any tensor at the origin. For example, the law of transformation of $C_{\mu\nu\sigma}$ gives

$$C'_{\mu\nu\sigma} = C_{\alpha\beta\gamma}\frac{\partial x_\alpha}{\partial x_\mu'}\frac{\partial x_\beta}{\partial x_\nu'}\frac{\partial x_\gamma}{\partial x_\sigma'} = C_{\alpha\beta\gamma} g^\alpha_\mu g^\beta_\nu g^\gamma_\sigma$$
$$= C_{\mu\nu\sigma}.$$

The transformation in fact alters the curvature and hypercurvature of the axes passing through the origin, but does not alter the angles of intersection.

Consider any tensor which contains only the $g_{\mu\nu}$ and their first and second derivatives. In canonical coordinates the first derivatives vanish and the second derivatives are linear functions of the $B^\epsilon_{\mu\nu\sigma}$, hence the whole tensor is a function of the $g_{\mu\nu}$ and the $B^\epsilon_{\mu\nu\sigma}$. But neither the tensor itself nor the $g_{\mu\nu}$ and $B^\epsilon_{\mu\nu\sigma}$ have been altered in the reduction to canonical coordinates, hence the same functional relation holds true in the original unrestricted coordinates. We have thus the important result—

The only fundamental tensors which do not contain derivatives of $g_{\mu\nu}$ beyond the second order are functions of $g_{\mu\nu}$ and $B^\epsilon_{\mu\nu\sigma}$.

This shows that our treatment of the tensors describing the character of space-time has been exhaustive as far as the second order. If for suitably chosen coordinates two surfaces have the same $g_{\mu\nu}$ and $B^{\epsilon}_{\mu\nu\sigma}$ at some point, they will be applicable to one another as far as cubes of the coordinates; the two tensors suffice to specify the whole metric round the point to this extent.

Having made the first derivatives vanish, we can by the linear transformation explained in § 4 give the $g_{\mu\nu}$ Galilean values at the selected point. The coordinates so obtained are called *natural coordinates* at the point and quantities referred to these coordinates are said to be expressed in *natural measure* Natural coordinates are thus equivalent to Galilean coordinates when only the $g_{\mu\nu}$ and their first derivatives are considered; the difference appears when we study phenomena involving the second derivatives

By making a Lorentz transformation (which leaves the coordinates still a natural system) we can reduce to rest the material located at the point, or an observer supposed to be stationed with his measuring appliances at the point. The *natural measure* is then further particularised as the *proper-measure* of the material, or observer. It may be noticed that the material will be at rest both as regards velocity and acceleration (unless it is acted on by electromagnetic forces) because there is no field of acceleration relative to natural coordinates.

To sum up this discussion of special systems of coordinates.—When the Riemann-Christoffel tensor vanishes, we can adopt Galilean coordinates throughout the region. When it does not vanish we can adopt coordinates which agree with Galilean coordinates at a selected point in the values of the $g_{\mu\nu}$ and their first derivatives but not in the second derivatives, these are called *natural coordinates* at the point. Either Galilean or natural coordinates can be subjected to Lorentz transformations, so that we can select a system with respect to which a particular observer is at rest; this system will be the *proper-coordinates* for that observer. Although we cannot in general make natural coordinates agree with Galilean coordinates in the second derivatives of the $g_{\mu\nu}$, we can impose 80 partially arbitrary conditions on the 100 second derivatives; and when these conditions are selected as in (36 7) the resulting coordinates have been called *canonical*.

There is another way of specialising coordinates which may be mentioned here for completeness. It is always possible to choose coordinates such that the determinant $g = -1$ everywhere (as in Galilean coordinates). This is explained in § 49.

We may also consider another class of specialised coordinates—those which are permissible in special problems. There are certain (non-Euclidean) coordinates found to be most convenient in dealing with the gravitational field of the sun, Einstein's or de Sitter's curved world, and so on. It must be remembered, however, that these refer to idealised problems, and coordinate-systems with simple properties can only be approximately realised in nature.

If possible a *static system* of coordinates is selected, the condition for this being that all the $g_{\mu\nu}$ are independent of one of the coordinates x_4 (which must be of timelike character*). In that case the interval corresponding to any displacement dx_μ is independent of the "time" x_4. Such a system can, of course, only be found if the relative configuration of the attracting masses is maintained unaltered. If in addition it is possible to make $g_{14}, g_{24}, g_{34} = 0$ the time will be reversible, and in particular the forward velocity of light along any track will be equal to the backward velocity; this renders the application of the name "time" to x_4 more just, since one of the alternative conventions of § 11 is satisfied. We shall if possible employ systems which are static and reversible in dealing with large regions of the world; problems in which this simplification is not permissible must generally be left aside as insoluble—e.g. the problem of two attracting bodies. For small regions of the world the greatest simplification is obtained by using natural coordinates.

37. Einstein's law of gravitation.

The contracted Riemann-Christoffel tensor is formed by setting $\epsilon = \sigma$ in $B^\epsilon_{\mu\nu\sigma}$. It is denoted by $G_{\mu\nu}$. Hence by (34·4)

$$G_{\mu\nu} = \{\mu\sigma, \alpha\}\{\alpha\nu, \sigma\} - \{\mu\nu, \alpha\}\{\alpha\sigma, \sigma\} + \frac{\partial}{\partial x_\nu}\{\mu\sigma, \sigma\} - \frac{\partial}{\partial x_\sigma}\{\mu\nu, \sigma\} \quad \text{...(37·1)}.$$

The symbols containing a duplicated suffix are simplified by (35·4), viz.

$$\{\mu\sigma, \sigma\} = \frac{\partial}{\partial x_\mu}\log\sqrt{-g}.$$

Hence, with some alterations of dummy suffixes,

$$G_{\mu\nu} = -\frac{\partial}{\partial x_\alpha}\{\mu\nu, \alpha\} + \{\mu\alpha, \beta\}\{\nu\beta, \alpha\} + \frac{\partial^2}{\partial x_\mu \partial x_\nu}\log\sqrt{-g} - \{\mu\nu, \alpha\}\frac{\partial}{\partial x_\alpha}\log\sqrt{-g} \quad \text{......(37·2)}.$$

Contraction by setting $\epsilon = \mu$ does not provide an alternative tensor, because

$$B^\mu_{\mu\nu\sigma} = g^{\mu\rho} B_{\mu\nu\sigma\rho} = 0,$$

owing to the antisymmetry of $B_{\mu\nu\sigma\rho}$ in μ and ρ.

The law $$G_{\mu\nu} = 0 \quad \text{......(37·3)},$$

in empty space, is chosen by Einstein for his law of gravitation.

We see from (37·2) that $G_{\mu\nu}$ is a symmetrical tensor; consequently the law provides 10 partial differential equations to determine the $g_{\mu\nu}$. It will be found later (§ 52) that there are 4 identical relations between them, so that the number of equations is effectively reduced to 6. The equations are of the second order and involve the second differential coefficients of $g_{\mu\nu}$ linearly. We proved in § 36 that tensors not containing derivatives beyond the second must necessarily be compounded from $g_{\mu\nu}$ and $B^\epsilon_{\mu\nu\sigma}$; so that, unless we are prepared

* dx_4 will be timelike if g_{44} is always positive.

to go beyond the second order, the choice of a law of gravitation is very limited, and we can scarcely avoid relying on the tensor $G_{\mu\nu}$*

Without introducing higher derivatives, which would seem out of place in this problem, we can suggest as an alternative to (37·3) the law

$$G_{\mu\nu} = \lambda g_{\mu\nu} \qquad \text{(37·4)},$$

where λ is a universal constant. There are theoretical grounds for believing that this is actually the correct form; but it is certain that λ must be an extremely small constant, so that in practical applications we still take (37·3) as sufficiently approximate. The introduction of the small constant λ leads to the spherical world of Einstein or de Sitter to which we shall return in Chapter V.

The spur

$$G = g^{\mu\nu} G_{\mu\nu} \qquad \text{(37·5)}$$

is called the Gaussian curvature, or simply the *curvature*, of space-time. It must be remembered, however, that the deviation from flatness is described in greater detail by the tensors $G_{\mu\nu}$ and $B_{\mu\nu\sigma\rho}$ (sometimes called *components of curvature*) and the vanishing of G is by no means a sufficient condition for flat space-time.

Einstein's law of gravitation expresses the fact that the geometry of an empty region of the world is not of the most general Riemannian type, but is limited. General Riemannian geometry corresponds to the quadratic form (2·1) with the g's entirely unrestricted functions of the coordinates; Einstein asserts that the natural geometry of an empty region is not of so unlimited a kind, and the possible values of the g's are restricted to those which satisfy the differential equations (37·3). It will be remembered that a field of force arises from the discrepancy between the natural geometry of a coordinate-system and the abstract Galilean geometry attributed to it; thus any law governing a field of force must be a law governing the natural geometry. That is why the law of gravitation must appear as a restriction on the possible natural geometry of the world. The inverse-square law, which is a plausible law of weakening of a supposed absolute force, becomes quite unintelligible (and indeed impossible) when expressed as a restriction on the intrinsic geometry of space-time; we have to substitute some law obeyed by the tensors which describe the world-conditions determining the natural geometry.

38. The gravitational field of an isolated particle.

We have now to determine a particular solution of the equations (37·3). The solution which we shall obtain will ultimately be shown to correspond to the field of an isolated particle continually at rest at the origin; and in seeking a solution we shall be guided by our general idea of the type of solution to be expected for such a particle. This preliminary argument need not be rigorous;

* The law $B_{\mu\nu\sigma\rho} = 0$ (giving flat space-time throughout all empty regions) would obviously be too stringent, since it does not admit of the existence of irreducible fields of force.

the final test is whether the formulae suggested by it satisfy the equations to be solved.

In flat space-time the interval, referred to spherical polar coordinates and time, is

$$ds^2 = -dr^2 - r^2 d\theta^2 - r^2 \sin^2\theta d\phi^2 + dt^2 \quad \text{.... (38·11).}$$

If we consider what modifications of this can be made without destroying the spherical symmetry in space, the symmetry as regards past and future time, or the static condition, the most general possible form appears to be

$$ds^2 = -U(r)\, dr^2 - V(r)\,(r^2 d\theta^2 + r^2 \sin^2\theta d\phi^2) + W(r)\, dt^2 \quad \text{(38·12),}$$

where U, V, W are arbitrary functions of r. Let

$$r_1^2 = r^2 V(r).$$

Then (38·12) becomes of the form

$$ds^2 = -U_1(r_1)\, dr_1^2 - r_1^2 d\theta^2 - r_1^2 \sin^2\theta d\phi^2 + W_1(r_1)\, dt^2 \quad \text{...(38·13),}$$

where U_1 and W_1 are arbitrary functions of r_1. There is no reason to regard r in (38·12) as more immediately the counterpart of r in (38·11) than r_1 is. If the functions U, V, W differ only slightly from unity, both r and r_1 will have approximately the properties of the radius-vector in Euclidean geometry; but no length in non-Euclidean space can have exactly the properties of a Euclidean radius-vector, and it is arbitrary whether we choose r or r_1 as its closest representative. We shall here choose r_1, and accordingly drop the suffix, writing (38·13) in the form

$$ds^2 = -e^\lambda dr^2 - r^2 d\theta^2 - r^2 \sin^2\theta d\phi^2 + e^\nu dt^2 \quad \text{......(38·2),}$$

where λ and ν are functions of r only.

Moreover since the gravitational field (or disturbance of flat space-time) due to a particle diminishes indefinitely as we go to an infinite distance, we must have λ and ν tend to zero as r tends to infinity. Formula (38·2) will then reduce to (38·11) at an infinite distance from the particle.

Our coordinates are

$$x_1 = r, \quad x_2 = \theta, \quad x_3 = \phi, \quad x_4 = t,$$

and the fundamental tensor is by (38·2)

$$g_{11} = -e^\lambda, \quad g_{22} = -r^2, \quad g_{33} = -r^2 \sin^2\theta, \quad g_{44} = e^\nu \quad \text{......(38·31),}$$

and

$$g_{\mu\nu} = 0 \quad \text{if} \quad \mu \neq \nu.$$

The determinant g reduces to its leading diagonal $g_{11}g_{22}g_{33}g_{44}$. Hence

$$-g = e^{\lambda+\nu} r^4 \sin^2\theta \quad \text{....................(38·32),}$$

and $g^{11} = 1/g_{11}$, etc., so that

$$g^{11} = -e^{-\lambda}, \quad g^{22} = -1/r^2, \quad g^{33} = -1/r^2 \sin^2\theta, \quad g^{44} = e^{-\nu} \quad \text{...(38·33).}$$

Since all the $g^{\mu\nu}$ vanish except when the two suffixes are the same, the summation disappears in the formula for the 3-index symbols (27·2), and

$$\{\mu\nu, \sigma\} = \tfrac{1}{2} g^{\sigma\sigma} \left(\frac{\partial g_{\mu\sigma}}{\partial x_\nu} + \frac{\partial g_{\nu\sigma}}{\partial x_\mu} - \frac{\partial g_{\mu\nu}}{\partial x_\sigma} \right) \quad \text{not summed.}$$

If μ, ν, σ denote *different* suffixes we get the following possible cases (the summation convention being suspended):

$$\left.\begin{aligned}
\{\mu\mu, \mu\} &= \tfrac{1}{2} g^{\mu\mu} \frac{\partial g_{\mu\mu}}{\partial x_\mu} = \tfrac{1}{2} \frac{\partial}{\partial x_\mu} (\log g_{\mu\mu}) \\
\{\mu\mu, \nu\} &= -\tfrac{1}{2} g^{\nu\nu} \frac{\partial g_{\mu\mu}}{\partial x_\nu} \\
\{\mu\nu, \nu\} &= \tfrac{1}{2} g^{\nu\nu} \frac{\partial g_{\nu\nu}}{\partial x_\mu} = \tfrac{1}{2} \frac{\partial}{\partial x_\mu} (\log g_{\nu\nu}) \\
\{\mu\nu, \sigma\} &= 0
\end{aligned}\right\} \quad \text{..............(38·4).}$$

It is now easy to go systematically through the 40 3-index symbols calculating the values of those which do not vanish. We obtain the following results, the accent denoting differentiation with respect to r:

$$\left.\begin{aligned}
\{11, 1\} &= \tfrac{1}{2}\lambda' \\
\{12, 2\} &= 1/r \\
\{13, 3\} &= 1/r \\
\{14, 4\} &= \tfrac{1}{2}\nu' \\
\{22, 1\} &= -re^{-\lambda} \\
\{23, 3\} &= \cot\theta \\
\{33, 1\} &= -r\sin^2\theta e^{-\lambda} \\
\{33, 2\} &= -\sin\theta\cos\theta \\
\{44, 1\} &= \tfrac{1}{2}e^{\nu-\lambda}\nu'
\end{aligned}\right\} \quad \text{......................(38·5).}$$

The remaining 31 symbols vanish. Note that $\{21, 2\}$ is the same as $\{12, 2\}$, etc.

These values must be substituted in (37·2). As there may be some pitfalls in carrying this out, we shall first write out the equations (37·2) in full, omitting the terms (223 in number) which now obviously vanish.

$$G_{11} = -\frac{\partial}{\partial r}\{11,1\} + \{11,1\}\{11,1\} + \{12,2\}\{12,2\} + \{13,3\}\{13,3\} + \{14,4\}\{14,4\}$$
$$+ \frac{\partial^2}{\partial r^2}\log\sqrt{-g} - \{11,1\}\frac{\partial}{\partial r}\log\sqrt{-g},$$

$$G_{22} = -\frac{\partial}{\partial r}\{22,1\} + 2\{22,1\}\{21,2\} + \{23,3\}\{23,3\} + \frac{\partial^2}{\partial\theta^2}\log\sqrt{-g}$$
$$-\{22,1\}\frac{\partial}{\partial r}\log\sqrt{-g},$$

$$G_{33} = -\frac{\partial}{\partial r}\{33,1\} - \frac{\partial}{\partial\theta}\{33,2\} + 2\{33,1\}\{31,3\} + 2\{33,2\}\{32,3\}$$
$$-\{33,1\}\frac{\partial}{\partial r}\log\sqrt{-g} - \{33,2\}\frac{\partial}{\partial\theta}\log\sqrt{-g},$$

$$G_{44} = -\frac{\partial}{\partial r}\{44,1\} + 2\{44,1\}\{41,4\} - \{44,1\}\frac{\partial}{\partial r}\log\sqrt{-g},$$

$$G_{12} = \{13,3\}\{23,3\} - \{12,2\}\frac{\partial}{\partial\theta}\log\sqrt{-g}.$$

The remaining components contain no surviving terms.

Substitute from (38·5) and (38·32) in these, and collect the terms The equations to be satisfied become

$$G_{11} = \tfrac{1}{2}\nu'' - \tfrac{1}{4}\lambda'\nu' + \tfrac{1}{4}\nu'^2 - \lambda'/r = 0 \qquad\qquad (38\cdot61),$$

$$G_{22} = e^{-\lambda}(1 + \tfrac{1}{2}r(\nu' - \lambda')) - 1 = 0 \qquad\qquad (38\cdot62),$$

$$G_{33} = \sin^2\theta \, . \, e^{-\lambda}(1 + \tfrac{1}{2}r(\nu' - \lambda')) - \sin^2\theta = 0 \qquad\qquad (38\cdot63),$$

$$-G_{44} = e^{\nu-\lambda}(-\tfrac{1}{2}\nu'' + \tfrac{1}{4}\lambda'\nu' - \tfrac{1}{4}\nu'^2 - \nu'/r) = 0 \qquad\qquad (38\cdot64),$$

$$G_{12} = 0 \qquad\qquad = 0 \qquad\qquad (38\cdot65).$$

We may leave aside (38·63) which is a mere repetition of (38·62); then there are left three equations to be satisfied by λ and ν. From (38·61) and (38·64) we have $\lambda' = -\nu'$. Since λ and ν are to vanish together at $r = \infty$, this requires that

$$\lambda = -\nu.$$

Then (38·62) becomes $\qquad e^{\nu}(1 + r\nu') = 1.$

Set $e^{\nu} = \gamma$, then $\qquad \gamma + r\gamma' = 1.$

Hence, integrating, $\qquad \gamma = 1 - \dfrac{2m}{r} \qquad\qquad (38\cdot7),$

where $2m$ is a constant of integration.

It will be found that all three equations are satisfied by this solution. Accordingly, substituting $e^{-\lambda} = e^{\nu} = \gamma$ in (38·2),

$$ds^2 = -\gamma^{-1}dr^2 - r^2 d\theta^2 - r^2\sin^2\theta\, d\phi^2 + \gamma dt^2 \qquad\qquad (38\cdot8),$$

where $\gamma = 1 - 2m/r$, is a particular solution of Einstein's gravitational equations $G_{\mu\nu} = 0$. The solution in this form was first obtained by Schwarzschild.

39. Planetary orbits.

According to (15·7) the track of a particle moving freely in the space-time given by (38·8) is determined by the equations of a geodesic (28·5), viz.

$$\frac{d^2x_\alpha}{ds^2} + \{\mu\nu, \alpha\}\frac{dx_\mu}{ds}\frac{dx_\nu}{ds} = 0 \qquad\qquad (39\cdot1).$$

Taking first $\alpha = 2$, the surviving terms are

$$\frac{d^2x_2}{ds^2} + \{12, 2\}\frac{dx_1}{ds}\frac{dx_2}{ds} + \{21, 2\}\frac{dx_2}{ds}\frac{dx_1}{ds} + \{33, 2\}\frac{dx_3}{ds}\frac{dx_3}{ds} = 0,$$

or using (38·5)

$$\frac{d^2\theta}{ds^2} + \frac{2}{r}\frac{dr}{ds}\frac{d\theta}{ds} - \cos\theta\sin\theta\left(\frac{d\phi}{ds}\right)^2 = 0 \qquad\qquad (39\cdot2).$$

Choose coordinates so that the particle moves initially in the plane $\theta = \tfrac{1}{2}\pi$. Then $d\theta/ds = 0$ and $\cos\theta = 0$ initially, so that $d^2\theta/ds^2 = 0$. The particle therefore continues to move in this plane, and we may simplify the remaining equations by putting $\theta = \tfrac{1}{2}\pi$ throughout. The equations for $\alpha = 1, 3, 4$ are found in like manner, viz.

$$\frac{d^2r}{ds^2} + \tfrac{1}{2}\lambda'\left(\frac{dr}{ds}\right)^2 - re^{-\lambda}\left(\frac{d\phi}{ds}\right)^2 + \tfrac{1}{2}e^{\nu-\lambda}\nu'\left(\frac{dt}{ds}\right)^2 = 0 \qquad (39\cdot31),$$

$$\frac{d^2\phi}{ds^2} + \frac{2}{r}\frac{dr}{ds}\frac{d\phi}{ds} = 0 \quad\text{.........................(39·32)},$$

$$\frac{d^2t}{ds^2} + \nu' \frac{dr}{ds}\frac{dt}{ds} = 0 \quad\text{.........................(39·33)}.$$

The last two equations may be integrated immediately, giving

$$r^2 \frac{d\phi}{ds} = h \quad\text{.................................(39·41)},$$

$$\frac{dt}{ds} = ce^{-\nu} = c/\gamma \quad\text{.........................(39·42)},$$

where h and c are constants of integration.

Instead of troubling to integrate (39·31) we can use in place of it (38·8) which plays here the part of an integral of energy. It gives

$$\gamma^{-1}\left(\frac{dr}{ds}\right)^2 + r^2\left(\frac{d\phi}{ds}\right)^2 - \gamma\left(\frac{dt}{ds}\right)^2 = -1 \quad\text{...........(39·43)}.$$

Eliminating dt and ds by means of (39·41) and (39·42)

$$\frac{1}{\gamma}\left(\frac{h}{r^2}\frac{dr}{d\phi}\right)^2 + \frac{h^2}{r^2} - \frac{c^2}{\gamma} = -1 \quad\text{.................(39·44)},$$

whence, multiplying through by γ or $(1 - 2m/r)$,

$$\left(\frac{h}{r^2}\frac{dr}{d\phi}\right)^2 + \frac{h^2}{r^2} = c^2 - 1 + \frac{2m}{r} + \frac{2m}{r}\cdot\frac{h^2}{r^2},$$

or writing $1/r = u$,

$$\left(\frac{du}{d\phi}\right)^2 + u^2 = \frac{c^2-1}{h^2} + \frac{2m}{h^2}u + 2mu^3 \quad\text{.............(39·5)}.$$

Differentiating with respect to ϕ, and removing the factor $\frac{du}{d\phi}$,

$$\frac{d^2u}{d\phi^2} + u = \frac{m}{h^2} + 3mu^2 \quad\text{.........................(39·61)},$$

with

$$r^2\frac{d\phi}{ds} = h \quad\text{.................................(39·62)}.$$

Compare these with the equations of a Newtonian orbit

$$\frac{d^2u}{d\phi^2} + u = \frac{m}{h^2} \quad\text{.............................(39·71)}$$

with

$$r^2\frac{d\phi}{dt} = h \quad\text{...........................(39·72)}.$$

In (39·61) the ratio of $3mu^2$ to m/h^2 is $3h^2u^2$, or by (39·62)

$$3\left(r\frac{d\phi}{ds}\right)^2.$$

For ordinary speeds this is an extremely small quantity—practically three times the square of the transverse velocity in terms of the velocity of light. For example, this ratio for the earth is ·00000003. In practical cases the extra term in (39·61) will represent an almost inappreciable correction to the Newtonian orbit (39·71).

Again in (39·62) and (39·72) the difference between ds and dt is equally insignificant, even if we were sure of what is meant by dt in the Newtonian theory. The *proper-time* for the body is ds, and it might perhaps be urged that dt in equation (39·72) is intended to refer to this; but on the other hand s cannot be used as a coordinate since ds is not a complete differential, and Newton's "time" is always assumed to be a coordinate.

Thus it appears that a particle moving in the field here discussed will behave as though it were under the influence of the Newtonian force exerted by a particle of gravitational mass m at the origin, the motion agreeing with the Newtonian theory to the order of accuracy for which that theory has been confirmed by observation.

By showing that our solution satisfies $G_{\mu\nu} = 0$, we have proved that it describes a possible state of the world which might be met with in nature under suitable conditions. By deducing the orbit of a particle, we have discovered how that state of the world would be recognised observationally if it did exist. In this way we conclude that the space-time field represented by (38·8) is the one which accompanies (or "is due to") a particle of mass m at the origin.

The gravitational mass m is the measure adopted in the Newtonian theory of the power of the particle in causing a field of acceleration around it, the units being here chosen so that the velocity of light and the constant of gravitation are both unity. It should be noticed that we have as yet given no reason to expect that m in the present chapter has anything to do with the m introduced in § 12 to measure the inertial properties of the particle.

For a circular orbit the Newtonian theory gives

$$m = \omega^2 r^3 = v^2 r,$$

the constant of gravitation being unity. Applying this to the earth, $v = 30$ km per sec. $= 10^{-4}$ in terms of the velocity of light, and $r = 1{\cdot}5 \cdot 10^8$ km. Hence the mass m of the sun is approximately 1·5 kilometres. The mass of the earth is 1/300,000th of this, or about 5 millimetres*.

More accurately, the mass of the sun, $1{\cdot}99 \,.\, 10^{33}$ grams, becomes in gravitational units 1·47 kilometres, and other masses are converted in a like proportion.

* Objection is sometimes taken to the use of a centimetre as a unit of gravitational (i.e. gravitation-exerting) mass, but the same objection would apply to the use of a gram, since the gram is properly a measure of a different property of the particle, viz. its *inertia*. Our constant of integration m is clearly a length and the reader may, if he wishes to make this clear, call it the gravitational radius instead of the gravitational mass. But when it is realised that the gravitational radius in centimetres, the inertia in grams, and the energy in ergs, are merely measure-numbers in different codes of the *same* intrinsic quality of the particle, it seems unduly pedantic to insist on the older discrimination of these units which grew up on the assumption that they measured qualities which were radically different.

40. The advance of perihelion.

The equation (39·5) for the orbit of a planet can be integrated in terms of elliptic functions; but we obtain the astronomical results more directly by a method of successive approximation. We proceed from equation (39·61)

$$\frac{d^2u}{d\phi^2}+u=\frac{m}{h^2}+3mu^2 \quad\text{.......................(40·1)}.$$

Neglecting the small term $3mu^2$, the solution is

$$u=\frac{m}{h^2}(1+e\cos(\phi-\varpi)) \quad\text{.....................(40·2)},$$

as in Newtonian dynamics. The constants of integration, e and ϖ, are the eccentricity and longitude of perihelion.

Substitute this first approximation in the small term $3mu^2$, then (40·1) becomes

$$\frac{d^2u}{d\phi^2}+u=\frac{m}{h^2}+3\frac{m^3}{h^4}+6\frac{m^3}{h^4}e\cos(\phi-\varpi)+\frac{3}{2}\frac{m^3}{h^4}e^2(1+\tfrac{1}{2}\cos 2(\phi-\varpi)) \quad\text{..... (40·3)}.$$

Of the additional terms the only one which can produce an effect within the range of observation is the term in $\cos(\phi-\varpi)$; this is of the right period to produce a continually increasing effect by resonance. Remembering that the particular integral of

$$\frac{d^2u}{d\phi^2}+u=A\cos\phi$$

is

$$u=\tfrac{1}{2}A\phi\sin\phi,$$

this term gives a part of u

$$u_1=3\frac{m^3}{h^4}e\phi\sin(\phi-\varpi) \quad\text{....................(40·4)},$$

which must be added to the complementary integral (40·2). Thus the second approximation is

$$u=\frac{m}{h^2}\left(1+e\cos(\phi-\varpi)+3\frac{m^2}{h^2}e\phi\sin(\phi-\varpi)\right)$$

$$=\frac{m}{h^2}(1+e\cos(\phi-\varpi-\delta\varpi)),$$

where

$$\delta\varpi=3\frac{m^2}{h^2}\phi \quad\text{..............................(40·5)},$$

and $(\delta\varpi)^2$ is neglected.

Whilst the planet moves through 1 revolution, the perihelion ϖ advances a fraction of a revolution equal to

$$\frac{\delta\varpi}{\phi}=\frac{3m^2}{h^2}=\frac{3m}{a(1-e^2)} \quad\text{......................(40·6)},$$

using the well-known equation of areas $h^2=ml=ma(1-e^2)$.

Another form is obtained by using Kepler's third law,

$$m = \left(\frac{2\pi}{T}\right)^2 a^3,$$

giving
$$\frac{\delta\varpi}{\phi} = \frac{12\pi^2 a^2}{c^2 T^2 (1 - e^2)} \quad \ldots\ldots\ldots\ldots\ldots\ldots\ldots (40{\cdot}7),$$

where T is the period, and the velocity of light c has been reinstated

This advance of the perihelion is appreciable in the case of the planet Mercury, and the predicted value is confirmed by observation.

For a circular orbit we put dr/ds, $d^2r/ds^2 = 0$, so that (39·31) becomes

$$-re^{-\lambda}\left(\frac{d\phi}{ds}\right)^2 + \tfrac{1}{2}e^{\nu-\lambda}\nu'\left(\frac{dt}{ds}\right)^2 = 0.$$

Whence
$$\left(\frac{d\phi}{dt}\right)^2 = \tfrac{1}{2}e^{\nu}\nu'/r = \tfrac{1}{2}\gamma'/r$$
$$= m/r^3,$$

so that Kepler's third law is *accurately* fulfilled. This result has no observational significance, being merely a property of the particular definition of r here adopted. Slightly different coordinate-systems exist which might with equal right claim to correspond to polar coordinates in flat space-time; and for these Kepler's third law would no longer be exact

We have to be on our guard against results of this latter kind which would only be of interest if the radius-vector were a directly measured quantity instead of a conventional coordinate. The advance of perihelion is a phenomenon of a different category. Clearly the number of years required for an eccentric orbit to make a complete revolution returning to its original position is capable of observational test, unaffected by any convention used in defining the exact length of the radius-vector

For the four inner planets the following table gives the corrections to the centennial motion of perihelion predicted by Einstein's theory:

	$\delta\varpi$	$e\,\delta\varpi$
Mercury	+42″·9	+8″·82
Venus	+ 8·6	+ 0·05
Earth	+ 3·8	+ 0·07
Mars	+ 1·35	+ 0·13

The product $e\,\delta\varpi$ is a better measure of the observable effect to be looked for, and the correction is only appreciable in the case of Mercury. After applying these corrections to $e\,\delta\varpi$, the following discrepancies between theory and observation remain in the secular changes of the elements of the inner planets, i and Ω being the inclination and the longitude of the node:

	$e\,\delta\varpi$	δe	$\sin i\,\delta\Omega$	δi
Mercury	−0″·58 ± 0″·29	−0″·88 ± 0″·33	+0″·46 ± 0″·34	+0″·38 ± 0″·54
Venus	− 0·11 ± 0·17	+ 0·21 ± 0·21	+ 0·53 ± 0·12	+ 0·38 ± 0·22
Earth	0·00 ± 0·09	+ 0·02 ± 0·07	... ...	− 0·22 ± 0·18
Mars	+ 0·51 ± 0·23	+ 0·29 ± 0·18	− 0·11 ± 0·15	− 0·01 ± 0·13

The probable errors here given include errors of observation, and also errors in the theory due to uncertainty of the masses of the planets. The positive sign indicates excess of observed motion over theoretical motion*.

Einstein's correction to the perihelion of Mercury has removed the principal discordance in the table, which on the Newtonian theory was nearly 30 times the probable error. Of the 15 residuals 8 exceed the probable error, and 3 exceed twice the probable error—as nearly as possible the proper proportion. But whereas we should expect the greatest residual to be about 3 times the probable error, the residual of the node of Venus is rather excessive at $4\frac{1}{2}$ times the probable error, and may perhaps be a genuine discordance. Einstein's theory throws no light on the cause of this discordance.

41. The deflection of light.

For motion with the speed of light $ds = 0$, so that by (39·62) $h = \infty$, and the orbit (39·61) reduces to

$$\frac{d^2u}{d\phi^2} + u = 3mu^2 \qquad \text{.................(41·1).}$$

The track of a light-pulse is also given by a geodesic with $ds = 0$ according to (15·8). Accordingly the orbit (41·1) gives the path of a ray of light.

We integrate by successive approximation. Neglecting $3mu^2$ the solution of the approximate equation

$$\frac{d^2u}{d\phi^2} + u = 0$$

is the straight line

$$u = \frac{\cos\phi}{R} \qquad \text{.........................(41·2)}$$

Substituting this in the small term $3mu^2$, we have

$$\frac{d^2u}{d\phi^2} + u = \frac{3m}{R^2}\cos^2\phi.$$

A particular integral of this equation is

$$u_1 = \frac{m}{R^2}(\cos^2\phi + 2\sin^2\phi),$$

so that the complete second approximation is

$$u = \frac{\cos\phi}{R} + \frac{m}{R^2}(\cos^2\phi + 2\sin^2\phi) \qquad \text{.............(41·3).}$$

Multiply through by rR,

$$R = r\cos\phi + \frac{m}{R}(r\cos^2\phi + 2r\sin^2\phi),$$

or in rectangular coordinates, $x = r\cos\phi$, $y = r\sin\phi$,

$$x = R - \frac{m}{R}\frac{x^2 + 2y^2}{\sqrt{(x^2 + y^2)}} \qquad \text{.................(41·4).}$$

* Newcomb, *Astronomical Constants*. His results have been slightly corrected by using a modern value of the constant of precession in the above table; see de Sitter, *Monthly Notices*, vol. 76, p. 728.

The second term measures the very slight deviation from the straight line $x = R$. The asymptotes are found by taking y very large compared with x. The equation then becomes

$$x = R - \frac{m}{R}(\pm 2y),$$

and the small angle between the asymptotes is (in circular measure)

$$\frac{4m}{R}.$$

For a ray grazing the sun's limb, $m = 1{\cdot}47$ km., $R = 697{,}000$ km., so that the deflection should be $1''{\cdot}75$. The observed values obtained by the British eclipse expeditions in 1919 were

Sobral expedition	$1''{\cdot}98 \pm 0''{\cdot}12$
Principe expedition	$1''{\cdot}61 \pm 0''{\cdot}30$

It has been explained in *Space, Time and Gravitation* that this deflection is double that which might have been predicted on the Newtonian theory. In this connection the following paradox has been remarked. Since the curvature of the light-track is doubled, the acceleration of the light at each point is double the Newtonian acceleration; whereas for a slowly moving object the acceleration is practically the same as the Newtonian acceleration. To a man in a lift descending with acceleration m/r^2 the tracks of ordinary particles will appear to be straight lines; but it looks as though it would require an acceleration $2m/r^2$ to straighten out the light-tracks. Does not this contradict the principle of equivalence?

The fallacy lies in a confusion between two meanings of the word "curvature." The *coordinate* curvature obtained from the equation of the track (41·4) is not the *geodesic* curvature. The latter is the curvature with which the local observer—the man in the lift—is concerned. Consider the curved light-track traversing the hummock corresponding to the sun's field; its curvature can be reckoned by projecting it either on the base of the hummock or on the tangent plane at any point. The curvatures of the two projections will generally be different. The projection into Euclidean coordinates (x, y) used in (41·4) is the projection on the base of the hummock; in applying the principle of equivalence the projection is on the tangent plane, since we consider a region of the curved world so small that it cannot be discriminated from its tangent plane.

42. Displacement of the Fraunhofer lines.

Consider a number of similar atoms vibrating at different points in the region. Let the atoms be momentarily at rest in our coordinate-system (r, θ, ϕ, t). The test of similarity of the atoms is that corresponding intervals should be equal, and accordingly the *interval* of vibration of all the atoms will be the same.

Since the atoms are at rest we set $dr, d\theta, d\phi = 0$ in (38·8), so that

$$ds^2 = \gamma dt^2 \qquad \text{(42·1)}.$$

Accordingly the *times* of vibration of the differently placed atoms will be inversely proportional to $\sqrt{\gamma}$.

Our system of coordinates is a *static system*, that is to say the $g_{\mu\nu}$ do not change with the time. (An arbitrary coordinate-system has not generally this property; and further when we have to take account of two or more attracting bodies, it is in most cases impossible to find a strictly static system of coordinates.) Taking an observer at rest in the system (r, θ, ϕ, t) a wave emitted by one of the atoms will reach him at a certain time δt after it leaves the atom; and owing to the static condition this time-lag remains constant for subsequent waves. Consequently the waves are received at the same time-periods as they are emitted. We are therefore able to compare the time-periods dt of the different atoms, by comparing the periods of the waves received from them, and can verify experimentally their dependence on the value of $\sqrt{\gamma}$ at the place where they were emitted. Naturally the most hopeful test is the comparison of the waves received from a solar and a terrestrial atom whose periods should be in the ratio 1·00000212 : 1. For wave-length 4000 Å, this amounts to a relative displacement of 0·0082 Å of the respective spectral lines. The verdict of experiment is not yet such as to secure universal assent; but it is now distinctly more favourable to Einstein's theory than when *Space, Time and Gravitation* was written.

The quantity dt is merely an auxiliary quantity introduced through the equation (38·8) which defines it. The fact that it is carried to us unchanged by light-waves is not of any physical interest, since dt was *defined* in such a way that this must happen. The absolute quantity ds, the interval of the vibration, is not carried to us unchanged, but becomes gradually modified as the waves take their course through the non-Euclidean space-time. It is in transmission through the solar system that the absolute difference is introduced into the waves, which the experiment hopes to detect.

The argument refers to *similar* atoms and the question remains whether, for example, a hydrogen atom on the sun is truly similar to a hydrogen atom on the earth. Strictly speaking it cannot be exactly similar because it is in a different kind of space-time, in which it would be impossible to make a finite structure exactly similar to one existing in the space-time near the earth. But if the interval of vibration of the hydrogen atom is modified by the kind of space-time in which it lies, the difference must be dependent on some invariant of the space-time. The simplest invariant which differs at the sun and the earth is the square of the length of the Riemann-Christoffel tensor, viz.

$$B^{\epsilon}_{\mu\nu\sigma} B_{\epsilon}^{\mu\nu\sigma}.$$

The value of this can be calculated from (38·8) by the method used in that section for calculating the $G_{\mu\nu}$. The result is

$$48 \frac{m^2}{r^6}.$$

By consideration of dimensions it seems clear that the proportionate change of ds would be of the order

$$\frac{\sigma^4 m^2}{r^6},$$

where σ is the radius of the atom; there does not seem to be any other length concerned. For a comparison of solar and terrestrial atoms this would be about 10^{-100}. In any case it seems impossible to construct from the invariants of space-time a term which would compensate the predicted shift of the spectral lines, which is proportional to m/r.

43. Isotropic coordinates.

We can transform the expression for the interval (38·8) by making the substitution

$$r = \left(1 + \frac{m}{2r_1}\right)^2 r_1 \quad \text{.................................(43·1)},$$

so that

$$dr = \left(1 - \frac{m^2}{4r_1^2}\right) dr_1,$$

$$\gamma = \left(1 - \frac{m}{2r_1}\right)^2 \Big/ \left(1 + \frac{m}{2r_1}\right)^2.$$

Then (38·8) becomes

$$ds^2 = -(1 + m/2r_1)^4 (dr_1^2 + r_1^2 d\theta^2 + r_1^2 \sin^2\theta\, d\phi^2) + \frac{(1 - m/2r_1)^2}{(1 + m/2r_1)^2} dt^2 \quad \text{...(43·2)}.$$

The coordinates (r_1, θ, ϕ) are called *isotropic* polar coordinates. The corresponding isotropic rectangular coordinates are obtained by putting

$$x = r_1 \sin\theta \cos\phi, \quad y = r_1 \sin\theta \sin\phi, \quad z = r_1 \cos\theta,$$

giving

$$ds^2 = -(1 + m/2r_1)^4 (dx^2 + dy^2 + dz^2) + \frac{(1 - m/2r_1)^2}{(1 + m/2r_1)^2} dt^2 \quad \text{...(43·3)},$$

with

$$r_1 = \sqrt{(x^2 + y^2 + z^2)}.$$

This system has some advantages. For example, to obtain the motion of a light-pulse we set $ds = 0$ in (43·3). This gives

$$\left(\frac{dx}{dt}\right)^2 + \left(\frac{dy}{dt}\right)^2 + \left(\frac{dz}{dt}\right)^2 = \frac{(1 - m/2r_1)^2}{(1 + m/2r_1)^6}.$$

At a distance r_1 from the origin the velocity of light is accordingly

$$\frac{(1 - m/2r_1)}{(1 + m/2r_1)^3} \quad \text{..............................(43·4)}$$

in all directions. For the original coordinates of (38·8) the velocity of light is not the same for the radial and transverse directions.

Again in the isotropic system the coordinate length $(\sqrt{(dx^2 + dy^2 + dz^2)})$ of a small rod which is rigid (ds = constant) does not alter when the orientation of the rod is altered. This system of coordinates is naturally arrived at when we partition space by rigid scales or by light-triangulations in a small region, e.g. in terrestrial measurements. Since the ultimate measurements involved in any observation are carried out in a terrestrial laboratory we ought, strictly speaking, always to employ the isotropic system which conforms to assumptions made in those measurements*. But on the earth the quantity m/r is negligibly small, so that the two systems coalesce with one another and with Euclidean coordinates. Non-Euclidean geometry is only required in the theoretical part of the investigation—the laws of planetary motion and propagation of light through regions where m/r is not negligible; as soon as the light-waves have been safely steered into the terrestrial observatory, the need for non-Euclidean geometry is at an end, and the difference between the isotropic and non-isotropic systems practically disappears.

In either system the forward velocity of light along any line is equal to the backward velocity. Consequently the coordinate t conforms to the convention (§ 11) that simultaneity may be determined by means of light-signals. If we have a clock at A and send a light-signal at time t_A which reaches B and is immediately reflected so as to return to A at time t_A', the time of arrival at B will be $\frac{1}{2}(t_A + t_A')$ just as in the special relativity theory. But the alternative convention, that simultaneity can be determined by slow transport of chronometers, breaks down when there is a gravitational field. This is evident from § 42, since the time-rate of a clock will depend on its position in the field. In any case slow transport of a clock is unrealisable because of the acceleration which all objects must submit to.

The isotropic system could have been found directly by seeking particular solutions of Einstein's equations having the form (38·12), or

$$ds^2 = -e^{\lambda}dr^2 - e^{\mu}(r^2 d\theta^2 + r^2 \sin^2\theta\, d\phi^2) + e^{\nu} dt^2,$$

where λ, μ, ν are functions of r. By the method of § 38, we find

$$\left.\begin{aligned}
G_{11} &= \mu'' + \tfrac{1}{2}\nu'' + \frac{2}{r}\mu' - \frac{1}{r}\lambda' + \tfrac{1}{2}\mu'^2 - \tfrac{1}{2}\lambda'\mu' - \tfrac{1}{4}\lambda'\nu' + \tfrac{1}{4}\nu'^2 \\
G_{22} &= e^{\mu-\lambda}\left[1 + 2r\mu' + \tfrac{1}{2}r(\nu' - \lambda') + \tfrac{1}{2}r^2\mu'' + \tfrac{1}{4}r^2\mu'(\mu' + \tfrac{1}{2}\nu' - \tfrac{1}{2}\lambda')\right] - 1 \\
G_{33} &= G_{22}\sin^2\theta \\
G_{44} &= -e^{\nu-\lambda}\left[\tfrac{1}{2}\nu'' + \frac{1}{r}\nu' + \tfrac{1}{2}\nu'\mu' - \tfrac{1}{4}\lambda'\nu' + \tfrac{1}{4}\nu'^2\right]
\end{aligned}\right\} \quad \ldots\ldots(43\cdot5)$$

The others are zero.

Owing to an identical relation between G_{11}, G_{22} and G_{44}, the vanishing of this tensor gives only two equations to determine the three unknowns λ, μ, ν. There exists therefore an infinite series of particular solutions, differing according to the third equation between λ, μ, ν which is at our disposal. The two solutions hitherto considered are obtained by taking $\mu = 0$, and $\lambda = \mu$, respectively. The same series of solutions is obtained in a simpler way by substituting arbitrary functions of r instead of r in (38·8).

* But the terrestrial laboratory is falling freely towards the sun, and is therefore accelerated relatively to the coordinates (x, y, z, t).

The possibility of substituting any function of r for r without destroying the spherical symmetry is obvious from the fact that a coordinate is merely an identification-number; but analytically this possibility is bound up with the existence of an identical relation between G_{11}, G_{22} and G_{44}, which makes the equations too few to determine a unique solution.

This introduces us to a theorem of great consequence in our later work. If Einstein's ten equations $G_{\mu\nu}=0$ were all independent, the ten $g_{\mu\nu}$ would be uniquely determined by them (the boundary conditions being specified). The expression for ds^2 would be unique and no transformation of coordinates would be possible. Since we know that we can transform coordinates as we please, there must exist identical relations between the ten $G_{\mu\nu}$; and these will be found in § 52.

44. Problem of two bodies—Motion of the moon.

The field described by the $g_{\mu\nu}$ may be (artificially) divided into a *field of pure inertia* represented by the Galilean values, and a *field of force* represented by the deviations of the $g_{\mu\nu}$ from the Galilean values. It is not possible to superpose the fields of force due to two attracting particles; because the sum of the two solutions will not satisfy $G_{\mu\nu}=0$, these equations being non-linear in the $g_{\mu\nu}$.

No solution of Einstein's equations has yet been found for a field with two singularities or particles. The simplest case to be examined would be that of two equal particles revolving in circular orbits round their centre of mass. Apparently there should exist a statical solution with two equal singularities; but the conditions at infinity would differ from those adopted for a single particle since the axes corresponding to the static solution constitute what is called a rotating system. The solution has not been found, and it is even possible that no such statical solution exists. I do not think it has yet been proved that two bodies can revolve without radiation of energy by gravitational waves. In discussions of this radiation problem there is a tendency to beg the question; it is not sufficient to constrain the particles to revolve uniformly, then calculate the resulting gravitational waves, and verify that the radiation of gravitational energy across an infinite sphere is zero. That shows that a statical solution is not obviously inconsistent with itself, but does not demonstrate its possibility.

The problem of two bodies on Einstein's theory remains an outstanding challenge to mathematicians—like the problem of three bodies on Newton's theory.

For practical purposes methods of approximation will suffice. We shall consider the problem of the field due to the combined attractions of the earth and sun, and apply it to find the modifications of the moon's orbit required by the new law of gravitation. The problem has been treated in considerable detail by de Sitter*. We shall not here attempt a complete survey of the

* *Monthly Notices*, vol. 77, p. 155.

problem; but we shall seek out the largest effects to be looked for in refined observations. There are three sources of fresh perturbations:

(1) The sun's attraction is not accurately given by Newton's law, and the solar perturbations of the moon's orbit will require corrections.

(2) Cross-terms between the sun's and the earth's fields of force will arise, since these are not additive.

(3) The earth's field is altered and would *inter alia* give rise to a motion of the lunar perigee analogous to the motion of Mercury's perihelion. It is easily calculated that this is far too small to be detected.

If Ω_S, Ω_E are the Newtonian potentials of the sun and earth, the leading terms of (1), (2), (3) will be relatively of order of magnitude

$$\Omega_S^2, \quad \Omega_S\Omega_E, \quad \Omega_E.$$

For the moon $\Omega_S = 750\Omega_E$. We may therefore confine attention to terms of type (1). If these prove to be too small to be detected, the others will presumably be not worth pursuing.

We were able to work out the planetary orbits from Einstein's law independently of the Newtonian theory; but in the problem of the moon's motion we must concentrate attention on the *difference* between Einstein's and Newton's formulae if we are to avoid repeating the whole labour of the classical lunar theory. In order to make this comparison we transform (39·31) and (39·32) so that t is used as the independent variable.

$$\frac{d^2}{ds^2} = \left(\frac{dt}{ds}\right)^2 \frac{d^2}{dt^2} + \frac{dt}{ds}\frac{d}{dt}\left(\frac{dt}{ds}\right)\frac{d}{dt}$$

$$= \left(\frac{dt}{ds}\right)^2 \left(\frac{d^2}{dt^2} + \lambda' \frac{dr}{dt}\frac{d}{dt}\right) \quad \text{by (39·42).}$$

Hence the equations (39·31) and (39·32) become

$$\frac{d^2r}{dt^2} + \tfrac{3}{2}\lambda'\left(\frac{dr}{dt}\right)^2 - re^{-\lambda}\left(\frac{d\phi}{dt}\right)^2 + \tfrac{1}{2}e^{2\nu}\nu' = 0,$$

$$\frac{d^2\phi}{dt^2} + \lambda'\frac{dr}{dt}\frac{d\phi}{dt} + \frac{2}{r}\frac{dr}{dt}\frac{d\phi}{dt} = 0.$$

Whence

$$\left.\begin{aligned} \frac{d^2r}{dt^2} - r\left(\frac{d\phi}{dt}\right)^2 + \frac{m}{r^2} &= R \\ r\left(\frac{d^2\phi}{dt^2} + \frac{2}{r}\frac{dr}{dt}\frac{d\phi}{dt}\right) &= \Phi \end{aligned}\right\} \quad \text{..................... (44·1),}$$

where

$$\left.\begin{aligned} R &= -\tfrac{3}{2}\lambda' u^2 - \frac{2m}{r^2}v^2 + \frac{2m^2}{r^3} \\ \Phi &= -\lambda' uv \end{aligned}\right\} \quad \text{.............. (44·21),}$$

and

$$u = dr/dt, \quad v = r\,d\phi/dt.$$

Equations (44·1) show that R and Φ are the radial and transverse perturbing forces which Einstein's theory adds to the classical dynamics. To a sufficient approximation $\lambda' = -2m/r^2$, so that

$$\left.\begin{aligned} R &= \frac{m}{r^2}(3u^2 - 2v^2) + \frac{2m^2}{r^3} \\ \Phi &= \frac{m}{r^2} \cdot 2uv \end{aligned}\right\} \quad \text{.........(44·22).}$$

In three-dimensional problems the perturbing forces become

$$\left.\begin{aligned} R &= \frac{m}{r^2}(3u^2 - 2v^2 - 2w^2) + \frac{2m^2}{r^3} \\ \Phi &= \frac{m}{r^2} \cdot 2uv \\ Z &= \frac{m}{r^2} \cdot 2uw \end{aligned}\right\} \quad \text{.........(44·23).}$$

It must be pointed out that these perturbing forces are Einstein's corrections to the law of central force m/r^2, where r is *the coordinate used in our previous work*. Whether these forces represent the actual differences between Einstein's and Newton's laws depends on what Newton's r is supposed to signify. De Sitter, making a slightly different choice of r, obtains different expressions for R, Φ*. One cannot say that one set of perturbing forces rather than the other represents the difference from the older theory, because the older theory was not sufficiently explicit. The classical lunar theory has been worked out on the basis of the law m/r^2, the ambiguous quantity r occurs in the results, and according as we have assigned to it one meaning or another, so we shall have to apply different corrections to those results. But the final comparison with observation does not depend on the choice of the intermediary quantity r.

Take fixed rectangular axes referred to the ecliptic with the sun as origin, and let

$(a, 0, 0)$ be the coordinates of the earth at the instant considered,

(x, y, z) the coordinates of the moon relative to the earth.

Taking the earth's orbit to be circular and treating the mass of the moon as infinitesimal, the earth's velocity will be $(0, v, 0)$, where $v^2 = m/a$.

To find the difference of the forces R, Φ, Z on the moon and on the earth, we differentiate (44·23) and set

$$\delta r = x, \quad \delta(u, v, w) = (dx/dt, dy/dt, dz/dt),$$

and, after the differentiation,

$$r = a, \quad (u, v, w) = (0, v, 0).$$

* *Monthly Notices*, vol. 76, p. 723, equations (53).

The result will give the perturbing forces on the moon's motion relative to the earth, viz.

$$\left.\begin{aligned} \delta R = X &= \frac{4mx}{a^3}v^2 - \frac{6m^2x}{a^4} - \frac{4m}{a^2}v\frac{dy}{dt} = -\frac{2m^2x}{a^4} - \frac{4m}{a^2}v\frac{dy}{dt} \\ \delta\Phi = Y &= \frac{2m}{a^2}v\frac{dx}{dt} \\ Z &= 0 \end{aligned}\right\} \quad \ldots (44\cdot3).$$

We shall omit the term $-2m^2x/a^4$ in X. It can be verified that it gives no important observable effects It produces only an apparent distortion of the orbit attributable to our use of non-isotropic coordinates (§43). Transforming to new axes (ξ, η) rotated through an angle θ with respect to (x, y) the remaining forces become

$$\left.\begin{aligned} \Xi &= \frac{m}{a^2}v\left(-2\cos\theta\sin\theta\frac{d\xi}{dt} - (4\cos^2\theta + 2\sin^2\theta)\frac{d\eta}{dt}\right) \\ \mathrm{H} &= \frac{m}{a^2}v\left(\;\;2\cos\theta\sin\theta\frac{d\eta}{dt} + (4\sin^2\theta + 2\cos^2\theta)\frac{d\xi}{dt}\right) \end{aligned}\right\} \quad \ldots (44\cdot4).$$

We keep the axes (ξ, η) permanently fixed; the angle θ which gives the direction of the sun (the old axis of x) will change uniformly, and in the long run take all values with equal frequency independently of the moon's position in its orbit We can only hope to observe the secular effects of the small forces Ξ, H, accumulated through a long period of time. Accordingly, averaging the trigonometrical functions, the secular terms are

$$\left.\begin{aligned} \Xi &= -3\frac{m}{a^2}v\frac{d\eta}{dt} = -2\omega\frac{d\eta}{dt} \\ \mathrm{H} &= \;\;3\frac{m}{a^2}v\frac{d\xi}{dt} = \;\;2\omega\frac{d\xi}{dt} \end{aligned}\right\} \quad \ldots\ldots\ldots\ldots\ldots\ldots\ldots (44\cdot5),$$

where

$$\omega = \tfrac{3}{2}mv/a^2 \quad \ldots\ldots\ldots\ldots\ldots\ldots (44\cdot6).$$

If (F_ξ, F_η) is the Newtonian force, the equations of motion including these secular perturbing forces will be

$$\frac{d^2\xi}{dt^2} + 2\omega\frac{d\eta}{dt} = F_\xi, \quad \frac{d^2\eta}{dt^2} - 2\omega\frac{d\xi}{dt} = F_\eta \quad \ldots\ldots\ldots\ldots (44\cdot7)$$

It is easily seen that ω is a very small quantity, so that ω^2 is negligible The equations (44·7) are then recognised as the Newtonian equations referred to axes rotating with angular velocity $-\omega$ Thus if we take the Newtonian orbit and give it an angular velocity $+\omega$, the result will be the solution of (44·7). The leading correction to the lunar theory obtained from Einstein's equations is a precessional effect, indicating that the classical results refer to a frame of reference advancing with angular velocity ω compared with the general inertial frame of the solar system.

From this cause the moon's node and perigee will advance with velocity ω. If Ω is the earth's angular velocity

$$\frac{\omega}{\Omega} = \frac{3}{2}\frac{m}{a} = \tfrac{3}{2}\,.\,10^{-8}.$$

Hence the advance of perigee and node in a century is

$$3\pi . 10^{-6} \text{ radians} = 1''{\cdot}94.$$

We may notice the very simple theoretical relation that Einstein's corrections cause an advance of the moon's perigee which is *one half* the advance of the earth's perihelion.

Neither the lunar theory nor the observations are as yet carried quite far enough to take account of this small effect; but it is only a little below the limit of detection. The result agrees with de Sitter's value except in the second decimal place which is only approximate.

There are well-known irregular fluctuations in the moon's longitude which attain rather large values, but it is generally considered that these are not of a type which can be explained by any amendment of gravitational theory and their origin must be looked for in other directions. At any rate Einstein's theory throws no light on them.

The advance of 1″·94 per century has not exclusive reference to the moon, in fact the elements of the moon's orbit do not appear in (44·6). It represents a property of the space surrounding the earth—a precession of the inertial frame in this region relative to the general inertial frame of the sidereal system. If the earth's rotation could be accurately measured by Foucault's pendulum or by gyrostatic experiments, the result would differ from the rotation relative to the fixed stars by this amount. This result seems to have been first pointed out by J. A. Schouten. One of the difficulties most often urged against the relativity theory is that the earth's rotation relative to the mean of the fixed stars appears to be an absolute quantity determinable by dynamical experiments on the earth*; it is therefore of interest to find that these two rotations are not exactly the same, and the earth's rotation relative to the stellar system (supposed to agree with the general inertial frame of the universe) *cannot be determined except by astronomical observations*.

The argument of the relativist is that the observed effect on Foucault's pendulum can be accounted for indifferently by a field of force or by rotation. The anti-relativist replies that the field of force is clearly a mathematical fiction, and the only possible *physical cause* must be absolute rotation. It is pointed out to him that nothing essential is gained by choosing the so-called non-rotating axes, because in any case the main part of the field of force remains, viz. terrestrial gravitation. He retorts that with his non-rotating axes he has succeeded in making the field of force vanish at infinity, so that the residuum is accounted for as a local disturbance by the earth; whereas, if axes fixed in the earth are admitted, the corresponding field of force becomes larger and larger as we recede from the earth, so that the relativist demands enormous forces in distant parts for which no physical cause can be assigned. Suppose, however, that the earth's rotation were much slower than it is now,

* *Space, Time and Gravitation*, p. 152.

and that Foucault's experiment had indicated a rotation of only $-1''\cdot 94$ per century. Our two disputants on the cloud-bound planet would no doubt carry on a long argument as to whether this was essentially an absolute rotation of the earth in space, the irony of the situation being that the earth all the while was non-rotating in the anti-relativist's sense, and the proposed transformation to allow for the Foucault rotation would actually have the effect of introducing the enormous field of force in distant parts of space which was so much objected to. When the origin of the $1''\cdot 94$ has been traced as in the foregoing investigation, the anti-relativist who has been arguing that the observed effect is definitely caused by rotation, must change his position and maintain that it is definitely due to a gravitational perturbation exerted by the sun on Foucault's pendulum; the relativist holds to his view that the two causes are not distinguishable.

45. Solution for a particle in a curved world.

In later work Einstein has adopted the more general equations (37·4)

$$G_{\mu\nu} = \alpha g_{\mu\nu} \quad \text{......................................(45·1).}$$

In this case we must modify (38·61), etc. by inserting $\alpha g_{\mu\nu}$ on the right. We then obtain

$$\tfrac{1}{2}\nu'' - \tfrac{1}{4}\lambda'\nu' + \tfrac{1}{4}\nu'^2 - \lambda'/r = -\alpha e^{\lambda} \quad \text{..............(45·21),}$$

$$e^{-\lambda}(1 + \tfrac{1}{2}r(\nu' - \lambda')) - 1 = -\alpha r^2 \quad \text{..............(45·22),}$$

$$e^{\nu-\lambda}(-\tfrac{1}{2}\nu'' + \tfrac{1}{4}\lambda'\nu' - \tfrac{1}{4}\nu'^2 - \nu'/r) = \alpha e^{\nu} \quad \text{..........(45·23).}$$

From (45·21) and (45·23), $\lambda' = -\nu'$, so that we may take $\lambda = -\nu$. An additive constant would merely amount to an alteration of the unit of time. Equation (45·22) then becomes

$$e^{\nu}(1 + r\nu') = 1 - \alpha r^2.$$

Let $e^{\nu} = \gamma$, then $$\gamma + r\gamma' = 1 - \alpha r^2$$

which on integration gives

$$\gamma = 1 - \frac{2m}{r} - \tfrac{1}{3}\alpha r^2 \quad \text{........................ (45·3).}$$

The only change is the substitution of this new value of γ in (38·8).

By recalculating the few steps from (39·44) to (39·61) we obtain the equation of the orbit

$$\frac{d^2u}{d\phi^2} + u = \frac{m}{h^2} + 3mu^2 - \frac{1}{3}\frac{\alpha}{h^2}u^{-3} \quad \text{..................(45·4).}$$

The effect of the new term in α is to give an additional motion of perihelion

$$\frac{\delta\varpi}{\phi} = \frac{1}{2}\frac{\alpha h^6}{m^4} = \frac{1}{2}\frac{\alpha a^3}{m}(1 - e^2)^3 \quad \text{.....................(45·5).}$$

At a place where γ vanishes there is an impassable barrier, since any change dr corresponds to an infinite distance ids surveyed by measuring-rods. The two roots of the quadratic (45·3) are approximately

$$r = 2m \quad \text{and} \quad r = \sqrt{(3/\alpha)}.$$

The first root would represent the boundary of the particle—if a genuine particle could exist—and give it the appearance of impenetrability The second barrier is at a very great distance and may be described as the *horizon* of the world

It is clear that the latter barrier (or illusion of a barrier) cannot be at a less distance than the most remote celestial objects observed, say 10^{25} cm. This makes α less than 10^{-50} (cm.)$^{-2}$. Inserting this value (in 45·5) we find that the additional motion of perihelion will be well below the limit of observational detection for all planets in the solar system*.

If in (45·3) we set $m = 0$, we abolish the particle at the origin and obtain the solution for an entirely empty world

$$ds^2 = -(1 - \tfrac{1}{3}\alpha r^2)^{-1} dr^2 - r^2 d\theta^2 - r^2 \sin^2\theta\, d\phi^2 + (1 - \tfrac{1}{3}\alpha r^2)\, dt^2 \quad\ldots(45\cdot6).$$

This will be further discussed in Chapter V.

46. Transition to continuous matter.

In the Newtonian theory of attractions the potential Ω in empty space satisfies the equation

$$\nabla^2 \Omega = 0,$$

of which the elementary solution is $\Omega = m/r$; then by a well-known procedure we are able to deduce that in continuous matter

$$\nabla^2 \Omega = -4\pi\rho \quad\ldots\ldots(46\cdot1).$$

We can apply the same principle to Einstein's potentials $g_{\mu\nu}$, which in empty space satisfy the equations $G_{\mu\nu} = 0$ The elementary solution has been found, and it remains to deduce the modification of the equations in continuous matter. The logical aspects of the transition from discrete particles to continuous density need not be discussed here, since they are the same for both theories

When the square of m/r is neglected, the isotropic solution (43·3) for a particle continually at rest becomes†

$$ds^2 = -\left(1 + \frac{2m}{r}\right)(dx^2 + dy^2 + dz^2) + \left(1 - \frac{2m}{r}\right) dt^2 \quad\ldots\ldots(46\cdot15).$$

The particle need not be at the origin provided that r is the distance from the particle to the point considered

Summing the fields of force of a number of particles, we obtain

$$ds^2 = -(1 + 2\Omega)(dx^2 + dy^2 + dz^2) + (1 - 2\Omega)\, dt^2 \quad\ldots\ldots(46\cdot2),$$

* This could scarcely have been asserted a few years ago, when it was not known that the stars extended much beyond 1000 parsecs distance A horizon distant 700 parsecs corresponds to a centennial motion of about 1″ in the earth's perihelion, and greater motion for the more distant planets in direct proportion to their periods.

† This approximation though sufficient for the present purpose is not good enough for a discussion of the perihelion of Mercury. The term in m^2/r^2 in the coefficient of dt^2 would have to be retained.

where

$$\Omega = \Sigma \frac{m}{r} = \text{Newtonian potential at the point considered.}$$

The inaccuracy in neglecting the interference of the fields of the particles is of the same order as that due to the neglect of m^2/r^2, if the number of particles is not unduly large.

Now calculate the $G_{\mu\nu}$ for the expression (46·2). We have

$$G_{\mu\nu} = g^{\sigma\rho} B_{\mu\nu\sigma\rho} = \tfrac{1}{2} g^{\sigma\rho} \left(\frac{\partial^2 g_{\mu\nu}}{\partial x_\rho \partial x_\sigma} + \frac{\partial^2 g_{\rho\sigma}}{\partial x_\mu \partial x_\nu} - \frac{\partial^2 g_{\mu\sigma}}{\partial x_\rho \partial x_\nu} - \frac{\partial^2 g_{\rho\nu}}{\partial x_\mu \partial x_\sigma} \right) \quad \ldots(46·3)$$

by (34·5). The non-linear terms are left out because they would involve Ω^2 which is of the order $(m/r)^2$ already neglected.

The only terms which survive are those in which the g's have like suffixes. Consider the last three terms in the bracket; for G_{11} they become

$$\frac{1}{2}\left(g^{11} \frac{\partial^2 g_{11}}{\partial x_1^2} + g^{22} \frac{\partial^2 g_{22}}{\partial x_1^2} + g^{33} \frac{\partial^2 g_{33}}{\partial x_1^2} + g^{44} \frac{\partial^2 g_{44}}{\partial x_1^2} - g^{11} \frac{\partial^2 g_{11}}{\partial x_1^2} - g^{11} \frac{\partial^2 g_{11}}{\partial x_1^2} \right).$$

Substituting for the g's from (46·2) we find that the result vanishes (neglecting Ω^2). For G_{44} the result vanishes for a different reason, viz. because Ω does not contain x_4 $(= t)$. Hence

$$G_{\mu\nu} = \tfrac{1}{2} g^{\sigma\rho} \frac{\partial^2 g_{\mu\nu}}{\partial x_\sigma \partial x_\rho} = \tfrac{1}{2} \Box g_{\mu\nu} \quad \text{as in (30·65)} \ldots(46·4).$$

Since time is not involved $\qquad \Box = -\nabla^2,$

$$G_{11}, G_{22}, G_{33}, G_{44} = -\tfrac{1}{2}\nabla^2 (g_{11}, g_{22}, g_{33}, g_{44})$$
$$= \nabla^2 \Omega \qquad \text{by (46·2).}$$

Hence, making at this point the transition to continuous matter,

$$G_{11}, G_{22}, G_{33}, G_{44} = -4\pi\rho \qquad \text{by (46·1)} \ldots\ldots\ldots\ldots(46·5).$$

Also
$$G = g^{\mu\nu} G_{\mu\nu} = -G_{11} - G_{22} - G_{33} + G_{44}$$
$$= 8\pi\rho$$

to the same approximation.

Consider the tensor defined by

$$-8\pi T_{\mu\nu} = G_{\mu\nu} - \tfrac{1}{2} g_{\mu\nu} G \ldots\ldots\ldots\ldots\ldots\ldots(46·6).$$

We readily find $\qquad T_{\mu\nu} = 0$, except $T_{44} = \rho$,

and raising the suffixes

$$T^{\mu\nu} = 0, \text{ except } T^{44} = \rho. \ldots\ldots\ldots(46·7),$$

since the $g^{\mu\nu}$ are Galilean to the order of approximation required.

Consider the expression

$$\rho_0 \frac{dx_\mu}{ds} \frac{dx_\nu}{ds},$$

where dx_μ/ds refers to the motion of the matter, and ρ_0 is the proper-density (an invariant). The matter is at rest in the coordinates hitherto used, and consequently

$$\frac{dx_1}{ds}, \frac{dx_2}{ds}, \frac{dx_3}{ds} = 0, \quad \frac{dx_4}{ds} = 1,$$

so that all components of the expression vanish, except the component $\mu, \nu = 4$ which is equal to ρ_0. Accordingly in these coordinates

$$T^{\mu\nu} = \rho_0 \frac{dx_\mu}{ds}\frac{dx_\nu}{ds} \quad \ldots\ldots \quad (46\cdot8),$$

since the density ρ in (46·7) is clearly the proper-density.

Now (46·8) is a tensor equation*, and since it has been verified for one set of coordinates it is true for all coordinate-systems. Equations (46·6) and (46·8) together give the extension of Einstein's law of gravitation for a region containing continuous matter of proper-density ρ_0 and velocity dx_μ/ds.

The question remains whether the neglect of m^2 causes any inaccuracy in these equations. In passing to continuous matter we diminish m for each particle indefinitely, but increase the number of particles in a given volume. To avoid increasing the number of particles we may diminish the volume, so that the formulae (46·5) will be true for the limiting case of a point inside a very small portion of continuous matter. Will the addition of surrounding matter in large quantities make any difference? This can contribute nothing directly to the tensor $G_{\mu\nu}$, since so far as this surrounding matter is concerned the point is in empty space; but Einstein's equations are non-linear and we must consider the possible cross-terms.

Draw a small sphere surrounding the point P which is being considered. Let $g_{\mu\nu} = \delta_{\mu\nu} + h_{\mu\nu} + h'_{\mu\nu}$, where $\delta_{\mu\nu}$ represents the Galilean values, and $h_{\mu\nu}$ and $h'_{\mu\nu}$ represent the fields of force contributed independently by the matter internal to and external to the sphere. By § 36 we can choose coordinates such that at P $h'_{\mu\nu}$ and its first derivatives vanish; and by the symmetry of the sphere the first derivatives of $h_{\mu\nu}$ vanish, whilst $h_{\mu\nu}$ itself tends to zero for an infinitely small sphere. Hence the cross-terms which are of the form

$$h'_{\sigma\tau}\frac{\partial^2 h_{\mu\nu}}{\partial x_\lambda \partial x_\rho}, \quad \frac{\partial h'_{\sigma\tau}}{\partial x_\lambda}\frac{\partial h_{\mu\nu}}{\partial x_\rho}, \quad \text{and} \quad h_{\sigma\tau}\frac{\partial^2 h'_{\mu\nu}}{\partial x_\lambda \partial x_\rho}$$

will all vanish at P. Accordingly with these limitations there are no cross-terms, and the sum of the two solutions $h_{\mu\nu}$ and $h'_{\mu\nu}$ is also a solution of the accurate equations. Hence the values (46·5) remain true. It will be seen that the limitation is that the coordinates must be "natural coordinates" at the point P. We have already paid heed to this in taking ρ to be the proper-density.

We have assumed that the matter at P is not accelerated with respect to these natural axes at P. (The original particles had to be *continually* at rest, otherwise the solution (46·15) does not apply.) If it were accelerated there would have to be a stress causing the acceleration. We shall find later that a stress contributes additional terms to the $G_{\mu\nu}$. The formulae (46·5) apply only strictly when there is no stress and the continuous medium is specified by one variable only, viz. the density.

* When an equation is stated to be a tensor equation, the reader is expected to verify that the covariant dimensions of both sides are the same.

The reader may feel that there is still some doubt as to the rigour of this justification of the neglect of m^2*. Lest he attach too great importance to the matter, we may state at once that the subsequent developments will not be based on this investigation. In the next chapter we shall arrive at the same formulae by a different line of argument, and proceed in the reverse direction from the laws of continuous matter to the particular case of an isolated particle.

The equation (46·2) is a useful expression for the gravitational field due to a static distribution of mass. It is only a first approximation correct to the order m/r, but *no second approximation exists* except in the case of a solitary particle. This is because when more than one particle is present accelerations necessarily occur, so that there cannot be an exact solution of Einstein's equations corresponding to a number of particles continually at rest. It follows that any constraint which could keep them at rest must necessarily be of such a nature as to contribute a gravitational field on its own account.

It will be useful to give the values of $G_{\mu\nu} - \frac{1}{2} g_{\mu\nu} G$ corresponding to the symmetrical formula for the interval (38·2). By varying λ and ν this can represent any distribution of continuous matter with spherical symmetry. We have

$$G = -e^{-\lambda}\left(\nu'' - \tfrac{1}{2}\lambda'\nu' + \tfrac{1}{2}\nu'^2 + 2(\nu' - \lambda')/r + 2(1 - e^{\lambda})/r^2\right)$$

$$\left.\begin{aligned} G_{11} - \tfrac{1}{2} g_{11} G &= -\nu'/r - (1 - e^{\lambda})/r^2 \\ G_{22} - \tfrac{1}{2} g_{22} G &= -r^2 e^{-\lambda}\left(\tfrac{1}{2}\nu'' - \tfrac{1}{4}\lambda'\nu' + \tfrac{1}{4}\nu'^2 + \tfrac{1}{2}(\nu' - \lambda')/r\right) \\ G_{33} - \tfrac{1}{2} g_{33} G &= -r^2 \sin^2\theta\, e^{-\lambda}\left(\tfrac{1}{2}\nu'' - \tfrac{1}{4}\lambda'\nu' + \tfrac{1}{4}\nu'^2 + \tfrac{1}{2}(\nu' - \lambda')/r\right) \\ G_{44} - \tfrac{1}{2} g_{44} G &= e^{\nu-\lambda}\left(-\lambda'/r + (1 - e^{\lambda})/r^2\right) \end{aligned}\right\} \quad (46·9).$$

47. Experiment and deductive theory.

So far as I am aware, the following is a complete list of the postulates which have been introduced into our mathematical theory up to the present stage.

1. The fundamental hypothesis of § 1.

2. The interval depends on a quadratic function of four coordinate-differences (§ 2).

3. The path of a freely moving particle is in all circumstances a geodesic (§ 15).

4. The track of a light-wave is a geodesic with $ds = 0$ (§ 15).

5. The law of gravitation for empty space is $G_{\mu\nu} = 0$, or more probably $G_{\mu\nu} = \lambda g_{\mu\nu}$, where λ is a very small constant (§ 37).

* To illustrate the difficulty, what exactly does ρ_0 mean, assuming that it is not *defined* by (46·6) and (46·7)? If the particles do not interfere with each other's fields, ρ_0 is Σm per unit volume, but if we take account of the interference, m is undefined—it is the constant of integration of an equation which does not apply. Mathematically, we cannot say what m would have been if the other particles had been removed; the question is nonsensical. Physically we could no doubt say what would have been the masses of the atoms if widely separated from one another, and compare them with the gravitational power of the atoms under actual conditions; but that involves laws of atomic structure which are quite outside the scope of the argument.

No. 4 includes the identification of the velocity of light with the fundamental velocity, which was originally introduced as a separate postulate in § 6.

In the mathematical theory we have two objects before us—to examine how we may test the truth of these postulates, and to discover how the laws which they express originate in the structure of the world. We cannot neglect either of these aims; and perhaps an ideal logical discussion would be divided into two parts, the one showing the gradual ascent from experimental evidence to the finally adopted specification of the structure of the world, the other starting with this specification and deducing all observational phenomena. The latter part is specially attractive to the mathematician for the proof may be made rigorous; whereas at each stage in the ascent some new inference or generalisation is introduced which, however plausible, can scarcely be considered incontrovertible. We can show that a certain structure will explain all the phenomena; we cannot show that nothing else will.

We may put to the experiments three questions in *crescendo*. Do they verify? Do they suggest? Do they (within certain limitations) compel the laws we adopt? It is when the last question is put that the difficulty arises for there are always limitations which will embarrass the mathematician who wishes to keep strictly to rigorous inference. What, for example, does experiment enable us to assert with regard to the gravitational field of a particle (the other four postulates being granted)? Firstly, we are probably justified in assuming that the interval can be expressed in the form (38·2), and experiment shows that λ and ν tend to zero at great distances. Provided that e^λ and e^ν are simple functions it will be possible to expand the coefficients in the form

$$ds^2 = -\left(1 + \frac{a_1}{r} + \frac{a_2}{r^2} + \dots\right)^{-1} dr^2 - r^2 d\theta^2 - r^2 \sin^2\theta\, d\phi^2 + \left(1 + \frac{b_1}{r} + \frac{b_2}{r^2} + \frac{b_3}{r^3} + \dots\right) dt^2.$$

Now reference to §§ 39, 40, 41 enables us to decide the following points:

(1) The Newtonian law of gravitation shows that $b_1 = -2m$.

(2) The observed deflection of light then shows that $a_1 = -2m$.

(3) The motion of perihelion of Mercury then shows that $b_2 = 0$.

The last two coefficients are not determined experimentally with any high accuracy; and we have no experimental knowledge of the higher coefficients. If the higher coefficients are zero we can proceed to deduce that this field satisfies $G_{\mu\nu} = 0$.

If small concessions are made, the case for the law $G_{\mu\nu} = 0$ can be strengthened. Thus if only one linear constant m is involved in the specification of the field, b_3 must contain m^3, and the corresponding term is of order $(m/r)^3$, an extremely small quantity. Whatever the higher coefficients may be, $G_{\mu\nu}$ will then vanish to a very high order of approximation.

Turning to the other object of our inquiry, we have yet to explain how these five laws originate in the structure of the world. In the next chapter we shall be concerned mainly with Nos. 3 and 5, which are not independent of one another. They will be replaced by a broader principle which contains them both and is of a more axiomatic character. No. 4 will be traced to its origin in the electromagnetic theory of Chapter VI. Finally a synthesis of these together with Nos 1 and 2 will be attempted in the closing chapter.

The following forward references will enable the reader to trace exactly what becomes of these postulates in the subsequent advance towards more primitive conceptions:

Nos. 1 and 2 are not further considered until § 97.

No. 3 is obtained directly from the law of gravitation in § 56.

No. 4 is obtained from the electromagnetic equations in § 74. These are traced to their origin in § 96.

No. 5 is obtained from the principle of identification in § 54, and more completely from the principle of measurement in § 66. The possibility of alternative laws is discussed in § 62

In the last century the ideal explanation of the phenomena of nature consisted in the construction of a mechanical model, which would act in the way observed. Whatever may be the practical helpfulness of a model, it is no longer recognised as contributing in any way to an ultimate explanation. A little later, the standpoint was reached that on carrying the analysis as far as possible we must ultimately come to a set of differential equations of which further explanation is impossible. We can then trace the *modus operandi*, but as regards ultimate causes we have to confess that "things happen so, because the world was made in that way." But in the kinetic theory of gases and in thermodynamics we have laws which can be explained much more satisfactorily. The principal laws of gases hold, not because a gas is made "that way," but because it is made "just anyhow." This is perhaps not to be taken quite literally; but if we could see that there was the same inevitability in Maxwell's laws and in the law of gravitation that there is in the laws of gases, we should have reached an explanation far more complete than an ultimate arbitrary differential equation. This suggests striving for an ideal—to show, not that the laws of nature come from a special construction of the ultimate basis of everything, but that the same laws of nature would prevail for the widest possible variety of structure of that basis. The complete ideal is probably unattainable and certainly unattained; nevertheless we shall be influenced by it in our discussion, and it appears that considerable progress in this direction is possible.

CHAPTER IV

RELATIVITY MECHANICS

48. The antisymmetrical tensor of the fourth rank.

A tensor $A_{\mu\nu}$ is said to be antisymmetrical if

$$A_{\nu\mu} = -A_{\mu\nu}.$$

It follows that $A_{11} = -A_{11}$, so that A_{11}, A_{22}, A_{33}, A_{44} must all be zero.

Consider a tensor of the fourth rank $E^{\alpha\beta\gamma\delta}$ which is antisymmetrical for all pairs of suffixes. Any component with two suffixes alike must be zero, since by the rule of antisymmetry $E^{\alpha\beta 11} = -E^{\alpha\beta 11}$. In the surviving components, $\alpha, \beta, \gamma, \delta$, being all different, must stand for the numbers 1, 2, 3, 4 in arbitrary order. We can pass from any of these components to E^{1234} by a series of interchanges of the suffixes in pairs, and each interchange merely reverses the sign. Writing E for E^{1234}, all the 256 components have one or other of the values

$$+E, \quad 0, \quad -E.$$

We shall write $$E^{\alpha\beta\gamma\delta} = E \,.\, \epsilon_{\alpha\beta\gamma\delta} \quad \text{.........................} (48\cdot1),$$

where

$\epsilon_{\alpha\beta\gamma\delta} = \;\; 0$, when the suffixes are not all different,

$= +1$, when they can be brought to the order 1, 2, 3, 4 by an even number of interchanges,

$= -1$, when an odd number of interchanges is needed.

It will appear later that E is not an invariant, consequently $\epsilon_{\alpha\beta\gamma\delta}$ is not a tensor.

The coefficient $\epsilon_{\alpha\beta\gamma\delta}$ is particularly useful for dealing with determinants. If $|k_{\mu\nu}|$ denotes the determinant formed with the elements $k_{\mu\nu}$ (which need not form a tensor), we have

$$4! \times |k_{\mu\nu}| = \epsilon_{\alpha\beta\gamma\delta}\, \epsilon_{\epsilon\zeta\eta\theta}\, k_{\alpha\epsilon}\, k_{\beta\zeta}\, k_{\gamma\eta}\, k_{\delta\theta} \quad \text{..............} (48\cdot2),$$

because the terms of the determinant are obtained by selecting four elements, one from each row ($\alpha, \beta, \gamma, \delta$, all different) and also from each column ($\epsilon, \zeta, \eta, \theta$, all different) and affixing the + or − sign to the product according as the order of the columns is brought into the order of the rows by an even or odd number of interchanges. The factor 4! appears because every possible permutation of the *same* four elements is included separately in the summation on the right.

It is possible by corresponding formulae to define and manipulate determinants in three dimensions (with 64 elements arranged in a cube) or in four dimensions.

Note that $$\epsilon_{\alpha\beta\gamma\delta}\, \epsilon_{\alpha\beta\gamma\delta} = 4! \quad \text{.........................} (48\cdot31).$$

The determinants with which we are most concerned are the fundamental determinant g and the Jacobian of a transformation

$$J = \frac{\partial (x_1', x_2', x_3', x_4')}{\partial (x_1, x_2, x_3, x_4)}.$$

By (48·2)

$$4!\, g = \epsilon_{\alpha\beta\gamma\delta}\, \epsilon_{\epsilon\zeta\eta\theta}\, g_{\alpha\epsilon}\, g_{\beta\zeta}\, g_{\gamma\eta}\, g_{\delta\theta} \quad \text{.................(48·32)},$$

$$4!\, J = \epsilon_{\alpha\beta\gamma\delta}\, \epsilon_{\epsilon\zeta\eta\theta} \frac{\partial x_\epsilon'}{\partial x_\alpha} \frac{\partial x_\zeta'}{\partial x_\beta} \frac{\partial x_\eta'}{\partial x_\gamma} \frac{\partial x_\theta'}{\partial x_\delta} \quad \text{..............(48·33)}.$$

To illustrate the manipulations we shall prove that*

$$g = J^2 g'.$$

By (48·32) and (48·33)

$$(4!)^3 J^2 g' = \epsilon_{\alpha\beta\gamma\delta}\, \epsilon_{\epsilon\zeta\eta\theta}\, g'_{\alpha\epsilon}\, g'_{\beta\zeta}\, g'_{\gamma\eta}\, g'_{\delta\theta} \,.\, \epsilon_{\iota\kappa\lambda\mu}\, \epsilon_{\nu\xi o\varpi} \frac{\partial x_\nu'}{\partial x_\iota} \frac{\partial x_\xi'}{\partial x_\kappa} \frac{\partial x_o'}{\partial x_\lambda} \frac{\partial x_\varpi'}{\partial x_\mu}$$

$$.\, \epsilon_{\rho\sigma\tau\upsilon}\, \epsilon_{\phi\chi\psi\omega} \frac{\partial x_\phi'}{\partial x_\rho} \frac{\partial x_\chi'}{\partial x_\sigma} \frac{\partial x_\psi'}{\partial x_\tau} \frac{\partial x_\omega'}{\partial x_\upsilon} \quad \text{......(48·41)}.$$

There are about 280 billion terms on the right, and we proceed to rearrange those which do not vanish.

For non-vanishing terms the letters ν, ξ, o, ϖ denote the same suffixes as α, β, γ, δ, but (usually) in a different order. Permute the four factors in which they occur so that they come into the same order; the suffixes of the denominators will then come into a new order, say, i, k, l, m. Thus

$$\frac{\partial x_\nu'}{\partial x_\iota} \frac{\partial x_\xi'}{\partial x_\kappa} \frac{\partial x_o'}{\partial x_\lambda} \frac{\partial x_\varpi'}{\partial x_\mu} = \frac{\partial x_\alpha'}{\partial x_i} \frac{\partial x_\beta'}{\partial x_k} \frac{\partial x_\gamma'}{\partial x_l} \frac{\partial x_\delta'}{\partial x_m} \quad \text{...........(48·42)}.$$

Since the number of interchanges of the denominators is the same as the number of interchanges of the numerators

$$\frac{\epsilon_{\nu\xi o\varpi}}{\epsilon_{\alpha\beta\gamma\delta}} = \pm 1 = \frac{\epsilon_{\iota\kappa\lambda\mu}}{\epsilon_{iklm}} \quad \text{.......................(48·43)},$$

so that the result of the transposition is

$$\epsilon_{\alpha\beta\gamma\delta}\, \epsilon_{\iota\kappa\lambda\mu} \frac{\partial x_\nu'}{\partial x_\iota} \frac{\partial x_\xi'}{\partial x_\kappa} \frac{\partial x_o'}{\partial x_\lambda} \frac{\partial x_\varpi'}{\partial x_\mu} = \epsilon_{\nu\xi o\varpi}\, \epsilon_{iklm} \frac{\partial x_\alpha'}{\partial x_i} \frac{\partial x_\beta'}{\partial x_k} \frac{\partial x_\gamma'}{\partial x_l} \frac{\partial x_\delta'}{\partial x_m} \quad \text{.. (48·5)}.$$

Making a similar transposition of the last four terms, (48·41) becomes

$$(4!)^3 J^2 g' = g'_{\alpha\epsilon}\, g'_{\beta\zeta}\, g'_{\gamma\eta}\, g'_{\delta\theta} \,.\, \frac{\partial x_\alpha'}{\partial x_i} \frac{\partial x_\beta'}{\partial x_k} \frac{\partial x_\gamma'}{\partial x_l} \frac{\partial x_\delta'}{\partial x_m} \,.\, \frac{\partial x_\epsilon'}{\partial x_r} \frac{\partial x_\zeta'}{\partial x_s} \frac{\partial x_\eta'}{\partial x_t} \frac{\partial x_\theta'}{\partial x_u}$$

$$.\, \epsilon_{iklm}\, \epsilon_{\nu\xi o\varpi}\, \epsilon_{\nu\xi o\varpi}\, \epsilon_{rstu}\, \epsilon_{\phi\chi\psi\omega}\, \epsilon_{\phi\chi\psi\omega}.$$

But by (23·22)

$$g'_{\alpha\epsilon} \frac{\partial x_\alpha'}{\partial x_i} \frac{\partial x_\epsilon'}{\partial x_r} = g_{ir}.$$

Hence

$$(4!)^3 J^2 g' = (4!)^2\, \epsilon_{iklm}\, \epsilon_{rstu}\, g_{ir}\, g_{ks}\, g_{lt}\, g_{mu}$$

$$= (4!)^3 g,$$

which proves the theorem.

* A shorter proof is given at the end of this section.

Returning to $E^{\alpha\beta\gamma\delta}$, its tensor-transformation law is

$$E'^{\mu\nu\sigma\tau} = E^{\alpha\beta\gamma\delta} \frac{\partial x_\mu'}{\partial x_\alpha} \frac{\partial x_\nu'}{\partial x_\beta} \frac{\partial x_\sigma'}{\partial x_\gamma} \frac{\partial x_\tau'}{\partial x_\delta}.$$

Whence multiplying by $\epsilon_{\mu\nu\sigma\tau}$ and using (48·1)

$$E' . \epsilon_{\mu\nu\sigma\tau} \epsilon_{\mu\nu\sigma\tau} = E . \epsilon_{\alpha\beta\gamma\delta} \epsilon_{\mu\nu\sigma\tau} \frac{\partial x_\mu'}{\partial x_\alpha} \frac{\partial x_\nu'}{\partial x_\beta} \frac{\partial x_\sigma'}{\partial x_\gamma} \frac{\partial x_\tau'}{\partial x_\delta},$$

so that by (48·31) and (48·33)

$$E' = JE \qquad \text{.............................(48·6).}$$

Thus E is not an invariant for transformations of coordinates.

Again $$E^{\alpha\beta\gamma\delta} E^{\epsilon\zeta\eta\theta} g_{\alpha\epsilon} g_{\beta\zeta} g_{\gamma\eta} g_{\delta\theta}$$

is seen by inspection to be an invariant. But this is equal to

$$E^2 \epsilon_{\alpha\beta\gamma\delta} \epsilon_{\epsilon\zeta\eta\theta} g_{\alpha\epsilon} g_{\beta\zeta} g_{\gamma\eta} g_{\delta\theta}$$
$$= 4!\, E^2 g.$$

Hence $E^2 g$ is an invariant ....(48·65).

Accordingly $E^2 g = E'^2 g' = (EJ)^2 g'$, by (48·6)

giving another proof that $g = J^2 g'$ ....(48·7).

Corollary. If a is the determinant formed from the components $a_{\mu\nu}$ of *any* covariant tensor, $E^2 a$ is an invariant and

$$a = J^2 a' \qquad \text{.........................(48·8).}$$

49. Element of volume. Tensor-density.

In § 32 we found that the surface-element corresponding to the parallelogram contained by two displacements, $\delta_1 x_\mu$, $\delta_2 x_\mu$, is the antisymmetrical tensor

$$dS^{\mu\nu} = \begin{vmatrix} \delta_1 x_\mu, & \delta_1 x_\nu \\ \delta_2 x_\mu, & \delta_2 x_\nu \end{vmatrix}.$$

Similarly we define the volume-element (four-dimensional) corresponding to the hyperparallelopiped contained by four displacements, $\delta_1 x_\mu$, $\delta_2 x_\mu$, $\delta_3 x_\mu$, $\delta_4 x_\mu$, as the tensor

$$dV^{\mu\nu\sigma\tau} = \begin{vmatrix} \delta_1 x_\mu, & \delta_1 x_\nu, & \delta_1 x_\sigma, & \delta_1 x_\tau \\ \delta_2 x_\mu, & \delta_2 x_\nu, & \delta_2 x_\sigma, & \delta_2 x_\tau \\ \delta_3 x_\mu, & \delta_3 x_\nu, & \delta_3 x_\sigma, & \delta_3 x_\tau \\ \delta_4 x_\mu, & \delta_4 x_\nu, & \delta_4 x_\sigma, & \delta_4 x_\tau \end{vmatrix} \qquad \text{.........(49·1).}$$

It will be seen that the determinant is an antisymmetrical tensor of the fourth rank, and its 256 components accordingly have one or other of the three values

$$+dV, \quad 0, \quad -dV,$$

where $dV = \pm dV^{1234}$. It follows from (48·65) that $(dV)^2 g$ is an invariant, so that

$$\sqrt{-g}\, dV \text{ is an invariant} \qquad \text{.................(49·2).}$$

Since the sign of dV^{1234} is associated with some particular cycle of enumeration of the edges of the parallelopiped, which is not usually of any importance, the single positive quantity dV is usually taken to represent the volume-element fully. Summing a number of infinitesimal volume-elements, we have

$$\iiiint \sqrt{-g}\,.\,dV \text{ is an invariant} \quad\quad (49\cdot3),$$

the integral being taken over any region defined independently of the coordinates.

When the quadruple integral is regarded as the limit of a sum, the infinitesimal parallelopipeds may be taken of any shape and orientation, but for analytical integration we choose them to be coincident with meshes of the coordinate-system that is being used, viz.

$$\delta_1 x_\mu = (dx_1, 0, 0, 0);\ \delta_2 x_\mu = (0, dx_2, 0, 0),\ \text{etc.}$$

Then (49·1) reduces to a single diagonal

$$dV = dx_1 dx_2 dx_3 dx_4.$$

We write $d\tau$ for the volume-element when chosen in this way, so that

$$d\tau \equiv dx_1 dx_2 dx_3 dx_4.$$

It is not usually necessary to discriminate between $d\tau$ and the more general expression dV, and we shall usually regard $\sqrt{-g}\,.\,d\tau$ as an invariant. Strictly speaking we mean that $\sqrt{-g}\,d\tau$ behaves as an invariant in volume-integration; whereas $\sqrt{-g}\,dV$ is intrinsically invariant.

For Galilean coordinates x, y, z, t, we have $\sqrt{-g} = 1$, so that

$$\sqrt{-g}\,d\tau = dx\,dy\,dz\,dt \quad\quad (49\cdot41).$$

Further if we take an observer at rest in this Galilean system, $dx\,dy\,dz$ is his element of proper-volume (three-dimensional) dW, and dt is his proper-time ds. Hence

$$\sqrt{-g}\,d\tau = dW\,ds \quad\quad (49\cdot42).$$

By (49·41) we see that $\sqrt{-g}\,d\tau$ is the volume in natural measure of the four-dimensional element. This natural or invariant volume is a physical conception—the result of physical measures made with unconstrained scales; it may be contrasted with the geometrical volume dV or $d\tau$, which expresses the number of unit meshes contained in the region.

Let T be a scalar, i.e. an invariant function of position, then, since $T\sqrt{-g}\,dV$ is an invariant,

$$\int T\sqrt{-g}\,d\tau \text{ is an invariant}$$

for any absolutely defined four-dimensional region. Each unit mesh (whose edges dx_1, dx_2, dx_3, dx_4 are unity) contributes the amount $T\sqrt{-g}$ to this invariant Accordingly we call $T\sqrt{-g}$ the *scalar-density** or *invariant-density*.

A nearly similar result is obtained for tensors. The integral

$$\int T^{\mu\nu}\sqrt{-g}\,d\tau$$

over an absolutely defined region is not a tensor; because, although it is the sum of a number of tensors, these tensors are not located at the same point and cannot be combined (§ 33). But in the limit as the region is made infinitely small its transformation law approaches more and more nearly that of a single tensor. Thus $T^{\mu\nu}\sqrt{-g}$ is a *tensor-density*, representing the amount per unit mesh of a tensor in the infinitesimal region round the point.

It is usual to represent the tensor-density corresponding to any tensor by the corresponding German letter; thus

$$\mathfrak{T}^{\mu\nu} \equiv T^{\mu\nu}\sqrt{-g}\,; \quad \mathfrak{T} \equiv T\sqrt{-g} \qquad \text{.................(49·5).}$$

By (48·1) $\quad \mathfrak{E}^{\alpha\beta\gamma\delta} = E^{\alpha\beta\gamma\delta}\sqrt{-g} = E\sqrt{-g}\,.\,\epsilon_{\alpha\beta\gamma\delta}$,

and since $E\sqrt{-g}$ is an invariant it follows that $\epsilon_{\alpha\beta\gamma\delta}$ is a tensor-density.

Physical quantities are of two main kinds, e.g.

Field of acceleration = *intensity* of some condition at a point,

Momentum = *quantity* of something in a volume.

The latter kind are naturally expressed as "so much per unit mesh." Hence *intensity* is naturally described by a tensor, and *quantity* by a tensor-density. We shall find $\sqrt{-g}$ continually appearing in our formulae; that is an indication that the physical quantities concerned are strictly tensor-densities rather than tensors. In the general theory tensor-densities are at least as important as tensors.

We can only speak of the amount of momentum in a large volume when a definite system of coordinates has been fixed. The total momentum is the sum of the momenta in different elements of volume, and for each element there will be different coefficients of transformation, when a change of coordinates is made. The only case in which we can state the amount of something in a large region without fixing a special system of coordinates is when we are dealing with an invariant, e.g. the amount of "Action" in a large region is independent of the coordinates. In short, tensor-analysis (except in the degenerate case of invariants) deals with things located at a point and not spread over a large region; that is why we usually have to use densities instead of quantities.

Alternatively we can express a physical quantity of the second kind as "so much per unit natural volume ($\sqrt{-g}\,d\tau$)"; it is then represented by a

* I have usually avoided the superfluous word "scalar," which is less expressive than its synonym "invariant." But it is convenient here in order to avoid confusion between the density *of an invariant* and a density *which is invariant*. The latter, ρ_0, has hitherto been called the invariant density (without the hyphen).

tensor. From the physical point of view it is perhaps as rational to express it in this way, as to express it by a tensor-density "so much per unit mesh ($d\tau$)." But analytically this is a somewhat hybrid procedure, because we seem to be employing simultaneously two systems of coordinates, the one openly for measuring the physical quantity, the other (a natural system) implicitly for measuring the volume containing it. It cannot be considered wrong in a physical sense to represent quantities of the second kind by tensors; but the analysis exposes our sub-conscious reference to $\sqrt{-g}\,d\tau$, by the repeated appearance of $\sqrt{-g}$ in the formulae.

In any kind of space-time it is possible to choose coordinates such that $\sqrt{-g}=1$ everywhere; for if three of the systems of partitions have been drawn arbitrarily, the fourth can be drawn so as to intercept meshes all of equal natural volume. In such coordinates tensors and tensor-densities become equivalent, and the algebra may be simplified; but although this simplification does not involve any loss of generality, it is liable to obscure the deeper significance of the theory, and it is not usually desirable to adopt it.

50. The problem of the rotating disc.

We may consider at this point a problem of some historic interest—

A disc made of homogeneous incompressible material is caused to rotate with angular velocity ω; to find the alteration in length of the radius.

The old paradox associated with this problem—that the circumference moving longitudinally might be expected to contract, whilst the radius moving transversely is unaltered—no longer troubles us*. But the general theory of relativity gives a quantitative answer to the problem, which was first obtained by Lorentz by a method different from that given here†.

We must first have a clear understanding of what is meant by the word incompressible. Let us isolate an element of the rotating disc, and refer it to axes with respect to which it has no velocity or acceleration (proper-measure); then except for the fact that it is under stress due to the cohesive forces of surrounding matter, it is relatively in the same state as an element of the non-rotating disc referred to fixed axes. Now the meaning of *incompressible* is that no stress-system can make any difference in the closeness of packing of the molecules; hence the particle-density σ (referred to proper-measure) is the same as for an element of the non-rotating disc. But the particle-density σ' referred to axes fixed in space may be different.

We might write down at once by (14·1)

$$\sigma' = \sigma (1 - \omega^2 r^2)^{-\frac{1}{2}},$$

since ωr is the velocity of the element. This would in fact give the right result. But in § 14 acceleration was not taken into account and we ought to

* *Space, Time and Gravitation*, p. 75. † *Nature*, vol. 106, p. 795.

proceed more rigorously. We use the accented coordinates of § 15 for our rotating system, and easily calculate from (15·4) that

$$\sqrt{-g'} = 1,$$

and since x_1', x_2', x_3' are constant for an element of the disc, the proper-time

$$ds = \sqrt{(1 - \omega^2 (x_1'^2 + x_2'^2))}\, dx_4'.$$

If dW is the proper-volume of the element, by (49·42)

$$dW\, ds = \sqrt{-g'} \,.\, dx_1' dx_2' dx_3' dx_4'.$$

Hence
$$dW = (1 - \omega^2 (x_1'^2 + x_2'^2))^{-\frac{1}{2}} dx_1' dx_2' dx_3'$$
$$= (1 - \omega^2 r'^2)^{-\frac{1}{2}} r' dr' d\theta' dx_3'.$$

If the thickness of the disc is $\delta x_3' = b$, and its boundary is given by $r' = a'$, the total number of particles in the disc will be

$$N = \int \sigma\, dW = 2\pi\sigma b \int_0^{a'} (1 - \omega^2 r'^2)^{-\frac{1}{2}} r' dr'.$$

Since this number is unaltered by the rotation, a' must be a function of ω such that

$$\int_0^{a'} (1 - \omega^2 r'^2)^{-\frac{1}{2}} r' dr' = \text{const.},$$

or
$$\frac{1}{\omega^2}(1 - \sqrt{(1 - \omega^2 a'^2)}) = \text{const.}$$

Expanding the square-root, this gives approximately

$$\tfrac{1}{2} a'^2 (1 + \tfrac{1}{4}\omega^2 a'^2) = \text{const.},$$

so that if a is the radius of the disc at rest

$$a' (1 + \tfrac{1}{8}\omega^2 a'^2) = a.$$

Hence to the same approximation

$$a' = a (1 - \tfrac{1}{8}\omega^2 a^2).$$

Note that a' is the radius of the rotating disc according to measurement with fixed scales, since the rotating and non-rotating coordinates have been connected by the elementary transformation (15·3).

We see that the contraction is one quarter of that predicted by a crude application of the FitzGerald formula to the circumference.

51. The divergence of a tensor.

In the elementary theory of vectors the divergence

$$\frac{\partial X}{\partial x} + \frac{\partial Y}{\partial y} + \frac{\partial Z}{\partial z}$$

is important; we can to some extent grasp its geometrical significance. In our general notation, this expression becomes

$$\frac{\partial A^\mu}{\partial x_\mu}.$$

But evidently a more fundamental operation is to take the covariant derivatives which will give an invariant

$$(A^\mu)_\mu.$$

We therefore define the *divergence* of a tensor as its contracted covariant derivative.

By (29·4)
$$(A^\mu)_\mu = \frac{\partial A^\mu}{\partial x_\mu} + \{\epsilon\mu, \mu\} A^\epsilon$$

$$= \frac{\partial A^\mu}{\partial x_\mu} + A^\epsilon \cdot \frac{1}{\sqrt{-g}} \frac{\partial}{\partial x_\epsilon} \sqrt{-g} \quad \text{by (35·4)}$$

$$= \frac{1}{\sqrt{-g}} \frac{\partial}{\partial x_\mu} (A^\mu \sqrt{-g}) \quad \text{.........(51·11)},$$

since ϵ may be replaced by μ. In terms of tensor-density this may be written

$$A^\mu_\mu \sqrt{-g} = \mathfrak{A}^\mu_\mu = \frac{\partial}{\partial x_\mu} \mathfrak{A}^\mu \quad \text{.........(51·12)}.$$

The divergence of A^ν_μ is by (30·2)

$$(A^\nu_\mu)_\nu = \frac{\partial}{\partial x_\nu} A^\nu_\mu + \{\alpha\nu, \nu\} A^\alpha_\mu - \{\mu\nu, \alpha\} A^\nu_\alpha$$

$$= \frac{1}{\sqrt{-g}} \frac{\partial}{\partial x_\nu} (A^\nu_\mu \sqrt{-g}) - \{\mu\nu, \alpha\} A^\nu_\alpha \quad \text{.........(51·2)},$$

by the same reduction as before. The last term gives

$$-\frac{1}{2}\left(\frac{\partial g_{\mu\beta}}{\partial x_\nu} + \frac{\partial g_{\nu\beta}}{\partial x_\mu} - \frac{\partial g_{\mu\nu}}{\partial x_\beta}\right) A^{\beta\nu}.$$

When $A^{\beta\nu}$ is a symmetrical tensor, two of the terms in the bracket cancel by interchange of β and ν, and we are left with $-\frac{1}{2} \frac{\partial g_{\beta\nu}}{\partial x_\mu} A^{\beta\nu}$.

Hence *for symmetrical tensors*

$$(A^\nu_\mu)_\nu = \frac{1}{\sqrt{-g}} \frac{\partial}{\partial x_\nu} (A^\nu_\mu \sqrt{-g}) - \frac{1}{2} \frac{\partial g_{\alpha\beta}}{\partial x_\mu} A^{\alpha\beta} \quad \text{.........(51·31)},$$

or, by (35·2),
$$(A^\nu_\mu)_\nu = \frac{1}{\sqrt{-g}} \frac{\partial}{\partial x_\nu} (A^\nu_\mu \sqrt{-g}) + \frac{1}{2} \frac{\partial g^{\alpha\beta}}{\partial x_\mu} A_{\alpha\beta} \quad \text{.........(51·32)}.$$

For *antisymmetrical tensors*, it is easier to use the contravariant associate,

$$(A^{\mu\nu})_\nu = \frac{\partial}{\partial x_\nu} A^{\mu\nu} + \{\alpha\nu, \nu\} A^{\mu\alpha} + \{\alpha\nu, \mu\} A^{\alpha\nu} \quad \text{.........(51·41)}.$$

The last term vanishes owing to the antisymmetry. Hence

$$(A^{\mu\nu})_\nu = \frac{1}{\sqrt{-g}} \frac{\partial}{\partial x_\nu} (A^{\mu\nu} \sqrt{-g}) \quad \text{.........(51·42)}.$$

Introducing tensor-densities our results become

$$\mathfrak{A}^{\nu}_{\mu\nu} = \frac{\partial}{\partial x_\nu}\mathfrak{A}^{\nu}_{\mu} - \tfrac{1}{2}\mathfrak{A}^{\alpha\beta}\frac{\partial g_{\alpha\beta}}{\partial x_\mu} \text{ (symmetrical tensors) ..(51 51)},$$

$$\mathfrak{A}^{\mu\nu}_{\nu} = \frac{\partial}{\partial x_\nu}\mathfrak{A}^{\mu\nu} \qquad \text{(antisymmetrical tensors) .. (51·52)}.$$

52. The four identities.

We shall now prove the fundamental theorem of mechanics—

The divergence of $G^{\nu}_{\mu} - \frac{1}{2}g^{\nu}_{\mu}G$ is identically zero ....(52).

In three dimensions the vanishing of the divergence is the condition of continuity of flux, e.g. in hydrodynamics $\partial u/\partial x + \partial v/\partial y + \partial w/\partial z = 0$. Adding a time-coordinate, this becomes the condition of *conservation* or *permanence*, as will be shown in detail later. *It will be realised how important for a theory of the material world is the discovery of a world-tensor which is inherently permanent.*

I think it should be possible to prove (52) by geometrical reasoning in continuation of the ideas of § 33. But I have not been able to construct a geometrical proof and must content myself with a clumsy analytical verification.

By the rules of covariant differentiation

$$(g^{\nu}_{\mu}G)_\nu = g^{\nu}_{\mu}\partial G/\partial x_\nu = \partial G/\partial x_\mu.$$

Thus the theorem reduces to

$$G^{\nu}_{\mu\nu} = \frac{1}{2}\frac{\partial G}{\partial x_\mu} \quad \text{.........................(52·1)}.$$

For $\mu = 1, 2, 3, 4$, these are the four identities referred to in § 37. By (51·32)

$$G^{\nu}_{\mu\nu} = \frac{1}{\sqrt{-g}}\frac{\partial}{\partial x_\nu}(G^{\nu}_{\mu}\sqrt{-g}) + \tfrac{1}{2}G_{\alpha\beta}\frac{\partial g^{\alpha\beta}}{\partial x_\mu},$$

and since $G = g^{\alpha\beta}G_{\alpha\beta}$

$$\frac{1}{2}\frac{\partial G}{\partial x_\mu} = \tfrac{1}{2}g^{\alpha\beta}\frac{\partial G_{\alpha\beta}}{\partial x_\mu} + \tfrac{1}{2}G_{\alpha\beta}\frac{\partial g^{\alpha\beta}}{\partial x_\mu}.$$

Hence, subtracting, we have to prove that

$$\frac{1}{\sqrt{-g}}\frac{\partial}{\partial x_\nu}(G^{\nu}_{\mu}\sqrt{-g}) = \tfrac{1}{2}g^{\alpha\beta}\frac{\partial G_{\alpha\beta}}{\partial x_\mu} \quad \text{.............. (52·2)}.$$

Since (52) is a tensor relation it is sufficient to show that it holds for a special coordinate-system; only we must be careful that our special choice of coordinate-system does not limit the kind of space-time and so spoil the generality of the proof. It has been shown in § 36 that in any kind of space-time, coordinates can be chosen so that all the first derivatives $\partial g_{\mu\nu}/\partial x_\sigma$ vanish at a particular point; we shall therefore lighten the algebra by taking coordinates such that at the point considered

$$\frac{\partial g_{\mu\nu}}{\partial x_\sigma} = 0 \quad \text{.................................(52·3)}.$$

This condition can, of course, only be applied after all differentiations have been performed. Then

$$\frac{1}{\sqrt{-g}}\frac{\partial}{\partial x_\nu}(G_\mu^\nu\sqrt{-g}) = \frac{1}{\sqrt{-g}}\frac{\partial}{\partial x_\nu}(g^{\nu\tau}g^{\sigma\rho}\sqrt{-g}\,.\,B_{\mu\tau\sigma\rho}).$$

Owing to (52·3) $g^{\nu\tau}g^{\sigma\rho}\sqrt{-g}$ can be taken outside the differential operator, giving

$$g^{\nu\tau}g^{\sigma\rho}\frac{\partial}{\partial x_\nu}B_{\mu\tau\sigma\rho},$$

which by (34·5) is equal to

$$\tfrac{1}{2}g^{\nu\tau}g^{\sigma\rho}\frac{\partial}{\partial x_\nu}\left(\frac{\partial^2 g_{\rho\sigma}}{\partial x_\mu\partial x_\tau} + \frac{\partial^2 g_{\mu\tau}}{\partial x_\rho\partial x_\sigma} - \frac{\partial^2 g_{\mu\sigma}}{\partial x_\rho\partial x_\tau} - \frac{\partial^2 g_{\rho\tau}}{\partial x_\mu\partial x_\sigma}\right)\text{.........(52·4).}$$

The rest of $B_{\mu\tau\sigma\rho}$ is omitted because it consists of products of two vanishing factors (3-index symbols), so that after differentiation by ∂x_ν one vanishing factor always remains.

By the double interchange σ for τ, ρ for ν, two terms in (52·4) cancel out, leaving

$$\frac{1}{\sqrt{-g}}\frac{\partial}{\partial x_\nu}(G_\mu^\nu\sqrt{-g}) = \tfrac{1}{2}g^{\nu\tau}g^{\sigma\rho}\frac{\partial}{\partial x_\nu}\left(\frac{\partial^2 g_{\rho\sigma}}{\partial x_\mu\partial x_\tau} - \frac{\partial^2 g_{\rho\tau}}{\partial x_\mu\partial x_\sigma}\right)\text{ ...(52·51).}$$

Similarly

$$\tfrac{1}{2}g^{\alpha\beta}\frac{\partial G_{\alpha\beta}}{\partial x_\mu} = \tfrac{1}{2}g^{\nu\tau}\frac{\partial G_{\nu\tau}}{\partial x_\mu} = \tfrac{1}{2}g^{\nu\tau}\frac{\partial}{\partial x_\mu}(g^{\sigma\rho}B_{\nu\tau\sigma\rho})$$

$$= \tfrac{1}{4}g^{\nu\tau}g^{\sigma\rho}\frac{\partial}{\partial x_\mu}\left(\frac{\partial^2 g_{\rho\sigma}}{\partial x_\nu\partial x_\tau} + \frac{\partial^2 g_{\nu\tau}}{\partial x_\rho\partial x_\sigma} - \frac{\partial^2 g_{\nu\sigma}}{\partial x_\rho\partial x_\tau} - \frac{\partial^2 g_{\rho\tau}}{\partial x_\nu\partial x_\sigma}\right)$$

$$= \tfrac{1}{2}g^{\nu\tau}g^{\sigma\rho}\frac{\partial}{\partial x_\mu}\left(\frac{\partial^2 g_{\rho\sigma}}{\partial x_\nu\partial x_\tau} - \frac{\partial^2 g_{\rho\tau}}{\partial x_\nu\partial x_\sigma}\right)\text{ ....(52·52),}$$

since the double interchange σ for τ, ρ for ν, causes two terms to become equal to the other two.

Comparing (52·51) and (52·52) we see that the required result is established for coordinates chosen so as to have the property (52·3) at the point considered; and since it is a tensor equation it must hold true for all systems of coordinates.

53. The material energy-tensor.

Let ρ_0 be the proper-density of matter, and let dx_μ/ds refer to the motion of the matter; we write, as in (46·8),

$$T^{\mu\nu} = \rho_0\frac{dx_\mu}{ds}\frac{dx_\nu}{ds}\text{ ....(53·1).}$$

Then $T^{\mu\nu}$ (with the associated mixed and covariant tensors) is called the *energy-tensor* of the matter.

For matter moving with any velocity relative to Galilean coordinates, the coordinate-density ρ is given by

$$\rho = \rho_0 \left(\frac{dt}{ds}\right)^2 \quad \text{.............................(53·2)},$$

for, as explained in (14·2), the FitzGerald factor $\beta = dt/ds$ appears twice, once for the increase of mass with velocity and once for the contraction of volume.

Hence in Galilean coordinates

$$T^{\mu\nu} = \rho \frac{dx_\mu}{dt} \frac{dx_\nu}{dt} \quad \text{...........................(53·3)},$$

so that if u, v, w are the components of velocity

$$T^{\mu\nu} = \begin{matrix} \rho u^2, & \rho vu, & \rho wu, & \rho u \\ \rho uv, & \rho v^2, & \rho wv, & \rho v \\ \rho uw, & \rho vw, & \rho w^2, & \rho w \\ \rho u, & \rho v, & \rho w, & \rho \end{matrix} \quad \text{...............(53·4)}.$$

In matter atomically constituted, a volume which is regarded as small for macroscopic treatment contains particles with widely divergent motions. Thus the terms in (53·4) should be summed for varying motions of the particles. For macroscopic treatment we express the summation in the following way.—Let (u, v, w) refer to the motion of the centre of mass of the element, and (u_1, v_1, w_1) be the internal motion of the particles relative* to the centre of mass. Then in a term of our tensor such as $\Sigma\rho(u + u_1)(v + v_1)$, the cross-products will vanish, leaving $\Sigma\rho uv + \Sigma\rho u_1 v_1$. Now $\Sigma\rho u_1 v_1$ represents the rate of transfer of u-momentum by particles crossing a plane perpendicular to the y-axis, and is therefore equal to the internal stress usually denoted by p_{xy}. We have therefore to add to (53·4) the tensor formed by the internal stresses, bordered by zeroes. The summation can now be omitted, ρ referring to the whole density, and u, v, w to the average or mass-motion of macroscopic elements. Accordingly

$$T^{\mu\nu} = \begin{matrix} p_{xx} + \rho u^2, & p_{yx} + \rho vu, & p_{zx} + \rho wu, & \rho u \\ p_{xy} + \rho uv, & p_{yy} + \rho v^2, & p_{zy} + \rho wv, & \rho v \\ p_{xz} + \rho uw, & p_{yz} + \rho vw, & p_{zz} + \rho w^2, & \rho w \\ \rho u, & \rho v, & \rho w, & \rho \end{matrix} \quad \text{......(53·5)}.$$

Consider the equations

$$\frac{\partial T^{\mu\nu}}{\partial x_\nu} = 0 \quad \text{.................................(53·6)}.$$

Taking first $\mu = 4$, this gives by (53·5)

$$\frac{\partial(\rho u)}{\partial x} + \frac{\partial(\rho v)}{\partial y} + \frac{\partial(\rho w)}{\partial z} + \frac{\partial \rho}{\partial t} = 0 \quad \text{..............(53·71)},$$

which is the usual "equation of continuity" in hydrodynamics.

* In the sense of elementary mechanics, i.e. the simple difference of the velocities.

For $\mu = 1$, we have

$$\begin{aligned}\frac{\partial p_{xx}}{\partial x} + \frac{\partial p_{xy}}{\partial y} + \frac{\partial p_{xz}}{\partial z} &= -\left(\frac{\partial (\rho u^2)}{\partial x} + \frac{\partial (\rho uv)}{\partial y} + \frac{\partial (\rho uw)}{\partial z} + \frac{\partial (\rho u)}{\partial t}\right) \\ &= -u\left(\frac{\partial (\rho u)}{\partial x} + \frac{\partial (\rho v)}{\partial y} + \frac{\partial (\rho w)}{\partial z} + \frac{\partial \rho}{\partial t}\right) \\ &\quad -\rho\left(u\frac{\partial u}{\partial x} + v\frac{\partial u}{\partial y} + w\frac{\partial u}{\partial z} + \frac{\partial u}{\partial t}\right) \\ &= -\rho\frac{Du}{Dt} \qquad \text{.................................(53·72)}\end{aligned}$$

by (53·71). Du/Dt is the acceleration of the element of the fluid.

This is the well-known equation of hydrodynamics when no body-force is acting. (By adopting Galilean coordinates any field of force acting on the mass of the fluid has been removed.)

Equations (53·71) and (53·72) express directly the conservation of mass and momentum, so that for Galilean coordinates these principles are contained in

$$\partial T^{\mu\nu}/\partial x_\nu = 0.$$

In fact $\partial T^{\mu\nu}/\partial x_\nu$ represents the rate of creation of momentum and mass in unit volume. In classical hydrodynamics momentum may be created in the volume (i.e. may appear in the volume without having crossed the boundary) by the action of a body-force ρX, ρY, ρZ; and these terms are added on the right-hand side of (53·72). The creation of mass is considered impossible. Accordingly the more general equations of *classical hydrodynamics* are

$$\frac{\partial T^{\mu\nu}}{\partial x_\nu} = (\rho X, \rho Y, \rho Z, 0) \qquad \text{.....................(53·81).}$$

In the *special relativity theory* mass is equivalent to energy, and the body-forces by doing work on the particles will also create mass, so that

$$\frac{\partial T^{\mu\nu}}{\partial x_\nu} = (\rho X, \rho Y, \rho Z, \rho S) \text{.....................(53·82),}$$

where ρS is the work done by the forces ρX, ρY, ρZ. These older formulae are likely to be only approximate; and the exact formulae must be deduced by extending the general relativity theory to the case when fields of force are present, viz. to non-Galilean coordinates.

It is often convenient to use the mixed tensor T_μ^ν in place of $T^{\mu\nu}$. For Galilean coordinates we obtain from (53·5)*

$$\begin{array}{lllll} T_\mu^\nu = & -p_{xx} - \rho u^2, & -p_{yx} - \rho vu, & -p_{zx} - \rho wu, & \rho u \\ \ulcorner\!\!\rightarrow \mu & -p_{xy} - \rho uv, & -p_{yy} - \rho v^2, & -p_{zy} - \rho wv, & \rho v \\ \downarrow & -p_{xz} - \rho uw, & -p_{yz} - \rho vw, & -p_{zz} - \rho w^2, & \rho w \\ \nu & \quad -\rho u \quad , & \quad -\rho v \quad , & \quad -\rho w \quad , & \rho \end{array} \qquad \text{...(53·91).}$$

* E.g. $T_2^1 = g_{\sigma 2} T^{\sigma 1} = 0 - T^{21} + 0 + 0$.

The equation equivalent to (53·82) is then

$$\frac{\partial T_\mu^\nu}{\partial x_\nu} = (-\rho X, -\rho Y, -\rho Z, \rho S) \quad\text{.................(53·92).}$$

That is to say $\partial T_\mu^\nu/\partial x_\nu$ is the rate of creation of negative momentum and of positive mass or energy in unit volume.

54. New derivation of Einstein's law of gravitation.

We have found that for Galilean coordinates

$$\partial T^{\mu\nu}/\partial x_\nu = 0 \quad\text{..............................(54·1).}$$

This is evidently a particular case of the tensor equation

$$(T^{\mu\nu})_\nu = 0 \quad\text{..............................(54·21).}$$

Or we may use the equivalent equation

$$(T_\mu^\nu)_\nu = 0 \quad\text{..............................(54·22),}$$

which results from lowering the suffix μ. In other words the divergence of the energy-tensor vanishes.

Taking the view that energy, stress, and momentum belong to the world (space-time) and not to some extraneous substance in the world, we must identify the energy-tensor with some fundamental tensor, i.e. a tensor belonging to the fundamental series derived from $g_{\mu\nu}$.

The fact that the divergence of T_μ^ν vanishes points to an identification with $(G_\mu^\nu - \frac{1}{2}g_\mu^\nu G)$ whose divergence vanishes *identically* (§ 52). Accordingly we set

$$G_\mu^\nu - \tfrac{1}{2}g_\mu^\nu G = -8\pi T_\mu^\nu \quad\text{......................(54·3),}$$

the factor 8π being introduced for later convenience in coordinating the units.

To pass from (54·1) to (54·21) involves an appeal to the hypothetical Principle of Equivalence; but by taking (54·3) as our fundamental equation of gravitation (54·21) becomes an identity requiring no hypothetical assumption.

We thus arrive at the law of gravitation for continuous matter (46·6) but with a different justification. Appeal is now made to a Principle of Identification. Our deductive theory starts with the interval (introduced by the fundamental axiom of § 1), from which the tensor $g_{\mu\nu}$ is immediately obtained. By pure mathematics we derive other tensors $G_{\mu\nu}$, $B_{\mu\nu\sigma\rho}$, and if necessary more complicated tensors. These constitute our world-building material; and the aim of the deductive theory is to construct from this a world which functions in the same way as the known physical world. If we succeed, mass, momentum, stress, etc. must be the vulgar names for certain analytical quantities in the deductive theory; and it is this stage of naming the analytical tensors which is reached in (54·3). If the theory provides a tensor $G_\mu^\nu - \frac{1}{2}g_\mu^\nu G$ which behaves in exactly the same way as the tensor summarising the mass, momentum and stress of matter is observed to behave, it is difficult to see how anything more could be required of it*.

By means of (53·91) and (54·3) the physical quantities ρ, u, v, w, p_{xx} .. p_{zz} are identified in terms of the fundamental tensors of space-time. There are 10 of these physical quantities and 10 different components of $G_\mu^\nu - \frac{1}{2}g_\mu^\nu G$, so that the identification is just sufficient. It will be noticed that this identification gives a dynamical, not a kinematical definition of the velocity of matter u, v, w; it is appropriate, for example, to the case of a rotating homogeneous and continuous fly-wheel, in which there is no velocity of matter in the kinematical sense, although a dynamical velocity is indicated by its gyrostatic properties†. The connection with the ordinary kinematical velocity, which determines the direction of the world-line of a particle in four dimensions, is followed out in § 56.

Contracting (54·3) by setting $\nu = \mu$, and remembering that $g_\mu^\mu = 4$, we have

$$G = 8\pi T \quad \text{.........................(54·4)},$$

so that an equivalent form of (54·3) is

$$G_\mu^\nu = -8\pi(T_\mu^\nu - \tfrac{1}{2}g_\mu^\nu T) \quad \text{.........................(54·5)}.$$

When there is no material energy-tensor this gives

$$G_\mu^\nu = 0,$$

which is equivalent to Einstein's law $G_{\mu\nu} = 0$ for empty space.

According to the new point of view Einstein's law of gravitation does not impose any limitation on the basal structure of the world. $G_{\mu\nu}$ may vanish or it may not. If it vanishes we say that space is empty; if it does not vanish we say that momentum or energy is present; and our practical test whether space is occupied or not—whether momentum and energy exist there—is the test whether $G_{\mu\nu}$ exists or not‡.

Moreover it is not an accident that it should be this particular tensor which is capable of being recognised by us. It is because its divergence vanishes—because it satisfies the law of conservation—that it fulfils the primary condition for being recognised as substantial. If we are to surround ourselves with a perceptual world at all, we must recognise as substance that which has some element of permanence. We may not be able to explain how the mind recognises as substantial the world-tensor $G_\mu^\nu - \frac{1}{2}g_\mu^\nu G$, but we can see that it could not well recognise anything simpler. There are no doubt

* For a complete theory it would be necessary to show that matter as now defined has a tendency to aggregate into atoms leaving large tracts of the world vacant. The relativity theory has not yet succeeded in finding any clue to the phenomenon of atomicity.

† *Space, Time and Gravitation*, p. 194.

‡ We are dealing at present with mechanics only, so that we can scarcely discuss the part played by electromagnetic fields (light) in conveying to us the impression that space is occupied by something. But it may be noticed that the *crucial* test is mechanical. A real image has the optical properties but not the mechanical properties of a solid body.

minds which have not this predisposition to regard as substantial the things which are permanent; but we shut them up in lunatic asylums.

The invariant
$$T = g_{\mu\nu} T^{\mu\nu}$$
$$= g_{\mu\nu} \cdot \rho_0 \frac{dx_\mu}{ds} \frac{dx_\nu}{ds}$$
$$= \rho_0,$$
since
$$g_{\mu\nu} dx_\mu dx_\nu = ds^2.$$
Thus
$$G = 8\pi T = 8\pi\rho_0 \quad \text{.........................(54·6).}$$

Einstein and de Sitter obtain a naturally curved world by taking instead of (54·3)
$$G_\mu^\nu - \tfrac{1}{2} g_\mu^\nu (G - 2\lambda) = -8\pi T_\mu^\nu \quad \text{.................(54·71),}$$
where λ is a constant. Since the divergence of g_μ^ν or of $g^{\mu\nu}$ vanishes, the divergence of this more general form will also vanish, and the laws of conservation of mass and momentum are still satisfied identically. Contracting (54·71), we have
$$G - 4\lambda = 8\pi T = 8\pi\rho_0 \quad \text{.................. (54·72).}$$
For empty space $G = 4\lambda$, and $T_\mu^\nu = 0$, and thus the equation reduces to
$$G_\mu^\nu = \lambda g_\mu^\nu,$$
or
$$G_{\mu\nu} = \lambda g_{\mu\nu},$$
as in (37·4).

When account is taken of the stresses in continuous matter, or of the molecular motions in discontinuous matter, the proper-density of the matter requires rather careful definition. There are at least three possible definitions which can be justified; and we shall denote the corresponding quantities by $\rho_0, \rho_{00}, \rho_{000}$.

(1) We define
$$\rho_0 = T.$$
By reference to (54·6) it will be seen that this represents the sum of the densities of the particles with different motions, *each particle being referred to axes with respect to which it is itself at rest.*

(2) We can sum the densities for the different particles referring them all to axes which are at rest in the matter as a whole. The result is denoted by ρ_{00}. Accordingly
$$\rho_{00} = T_{44} \text{ referred to axes at rest in the matter as a whole.}$$

(3) If a perfect fluid is referred to axes with respect to which it is at rest, the stresses p_{xx}, p_{yy}, p_{zz} are each equal to the hydrostatic pressure p. The energy-tensor (53·5) accordingly becomes
$$T^{\mu\nu} = \begin{matrix} p & 0 & 0 & 0 \\ 0 & p & 0 & 0 \\ 0 & 0 & p & 0 \\ 0 & 0 & 0 & \rho_{00} \end{matrix}$$

Writing $\rho_{00} = \rho_{000} - p$, the pressure-terms give a tensor $-g^{\mu\nu}p$. Accordingly we have the tensor equation applicable to any coordinate-system

$$T^{\mu\nu} = \rho_{000} \frac{dx_\mu}{ds} \frac{dx_\nu}{ds} - g^{\mu\nu} p \quad \text{.....................(54·81).}$$

Thus if the energy-tensor is analysed into two terms depending respectively on two invariants specifying the state of the fluid, we must take these invariants to be p and ρ_{000}.

The three quantities are related by

$$\rho_0 = \rho_{00} - 3p = \rho_{000} - 4p \quad \text{.....................(54·82).}$$

If a fluid is *incompressible*, i.e. if the closeness of packing of the particles is independent of p, the condition must be that ρ_0 is constant*. Incompressibility is concerned with constancy not of mass-density but of particle-density, so that no account should be taken of increases of mass of the particles due to motion relative to the centre of mass of the matter as a whole.

For a liquid or solid the stress does not arise entirely from molecular motions, but is due mainly to direct repulsive forces between the molecules held in proximity. These stresses must, of course, be included in the energy-tensor (which would otherwise not be conserved) just as the gaseous pressure is included. It will be shown later that if these repulsive forces are Maxwellian electrical forces they contribute nothing to ρ_0, so that ρ_0 arises entirely from the molecules individually (probably from the electrons individually) and is independent of the circumstances of packing.

Since ρ_0 is the most useful of the three quantities in theoretical investigations we shall in future call it the proper-density (or invariant density) without qualification.

55. The force.

By (51·2) the equation $(T_\mu^\nu)_\nu = 0$ becomes

$$\frac{1}{\sqrt{-g}} \frac{\partial}{\partial x_\nu} (T_\mu^\nu \sqrt{-g}) = \{\mu\nu, \alpha\}\, T_\alpha^\nu \quad \text{.................(55·1).}$$

Let us choose coordinates so that $\sqrt{-g} = 1$; then

$$\frac{\partial}{\partial x_\nu} T_\mu^\nu = \{\mu\nu, \alpha\}\, T_\alpha^\nu \quad \text{...........................(55·2).}$$

In most applications the velocity of the matter is extremely small compared with the velocity of light, so that on the right of this equation $T_4^4 = \rho$ is much larger than the other components of T_α^ν. As a first approximation we neglect the other components, so that

$$\frac{\partial}{\partial x_\nu} T_\mu^\nu = \{\mu 4, 4\}\, \rho \quad \text{...........................(55·3).}$$

* Many writers seem to have defined incompressibility by the condition ρ_{00} = constant. This is surely a most misleading definition.

This will agree with classical mechanics (53·92) if

$$-X,\ -Y,\ -Z = \{14, 4\},\ \{24, 4\},\ \{34, 4\} \qquad \text{.............(55·4)}$$

The 3-index symbols can thus be interpreted as components of the field of force. The three quoted are the leading components which act proportionately to the mass or energy; the others, neglected in Newtonian mechanics, are evoked by the momenta and stresses which form the remaining components of the energy-tensor.

The limitation $\sqrt{-g} = 1$ is not essential if we take account of the confusion of tensor-densities with tensors referred to at the end of § 49. It will be remembered that the force (X, Y, Z) occurs because we attribute to our mesh-system an abstract Galilean geometry which is not the natural geometry. Either inadvertently or deliberately we place ourselves in the position of an observer who has mistaken his non-Galilean mesh-system for rectangular coordinates and time. We therefore mistake the unit mesh for the unit of natural volume, and the density of the energy-tensor $\mathfrak{T}_\mu^\nu$ reckoned per unit mesh is mistaken for the energy-tensor itself T_μ^ν reckoned per unit natural volume. For this reason the conservation of the supposed energy-tensor should be expressed analytically by $\partial \mathfrak{T}_\mu^\nu / \partial x_\nu = 0$; and when a field of force intervenes the equations of classical hydrodynamics should be written

$$\frac{\partial}{\partial x_\nu} \mathfrak{T}_\mu^\nu = \mathfrak{T}_4^4 (-X,\ -Y,\ -Z,\ 0) \qquad \text{.............(55·51)},$$

the supposed density ρ being really the "density-density" $\rho\sqrt{-g}$ or $\mathfrak{T}_4^4$*.

Since (55·1) is equivalent to

$$\frac{\partial}{\partial x_\nu} \mathfrak{T}_\mu^\nu = \{\mu\nu, \alpha\}\, \mathfrak{T}_\alpha^\nu \qquad \text{.......................(55·52)},$$

the result (55·4) follows irrespective of the value of $\sqrt{-g}$.

The alternative formula (51·51) may be used to calculate $T^\nu_{\mu\nu}$, giving

$$\frac{\partial}{\partial x_\nu} \mathfrak{T}_\mu^\nu = \tfrac{1}{2} \mathfrak{T}^{\alpha\beta} \frac{\partial g_{\alpha\beta}}{\partial x_\mu} \qquad \text{........ .... (55·6)}.$$

Retaining on the right only $\mathfrak{T}^{44}$, we have by comparison with (55·51)

$$X,\ Y,\ Z = -\frac{1}{2}\frac{\partial g_{44}}{\partial x},\ -\frac{1}{2}\frac{\partial g_{44}}{\partial y},\ -\frac{1}{2}\frac{\partial g_{44}}{\partial z} \qquad \text{............(55·7)}.$$

* It might seem preferable to avoid this confusion by immediately identifying the energy, momentum and stress with the components of $\mathfrak{T}_\mu^\nu$, instead of adopting the roundabout procedure of identifying them with T_μ^ν and noting that in practice $\mathfrak{T}_\mu^\nu$ is inadvertently substituted. The inconvenience is that we do not always attribute abstract Galilean geometry to our coordinate-system. For example, if polar coordinates are used, there is no tendency to confuse the mesh $dr\,d\theta\,d\phi$ with the natural volume $r^2 \sin\theta\, dr\, d\theta\, d\phi$; in such a case it is much more convenient to take T_μ^ν as the measure of the density of energy, momentum and stress. It is when by our attitude of mind we attribute abstract Galilean geometry to coordinates whose natural geometry is not accurately Galilean, that the automatic substitution of $\mathfrak{T}_\mu^\nu$ for the quantity intended to represent T_μ^ν occurs.

Hence, for a static coordinate-system

$$Xdx + Ydy + Zdz = -\frac{1}{2}\left(\frac{\partial g_{44}}{\partial x}dx + \frac{\partial g_{44}}{\partial y}dy + \frac{\partial g_{44}}{\partial z}dz\right)$$
$$= -\tfrac{1}{2}dg_{44},$$

so that X, Y, Z are derivable from a potential

$$\Omega = -\tfrac{1}{2}g_{44} + \text{const.}$$

Choosing the constant so that $g_{44} = 1$ when $\Omega = 0$

$$g_{44} = 1 - 2\Omega \quad\text{.............................(55·8).}$$

Special cases of this result will be found in (15·4) and (38·8), Ω being the potential of the centrifugal force and of the Newtonian gravitational force respectively.

Let us now briefly review the principal steps in our new derivation of the laws of mechanics and gravitation. We concentrate attention on the world-tensor T_μ^ν *defined* by

$$T_\mu^\nu = -\frac{1}{8\pi}(G_\mu^\nu - \tfrac{1}{2}g_\mu^\nu G).$$

The question arises how this tensor would be recognised in nature—what names has the practical observer given to its components? We suppose tentatively that when Galilean or natural coordinates are used T_4^4 is recognised as the amount of mass or energy per unit volume, T_1^4, T_2^4, T_3^4 as the negative momentum per unit volume, and the remaining components contain the stresses according to the detailed specifications in (53·91). This can only be tested by examining whether the components of T_μ^ν do actually obey the laws which mass, momentum and stress are known by observation to obey. For natural coordinates the empirical laws are expressed by $\partial T_\mu^\nu/\partial x_\nu = 0$, which is satisfied because our tensor from its definition has been proved to satisfy $(T_\mu^\nu)_\nu = 0$ identically. When the coordinates are not natural, the identity $T_{\mu\nu}^\nu = 0$ gives the more general law

$$\frac{\partial}{\partial x_\nu}\mathfrak{T}_\mu^\nu = \frac{1}{2}\frac{\partial g_{\alpha\beta}}{\partial x_\mu}\mathfrak{T}^{\alpha\beta}.$$

We attribute an abstract Galilean geometry to these coordinates, and should accordingly identify the components of T_μ^ν as before, just as though the coordinates were natural; but owing to the resulting confusion of unit mesh with unit natural volume, the tensor-densities $\mathfrak{T}_1^4$, $\mathfrak{T}_2^4$, $\mathfrak{T}_3^4$, $\mathfrak{T}_4^4$ will now be taken to represent the negative momentum and energy per unit volume.

In accordance with the definition of force as rate of change of momentum, the quantity on the right will be recognised as the (negative) body-force acting on unit volume, the three components of the force being given by $\mu = 1, 2, 3$. When the velocity of the matter is very small compared with the velocity of light as in most ordinary problems, we need only consider on the right the component $\mathfrak{T}^{44}$ or ρ; and the force is then due to a field of acceleration of the usual type with components $-\frac{1}{2}\partial g_{44}/\partial x_1$, $-\frac{1}{2}\partial g_{44}/\partial x_2$, $-\frac{1}{2}\partial g_{44}/\partial x_3$. The potential Ω of the field of acceleration is thus connected with g_{44} by the relation $g_{44} = 1 - 2\Omega$. When this approximation is not sufficient there is no simple field of acceleration; the acceleration of the matter depends not only on its position but also on its velocity and even on its state of stress. Einstein's law of gravitation for empty space $G_{\mu\nu} = 0$ follows at once from the above identification of T^{ν}_{μ}.

56. Dynamics of a particle.

An isolated particle is a narrow tube in four dimensions containing a non-zero energy-tensor and surrounded by a region where the energy-tensor is zero. The tube is the world-line or track of the particle in space-time.

The momentum and mass of the particle are obtained by integrating $\mathfrak{T}^4_\mu$ over a three-dimensional volume; if the result is written in the form

$$-Mu, \quad -Mv, \quad -Mw, \quad M,$$

then M is the mass (relative to the coordinate system), and (u, v, w) is the *dynamical velocity* of the particle, i.e. the ratio of the momenta to the mass.

The *kinematical velocity* of the particle is given by the direction of the tube in four dimensions, viz. $\left(\frac{dx_1}{dx_4}, \frac{dx_2}{dx_4}, \frac{dx_3}{dx_4}\right)$ along the tube. For completely continuous matter there is no division of the energy-tensor into tubes and the notion of kinematical velocity does not arise.

It does not seem to be possible to deduce without special assumptions that the dynamical velocity of a particle is equal to the kinematical velocity. The law of conservation merely shows that (Mu, Mv, Mw, M) is constant along the tube when no field of force is acting; it does not show that the direction of this vector is the direction of the tube.

I think there is no doubt that in nature the dynamical and kinematical velocities are the same, but the reason for this must be sought in the symmetrical properties of the ultimate particles of matter. If we assume as in § 38 that the particle is the nucleus of a symmetrical field, the result becomes obvious. A symmetrical particle which is kinematically at rest cannot have any momentum since there is no preferential direction in which the momentum could point; in that case the tube is along the t-axis, and so also is the vector $(0, 0, 0, M)$. It is not necessary to assume complete spherical symmetry; three perpendicular planes of symmetry would suffice. The ultimate particle may for example have the symmetry of an anchor-ring.

It might perhaps be considered sufficient to point out that a "particle" in practical dynamics always consists of a large number of ultimate particles or atoms, so that the symmetry may be merely a consequence of haphazard averages. But we shall find in § 80, that the same difficulty occurs in understanding how an electrical field affects the direction of the world-line of a charged particle, and the two problems seem to be precisely analogous. In the electrical problem the motions of the ultimate particles (electrons) have been experimented on individually, and there has been no opportunity of introducing the symmetry by averaging. I think therefore that the symmetry exists in each particle independently.

It seems necessary to suppose that it is an essential condition for the existence of an actual particle that it should be the nucleus of a *symmetrical* field, and its world-line must be so directed and curved as to assure this symmetry. A satisfactory explanation of this property will be reached in § 66.

With this understanding we may use the equation (53·1), involving kinematical velocity,

$$T^{\mu\nu} = \rho_0 \frac{dx_\mu}{ds} \frac{dx_\nu}{ds} \qquad \text{.........................(56·1)},$$

in place of (53·4), involving dynamical velocity. From the identity $T^{\mu\nu}_{\nu} = 0$, we have by (51·41)

$$\frac{\partial}{\partial x_\nu}(T^{\mu\nu}\sqrt{-g}) = -\{\alpha\nu, \mu\} T^{\alpha\nu}\sqrt{-g} \qquad \text{.............(56·2)}.$$

Integrate this through a very small four-dimensional volume. The left-hand side can be integrated once, giving

$$\left[\iiint T^{\mu 1}\sqrt{-g}\, dx_2 dx_3 dx_4 + \iiint T^{\mu 2}\sqrt{-g}\, dx_1 dx_3 dx_4 + \ldots\right]$$

$$= -\iiiint \{\alpha\nu, \mu\} T^{\alpha\nu} . \sqrt{-g}\, d\tau \qquad \text{.....................(56·3)}.$$

Suppose that in this volume there is only a single particle, so that the energy-tensor vanishes everywhere except in a narrow tube. By (56·1) the quadruple integral becomes

$$-\iiiint \{\alpha\nu, \mu\} \frac{dx_\alpha}{ds}\frac{dx_\nu}{ds} \rho_0 \sqrt{-g}\, d\tau = -\{\alpha\beta, \mu\} \frac{dx_\alpha}{ds}\frac{dx_\beta}{ds} m\, ds \ldots\text{(56·4)},$$

since $\rho_0\sqrt{-g}\,d\tau = \rho_0 dW . ds = dm . ds$, where dm is the proper-mass.

On the left the triple integrals vanish except at the two points where the world-line intersects the boundary of the region. For convenience we draw the boundary near these two points in the planes $dx_1 = 0$, so that only the first of the four integrals survives. The left-hand side of (56·3) becomes

$$\left[\iiint \rho_0 \sqrt{-g} \frac{dx_\mu}{ds}\frac{dx_1}{ds} dx_2 dx_3 dx_4\right] \qquad \text{...............(56·51)},$$

the bracket denoting the difference at the two ends of the world-line.

The geometrical volume of the oblique cylinder cut off from the tube by sections $dx_2 dx_3 dx_4$ at a distance apart ds measured along the tube is

$$\frac{dx_1}{ds} . ds\, dx_2 dx_3 dx_4.$$

Multiplying by $\rho_0\sqrt{-g}$ we get the amount of ρ_0 contained*, which is $dmds$. Hence (56·51) reduces to

$$\left[m\frac{dx_\mu}{ds}\right].$$

The difference at the two limits is

$$\frac{d}{ds}\left(m\frac{dx_\mu}{ds}\right)ds \quad\text{.........................(56·52)},$$

where ds is now the length of track between the two limits as in (56·4).

By (56·4) and (56·52) the equation reduces to

$$\frac{d}{ds}\left(m\frac{dx_\mu}{ds}\right) = -m\,\{\alpha\beta,\mu\}\frac{dx_\alpha}{ds}\frac{dx_\beta}{ds} \quad\text{...............(56·6)}.$$

Provided that m is constant this gives the equations of a geodesic (28·5), showing that the track of an isolated particle is a geodesic. The constancy of m can be proved formally as follows—

From (56·6)

$$mg_{\mu\nu}\frac{dx_\nu}{ds}\cdot\frac{d}{ds}\left(m\frac{dx_\mu}{ds}\right) = -m^2[\alpha\beta,\nu]\frac{dx_\nu}{ds}\frac{dx_\alpha}{ds}\frac{dx_\beta}{ds}$$

$$= -\tfrac{1}{2}m^2\frac{\partial g_{\alpha\nu}}{\partial x_\beta}\frac{dx_\beta}{ds}\frac{dx_\alpha}{ds}\frac{dx_\nu}{ds}$$

$$= -\tfrac{1}{2}m^2\frac{dg_{\alpha\nu}}{ds}\cdot\frac{dx_\alpha}{ds}\frac{dx_\nu}{ds}$$

$$= -\tfrac{1}{2}m^2\frac{dg_{\mu\nu}}{ds}\frac{dx_\mu}{ds}\frac{dx_\nu}{ds}.$$

Adding the same equation with μ and ν interchanged

$$g_{\mu\nu}\,.\,m\frac{dx_\nu}{ds}\cdot\frac{d}{ds}\left(m\frac{dx_\mu}{ds}\right) + g_{\mu\nu}\,.\,m\frac{dx_\mu}{ds}\cdot\frac{d}{ds}\left(m\frac{dx_\nu}{ds}\right) + m\,.\frac{dx_\mu}{ds}\,.\,m\frac{dx_\nu}{ds}\cdot\frac{dg_{\mu\nu}}{ds} = 0$$

or

$$\frac{d}{ds}\left(g_{\mu\nu}\,.\,m\frac{dx_\mu}{ds}\,.\,m\frac{dx_\nu}{ds}\right) = 0.$$

By (22·1) this gives $dm^2/ds = 0$. Accordingly the invariant mass of an isolated particle remains constant.

The present proof does not add very much to the argument in § 17 that the particle follows a geodesic because that is the only track which is absolutely defined. Here we postulate symmetrical properties for the particle (referred to proper-coordinates), this has the effect that there is no means of fixing a direction in which it could deviate from a geodesic. For further enlightenment we must wait until Chapter V.

* The *amount* of density in a four-dimensional volume is, of course, not the mass but a quantity of dimensions mass × time.

57. Equality of gravitational and inertial mass. Gravitational waves.

The term gravitational mass can be used in two senses; it may refer to (*a*) the response of a particle to a gravitational field of force, or (*b*) to its power of producing a gravitational field of force. In the sense (*a*) its identity with inertial mass is axiomatic in our theory, the separation of the field of force from the inertial field being dependent on our arbitrary choice of an abstract geometry. We accordingly use the term exclusively in the sense (*b*), and we have shown in §§ 38, 39 that the constant of integration m represents the gravitational mass. But in the present discussion the ρ_0 which occurs in the tensor $T_{\mu\nu}$ refers to inertial mass defined by the conservation of energy and momentum. The connection is made *via* equation (54·3), where on the left the mass appears in terms of $g_{\mu\nu}$, i.e. in terms of its power of exerting (or being accompanied by) a gravitational field; and on the right it appears in the energy-tensor which comprises ρ_0 according to (53·1). But it will be remembered that the factor 8π in (54·3) was chosen arbitrarily, and this must now be justified*. This coefficient of proportionality corresponds to the Newtonian constant of gravitation.

The proportionality of gravitational and inertial mass, and the "constant of gravitation" which connects them, are conceptions belonging to the approximate Newtonian scheme, and therefore presuppose that the gravitational fields are so weak that the equations can be treated as linear. For more intense fields the Newtonian terminology becomes ambiguous, and it is idle to inquire whether the constant of gravitation really remains constant when the mass is enormously great. Accordingly we here discuss only the limiting case of very weak fields, and set

$$g_{\mu\nu} = \delta_{\mu\nu} + h_{\mu\nu} \quad \text{..........................(57·1)},$$

where $\delta_{\mu\nu}$ represents Galilean values, and $h_{\mu\nu}$ will be a small quantity of the first order whose square is neglected. The derivatives of the $g_{\mu\nu}$ will be small quantities of the first order.

We have, correct to the first order,

$$G_{\mu\nu} = g^{\sigma\rho} B_{\mu\nu\sigma\rho} = \tfrac{1}{2} g^{\sigma\rho} \left(\frac{\partial^2 g_{\mu\nu}}{\partial x_\sigma \partial x_\rho} + \frac{\partial^2 g_{\sigma\rho}}{\partial x_\mu \partial x_\nu} - \frac{\partial^2 g_{\mu\sigma}}{\partial x_\nu \partial x_\rho} - \frac{\partial^2 g_{\nu\rho}}{\partial x_\mu \partial x_\sigma} \right) \text{...(57·2)}$$

by (34·5).

We shall try to satisfy this by breaking it up into two equations

$$G_{\mu\nu} = \tfrac{1}{2} g^{\sigma\rho} \frac{\partial^2 g_{\mu\nu}}{\partial x_\sigma \partial x_\rho} \quad \text{..........................(57·31)}$$

and

$$0 = g^{\sigma\rho} \left(\frac{\partial^2 g_{\sigma\rho}}{\partial x_\mu \partial x_\nu} - \frac{\partial^2 g_{\mu\sigma}}{\partial x_\nu \partial x_\rho} - \frac{\partial^2 g_{\nu\rho}}{\partial x_\mu \partial x_\sigma} \right) \quad \text{..............(57·32)}.$$

* It has been justified in § 46, which has a close connection with the present paragraph; but the argument is now proceeding in the reverse direction.

The second equation becomes, correct to the first order,

$$0 = \delta^{\sigma\rho}\left(\frac{\partial^2 h_{\sigma\rho}}{\partial x_\mu \partial x_\nu} - \frac{\partial^2 h_{\mu\sigma}}{\partial x_\nu \partial x_\rho} - \frac{\partial^2 h_{\nu\rho}}{\partial x_\mu \partial x_\sigma}\right)$$

$$= \frac{\partial^2 h}{\partial x_\mu \partial x_\nu} - \frac{\partial^2 h^\rho_\mu}{\partial x_\nu \partial x_\rho} - \frac{\partial^2 h^\sigma_\nu}{\partial x_\mu \partial x_\sigma},$$

where $h^\rho_\mu = \delta^{\sigma\rho} h_{\mu\sigma}, \quad h = h^\rho_\rho = \delta^{\sigma\rho} h_{\sigma\rho}$.

This is satisfied if

$$\frac{\partial h^\alpha_\mu}{\partial x_\alpha} = \frac{1}{2}\frac{\partial h}{\partial x_\mu}$$

or $$\frac{\partial}{\partial x_\alpha}(h^\alpha_\mu - \tfrac{1}{2}\delta^\alpha_\mu h) = 0 \quad \text{.....................(57·4)}.$$

The other equation (57·31) may be written

$$\Box h_{\mu\nu} = 2G_{\mu\nu}$$

or $$\Box h^\alpha_\mu = 2G^\alpha_\mu,$$

showing that G^α_μ is a small quantity of the first order. Hence

$$\Box(h^\alpha_\mu - \tfrac{1}{2}\delta^\alpha_\mu h) = 2(G^\alpha_\mu - \tfrac{1}{2}g^\alpha_\mu G)$$

$$= -16\pi T^\alpha_\mu \quad \text{.........................(57·5)}.$$

This "equation of wave-motion" can be integrated. Since we are dealing with small quantities of the first order, the effect of the deviations from Galilean geometry will only affect the results to the second order; accordingly the well-known solution* may be used, viz.

$$h^\alpha_\mu - \tfrac{1}{2}\delta^\alpha_\mu h = \frac{1}{4\pi}\int \frac{(-16\pi T^\alpha_\mu)' \, dV'}{r'} \quad \text{.................(57·6)},$$

the integral being taken over each element of space-volume dV' at a coordinate distance r' from the point considered and at a time $t - r'$, i.e. at a time such that waves propagated from dV' with unit velocity can reach the point at the time considered.

If we calculate from (57·6) the value of

$$\frac{\partial}{\partial x_\alpha}(h^\alpha_\mu - \tfrac{1}{2}\delta^\alpha_\mu h),$$

the operator $\partial/\partial x_\alpha$ indicates a displacement in space and time of the point considered, involving a change of r'. We may, however, keep r' constant on the right-hand side and displace to the same extent the element dV' where $(T^\alpha_\mu)'$ is calculated. Thus

$$\frac{\partial}{\partial x_\alpha}(h^\alpha_\mu - \tfrac{1}{2}\delta^\alpha_\mu h) = -4\int\left\{\frac{\partial}{\partial x_\alpha}(T^\alpha_\mu)\right\}' \frac{dV'}{r'}.$$

But by (55·2) $\partial T^\alpha_\mu/\partial x_\alpha$ is of the second order of small quantities, so that to our approximation (57·4) is satisfied.

* Rayleigh, *Theory of Sound*, vol. II, p. 104, equation (3).

The result is that $\Box h_{\mu\nu} = 2G_{\mu\nu}$ ....(57·7)

satisfies the gravitational equations correctly to the first order, because both the equations into which we have divided (57·2) then become satisfied. Of course there may be other solutions of (57·2), which do not satisfy (57·31) and (57·32) separately.

For a static field (57·7) reduces to

$$-\nabla^2 h_{\mu\nu} = 2G_{\mu\nu}$$
$$= -16\pi (T_{\mu\nu} - \tfrac{1}{2}\delta_{\mu\nu} T) \qquad \text{by (54·5)}.$$

Also for matter at rest $T = T_{44} = \rho$ (the *inertial* density) and the other components of $T_{\mu\nu}$ vanish; thus

$$\nabla^2 (h_{11}, h_{22}, h_{33}, h_{44}) = 8\pi\rho\,(1, 1, 1, 1).$$

For a single particle the solution of this equation is well known to be

$$h_{11}, h_{22}, h_{33}, h_{44} = -\frac{2m}{r}.$$

Hence by (57·1) the complete expression for the interval is

$$ds^2 = -\left(1 + \frac{2m}{r}\right)(dx^2 + dy^2 + dz^2) + \left(1 - \frac{2m}{r}\right)dt^2 \quad \text{......(57·8)},$$

agreeing with (46·15). But m as here introduced is the inertial mass and not merely a constant of integration. We have shown in §§ 38, 39 that the m in (46·15) is the gravitational mass reckoned with constant of gravitation unity. Hence we see that inertial mass and gravitational mass are equal and expressed in the same units, when the constant of proportionality between the world-tensor and the physical-tensor is chosen to be 8π as in (54·3).

In empty space (57·7) becomes

$$\Box h_{\mu\nu} = 0,$$

showing that the deviations of the gravitational potentials are propagated as waves with unit velocity, i.e. the velocity of light (§ 30). But it must be remembered that this representation of the propagation, though always permissible, is not unique. In replacing (57·2) by (57·31) and (57·32), we introduce a restriction which amounts to choosing a special coordinate-system. Other solutions of (57·2) are possible, corresponding to other coordinate-systems. All the coordinate-systems differ from Galilean coordinates by small quantities of the first order. The potentials $g_{\mu\nu}$ pertain not only to the gravitational influence which has objective reality, but also to the coordinate-system which we select arbitrarily. We can "propagate" coordinate-changes with the *speed of thought*, and these may be mixed up at will with the more dilatory propagation discussed above. There does not seem to be any way of distinguishing a physical and a conventional part in the changes of the $g_{\mu\nu}$.

The statement that in the relativity theory gravitational waves are propagated with the speed of light has, I believe, been based entirely on the foregoing investigation; but it will be seen that it is only true in a very conventional sense. If coordinates are chosen so as to satisfy a certain condition which has no very clear geometrical importance, the speed is that of light; if the coordinates are slightly different the speed is altogether different from that of light. The result stands or falls by the choice of coordinates and, so far as can be judged, the coordinates here used were purposely introduced in order to obtain the simplification which results from representing the propagation as occurring with the speed of light. The argument thus follows a vicious circle.

Must we then conclude that the speed of propagation of gravitation is necessarily a conventional conception without absolute meaning? I think not. The speed of gravitation is quite definite; only the problem of determining it does not seem to have yet been tackled correctly. To obtain a speed independent of the coordinate-system chosen, we must consider the propagation not of a world-tensor but of a world-invariant. The simplest world-invariant for this purpose is $B^{\epsilon}_{\mu\nu\sigma}B^{\mu\nu\sigma}_{\epsilon}$, since G and $G_{\mu\nu}G^{\mu\nu}$ vanish in empty space. It is scarcely possible to treat of the propagation of an isolated pulse of gravitational influence, because there seems to be no way of starting a sudden pulse without calling in supernatural agencies which violate the equations of mechanics. We may consider the regular train of waves caused by the earth in its motion round the sun. At a distant point in the ecliptic $B^{\epsilon}_{\mu\nu\sigma}B^{\mu\nu\sigma}_{\epsilon}$ will vary with an annual periodicity; if it has a maximum or minimum value at the instant when the earth is *seen* to transit the sun, the inference is that the wave of disturbance has travelled to us at the same speed as the light. (It may perhaps be objected that there is no proof that the disturbance has been propagated from the earth; it might be a stationary wave permanently located round the sun which is as much the cause as the effect of the earth's annual motion. I do not think the objection is valid, but it requires examination.) There does not seem to be any grave difficulty in treating this problem; and it deserves investigation.

58. Lagrangian form of the gravitational equations.

The Lagrangian function $\mathfrak{L}$ is defined by

$$\mathfrak{L} = g^{\mu\nu}\sqrt{-g}\,(\{\mu\alpha, \beta\}\{\nu\beta, \alpha\} - \{\mu\nu, \alpha\}\{\alpha\beta, \beta\}) \quad \ldots\ldots\ldots(58\cdot1),$$

which forms part of the expression for $\mathfrak{G}\,(= g^{\mu\nu}G_{\mu\nu}\sqrt{-g})$. For any small variation of $\mathfrak{L}$

$$\begin{aligned}\delta\mathfrak{L} = {} & \{\mu\alpha, \beta\}\,\delta(g^{\mu\nu}\sqrt{-g}\,\{\nu\beta, \alpha\}) + \{\nu\beta, \alpha\}\,\delta(g^{\mu\nu}\sqrt{-g}\,\{\mu\alpha, \beta\}) \\ & - \{\mu\nu, \alpha\}\,\delta(g^{\mu\nu}\sqrt{-g}\,\{\alpha\beta, \beta\}) - \{\alpha\beta, \beta\}\,\delta(g^{\mu\nu}\sqrt{-g}\,\{\mu\nu, \alpha\}) \\ & - (\{\mu\alpha, \beta\}\{\nu\beta, \alpha\} - \{\mu\nu, \alpha\}\{\alpha\beta, \beta\})\,\delta(g^{\mu\nu}\sqrt{-g}) \quad \ldots\ldots\ldots(58\cdot2)\end{aligned}$$

The first term in (58·2)

$$= \tfrac{1}{2}\{\mu\alpha, \beta\}\, \delta\left(\sqrt{-g}\,.\, g^{\mu\nu} g^{\alpha\epsilon}\left(\frac{\partial g_{\nu\epsilon}}{\partial x_\beta} + \frac{\partial g_{\beta\epsilon}}{\partial x_\nu} - \frac{\partial g_{\beta\nu}}{\partial x_\epsilon}\right)\right)$$

$$= \tfrac{1}{2}\{\mu\alpha, \beta\}\, \delta\left(\sqrt{-g}\,.\, g^{\mu\nu} g^{\alpha\epsilon}\frac{\partial g_{\nu\epsilon}}{\partial x_\beta}\right)$$

$$= -\tfrac{1}{2}\{\mu\alpha, \beta\}\, \delta\left(\sqrt{-g}\,.\, \frac{\partial g^{\mu\alpha}}{\partial x_\beta}\right) \quad \text{by (35·11)}$$

$$= -\tfrac{1}{2}\{\mu\nu, \alpha\}\, \delta\left(\sqrt{-g}\,.\, \frac{\partial g^{\mu\nu}}{\partial x_\alpha}\right) \quad \text{.........................(58·31).}$$

The second term reduces to the same.

The third term becomes by (35·4)

$$-\{\mu\nu, \alpha\}\, \delta\left(g^{\mu\nu} \frac{\partial}{\partial x_\alpha}\sqrt{-g}\right) \quad \text{..................(58·32)}$$

In the fourth term we have

$$g^{\mu\nu}\sqrt{-g}\,\{\mu\nu, \alpha\} = -\frac{\partial}{\partial x_\nu}(g^{\alpha\nu}\sqrt{-g}),$$

by (51·41), since the divergence of $g^{\alpha\nu}$ vanishes. Hence with some alterations of dummy suffixes, the fourth term becomes

$$\{\nu\beta, \beta\}\, g^\alpha_\mu\, \delta\left(\frac{\partial}{\partial x_\alpha}(g^{\mu\nu}\sqrt{-g})\right) \quad \text{..................(58·33).}$$

Substituting these values in (58·2), we have

$$\delta\mathfrak{L} = [-\{\mu\nu, \alpha\} + g^\alpha_\mu\{\nu\beta, \beta\}]\, \delta\left(\frac{\partial}{\partial x_\alpha}(g^{\mu\nu}\sqrt{-g})\right)$$

$$-[\{\mu\alpha, \beta\}\{\nu\beta, \alpha\} - \{\mu\nu, \alpha\}\{\alpha\beta, \beta\}]\, \delta(g^{\mu\nu}\sqrt{-g}) \text{...(58·4).}$$

We write $$\mathfrak{g}^{\mu\nu} = g^{\mu\nu}\sqrt{-g}\,; \quad \mathfrak{g}^{\mu\nu}_\alpha = \frac{\partial}{\partial x_\alpha}(g^{\mu\nu}\sqrt{-g}) \quad \text{............(58·45).}$$

Then when $\mathfrak{L}$ is expressed as a function of the $\mathfrak{g}^{\mu\nu}$ and $\mathfrak{g}^{\mu\nu}_\alpha$, (58·4) gives

$$\frac{\partial\mathfrak{L}}{\partial\mathfrak{g}^{\mu\nu}} = -[\{\mu\alpha, \beta\}\{\nu\beta, \alpha\} - \{\mu\nu, \alpha\}\{\alpha\beta, \beta\}] \quad \text{.........(58·51),}$$

$$\frac{\partial\mathfrak{L}}{\partial\mathfrak{g}^{\mu\nu}_\alpha} = [-\{\mu\nu, \alpha\} + g^\alpha_\mu\{\nu\beta, \beta\}] \quad \text{..........(58·52)}$$

Comparing with (37·2) we have

$$G_{\mu\nu} = \frac{\partial}{\partial x_\alpha}\frac{\partial\mathfrak{L}}{\partial\mathfrak{g}^{\mu\nu}_\alpha} - \frac{\partial\mathfrak{L}}{\partial\mathfrak{g}^{\mu\nu}} \quad \text{......................(58·6).}$$

This form resembles that of Lagrange's equations in dynamics. Regarding $\mathfrak{g}^{\mu\nu}$ as a coordinate q, and x_α as a four-dimensional time t, so that $\mathfrak{g}^{\mu\nu}_\alpha$ is a velocity q', the gravitational equations $G_{\mu\nu} = 0$ correspond to the well-known form

$$\frac{d}{dt}\frac{\partial\mathfrak{L}}{\partial q'} - \frac{\partial\mathfrak{L}}{\partial q} = 0.$$

The two following formulae express important properties of the Lagrangian function:

$$\mathfrak{g}^{\mu\nu}\frac{\partial\mathfrak{L}}{\partial\mathfrak{g}^{\mu\nu}} = -\mathfrak{L} \quad \text{..........................(58·71)},$$

$$\mathfrak{g}^{\mu\nu}_{\alpha}\frac{\partial\mathfrak{L}}{\partial\mathfrak{g}^{\mu\nu}_{\alpha}} = 2\mathfrak{L} \quad \text{..........................(58·72)}.$$

The first is obvious from (58·51). To prove the second, we have

$$\mathfrak{g}^{\mu\nu}_{\alpha} = \frac{\partial}{\partial x_\alpha}(g^{\mu\nu}\sqrt{-g}) = \sqrt{-g}\frac{\partial g^{\mu\nu}}{\partial x_\alpha} + g^{\mu\nu}\sqrt{-g}\,\{\alpha\epsilon, \epsilon\}$$

$$= \sqrt{-g}\,[-\{\epsilon\alpha, \mu\}\,g^{\epsilon\nu} - \{\epsilon\alpha, \nu\}\,g^{\mu\epsilon} + \{\alpha\epsilon, \epsilon\}\,g^{\mu\nu}]$$

by (30·1) since the covariant derivative of $g^{\mu\nu}$ vanishes.

Hence by (58·52)

$$\mathfrak{g}^{\mu\nu}_{\alpha}\frac{\partial\mathfrak{L}}{\partial\mathfrak{g}^{\mu\nu}_{\alpha}} = \sqrt{-g}\,[\{\mu\nu, \alpha\}\,\{\epsilon\alpha, \mu\}\,g^{\epsilon\nu} + \{\mu\nu, \alpha\}\,\{\epsilon\alpha, \nu\}\,g^{\epsilon\mu} - \{\mu\nu, \alpha\}\,\{\alpha\epsilon, \epsilon\}\,g^{\mu\nu}$$

$$- \{\nu\beta, \beta\}\,g^{\alpha}_{\mu}\,\{\epsilon\alpha, \mu\}\,g^{\epsilon\nu} - \{\nu\beta, \beta\}\,g^{\alpha}_{\mu}\,\{\epsilon\alpha, \nu\}\,g^{\epsilon\mu} + \{\nu\beta, \beta\}\,g^{\alpha}_{\mu}\,\{\alpha\epsilon, \epsilon\}\,g^{\mu\nu}],$$

which by change of dummy suffixes becomes

$$= \sqrt{-g}\,[\{\beta\nu, \alpha\}\,\{\mu\alpha, \beta\}\,g^{\mu\nu} + \{\mu\beta, \alpha\}\,\{\nu\alpha, \beta\}\,g^{\nu\mu} - \{\mu\nu, \alpha\}\,\{\alpha\beta, \beta\}\,g^{\mu\nu}$$

$$- \{\nu\beta, \beta\}\,\{\mu\alpha, \alpha\}\,g^{\mu\nu} - \{\alpha\beta, \beta\}\,\{\nu\mu, \alpha\}\,g^{\nu\mu} + \{\nu\beta, \beta\}\,\{\mu\epsilon, \epsilon\}\,g^{\mu\nu}]$$

$$= 2\mathfrak{L} \qquad \text{by (58·1)}.$$

The equations (58·71) and (58·72) show that the Lagrangian function is a homogeneous function of degree -1 in the "coordinates" and of degree 2 in the "velocities."

We can derive a useful expression for $\mathfrak{G}$

$$\mathfrak{G} = \mathfrak{g}^{\mu\nu}G_{\mu\nu}$$

$$= \mathfrak{g}^{\mu\nu}\frac{\partial}{\partial x_\alpha}\frac{\partial\mathfrak{L}}{\partial\mathfrak{g}^{\mu\nu}_{\alpha}} - \mathfrak{g}^{\mu\nu}\frac{\partial\mathfrak{L}}{\partial\mathfrak{g}^{\mu\nu}} \qquad \text{by (58·6)}$$

$$= \frac{\partial}{\partial x_\alpha}\left(\mathfrak{g}^{\mu\nu}\frac{\partial\mathfrak{L}}{\partial\mathfrak{g}^{\mu\nu}_{\alpha}}\right) - \mathfrak{g}^{\mu\nu}_{\alpha}\frac{\partial\mathfrak{L}}{\partial\mathfrak{g}^{\mu\nu}_{\alpha}} - \mathfrak{g}^{\mu\nu}\frac{\partial\mathfrak{L}}{\partial\mathfrak{g}^{\mu\nu}}$$

$$= \frac{\partial}{\partial x_\alpha}\left(\mathfrak{g}^{\mu\nu}\frac{\partial\mathfrak{L}}{\partial\mathfrak{g}^{\mu\nu}_{\alpha}}\right) - \mathfrak{L} \quad \text{..................................(58·8)}$$

by (58·71) and (58·72).

It will be seen that $(\mathfrak{G} + \mathfrak{L})$ has the form of a *divergence* (51·12); but the quantity of which it is the divergence is not a vector-density, nor is $\mathfrak{L}$ a scalar-density.

We shall derive another formula which will be needed in § 59,

$$d\,(g^{\mu\nu}\sqrt{-g}) = \sqrt{-g}\,(dg^{\mu\nu} + g^{\mu\nu}\,.\,\tfrac{1}{2}g^{\alpha\beta}\,dg_{\alpha\beta}) \qquad \text{by (35·3)}.$$

Hence, using (35·2),

$$G_{\mu\nu}d\,(g^{\mu\nu}\sqrt{-g}) = \sqrt{-g}\,(-G^{\mu\nu}dg_{\mu\nu} + \tfrac{1}{2}Gg^{\alpha\beta}\,dg_{\alpha\beta})$$

$$= -(G^{\mu\nu} - \tfrac{1}{2}g^{\mu\nu}G)\,\sqrt{-g}\,.\,dg_{\mu\nu}$$

$$= 8\pi\mathfrak{T}^{\mu\nu}dg_{\mu\nu} \quad \text{..................................(58·91)}.$$

Accordingly

$$8\pi\mathfrak{T}^{\mu\nu}\frac{\partial g_{\mu\nu}}{\partial x_\alpha} = G_{\mu\nu}\mathfrak{g}_\alpha^{\mu\nu}$$

$$= \mathfrak{g}_\alpha^{\mu\nu}\left(\frac{\partial}{\partial x_\beta}\frac{\partial\mathfrak{L}}{\partial\mathfrak{g}_\beta^{\mu\nu}} - \frac{\partial\mathfrak{L}}{\partial\mathfrak{g}^{\mu\nu}}\right)$$

$$= \frac{\partial}{\partial x_\beta}\left(\mathfrak{g}_\alpha^{\mu\nu}\frac{\partial\mathfrak{L}}{\partial\mathfrak{g}_\beta^{\mu\nu}}\right) - \frac{\partial}{\partial x_\beta}\mathfrak{g}_\alpha^{\mu\nu}\cdot\frac{\partial\mathfrak{L}}{\partial\mathfrak{g}_\beta^{\mu\nu}} - \mathfrak{g}_\alpha^{\mu\nu}\frac{\partial\mathfrak{L}}{\partial\mathfrak{g}^{\mu\nu}} \quad \text{...(58·92).}$$

Now

$$\frac{\partial\mathfrak{L}}{\partial x_\alpha} = \frac{\partial\mathfrak{L}}{\partial\mathfrak{g}^{\mu\nu}}\frac{\partial\mathfrak{g}^{\mu\nu}}{\partial x_\alpha} + \frac{\partial\mathfrak{L}}{\partial\mathfrak{g}_\beta^{\mu\nu}}\frac{\partial\mathfrak{g}_\beta^{\mu\nu}}{\partial x_\alpha},$$

and since

$$\frac{\partial\mathfrak{g}_\beta^{\mu\nu}}{\partial x_\alpha} = \frac{\partial^2\mathfrak{g}^{\mu\nu}}{\partial x_\alpha\partial x_\beta} = \frac{\partial\mathfrak{g}_\alpha^{\mu\nu}}{\partial x_\beta},$$

we see that (58·92) reduces to

$$8\pi\mathfrak{T}^{\mu\nu}\frac{\partial g_{\mu\nu}}{\partial x_\alpha} = \frac{\partial}{\partial x_\beta}\left(\mathfrak{g}_\alpha^{\mu\nu}\frac{\partial\mathfrak{L}}{\partial\mathfrak{g}_\beta^{\mu\nu}}\right) - \frac{\partial\mathfrak{L}}{\partial x_\alpha}$$

$$= \frac{\partial}{\partial x_\beta}\left\{\mathfrak{g}_\alpha^{\mu\nu}\frac{\partial\mathfrak{L}}{\partial\mathfrak{g}_\beta^{\mu\nu}} - g_\alpha^\beta\mathfrak{L}\right\} \quad \text{..............(58·93).}$$

59. Pseudo-energy-tensor of the gravitational field.

The formal expression of the conservation of the material energy and momentum is contained in the equations

$$\frac{\partial\mathfrak{T}_\mu^\nu}{\partial x_\nu} = 0 \quad \text{..............................(59·1),}$$

or, if we name the coordinates x, y, z, t,

$$\frac{\partial}{\partial x}\mathfrak{T}_\mu^1 + \frac{\partial}{\partial y}\mathfrak{T}_\mu^2 + \frac{\partial}{\partial z}\mathfrak{T}_\mu^3 + \frac{\partial}{\partial t}\mathfrak{T}_\mu^4 = 0.$$

Multiply by $dxdydz$ and integrate through a given three-dimensional region. The last term is

$$\frac{\partial}{\partial t}\iiint\mathfrak{T}_\mu^4\,dxdydz.$$

The other three terms yield surface-integrals over the boundary of the region. Thus the law (59·1) states that the rate of change of $\iiint\mathfrak{T}_\mu^4\,dxdydz$ is equal to certain terms which describe something going on at the boundary of the region. In other words, changes of this integral cannot be created in the interior of the region, but are always traceable to transmission across the boundary. This is clearly what is meant by conservation of the integral.

This equation (59·1) applies only in the special case when the coordinates are such that there is no field of force. We have generalised it by substituting the corresponding tensor equation $T_{\mu\nu}^\nu = 0$; but this is no longer a formal expression of the conservation of anything. It is of interest to compare the traditional method of generalising (59·1) in which formal conservation is adhered to.

In classical mechanics the law of conservation is restored by recognising another form of energy—potential energy—which is not included in $\mathfrak{T}_\mu^\nu$. This is supposed to be stored up in the gravitational field, and similarly the momentum and stress components may have their invisible complements in the gravitational field. We have therefore to add to $\mathfrak{T}_\mu^\nu$ a complementary expression $\mathfrak{t}_\mu^\nu$ denoting potential energy, momentum and stress; and conservation is only asserted for the sum. If

$$\mathfrak{S}_\mu^\nu = \mathfrak{T}_\mu^\nu + \mathfrak{t}_\mu^\nu \quad \text{.............................(59·2)},$$

then (59·1) is generalised in the form

$$\frac{\partial \mathfrak{S}_\mu^\nu}{\partial x_\nu} = 0 \quad \text{...........................(59·3)}.$$

Accordingly the difference between the relativity treatment and the classical treatment is as follows. In both theories it is recognised that in certain cases $\mathfrak{T}_\mu^\nu$ is conserved, but that in the general case this conservation breaks down. The relativity theory treats the general case by discovering a more exact formulation of what happens to $\mathfrak{T}_\mu^\nu$ when it is not strictly conserved, viz. $\mathfrak{T}_{\mu\nu}^\nu = 0$. The classical theory treats it by introducing a supplementary energy, so that conservation is still maintained but for a different quantity, viz. $\partial \mathfrak{S}_\mu^\nu / \partial x_\nu = 0$. The relativity treatment adheres to the physical quantity and modifies the law; the classical treatment adheres to the law and modifies the physical quantity. Of course, both methods should be expressible by equivalent formulae; and we have in our previous work spoken of $\mathfrak{T}_{\mu\nu}^\nu = 0$ as the law of conservation of energy and momentum, because, although it is not formally a law of conservation, it expresses exactly the phenomena which classical mechanics attributes to conservation.

The relativity treatment has enabled us to discover the exact equations, and we may now apply these to obtain the corresponding exact expression for the quantity $\mathfrak{S}_\mu^\nu$ introduced in the classical treatment.

It is clear that $\mathfrak{t}_\mu^\nu$ and therefore $\mathfrak{S}_\mu^\nu$ cannot be tensor-densities, because $\mathfrak{t}_\mu^\nu$ vanishes when natural coordinates are used at a point, and would therefore always vanish if it were a tensor-density. We call $\mathfrak{t}_\mu^\nu$ the pseudo-tensor-density of potential energy.

The explicit value of $\mathfrak{t}_\mu^\nu$ must be calculated from the condition (59·3), or

$$\begin{aligned} \frac{\partial \mathfrak{t}_\mu^\nu}{\partial x_\nu} &= -\frac{\partial \mathfrak{T}_\mu^\nu}{\partial x_\nu} \\ &= -\tfrac{1}{2}\mathfrak{T}^{\alpha\beta}\frac{\partial g_{\alpha\beta}}{\partial x_\mu} \qquad \text{by (55·6)} \\ &= -\frac{1}{16\pi}\frac{\partial}{\partial x_\nu}\left\{\mathfrak{g}_\mu^{\alpha\beta}\frac{\partial \mathfrak{L}}{\partial \mathfrak{g}_\nu^{\alpha\beta}} - g_\mu^\nu \mathfrak{L}\right\} \qquad \text{by (58·93)}. \end{aligned}$$

Hence

$$16\pi \mathfrak{t}_\mu^\nu = g_\mu^\nu \mathfrak{L} - \mathfrak{g}_\mu^{\alpha\beta}\frac{\partial \mathfrak{L}}{\partial \mathfrak{g}_\nu^{\alpha\beta}} \quad \text{.......................(59·4)}.$$

This may remind us of the Hamiltonian integral of energy

$$-h = L - \Sigma q' \frac{\partial L}{\partial q'}$$

in general dynamics.

We can form a pseudo-scalar-density by contraction of (59·4)

$$16\pi \mathfrak{t} = 4\mathfrak{L} - \mathfrak{g}^{\alpha\beta}_{\mu} \frac{\partial \mathfrak{L}}{\partial \mathfrak{g}^{\alpha\beta}_{\mu}}$$

$$= 2\mathfrak{L}, \quad \text{by (58·72)}.$$

Thus we obtain the interesting comparison with (54·4)

$$\left.\begin{aligned} \mathfrak{L} &= 8\pi\mathfrak{t} \\ \mathfrak{G} &= 8\pi\mathfrak{T} \end{aligned}\right\} \quad \text{.............................(59·5)}.$$

It should be understood that in this section we have been occupied with the transition between the old and new points of view. The quantity $\mathfrak{t}_\mu^\nu$ represents the potential energy of classical mechanics, but we do not ourselves recognise it as an energy of any kind. It is not a tensor-density, and it can be made to vanish at any point by suitably choosing the coordinates; we do not associate it with any absolute feature of world-structure. In fact finite values of $\mathfrak{t}_\mu^\nu$ can be produced in an empty world containing no gravitating matter merely by choice of coordinates. The tensor-density $\mathfrak{T}_\mu^\nu$ comprises all the energy which we recognise; and we call it gravitational or material energy indiscriminately according as it is expressed in terms of $g_{\mu\nu}$ or ρ_0, u, v, w.

This difference between the classical and the relativity view of energy recalls the remarks on the definition of physical quantities made in the Introduction. As soon as the principle of conservation of energy was grasped, the physicist practically made it his definition of energy, so that energy was that *something* which obeyed the law of conservation. He followed the practice of the pure mathematician, defining energy by the properties he wished it to have, instead of describing how he had measured it. This procedure has turned out to be rather unlucky in the light of the new developments. It is true that a quantity $\mathfrak{S}_\mu^\nu$ can be found which obeys the definition, but it is not a tensor and is therefore not a direct measure of an intrinsic condition of the world. Rather than saddle ourselves with this quantity, which is not now of primary interest, we go back to the more primitive idea of *vis viva*—generalised, it is true, by admitting heat or molecular *vis viva* but not potential energy. We find that this is not in all cases formally conserved, but it obeys the law that its divergence vanishes; and from our new point of view this is a simpler and more significant property than strict conservation.

Integrating over an isolated material body we may set

$$\iiint \mathfrak{T}_\mu^4 \, dx\,dy\,dz = -Mu, \ -Mv, \ -Mw, \ M,$$

$$\iiint \mathfrak{S}_\mu^4 \, dx\,dy\,dz = -M'u', \ -M'v', \ -M'w', \ M',$$

where the latter expression includes the potential energy and momentum of the body. Changes of $M'u'$, etc. can only occur by transfer from regions outside the body by action passing through the boundary; whereas changes of Mu, etc can be produced by the mutual attractions of the particles of the body. It is clear that the kinematical velocity, or direction of the world-line of the body, corresponds to $u:v:w:1$; the direction of $u':v':w':1$ can be varied at will by choosing different coordinate-systems.

In empty space the expression for $\mathfrak{t}_\mu^\nu$ can be simplified. Since $\mathfrak{G}=0$, (58·8) becomes

$$\mathfrak{L} = \frac{\partial}{\partial x_\nu}\left(\mathfrak{g}^{\alpha\beta}\frac{\partial \mathfrak{L}}{\partial \mathfrak{g}^{\alpha\beta}_\nu}\right).$$

Hence

$$16\pi \mathfrak{t}_\mu^\nu = \frac{\partial}{\partial x_\mu}\left(\mathfrak{g}^{\alpha\beta}\frac{\partial \mathfrak{L}}{\partial \mathfrak{g}^{\alpha\beta}_\nu}\right) - \mathfrak{g}^{\alpha\beta}_\mu \frac{\partial \mathfrak{L}}{\partial \mathfrak{g}^{\alpha\beta}_\nu}$$

$$= \mathfrak{g}^{\alpha\beta}\frac{\partial}{\partial x_\mu}\frac{\partial \mathfrak{L}}{\partial \mathfrak{g}^{\alpha\beta}_\nu}$$

$$= \mathfrak{g}^{\alpha\beta}\frac{\partial}{\partial x_\mu}\left[-\{\alpha\beta, \nu\} + g^\nu_\alpha \frac{\partial}{\partial x_\beta}\log\sqrt{-g}\right] \quad \text{........ (59·6)}$$

by (58·52).

60. Action.

The invariant integral

$$A = \iiiint \rho_0 \sqrt{-g}\, d\tau \quad \text{.............................(60·11)}$$

represents the *action* of the matter in a four-dimensional region.

By (49·42),

$$A = \iiiint \rho_0 dW ds$$

$$= \iint dm\, ds \quad \text{...............................(60·12),}$$

where m is the invariant mass or energy.

Thus the action of a particle having energy m for a proper-time ds is equal to mds, agreeing with the definition of action in ordinary mechanics as energy multiplied by time. By (54·6) another form is

$$A = \frac{1}{8\pi}\iiiint G\sqrt{-g}\, d\tau \quad \text{.............................(60·2),}$$

so that (ignoring the numerical factor) $G\sqrt{-g}$, or $\mathfrak{G}$, represents the action-density of the gravitational field. Note that material action and gravitational action are alternative aspects of the same thing; they are not to be added together to give a total action.

But in stating that the gravitational action and the material action are necessarily the same thing, we have to bear in mind a very peculiar conception which is almost always associated with the term Action. From its first introduction, action has always been looked upon as something whose sole *raison d'être* is to be varied—and, moreover, *varied in such a way as to defy the laws of nature!* We have thus to remember that when a writer begins to talk about action, he is probably going to consider impossible conditions of the world. (That does not mean that he is talking nonsense—he brings out the important features of the possible conditions by comparing them with impossible conditions.) Thus we may not always *disregard* the difference between material and gravitational action; it is impossible that there should be any difference, but then we are about to discuss impossibilities.

We have to bear in mind the two aspects of action in this subject. It is primarily a physical quantity having a definite numerical value, given indifferently by (60·11) or (60·2), which is of special importance because it is invariant. But it also denotes a mathematical function of the variables; the functional form, which is all important, will differ according to which of the two expressions is used. In particular we have to consider the partial derivatives, and these will depend on the variables in terms of which the action is expressed.

The Hamiltonian method of variation of an integral is of great importance in this subject; several examples of it will be given presently. I think it is unfortunate that this valuable method is nearly always applied in the form of a principle of stationary action. By considering the variation of the integral for small variations of the $g_{\mu\nu}$, or other variables, we obtain a kind of generalised differential coefficient which I will call the Hamiltonian derivative. It may be possible to construct integrals for which the Hamiltonian derivatives vanish, so that the integral has the stationary property. But just as in the ordinary differential calculus we are not solely concerned with problems of maxima and minima, and we take some interest in differential coefficients which do not vanish; so Hamiltonian derivatives may be worthy of attention even when they disappoint us by failing to vanish.

Let us consider the variation of the gravitational action in a region, viz.

$$8\pi\,\delta A = \delta\int G\sqrt{-g}\,d\tau,$$

for arbitrary small variations $\delta g_{\mu\nu}$ which vanish at and near* the boundary of the region. By (58·8)

$$\delta\int G\sqrt{-g}\,d\tau = -\,\delta\int \mathfrak{L}\,d\tau + \delta\int \frac{\partial}{\partial x_\alpha}\left(\mathfrak{g}^{\mu\nu}\frac{\partial \mathfrak{L}}{\partial \mathfrak{g}^{\mu\nu}_\alpha}\right)d\tau.$$

Also since $\mathfrak{L}$ is a function of $\mathfrak{g}^{\mu\nu}$ and $\mathfrak{g}^{\mu\nu}_\alpha$

$$\int \delta\mathfrak{L}\,d\tau = \int\left(\frac{\partial \mathfrak{L}}{\partial \mathfrak{g}^{\mu\nu}}\,\delta\mathfrak{g}^{\mu\nu} + \frac{\partial \mathfrak{L}}{\partial \mathfrak{g}^{\mu\nu}_\alpha}\,\delta\mathfrak{g}^{\mu\nu}_\alpha\right)d\tau,$$

and, by partial integration of the second term,

$$= \int\left(\frac{\partial \mathfrak{L}}{\partial \mathfrak{g}^{\mu\nu}} - \frac{\partial}{\partial x_\alpha}\frac{\partial \mathfrak{L}}{\partial \mathfrak{g}^{\mu\nu}_\alpha}\right)\delta\mathfrak{g}^{\mu\nu}\,d\tau + \int \frac{\partial}{\partial x_\alpha}\left(\frac{\partial \mathfrak{L}}{\partial \mathfrak{g}^{\mu\nu}_\alpha}\,\delta\mathfrak{g}^{\mu\nu}\right)d\tau.$$

* So that their first derivatives also vanish.

By (58·6) the first integrand becomes $-G_{\mu\nu}\delta\mathfrak{g}^{\mu\nu}$, so that we have

$$\delta\int G\sqrt{-g}\,d\tau = \int G_{\mu\nu}\,\delta\,(g^{\mu\nu}\sqrt{-g})\,d\tau + \int \frac{\partial}{\partial x_\alpha}\left(\mathfrak{g}^{\mu\nu}\,\delta\left(\frac{\partial\mathfrak{L}}{\partial\mathfrak{g}^{\mu\nu}_\alpha}\right)\right)d\tau \quad\ldots(60{\cdot}3).$$

The second term can be integrated immediately giving a triple integral over the boundary of the four-dimensional region; and it vanishes because all variations vanish at the boundary by hypothesis. Hence

$$\delta\int G\sqrt{-g}\,d\tau = \int G_{\mu\nu}\,\delta\,(g^{\mu\nu}\sqrt{-g})\,d\tau \quad\ldots\ldots\ldots\ldots\ldots\ldots\ldots(60{\cdot}41)$$

$$= -\int (G^{\mu\nu} - \tfrac{1}{2}g^{\mu\nu}G)\,\delta g_{\mu\nu}\sqrt{-g}\,d\tau \quad\ldots\ldots\ldots(60{\cdot}42)$$

by (58·91).

I call the coefficient $-(G^{\mu\nu} - \tfrac{1}{2}g^{\mu\nu}G)$ the *Hamiltonian derivative* of G with respect to $g_{\mu\nu}$, writing it symbolically

$$\frac{\mathfrak{h}G}{\mathfrak{h}g_{\mu\nu}} = -(G^{\mu\nu} - \tfrac{1}{2}g^{\mu\nu}G) = 8\pi T^{\mu\nu} \quad\ldots\ldots\ldots\ldots\ldots\ldots(60{\cdot}43).$$

We see from (60·42) that the action A is only stationary when the energy-tensor $T^{\mu\nu}$ vanishes, that is to say in empty space. In fact action is only stationary when it does not exist—and not always then.

It would thus appear that the Principle of Stationary Action is in general untrue. Nevertheless some modified statement of the principle appears to have considerable significance. In the actual world the space occupied by matter (electrons) is extremely small compared with the empty regions. Thus the Principle of Stationary Action, although not universally true, expresses a very general tendency—a tendency with exceptions*. Our theory does not account for this atomicity of matter; and in the stationary variation of action we seem to have an indication of a way of approaching this difficult problem, although the precise formulation of the law of atomicity is not yet achieved. It is suspected that it may involve an "action" which is capable only of discontinuous variation.

It is not suggested that there is anything incorrect in the principle of least action as used in classical mechanics. The break-down occurs when we attempt to generalise it for variations of the state of the system beyond those hitherto contemplated. Indeed it is obvious that the principle must break down if pressed to extreme generality. We may discriminate (*a*) possible states of the world, (*b*) states which although impossible are contemplated, (*c*) impossible states which are not contemplated. Generalisation of the principle consists in transferring states from class (*c*) to class (*b*); there must be some limit to this, for otherwise we should find ourselves asserting that the equation $\delta A \neq 0$ is not merely not a possible equation but also not even an impossible equation.

* I do not regard electromagnetic fields as constituting an exception, because they have not yet been taken into account in our work. But the action of matter has been fully included, so that the break-down of the principle as applied to matter is a definite exception.

61. A property of invariants.

Let K be any invariant function of the $g_{\mu\nu}$ and their derivatives up to any order, so that

$$\int K\sqrt{-g}\,d\tau \text{ is an invariant}$$

The small variations $\delta(K\sqrt{-g})$ can be expressed as a linear sum of terms involving $\delta g_{\mu\nu}$, $\delta(\partial g_{\mu\nu}/\partial x_\alpha)$, $\delta(\partial^2 g_{\mu\nu}/\partial x_\alpha \partial x_\beta)$, etc. By the usual method of partial integration employed in the calculus of variations, these can all be reduced to terms in $\delta g_{\mu\nu}$, together with complete differentials.

Thus for variations which vanish at the boundary of the region, we can write

$$\delta\int K\sqrt{-g}\,d\tau = \int P^{\mu\nu}\,\delta g_{\mu\nu}\sqrt{-g}\,d\tau \quad \text{............(61·1)},$$

where the coefficients, here written $P^{\mu\nu}$, can be evaluated when the analytical expression for K is given. The complete differentials yield surface-integrals over the boundary, so that they do not contribute to the variations In accordance with our previous notation (60·43), we have

$$P^{\mu\nu} = \frac{\mathfrak{h}K}{\mathfrak{h}g_{\mu\nu}} \quad \text{...........................(61·2)}.$$

We take $P^{\mu\nu}$ to be symmetrical in μ and ν, since any antisymmetrical part would be meaningless owing to the inner multiplication by $\delta g_{\mu\nu}$. Also since $\delta g_{\mu\nu}$ is an arbitrary tensor $P^{\mu\nu}$ must be a tensor.

Consider the case in which the $\delta g_{\mu\nu}$ arise merely from a transformation of coordinates. Then (61·1) vanishes, not from any stationary property, but because of the invariance of K. The $\delta g_{\mu\nu}$ are not now arbitrary independent variations, so that it does not follow that $P^{\mu\nu}$ vanishes.

Comparing $g_{\mu\nu}$ and $g_{\mu\nu} + \delta g_{\mu\nu}$ by (23·22), since they correspond to a transformation of coordinates,

$$g_{\mu\nu} = (g_{\alpha\beta} + \delta g_{\alpha\beta})\frac{\partial(x_\alpha + \delta x_\alpha)}{\partial x_\mu}\cdot\frac{\partial(x_\beta + \delta x_\beta)}{\partial x_\nu}$$

$$= (g_{\alpha\beta} + \delta g_{\alpha\beta})\frac{\partial x_\alpha}{\partial x_\mu}\frac{\partial x_\beta}{\partial x_\nu} + g_{\alpha\beta}\frac{\partial x_\alpha}{\partial x_\mu}\frac{\partial(\delta x_\beta)}{\partial x_\nu} + g_{\alpha\beta}\frac{\partial x_\beta}{\partial x_\nu}\frac{\partial(\delta x_\alpha)}{\partial x_\mu}.$$

But $$\frac{\partial x_\alpha}{\partial x_\mu} = g_\mu^\alpha,\quad \frac{\partial x_\beta}{\partial x_\nu} = g_\nu^\beta \text{ by (22·3)}.$$

Hence $$g_{\mu\nu} = g_{\mu\nu} + \delta g_{\mu\nu} + g_{\mu\beta}\frac{\partial(\delta x_\beta)}{\partial x_\nu} + g_{\alpha\nu}\frac{\partial(\delta x_\alpha)}{\partial x_\mu}.$$

This is a comparison of the fundamental tensor at $x_\alpha + \delta x_\alpha$ in the new coordinate-system with the value at x_α in the old system. There would be no objection to using this value of $\delta g_{\mu\nu}$ provided that we took account of the corresponding $\delta(d\tau)$. We prefer, however, to keep $d\tau$ fixed in the comparison, and must compare the values at x_α in both systems. It is therefore necessary to subtract the change $\delta x_\alpha \cdot \partial g_{\mu\nu}/\partial x_\alpha$ of $g_{\mu\nu}$ in the distance δx_α; hence

$$-\delta g_{\mu\nu} = g_{\mu\beta}\frac{\partial(\delta x_\beta)}{\partial x_\nu} + g_{\alpha\nu}\frac{\partial(\delta x_\alpha)}{\partial x_\mu} + \frac{\partial g_{\mu\nu}}{\partial x_\alpha}\delta x_\alpha \quad \text{............} (61\cdot3).$$

Hence (61·1) becomes

$$\delta\int K\sqrt{-g}\,d\tau = -\int P^{\mu\nu}\sqrt{-g}\left(g_{\mu\alpha}\frac{\partial}{\partial x_\nu}(\delta x_\alpha) + g_{\nu\alpha}\frac{\partial}{\partial x_\mu}(\delta x_\alpha) + \frac{\partial g_{\mu\nu}}{\partial x_\alpha}\delta x_\alpha\right)d\tau$$

which, by partial integration,

$$= \int\left\{\frac{\partial}{\partial x_\nu}(g_{\mu\alpha}P^{\mu\nu}\sqrt{-g}) + \frac{\partial}{\partial x_\mu}(g_{\nu\alpha}P^{\mu\nu}\sqrt{-g}) - P^{\mu\nu}\sqrt{-g}\frac{\partial g_{\mu\nu}}{\partial x_\alpha}\right\}\delta x_\alpha\,d\tau$$

$$= 2\int\left\{\frac{\partial}{\partial x_\nu}\mathfrak{P}^\nu_\alpha - \tfrac{1}{2}\mathfrak{P}^{\mu\nu}\frac{\partial g_{\mu\nu}}{\partial x_\alpha}\right\}\delta x_\alpha\,d\tau$$

$$= 2\int P^\nu_{\alpha\nu}\delta x_\alpha\sqrt{-g}\,d\tau \text{ by } (51\cdot51) \quad \text{............} (61\cdot4).$$

This has to vanish for all arbitrary variations δx_α—deformations of the mesh-system—and accordingly

$$(P^\nu_\alpha)_\nu = 0 \quad \text{............} (61\cdot5).$$

We have thus demonstrated the general theorem—

The Hamiltonian derivative of any fundamental invariant is a tensor whose divergence vanishes

The theorem of § 52 is a particular case, since $T^{\mu\nu}$ is the Hamiltonian derivative of G by (60·43).

62. Alternative energy-tensors.

We have hitherto identified the energy-tensor with $G^\nu_\mu - \frac{1}{2}g^\nu_\mu G$ mainly because the divergence of the latter vanishes identically; but the theorem just proved enables us to derive other fundamental tensors whose divergence vanishes, so that alternative identifications of the energy-tensor would seem to be possible. The three simplest fundamental invariants are

$$K = G, \quad K' = G_{\mu\nu}G^{\mu\nu}, \quad K'' = B^\rho_{\mu\nu\sigma}B^{\mu\nu\sigma}_\rho \quad \text{............} (62\cdot1).$$

Hitherto we have taken $\mathfrak{h}K/\mathfrak{h}g_{\mu\nu}$ to be the energy-tensor; but if $\mathfrak{h}K'/\mathfrak{h}g_{\mu\nu}$ were substituted, the laws of conservation of energy and momentum would be satisfied, since the divergence vanishes. Similarly $\mathfrak{h}K''/\mathfrak{h}g_{\mu\nu}$ could be used.

The condition for empty space is given by the vanishing of the energy-tensor. Hence for the three possible hypotheses, the law of gravitation in empty space is

$$\frac{\mathfrak{h}K}{\mathfrak{h}g_{\mu\nu}}, \quad \frac{\mathfrak{h}K'}{\mathfrak{h}g_{\mu\nu}}, \quad \frac{\mathfrak{h}K''}{\mathfrak{h}g_{\mu\nu}} = 0 \quad \text{............} (62\cdot2)$$

respectively.

It is easy to see that the last two tensors contain fourth derivatives of the $g_{\mu\nu}$, so that if we can lay it down as an essential condition that the law of gravitation in empty space must be expressed by differential equations of the second order, the only possible energy-tensor is the one hitherto accepted. For fourth-order equations the question of the nature of the boundary conditions necessary to supplement the differential equations would become very difficult; but this does not seem to be a conclusive reason for rejecting such equations.

The two alternative tensors are excessively complicated expressions; but when applied to determine the field of an isolated particle, they become not unmanageable. The field, being symmetrical, must be of the general form (38·2), so that we have only to determine the disposable coefficients λ and ν both of which must be functions of r only. K' can be calculated in terms of λ and ν without difficulty from equations (38·6); but the expression for K'' turns out to be rather simpler and I shall deal with it. By the method of § 38, we find

$$\mathfrak{K}'' = K''\sqrt{-g} = 2e^{\frac{1}{2}(\lambda+\nu)}\sin\theta\,\{e^{-2\lambda}(\lambda'^2+\nu'^2) + 2r^2e^{-2\lambda}(\tfrac{1}{4}\lambda'\nu' - \tfrac{1}{4}\nu'^2 - \tfrac{1}{2}\nu'')^2 + 2(1-e^{-\lambda})^2/r^2\} \quad\text{.........(62·3)}$$

It is clear that the integral of $\mathfrak{K}''$ will be stationary for variations from the symmetrical condition, so that we need only consider variations of λ and ν and their derivatives with respect to r. Thus the gravitational equations $\mathfrak{h}K''/\mathfrak{h}g_{\mu\nu}=0$ are equivalent to

$$\frac{\mathfrak{h}K''}{\mathfrak{h}\lambda}=0, \quad \frac{\mathfrak{h}K''}{\mathfrak{h}\nu}=0 \quad\text{.........................(62·4).}$$

Now for a variation of λ

$$\delta\int\mathfrak{K}\,d\tau = \int\left(\frac{\partial\mathfrak{K}}{\partial\lambda}\delta\lambda + \frac{\partial\mathfrak{K}}{\partial\lambda'}\delta\lambda' + \frac{\partial\mathfrak{K}}{\partial\lambda''}\delta\lambda''\right)d\tau$$

$$= \int\left\{\frac{\partial\mathfrak{K}}{\partial\lambda} - \frac{\partial}{\partial r}\left(\frac{\partial\mathfrak{K}}{\partial\lambda'}\right) + \frac{\partial^2}{\partial r^2}\left(\frac{\partial\mathfrak{K}}{\partial\lambda''}\right)\right\}\delta\lambda\,d\tau + \text{surface-integrals.}$$

Hence our equations (62·4) take the Lagrangian form

$$\left.\begin{aligned}\frac{\mathfrak{h}K''}{\mathfrak{h}\lambda} &= \frac{\partial\mathfrak{K}''}{\partial\lambda} - \frac{\partial}{\partial r}\frac{\partial\mathfrak{K}''}{\partial\lambda'} + \frac{\partial^2}{\partial r^2}\frac{\partial\mathfrak{K}''}{\partial\lambda''} = 0\\ \frac{\mathfrak{h}K''}{\mathfrak{h}\nu} &= \frac{\partial\mathfrak{K}''}{\partial\nu} - \frac{\partial}{\partial r}\frac{\partial\mathfrak{K}''}{\partial\nu'} + \frac{\partial^2}{\partial r^2}\frac{\partial\mathfrak{K}''}{\partial\nu''} = 0\end{aligned}\right\} \quad\text{..............(62·5).}$$

From these λ and ν are to be determined.

It can be shown that one exact solution is the same as in § 38, viz.

$$e^{-\lambda} = e^{\nu} = \gamma = 1 - 2m/r \quad\text{.........................(62·6).}$$

For taking the partial derivatives of (62·3), and applying (62·6) after the differentiation,

$$\frac{\partial\mathfrak{K}''}{\partial\lambda} = -\tfrac{3}{2}\mathfrak{K}'' + 4\frac{(1-e^{-\lambda})}{r^2}\,.\,2e^{\frac{1}{2}(\lambda+\nu)}\sin\theta = \left(-72\frac{m^2}{r^4} + 16\frac{m}{r^3}\right)\sin\theta,$$

$$\frac{\partial\mathfrak{K}''}{\partial\lambda'} = 2e^{\frac{1}{2}(\lambda+\nu)}\sin\theta\,\{2e^{-2\lambda}\lambda' + r^2e^{-2\lambda}(\tfrac{1}{4}\lambda'\nu' - \tfrac{1}{4}\nu'^2 - \tfrac{1}{2}\nu'')\,\nu'\}$$

$$= \left(24\frac{m^2}{r^3} - 8\frac{m}{r^2}\right)\sin\theta,$$

$$\frac{\partial \mathfrak{K}''}{\partial \lambda''} = 0,$$

$$\frac{\partial \mathfrak{K}''}{\partial \nu} = \tfrac{1}{2}\mathfrak{K}'' = 24\frac{m^2}{r^4}\sin\theta,$$

$$\frac{\partial \mathfrak{K}''}{\partial \nu'} = 2e^{\frac{1}{2}(\lambda+\nu)}\sin\theta\,\{2e^{-2\lambda}\nu' + 4r^2e^{-2\lambda}(\tfrac{1}{4}\lambda'\nu' - \tfrac{1}{4}\nu'^2 - \tfrac{1}{2}\nu'')(\tfrac{1}{4}\lambda' - \tfrac{1}{2}\nu')\}$$

$$= \left(-40\frac{m^2}{r^3} + 8\frac{m}{r^2}\right)\sin\theta,$$

$$\frac{\partial \mathfrak{K}''}{\partial \nu''} = -2e^{\frac{1}{2}(\lambda+\nu)}\sin\theta\,.\,2r^2e^{-2\lambda}(\tfrac{1}{4}\lambda'\nu' - \tfrac{1}{4}\nu'^2 - \tfrac{1}{2}\nu'') = \left(16\frac{m^2}{r^2} - 8\frac{m}{r}\right)\sin\theta.$$

On substituting these values, (62·5) is verified exactly.

The alternative law $\mathfrak{h}K'/\mathfrak{h}g_{\mu\nu} = 0$ is also satisfied by the same solution. For

$$\delta(G_{\mu\nu}G^{\mu\nu}\sqrt{-g}) = G_{\mu\nu}\delta(G^{\mu\nu}\sqrt{-g}) + G^{\mu\nu}\sqrt{-g}\,\delta G_{\mu\nu},$$

hence the variation of $K'\sqrt{-g}$ vanishes wherever $G_{\mu\nu} = 0$. Any field of gravitation agreeing with Einstein's law will satisfy the alternative law proposed, but not usually *vice versa*.

There are doubtless other symmetrical solutions for the alternative laws of gravitation which are not permitted by Einstein's law, since the differential equations are now of the fourth order and involve two extra boundary conditions either at the particle or at infinity It may be asked, Why should these be excluded in nature? We can only answer that it may be for the same reason that negative mass, doublets, electrons of other than standard mass, or other theoretically possible singularities in the world, do not occur, the ultimate particle satisfies conditions which are at present unknown to us.

It would seem therefore that there are three admissible laws of gravitation (62·2) Each can give precisely the same gravitational field of the sun, and all astronomical phenomena are the same whichever law is used Small differences may appear in the cross-terms due to two or more attracting bodies; but as was shown in our discussion of the lunar theory these are too small to be detected by astronomical observation. Each law gives precisely the same mechanical phenomena, since the conservation of energy and momentum is satisfied. When we ask which of the three is the law of the actual world, I am not sure that the question has any meaning The subject is very mystifying, and the following suggestions are put forward very tentatively.

The energy-tensor has been regarded as giving the definition of matter, since it comprises the properties by which matter is described in physics. Our three energy-tensors give us three alternative material worlds; and the question is which of the three are we looking at when we contemplate the world around us; but if these three material worlds are each doing the same thing (within the limits of observational accuracy) it seems impossible to decide whether we are observing one or other or all three.

To put it another way, an observation involves the relation of the T_μ^ν of our bodies to the T_μ^ν of external objects, or alternatively of the respective T'^ν_μ or T''^ν_μ. If these are the same relation it seems meaningless to ask which of the three bodies and corresponding worlds the relation is between. After all it is the relation which is the reality. In accepting T_μ^ν as the energy-tensor we are simply choosing the simplest of three possible modes of representing the observation.

One cannot but suspect that there is some identical relation between the Hamiltonian derivatives of the three fundamental invariants. If this relation were discovered it would perhaps clear up a rather mysterious subject.

63. Gravitational flux from a particle.

Let us consider an empty region of the world, and try to create in it one or more particles of small mass δm by variations of the $g_{\mu\nu}$ within the region. By (60·12) and (60·2),

$$\delta \int G \sqrt{-g}\, d\tau = 8\pi \Sigma\, \delta m \,.\, ds \quad\quad (63\cdot 1),$$

and by (60·42) the left-hand side is zero because the space is initially empty. In the actual world particles for which $\delta m\ ds$ is negative do not exist, hence it is impossible to create any particles in an empty region, so long as we adhere to the condition that the $g_{\mu\nu}$ and their first derivatives must not be varied on the boundary. To permit the creation of particles we must give up this restriction and accordingly resurrect the term

$$\delta \int G \sqrt{-g}\, d\tau = \int \frac{\partial}{\partial x_\alpha}\left(\mathfrak{g}^{\mu\nu}\delta\left(\frac{\partial \mathfrak{L}}{\partial \mathfrak{g}^{\mu\nu}_\alpha}\right)\right) d\tau \quad\quad (63\cdot 2)$$

which was discarded from (60·3). On performing the first integration, (63·2) gives the flux of the normal component of

$$\mathfrak{g}^{\mu\nu}\delta\left(\frac{\partial \mathfrak{L}}{\partial \mathfrak{g}^{\mu\nu}_\alpha}\right) = g^{\mu\nu}\sqrt{-g}\,\delta\left[-\{\mu\nu, \alpha\} + g^\alpha_\mu \{\nu\beta, \beta\}\right] \quad\quad (63\cdot 3)$$

across the three-dimensional surface of the region. The close connection of this expression with the value of $\mathfrak{t}_\mu^\nu$ in (59·6) should be noticed.

Take the region in the form of a long tube and create a particle of gravitational mass δm along its axis. The flux (63·3) is an invariant, since $\delta m \,.\, ds$ is invariant, so we may choose the special coordinates of § 38 for which the particle is at rest. Take the tube to be of radius r and calculate the flux for a length of tube $dt = ds$. The normal component of (63·3) is given by $\alpha = 1$ and accordingly the flux is

$$\iiint g^{\mu\nu}\sqrt{-g}\,\delta\left[-\{\mu\nu, 1\} + g^1_\mu\{\nu\beta, \beta\}\right] d\theta\, d\phi\, dt$$

$$= 4\pi r^2 ds \,.\left[-g^{\mu\nu}\delta\{\mu\nu, 1\} + g^{1\nu}\delta\left(\frac{\partial}{\partial x_\nu}\log\sqrt{-g}\right)\right] \quad\quad (63\cdot 4),$$

which by (38·5)

$$=4\pi r^2 ds\left\{e^{-\lambda}\delta\left(\tfrac{1}{2}\lambda'\right)-\frac{1}{r^2}\delta\left(r e^{-\lambda}\right)-\frac{1}{r^2\sin^2\theta}\delta\left(r\sin^2\theta\, e^{-\lambda}\right)-e^{-\nu}\delta\left(\tfrac{1}{2}e^{\nu-\lambda}\nu'\right)-e^{-\lambda}\delta\left(\frac{2}{r}\right)\right\} \quad \text{.................. (63·5).}$$

Remembering that the variations involve only δm, this reduces to

$$4\pi r^2 ds\left(-\delta\gamma'-\frac{2}{r}\delta\gamma\right)$$

$$=8\pi\,\delta m\,.\,ds \quad \text{.............................. (63·6).}$$

We have ignored the flux across the two ends of the tube. It is clear that these will counterbalance one another.

This verification of the general result (63·1) for the case of a single particle gives another proof of the identity of gravitational mass with inertial mass.

We see then that a particle is attended by a certain flux of the quantity (63·3) across all surrounding surfaces. It is this flux which makes the presence of a massive particle known to us, and characterises it; in an observational sense the flux *is* the particle. So long as the space is empty the flux is the same across all surrounding surfaces however distant, the radius r of the tube having disappeared in the result; so that in a sense the Newtonian law of the inverse square has a direct analogue in Einstein's theory.

In general the flux is modified in passing through a region containing other particles or continuous matter, since the first term on the right of (60·3) no longer vanishes. This may be ascribed analytically to the non-linearity of the field equations, or physically to the fact that the outflowing influence can scarcely exert its action on other matter without being modified in the process. In our verification for the single particle the flux due to δm was independent of the value of m originally present; but this is an exceptional case due to symmetrical conditions which cause the integral of $T^{\mu\nu}\delta g_{\mu\nu}$ to vanish although $T^{\mu\nu}$ is not zero. Usually the flux due to δm will be modified if other matter is initially present.

For an isolated particle $m\,ds$ in any region is stationary for variations of its track, this condition being equivalent to (56·6). Hence for this kind of variation the action $8\pi\Sigma m\,ds$ in a region is stationary. The question arises how this is to be reconciled with our previous result (§ 60) that the principle of stationary action is untrue for regions containing matter. The reason is this:—when we give arbitrary variations to the $g_{\mu\nu}$, the matter in the tube will in general cease to be describable as a *particle*, because it has lost the symmetry of its field*. The action therefore is only stationary for a special kind of variation of $g_{\mu\nu}$ in the neighbourhood of each particle which deforms the track without destroying the symmetry of the particle; it is not stationary for unlimited variations of the $g_{\mu\nu}$.

* It will be remembered that in deriving (56·6) we had to assume the symmetry of the particle.

The fact that the variations which cause the failure of the principle of stationary action—those which violate the symmetry of the particles—are impossible in the actual world is irrelevant. Variations of the track of the particle are equally impossible, since in the actual world a particle cannot move in any other way than that in which it does move. The whole point of the Principle of Stationary Action is to show the relation of an actual state of the world to slightly varied states which cannot occur. Thus the breakdown of the principle cannot be excused. But we can see now why it gives correct results in ordinary mechanics, which takes the tracks of the particles as the sole quantities to be varied, and disregards the more general variations of the state of the world for which the principle ceases to be true.

64. Retrospect.

We have developed the mathematical theory of a continuum of four dimensions in which the points are connected in pairs by an absolute relation called the interval. In order that this theory may not be merely an exercise in pure mathematics, but may be applicable to the actual world, the quantities appearing in the theory must at some point be tied on to the things of experience. In the earlier chapters this was done by identifying the mathematical interval with a quantity which is the result of practical measurement with scales and clocks. In the present chapter this point of contact of theory and experience has passed into the background, and attention has been focussed on another opportunity of making the connection. The quantity $G_\mu^\nu - \frac{1}{2}g_\mu^\nu G$ appearing in the theory is, on account of its property of conservation, now identified with matter, or rather with the mechanical abstraction of matter which comprises the measurable properties of mass, momentum and stress sufficing for all mechanical phenomena. By making the connection between mathematical theory and the actual world at this point, we obtain a great lift forward.

Having now two points of contact with the physical world, it should become possible to construct a complete cycle of reasoning. There is one chain of pure deduction passing from the mathematical interval to the mathematical energy-tensor. The other chain binds the physical manifestations of the energy-tensor and the interval; it passes from matter as now defined by the energy-tensor to the interval regarded as the result of measurements made with this matter. The discussion of this second chain still lies ahead of us.

If actual matter had no other properties save such as are implied in the functional form of $G_\mu^\nu - \frac{1}{2}g_\mu^\nu G$, it would, I think, be impossible to make measurements with it. The property which makes it serviceable for measurement is discontinuity (not necessarily in the strict sense, but discontinuity from the macroscopic standpoint, i.e. atomicity). So far our only attempt to employ the new-found matter for measuring intervals has been in the study of the dynamics of a particle in § 56; we had there to assume that discrete particles exist and further that they have necessarily a symmetry of field; on this understanding we have completed the cycle for one of our most important test-bodies—the moving particle—the geodesic motion of which is used, especially in astronomy, for comparing intervals. But the theory of the use of matter for the purpose of measuring intervals will be taken up in a more general way at the beginning of the next chapter, and it will be seen how profoundly the existence of the complete cycle has determined that outlook on the world which we express in our formulation of the laws of mechanics.

It is a feature of our attitude towards nature that we pay great regard to that which is permanent; and for the same reason the creation of anything in the midst of a region is signalised by us as more worthy of remark than its entry in the orthodox manner through the boundary. Thus when we consider how an invariant depends on the variables used to describe the world, we attach more importance to changes which result in creation than to changes which merely involve transfer from elsewhere. It is perhaps for this reason that the Hamiltonian derivative of an invariant gives a quantity of greater significance for us than, for example, the ordinary derivative. The Hamiltonian derivative has a creative quality, and thus stands out in our minds as an active agent working in the passive field of space-time. Unless this idiosyncrasy of our practical outlook is understood, the Hamiltonian method with its casting away of boundary integrals appears somewhat artificial; but it is actually the natural method of deriving physical quantities prominent in our survey of the world, because it is guided by those principles which have determined their prominence. The particular form of the Hamiltonian method known as Least Action, in which special search is made for Hamiltonian derivatives which vanish, does not appear at present to admit of any very general application. In any case it seems better adapted to give neat mathematical formulae than to give physical insight; to grasp the equality or identity of two physical quantities is simpler than to ponder over the behaviour of the quantity which is their difference—distinguished though it may be by the important property of being incapable of existing!

According to the views reached in this chapter the law of gravitation $G_{\mu\nu} = 0$ is not to be regarded as an expression for the natural texture of the continuum, which can only be forcibly broken at points where some extraneous agent (matter) is inserted. The differentiation of occupied and unoccupied space arises from our particular outlook on the continuum, which, as explained above, is such that the Hamiltonian derivatives of the principal invariant G stand out as active agents against the passive background. It is therefore the regions in which these derivatives vanish which are regarded by us as unoccupied; and the law $G_{\mu\nu} = 0$ merely expresses the discrimination made by this process.

Among the minor points discussed, we have considered the speed of propagation of gravitational influence. It is presumed that the speed is that of light, but this does not appear to have been established rigorously. Any absolute influence must be measured by an invariant, particularly the invariant $B^{\epsilon}_{\mu\nu\sigma} B^{\mu\nu\sigma}_{\epsilon}$. The propagation of this invariant does not seem to have been investigated.

The ordinary potential energy of a weight raised to a height is not counted as energy in our theory and does not appear in our energy-tensor. It is found superfluous because the property of our energy-tensor has been formulated as a general law which from the absolute point of view is simpler than the formal law of conservation. The potential energy and momentum t^{ν}_{μ} needed if the formal law of conservation is preserved is not a tensor, and must be regarded as a mathematical fiction, not as representing any significant condition of the world. The pseudo-energy-tensor t^{ν}_{μ} can be created and destroyed at will by changes of coordinates; and even in a world containing no attracting matter (flat space-time) it does not necessarily vanish. It is therefore impossible to regard it as of a nature homogeneous with the proper energy-tensor.

CHAPTER V

CURVATURE OF SPACE AND TIME

65. Curvature of a four-dimensional manifold.

In the general Riemannian geometry admitted in our theory the $g_{\mu\nu}$ may be any 10 functions of the four coordinates x_μ.

A four-dimensional continuum obeying Riemannian geometry can be represented graphically as a surface of four dimensions drawn in a Euclidean hyperspace of a sufficient number of dimensions. Actually 10 dimensions are required, corresponding to the number of the $g_{\mu\nu}$. For let $(y_1, y_2, y_3, \ldots y_{10})$ be rectangular Euclidean coordinates, and (x_1, x_2, x_3, x_4) parameters on the surface, the equations of the surface will be of the form

$$y_1 = f_1(x_1, x_2, x_3, x_4), \ \ldots\ldots, \ y_{10} = f_{10}(x_1, x_2, x_3, x_4).$$

For an interval on the surface, the Euclidean geometry of the y's gives

$$\begin{aligned} -ds^2 &= dy_1^2 + dy_2^2 + dy_3^2 + \ldots + dy_{10}^2 \\ &= \left\{\left(\frac{\partial f_1}{\partial x_1}\right)^2 + \left(\frac{\partial f_2}{\partial x_1}\right)^2 + \ldots + \left(\frac{\partial f_{10}}{\partial x_1}\right)^2\right\} dx_1^2 + \ldots \\ &\quad + \left\{\frac{\partial f_1}{\partial x_1}\frac{\partial f_1}{\partial x_2} + \ldots + \frac{\partial f_{10}}{\partial x_1}\frac{\partial f_{10}}{\partial x_2}\right\} 2dx_1 dx_2 + \ldots. \end{aligned}$$

Equating the coefficients to the given functions $g_{\mu\nu}$, we have 10 partial differential equations of the form

$$\frac{\partial f_1}{\partial x_\mu}\frac{\partial f_1}{\partial x_\nu} + \ldots + \frac{\partial f_{10}}{\partial x_\mu}\frac{\partial f_{10}}{\partial x_\nu} = g_{\mu\nu},$$

to be satisfied by the 10 f's. Clearly it would not be possible to satisfy these equations with less than 10 f's except in special cases.

When we use the phrase "curvature" in connection with space-time, we always think of it as embedded in this way in a Euclidean space of higher dimensions. It is not suggested that the higher space has any existence; the purpose of the representation is to picture more vividly the metrical properties of the world. It must be remembered too that a great variety of four-dimensional surfaces in 10 dimensions will possess the same metric, i e be applicable to one another by bending without stretching, and any one of these can be chosen to represent the metric of space-time. Thus a geometrical property of the chosen representative surface need not necessarily be a property belonging intrinsically to the space-time continuum.

A four-dimensional surface free to twist about in six additional dimensions has bewildering possibilities. We consider first the simple case in which the surface, or at least a small portion of it, can be drawn in Euclidean space of five dimensions.

Take a point on the surface as origin Let (x_1, x_2, x_3, x_4) be rectangular coordinates in the tangent plane (four-dimensional) at the origin, and let the fifth rectangular axis along the normal be z. Then by Euclidean geometry

$$-ds^2 = dx_1^2 + dx_2^2 + dx_3^2 + dx_4^2 + dz^2 \qquad (65\cdot1),$$

imaginary values of ds corresponding as usual to real distances in space. The four-dimensional surface will be specified by a single equation between the five coordinates, which we may take to be

$$z = f(x_1, x_2, x_3, x_4).$$

If the origin is a regular point this can be expanded in powers of the x's. The deviation from the tangent plane is of the second order compared with distances parallel to the plane; consequently z does not contain linear terms in the x's The expansion accordingly starts with a homogeneous quadratic function, and the equation is of the form

$$2z = a_{\mu\nu} x_\mu x_\nu \qquad (65\cdot2),$$

correct to the second order. For a fixed value of z the quadric (65·2) is called the *indicatrix*.

The radius of curvature of any normal section of the surface is found by the well-known method. If t is the radius of the indicatrix in the direction of the section (direction cosines l_1, l_2, l_3, l_4), the radius of curvature is

$$\rho = \frac{t^2}{2z} = \frac{1}{a_{\mu\nu} l_\mu l_\nu}.$$

In particular, if the axes are rotated so as to coincide with the principal axes of the indicatrix, (65·2) becomes

$$2z = k_1 x_1^2 + k_2 x_2^2 + k_3 x_3^2 + k_4 x_4^2 \qquad (65\cdot3),$$

and the principal radii of curvature of the surface are the reciprocals of k_1, k_2, k_3, k_4.

Differentiating (65·2)

$$dz = a_{\mu\nu} x_\mu dx_\nu, \quad dz^2 = a_{\mu\nu} x_\mu dx_\nu \cdot a_{\sigma\tau} x_\sigma dx_\tau.$$

Hence, substituting in (65·1)

$$-ds^2 = dx_1^2 + dx_2^2 + dx_3^2 + dx_4^2 + (a_{\mu\nu} a_{\sigma\tau} x_\mu x_\sigma)\, dx_\nu dx_\tau$$

for points in the four-dimensional continuum Accordingly

$$-g_{\nu\tau} = g_\nu^\tau + a_{\mu\nu} a_{\sigma\tau} x_\mu x_\sigma \qquad (65\cdot4).$$

Hence at the origin the $g_{\mu\nu}$ are Euclidean; their first derivatives vanish and their second derivatives are given by

$$\frac{\partial^2 g_{\nu\tau}}{\partial x_\mu \partial x_\sigma} = -(a_{\mu\nu} a_{\sigma\tau} + a_{\sigma\nu} a_{\mu\tau}),$$

by (35·5)

Calculating the Riemann-Christoffel tensor by (34·5), since the first derivatives vanish,

$$B_{\mu\nu\sigma\rho} = \frac{1}{2}\left(\frac{\partial^2 g_{\sigma\rho}}{\partial x_\mu \partial x_\nu} + \frac{\partial^2 g_{\mu\nu}}{\partial x_\sigma \partial x_\rho} - \frac{\partial^2 g_{\mu\sigma}}{\partial x_\nu \partial x_\rho} - \frac{\partial^2 g_{\nu\rho}}{\partial x_\mu \partial x_\sigma}\right)$$

$$= a_{\mu\nu} a_{\sigma\rho} - a_{\mu\sigma} a_{\nu\rho} \qquad (65\cdot51).$$

Hence, remembering that the $g^{\tau\rho}$ have Euclidean values $-g^{\rho}_{\sigma}$,

$$G_{\mu\nu} = g^{\tau\rho} B_{\mu\nu\sigma\rho} = -a_{\mu\nu}(a_{11}+a_{22}+a_{33}+a_{44}) + a_{\mu\sigma}a_{\nu\sigma} \quad \ldots\ldots (65\cdot52).$$

In particular

$$G_{11} = -a_{11}(a_{11}+a_{22}+a_{33}+a_{44}) + a^2_{11} + a^2_{12} + a^2_{13} + a^2_{14}$$
$$= (a^2_{12} - a_{11}a_{22}) + (a^2_{13} - a_{11}a_{33}) + (a^2_{14} - a_{11}a_{44}) \quad \ldots\ldots (65\cdot53).$$

Also

$$G = g^{\mu\nu}G_{\mu\nu} = -G_{11} - G_{22} - G_{33} - G_{44}$$
$$= -2\{(a^2_{12}-a_{11}a_{22}) + (a^2_{13}-a_{11}a_{33}) + (a^2_{14}-a_{11}a_{44}) + (a^2_{23}-a_{22}a_{33})$$
$$+ (a^2_{24}-a_{22}a_{44}) + (a^2_{34}-a_{33}a_{44})\} \quad \ldots\ldots (65\cdot54).$$

When the principal axes are taken as in (65·3), these results become

$$\left.\begin{aligned} G_{11} &= -k_1(k_2+k_3+k_4) \\ G_{22} &= -k_2(k_1+k_3+k_4);\ \text{etc.} \end{aligned}\right\} \quad \ldots\ldots (65\cdot55)$$

and $$G = 2(k_1k_2 + k_1k_3 + k_1k_4 + k_2k_3 + k_2k_4 + k_3k_4) \quad \ldots\ldots (65\cdot6).$$

The invariant G has thus a comparatively simple interpretation in terms of the principal radii of curvature. It is a generalisation of the well-known invariant for two-dimensional surfaces $1/\rho_1\rho_2$, or k_1k_2. But this interpretation is only possible in the simple case of five dimensions. In general five dimensions are not sufficient to represent even the small portion of the surface near the origin; for if we set $G_{\mu\nu}=0$ in (65·55), we obtain $k_\mu = 0$, and hence by (65·51) $B_{\mu\nu\sigma\rho}=0$. Thus it is not possible to represent a natural gravitational field ($G_{\mu\nu}=0$, $B_{\mu\nu\sigma\rho}\neq 0$) in five Euclidean dimensions.

In the more general case we continue to call the invariant G the Gaussian curvature although the interpretation in terms of normal curvatures no longer holds. It is convenient also to introduce a quantity called the *radius of spherical curvature*, viz. the radius of a hypersphere which has the same Gaussian curvature as the surface considered*.

Considering the geometry of the general case, in 10 dimensions the normal is a six-dimensional continuum in which we can take rectangular axes $z_1, z_2, \ldots z_6$. The surface is then defined by six equations which near the origin take the form

$$2z_r = a_{r\mu\nu}x_\mu x_\nu \qquad (r = 1, 2 \ldots 6).$$

The radius of curvature of a normal section in the direction l_μ is then

$$\rho = \frac{t^2}{2\sqrt{(z_1^2+z_2^2+\ldots+z_6^2)}} = \frac{1}{\sqrt{\{(a_{1\mu\nu}l_\mu l_\nu)^2+\ldots+(a_{6\mu\nu}l_\mu l_\nu)^2\}}}.$$

It is, however, of little profit to develop the properties of normal curvature, which depend on the surface chosen to represent the metric of space-time and are not intrinsic in the metric itself. We therefore follow a different plan, introducing the radius of spherical curvature which has invariant properties.

* A hypersphere of four dimensions is by definition a four-dimensional surface drawn in five dimensions so that (65·6) applies to it. Accordingly if its radius is R, we have $G=12/R^2$. For three dimensions $G=6/R^2$; for two dimensions $G=2/R^2$.

Reverting for the moment to five dimensions, consider the *three-dimensional* space formed by the section of our surface by $x_1=0$. Let $G_{(1)}$ be its Gaussian curvature. Then $G_{(1)}$ is formed from G by dropping all terms containing the suffix 1—a dimension which no longer enters into consideration. Accordingly $G-G_{(1)}$ consists of those terms of G which contain the suffix 1; and by (65·53) and (65·54) we have

$$\tfrac{1}{2}(G-G_{(1)})=-G_{11} \quad \text{.................(65·71).}$$

Introducing the value $g_{11}=-1$ at the origin

$$G_{11}-\tfrac{1}{2}g_{11}G=\tfrac{1}{2}G_{(1)} \quad \text{...... (65·72)}$$

This result obtained for five dimensions is perfectly general From the manner in which (65·4) was obtained, it will be seen that each of the six z's will make contributions to $g_{\nu\tau}$ which are simply additive; we have merely to sum $a_{\mu\nu}a_{\sigma\tau}x_\mu x_\sigma$ for the six values of $a_{\mu\nu}a_{\sigma\tau}$ contributed by the six terms dz_r^2. All the subsequent steps involve linear equations and the work will hold for six z's just as well as for one z. Hence (65·72) is true in the general case when the representation requires 10 dimensions.

Now consider the invariant quadric

$$(G_{\mu\nu}-\tfrac{1}{2}g_{\mu\nu}G)\,dx_\mu dx_\nu=3 \quad \text{.............. (65·81)}$$

Let ρ_1 be the radius of this quadric in the x_1 direction, so that $dx_\mu=(\rho_1, 0, 0, 0)$ is a point on the quadric; the equation gives

$$(G_{11}-\tfrac{1}{2}g_{11}G)\,\rho_1^2=3,$$

so that by (65·72)

$$G_{(1)}=\frac{6}{\rho_1^2} \quad \text{.............................. (65·82).}$$

But for a hypersphere of radius R of *three* dimensions ($k_1=k_2=k_3=1/R$; k_4 disappears) the Gaussian curvature is $6/R^2$. Hence ρ_1 is the radius of spherical curvature of the three-dimensional section of the world perpendicular to the axis x_1.

Now the quadric (65·81) is invariant, so that the axis x_1 may be taken in any arbitrary direction Accordingly we see that—

The radius of the quadric $(G_{\mu\nu}-\tfrac{1}{2}g_{\mu\nu}G)\,dx_\mu dx_\nu=3$ *in any direction is equal to the radius of spherical curvature of the corresponding three-dimensional section of the world*

We call this quadric the *quadric of curvature.*

66. Interpretation of Einstein's law of gravitation.

We take the later form of Einstein's law (37·4)

$$G_{\mu\nu}=\lambda g_{\mu\nu} \quad \text{.............................(66·1)}$$

in empty space, λ being a universal constant at present unknown but so small as not to upset the agreement with observation established for the original form $G_{\mu\nu}=0$ We at once obtain $G=4\lambda$, and hence

$$G_{\mu\nu}-\tfrac{1}{2}g_{\mu\nu}G=-\lambda g_{\mu\nu}.$$

Substituting in (65·81) the quadric of curvature becomes

$$-\lambda g_{\mu\nu} dx_\mu dx_\nu = 3,$$

or

$$-ds^2 = 3/\lambda \qquad (66{\cdot}2)$$

That is to say, the quadric of curvature is a sphere of radius $\sqrt{(3/\lambda)}$, and the radius of curvature in every direction* and at every point in empty space has the constant length $\sqrt{(3/\lambda)}$.

Conversely if the directed radius of curvature in empty space is homogeneous and isotropic Einstein's law will hold.

The statement that the radius of curvature is a constant length requires more consideration before its full significance is appreciated. Length is not absolute, and the result can only mean *constant relative to the material standards of length* used in all our measurements and in particular in those measurements which verify $G_{\mu\nu} = \lambda g_{\mu\nu}$. In order to make a direct comparison the material unit must be conveyed to the place and pointed in the direction of the length to be measured. It is true that we often use indirect methods avoiding actual transfer or orientation; but the justification of these indirect methods is that they give the same result as a direct comparison, and their validity depends on the truth of the fundamental laws of nature. We are here discussing the most fundamental of these laws, and to admit the validity of the indirect methods of comparison at this stage would land us in a vicious circle. Accordingly the precise statement of our result is that the radius of curvature at any point and in any direction is in constant proportion to the length of a specified material unit placed at the same point and orientated in the same direction.

This becomes more illuminating if we invert the comparison—

The length of a specified material structure bears a constant ratio to the radius of curvature of the world at the place and in the direction in which it lies .... (66·3).

The law no longer appears to have any reference to the constitution of an empty continuum. It is a law of material structure showing what dimensions a specified collection of molecules must take up in order to adjust itself to equilibrium with surrounding conditions of the world.

The possibility of the existence of an electron in space is a remarkable phenomenon which we do not yet understand. The details of its structure must be determined by some unknown set of equations, which apparently admit of only two discrete solutions, the one giving a negative electron and the other a positive electron or proton. If we solve these equations to find

* For brevity I use the phrase "radius of curvature in a direction" to mean the radius of spherical curvature of the three-dimensional section of the world at right angles to that direction. There is no other radius of curvature *associated with a direction* likely to be confused with it.

the radius of the electron in any direction, the result must necessarily take the form

radius of electron in given direction = numerical constant × some function of the conditions in the space into which the electron was inserted.

And since the quantity on the left is a directed length, the quantity on the right must be a directed length. We have just found one directed length characteristic of the empty space in which the electron was introduced, viz. the radius of spherical curvature of a corresponding section of the world. Presumably by going to third or fourth derivatives of the $g_{\mu\nu}$ other independent directed lengths could be constructed; but that seems to involve an unlikely complication There is strong ground then for anticipating that the solution of the unknown equations will be

radius of electron in any direction = numerical constant × radius of curvature of space-time in that direction.

This leads at once to the law (66·3).

As with the electron, so with the atom and aggregations of atoms forming the practical units of material structure. Thus we see that Einstein's law of gravitation is the almost inevitable outcome of the use of material measuring-appliances for surveying the world, whatever may be the actual laws under which material structures are adjusted in equilibrium with the empty space around them.

Imagine first a world in which the curvature, referred to some chosen (non-material) standard of measurement, was not isotropic. An electron inserted in this would need to have the same anisotropy in order that it might obey the same detailed conditions of equilibrium as a symmetrical electron in an isotropic world. The same anisotropy persists in any material structure formed of these electrons Finally when we *measure* the world, i.e. make comparisons with material structures, the anisotropy occurs on both sides of the comparison and is eliminated. Einstein's law of gravitation expresses the result of this elimination. The symmetry and homogeneity expressed by Einstein's law is not a property of the external world, but a property of the operation of measurement.

From this point of view it is inevitable that the constant λ cannot be zero; so that empty space has a finite radius of curvature relative to familiar standards. An electron could never decide how large it ought to be unless there existed some length independent of itself for it to compare itself with.

It will be noticed that our rectangular coordinates (x_1, x_2, x_3, x_4) in this and the previous section approximate to Euclidean, not Galilean, coordinates. Consequently x_4 is imaginary time, and $G_{(4)}$ is not in any real direction in the world. There is no radius of curvature in a real timelike direction. This does not mean that our discussion is limited to three dimensions; it includes all directions in the four-dimensional world outside the light-cone, and applies to the space-dimensions of material structures moving with any speed up to the speed of light The real quadric of curvature terminates at the light-cone, and the mathematical continuation of it lies not inside the cone but in directions of imaginary time which do not concern us

By consideration of extension in timelike directions we obtain a confirmation of these views, which is, I think, not entirely fantastic. We have said that an electron would not know how large it ought to be unless there existed independent lengths in space for it to measure itself against. Similarly it would not know how long it ought to exist unless there existed a length in time for it to measure itself against. But there is no radius of curvature in a time-like direction; so the electron does *not* know how long it ought to exist. Therefore it just goes on existing indefinitely.

The alternative laws of gravitation discussed in § 62 would be obtained if the radius of the unit of material structure adjusted itself as a definite fraction not of the radius of curvature, but of other directed lengths (of a more complex origin) characteristic of empty space-time.

In § 56 it was necessary to postulate that the gravitational field due to an ultimate particle of matter has symmetrical properties. This has now been justified. We have introduced a new and far-reaching principle into the relativity theory, viz. that symmetry itself can only be relative; and the particle, which so far as mechanics is concerned is to be identified with its gravitational field, is the standard of symmetry. We reach the same result if we attempt to define symmetry by the propagation of light, so that the cone $ds=0$ is taken as the standard of symmetry. It is clear that if the locus $ds=0$ has complete symmetry about an axis (taken as the axis of t) ds^2 must be expressible by the formula (38·12).

The double-linkage of field and matter, matter and field, will now be realised Matter is derived from the fundamental tensor $g_{\mu\nu}$ by the expression $G_\mu^\nu - \frac{1}{2}g_\mu^\nu G$; but it is matter so derived which is initially used to measure the fundamental tensor $g_{\mu\nu}$. We have in this section considered one simple consequence of this cycle—the law of gravitation It needs a broader analysis to follow out the full consequences, and this will be attempted in Chapter VII, Part II.

67. Cylindrical and spherical space-time.

According to the foregoing section λ does not vanish, and there is a small but finite curvature at every point of space and time. This suggests the consideration of the shape and size of the world as a whole.

Two forms of the world have been suggested—

(1) Einstein's cylindrical world. Here the space-dimensions correspond to a sphere, but the time-dimension is uncurved.

(2) De Sitter's spherical world. Here all dimensions are spherical; but since it is imaginary time which is homogeneous with the space-coordinates, sections containing real time become hyperbolas instead of circles

We must describe these two forms analytically. A point on the surface of a sphere of radius R is described by two angular variables θ, ϕ, such that

$$-ds^2 = R^2(d\theta^2 + \sin^2\theta d\phi^2).$$

Extending this to three dimensions, we have three angular variables such that

$$-ds^2 = R^2\{d\chi^2 + \sin^2\chi(d\theta^2 + \sin^2\theta d\phi^2)\} \quad \text{.........(67·11).}$$

Accordingly in Einstein's form the interval is given by

$$ds^2 = -R^2 d\chi^2 - R^2\sin^2\chi(d\theta^2 + \sin^2\theta d\phi^2) + dt^2 \quad \text{......(67·12).}$$

Of course this form applies only to a survey of the world on the grand scale. Trifling irregularities due to the aggregation of matter into stars and stellar systems are treated as local deviations which can be disregarded.

Proceeding from the origin in any direction, $R\chi$ is the distance determined by measurement with rigid scales. But the measured area of a sphere of radius $R\chi$ is not $4\pi R^2\chi^2$ but $4\pi R^2\sin^2\chi$. There is not so much elbow-room in distant parts as Euclid supposed. We reach a "greatest sphere" at the distance $\frac{1}{2}\pi R$; proceeding further, successive spheres contract and decrease to a single point at a distance πR—the greatest distance which can exist.

The whole volume of space (determined by rigid scales) is finite and equal to

$$\int_0^\pi 4\pi R^2\sin^2\chi \,.\, R d\chi = 2\pi^2 R^3 \quad \text{..............(67·2).}$$

Although the volume of space is finite, there is no boundary; nor is there any centre of spherical space. Every point stands in the same relation to the rest of space as every other point.

To obtain de Sitter's form, we generalise (67·11) to four dimensions (i.e. a spherical four-dimensional surface drawn in Euclidean space of five dimensions). We have four angular variables ω, ζ, θ, ϕ, and

$$-ds^2 = R^2[d\omega^2 + \sin^2\omega\{d\zeta^2 + \sin^2\zeta(d\theta^2 + \sin^2\theta d\phi^2)\}] \quad \text{...(67·31).}$$

In order to obtain a coordinate-system whose physical interpretation is more easily recognisable, we make the transformation

$$\cos\omega = \cos\chi\cos it,$$
$$\cot\zeta = \cot\chi\sin it,$$

which gives

$$\left.\begin{aligned}\sin\chi &= \sin\zeta\sin\omega\\ \tan it &= \cos\zeta\tan\omega\end{aligned}\right\} \quad \text{......................(67·32).}$$

Working out the results of this substitution, we obtain

$$ds^2 = -R^2 d\chi^2 - R^2\sin^2\chi(d\theta^2 + \sin^2\theta d\phi^2) + R^2\cos^2\chi \,.\, dt^2 \text{...(67·33).}$$

So far as space (χ, θ, ϕ) is concerned, this agrees with Einstein's form (67·12); but the variable t, which will be regarded as the "time"* in this world, has different properties. For a clock at rest (χ, θ, ϕ = const.) we have

$$ds = R\cos\chi dt \quad \text{.........................(67·4),}$$

* The velocity of light at the origin is now R. In the usual units the time would be Rt.

so that the "time" of any cycle is proportional to $\sec \chi$ The clock-beats become longer and longer as we recede from the origin, in particular the vibrations of an atom become slower Moreover we can detect by practical measurement this slowing down of atomic vibrations, because it is preserved in the transmission of the light to us. The coordinates (67·33) form a statical system, the velocity of light being independent of t, hence the light-pulses are all delayed in transmission by the same "time" and reach us at the same intervals of t as they were emitted. Spectral lines emanating from distant sources at rest should consequently appear displaced towards the red.

At the "horizon" $\chi = \frac{1}{2}\pi$, any finite value of ds corresponds to an infinite dt. It takes an infinite "time" for anything to happen. All the processes of nature have come to a standstill so far as the observer at the origin can have evidence of them.

But we must recall that by the symmetry of the original formula (67·31), any point of space and time could be chosen as origin with similar results. Thus there can be no actual difference in the natural phenomena at the horizon and at the origin. The observer on the horizon does not perceive the stoppage —in fact he has a horizon of his own at a distance $\frac{1}{2}\pi R$ where things appear to him to have come to a standstill

Let us send a ray of light from the origin to the horizon and back again (We take the double journey because the time-lapse can then be recorded by a single clock at the origin; the physical significance of the time for a single journey is less obvious) Setting $ds = 0$, the velocity of the light is given by

$$0 = -R^2 d\chi^2 + R^2 \cos^2 \chi \, dt^2,$$

so that

$$dt = \pm \sec \chi \, d\chi,$$

whence

$$t = \pm \log \tan \left(\tfrac{1}{4}\pi + \tfrac{1}{2}\chi\right) \quad \text{.................... (67·5).}$$

This must be taken between the limits $\chi = 0$ and $\frac{1}{2}\pi$, and again with reversed sign between the limits $\frac{1}{2}\pi$ and 0. The result is infinite, and the journey can never be completed.

De Sitter accordingly dismisses the paradox of the arrest of time at the horizon with the remark that it only affects events which happen before the beginning or after the end of eternity. But we shall discuss this in greater detail in § 70.

68. Elliptical space.

The equation (67·11) for spherical space, which appears in both de Sitter's and Einstein's form of the interval, can also be construed as representing a slightly modified kind of space called "elliptical space." From the modern standpoint the name is rather unfortunate, and does not in any way suggest its actual nature. We can approach the problem of elliptical space in the following way—

Suppose that in spherical space the physical processes going on at every point are exactly the same as those going on at the antipodal point, so that one half of the world is an exact replica of the other half Let $ABA'B'$ be four points 90° apart on a great circle. Let us proceed from B', *via* A, to B; on continuing the journey along BA' it is impossible to tell that we are not repeating the journey $B'A$ already performed We should be tempted to think that the arc $B'A$ was in fact the immediate continuation of AB, B and B' being the same point and only represented as wide apart through some fault in our projective representation—just as in a Mercator Chart we see the same Behring Sea represented at both edges of the map. We may leave to the metaphysicist the question whether two objects can be exactly alike, both intrinsically and in relation to all surroundings, and yet differ in identity, physics has no conception of what is meant by this mysterious differentiation of identity, and in the case supposed, physics would unhesitatingly declare that the observer was re-exploring the same hemisphere.

Thus the spherical world in the case considered does not consist of two similar halves, but of a single hemisphere imagined to be repeated twice over for convenience of projective representation. The differential geometry is the same as for a sphere, as given by (67 11), but the *connectivity* is different; just as a plane and a cylinder have the same differential geometry but different connectivity. At the limiting circle of any hemisphere there is a cross-connection of opposite ends of the diameters which it is impossible to represent graphically, but that is, of course, no reason against the existence of the cross-connection.

This hemisphere which returns on itself by cross-connections is the type of elliptical space. In what follows we shall not need to give separate consideration to elliptical space. It is sufficient to bear in mind that in adopting spherical space we may be representing the physical world in duplicate, for example, the volume $2\pi^2R^3$ already given may refer to the duplicated world.

The difficulty in conceiving spherical or elliptical space arises mainly because we think of space as a continuum in which objects are *located*. But it was explained in § 1 that location is not the primitive conception, and is of the nature of a computational result based on the more fundamental notion of extension or distance. In using the word "space" it is difficult to repress irrelevant ideas, therefore let us abandon the word and state explicitly that we are considering a *network of intervals* (or distances, since at present we are not dealing with time). The relation of interval or distance between two points is of some transcendental character comparable, for example, with a difference of potential or with a chemical affinity, the reason why this particular relation is always associated with geometrical ideas must be sought in human psychology rather than in its intrinsic nature. We apply measure-numbers to the interval as we should apply them to any other relation of the two points; and we thus obtain a network with a number attached to every chord of the net. We could then make a string model of the network, the length of each string corresponding to the measure-number of the interval.

Clearly the form of this model—the existence or non-existence of unexpected cross-connections—cannot be predicted *a priori*; it must be the subject of observation and experiment. It may turn out to correspond to a lattice drawn by the mathematician in a Euclidean space; or it may be cross-connected in a way which cannot be represented in a lattice of that kind. Graphical representation is serviceable as a tool but is dangerous as an obsession. If we can find a graphical representation which conforms to the actual character of the network, we may employ it; but we must not imagine that any considerations as to suitability for graphical representation have determined the design of the network. From experience we know that small portions of the network do admit of easy representation as a lattice in flat space, just as small portions of the earth's surface can be mapped on a flat sheet. It does not follow that the whole earth is flat, or that the whole network can be represented in a space without multiple connection.

69. Law of gravitation for curved space-time.

By means of the results (43·5) the $G_{\mu\nu}$ can be calculated for either Einstein's or de Sitter's forms of the world. De Sitter's equation (67·33) is of the standard form with χ substituted for r, and

$$e^{\lambda} = R^2, \quad e^{\mu} = R^2 \sin^2\chi/\chi^2, \quad e^{\nu} = R^2\cos^2\chi,$$

thus

$$\lambda' = 0, \quad \mu' = 2\cot\chi - 2/\chi, \quad \nu' = -2\tan\chi,$$

$$\mu'' = -2\operatorname{cosec}^2\chi + 2/\chi^2, \quad \nu'' = -2\sec^2\chi.$$

Hence by (43·5) we find after an easy reduction

$$G_{11} = -3, \quad G_{22} = -3\sin^2\chi, \quad G_{33} = -3\sin^2\chi\sin^2\theta, \quad G_{44} = 3\cos^2\chi.$$

These are equivalent to

$$G_{\mu\nu} = \frac{3}{R^2} g_{\mu\nu} \quad \text{.......................} (69{\cdot}11).$$

De Sitter's world thus corresponds to the revised form of the law of gravitation

$$G_{\mu\nu} = \lambda g_{\mu\nu},$$

and its radius is given by

$$\lambda = \frac{3}{R^2} \quad \text{.............................} (69{\cdot}12).$$

Einstein's form (67·12) gives similarly

$$e^{\lambda} = R^2, \quad e^{\mu} = R^2\sin^2\chi/\chi^2, \quad e^{\nu} = 1,$$

from which by (43·5)

$$G_{11} = -2, \quad G_{22} = -2\sin^2\chi, \quad G_{33} = -2\sin^2\chi\sin^2\theta, \quad G_{44} = 0 \quad ..(69{\cdot}21),$$

$$G = 6/R^2 \text{..............................} (69{\cdot}22).$$

It is not possible to reconcile these values with the law $G_{\mu\nu} = \lambda g_{\mu\nu}$, owing to the vanishing of G_{44}. Einstein's form cannot be the natural form of empty space; but it may nevertheless be the actual form of the world if the matter in the world is suitably distributed. To determine the necessary distribution we must calculate the energy-tensor (54·71)

$$-8\pi T_{\mu\nu} = G_{\mu\nu} - \tfrac{1}{2} g_{\mu\nu} G + \lambda g_{\mu\nu}.$$

We find

$$\left.\begin{aligned} -8\pi T_{11} &= \left(-\frac{1}{R^2}+\lambda\right) g_{11} \\ -8\pi T_{22} &= \left(-\frac{1}{R^2}+\lambda\right) g_{22} \\ -8\pi T_{33} &= \left(-\frac{1}{R^2}+\lambda\right) g_{33} \\ -8\pi T_{44} &= \left(-\frac{3}{R^2}+\lambda\right) g_{44} \end{aligned}\right\} \qquad \text{.................(69·3).}$$

Since λ is still at our disposal, the distribution of this energy-tensor is indeterminate. But it is noted that within the stellar system the speed of matter, whether of molecules or of stars, is generally small compared with the velocity of light There is perhaps a danger of overstressing this evidence, since astronomical research seems to show that the greater the scale of our exploration the more divergent are the velocities; thus the spiral nebulae, which are perhaps the most remote objects observed, have speeds of the order 500 km per sec.—at least ten times greater than the speeds observed in the stellar system. It seems possible that at still greater distances the velocities may increase further However in Einstein's solution we assume that the average velocity of the material particles is always small compared with the velocity of light, so the general features of the world correspond to

$$T_{11} = T_{22} = T_{33} = 0, \quad T_{44} = \rho, \quad T = \rho_0,$$

where ρ_0 is the average density (in natural measure) of the matter in space.

Hence by (69 3) $$\lambda = \frac{1}{R^2}, \quad 8\pi\rho_0 = \frac{2}{R^2} \qquad \text{.............(69·4)}$$

Accordingly if M is the total mass in the universe, we have by (67 2)

$$\begin{aligned} M &= 2\pi^2 R^3 \rho_0 \\ &= \tfrac{1}{2}\pi R \qquad \text{.............................(69·5)} \end{aligned}$$

R can scarcely be less than 10^{18} kilometres since the distances of some of the globular clusters exceed this. Remembering that the gravitational mass of the sun is 1·5 kilometres, the mass of the matter in the world must be equivalent to at least a trillion suns, if Einstein's form of the world is correct

It seems natural to regard de Sitter's and Einstein's forms as two limiting cases, the circumstances of the actual world being intermediate between them. De Sitter's empty world is obviously intended only as a limiting case; and the presence of stars and nebulae must modify it, if only slightly, in the direction of Einstein's solution. Einstein's world containing masses far exceeding anything imagined by astronomers, might be regarded as the other extreme—a world containing as much matter as it can hold This view denies any fundamental cleavage of the theory in regard to the two forms, regarding it as a mere accident, depending on the amount of matter which happens to have been created, whether de Sitter's or Einstein's form is the nearer approximation to the truth. But this compromise has been strongly challenged, as we shall see

70. Properties of de Sitter's spherical world.

If in (67·33) we write

$$r = R \sin \chi,$$

we obtain
$$\left.\begin{aligned} ds^2 &= -\gamma^{-1} dr^2 - r^2 d\theta^2 - r^2 \sin^2 \theta \, d\phi^2 + \gamma dt^2 \\ \gamma &= 1 - r^2/R^2 = 1 - \tfrac{1}{3}\lambda r^2 \end{aligned}\right\} \quad \text{.........(70·1)},$$
where

and the customary unit of t has been restored. This solution for empty space has already been given, equation (45·6).

We have merely to substitute this value of γ in the investigations of §§ 38, 39, in order to obtain the motion of material particles and of light-waves in de Sitter's empty world. Thus (39·31) may be written

$$\frac{d^2 r}{ds^2} - \frac{1}{2}\frac{\gamma'}{\gamma}\left(\frac{dr}{ds}\right)^2 - r\gamma\left(\frac{d\phi}{ds}\right)^2 + \tfrac{1}{2}\gamma\gamma'\left(\frac{dt}{ds}\right)^2 = 0.$$

Whence

$$\frac{d^2 r}{ds^2} = -\frac{\tfrac{1}{3}\lambda r}{1 - \tfrac{1}{3}\lambda r^2}\left(\frac{dr}{ds}\right)^2 + r\left(1 - \tfrac{1}{3}\lambda r^2\right)\left(\frac{d\phi}{ds}\right)^2 + \tfrac{1}{3}\lambda r\left(1 - \tfrac{1}{3}\lambda r^2\right)\left(\frac{dt}{ds}\right)^2$$
......(70·21).

For a particle at rest

$$\frac{dr}{ds} = 0, \quad \frac{d\phi}{ds} = 0, \quad \left(\frac{dt}{ds}\right)^2 = \gamma^{-1}.$$

Hence
$$\frac{d^2 r}{ds^2} = \tfrac{1}{3}\lambda r \quad \text{.............................. (70·22)}.$$

Thus a particle at rest will not remain at rest unless it is at the origin; but will be repelled from the origin with an acceleration increasing with the distance. A number of particles initially at rest will tend to scatter, unless their mutual gravitation is sufficient to overcome this tendency.

It can easily be verified that there is no such tendency in Einstein's world. A particle placed anywhere will remain at rest. This indeed is necessary for the self-consistency of Einstein's solution, for he requires the world to be filled with matter having negligible velocity. It is sometimes urged against de Sitter's world that it becomes non-statical as soon as any matter is inserted in it But this property is perhaps rather in favour of de Sitter's theory than against it.

One of the most perplexing problems of cosmogony is the great speed of the spiral nebulae. Their radial velocities average about 600 km. per sec and there is a great preponderance of velocities of recession from the solar system It is usually supposed that these are the most remote objects known (though this view is opposed by some authorities), so that here if anywhere we might look for effects due to a general curvature of the world. De Sitter's theory gives a double explanation of this motion of recession; first, there is the general tendency to scatter according to equation (70·22); second, there is the general displacement of spectral lines to the red in distant objects due to the slowing down of atomic vibrations (67·4) which would be erroneously interpreted as a motion of recession.

The most extensive measurements of radial velocities of spiral nebulae have been made by Prof V. M Slipher at the Lowell Observatory. He has kindly prepared for me the following table, containing many unpublished results It is believed to be complete up to date (Feb 1922). For the nebulae marked (*) the results have been closely confirmed at other observatories; those marked (†) are not so accurate as the others The number in the first column refers to the "New General Catalogue," *Memoirs R A S*, vol 49 One additional nebula N.G C. 1700 has been observed by Pease, who found a large receding velocity but gave no numerical estimate.

Radial Velocities of Spiral Nebulae

+ indicates receding, − approaching

N G C	R. A	Dec.	Rad. Vel.	N G C	R A	Dec	Rad. Vel.
	h m	° ′	km. per sec.		*h m*	° ′	km per sec
221	0 38	+40 26	− 300	4151*	12 6	+39 51	+ 980
224*	0 38	+40 50	− 300	4214	12 12	+36 46	+ 300
278†	0 47	+47 7	+ 650	4258	12 15	+47 45	+ 500
404	1 5	+35 17	− 25	4382†	12 21	+18 38	+ 500
584†	1 27	− 7 17	+1800	4449	12 24	+44 32	+ 200
598*	1 29	+30 15	− 260	4472	12 25	+ 8 27	+ 850
936	2 24	− 1 31	+1300	4486†	12 27	+12 50	+ 800
1023	2 35	+38 43	+ 300	4526	12 30	+ 8 9	+ 580
1068*	2 39	− 0 21	+1120	4565†	12 32	+26 26	+1100
2683	8 48	+33 43	+ 400	4594*	12 36	−11 11	+1100
2841†	9 16	+51 19	+ 600	4649	12 40	+12 0	+1090
3031	9 49	+69 27	− 30	4736	12 47	+41 33	+ 290
3034	9 49	+70 5	+ 290	4826	12 53	+22 7	+ 150
3115†	10 1	− 7 20	+ 600	5005	13 7	+37 29	+ 900
3368	10 42	+12 14	+ 940	5055	13 12	+42 37	+ 450
3379*	10 43	+13 0	+ 780	5194	13 26	+47 36	+ 270
3489†	10 56	+14 20	+ 600	5195†	13 27	+47 41	+ 240
3521	11 2	+ 0 24	+ 730	5236†	13 32	−29 27	+ 500
3623	11 15	+13 32	+ 800	5866	15 4	+56 4	+ 650
3627	11 16	+13 26	+ 650	7331	22 33	+33 23	+ 500
4111†	12 3	+43 31	+ 800				

The great preponderance of positive (receding) velocities is very striking, but the lack of observations of southern nebulae is unfortunate, and forbids a final conclusion. Even if these also show a preponderance of receding velocities the cosmogonical difficulty is perhaps not entirely removed by de Sitter's theory. It will be seen that two‡ nebulae (including the great Andromeda nebula) are approaching with rather high velocity and these velocities happen to be exceptionally well determined. In the full formula (70·21) there are no terms which under any reasonable conditions encourage motion towards the origin§. It is therefore difficult to account for these motions even as exceptional phenomena; on the other hand an approaching velocity of 300 km. per sec. is about the limit occasionally attained by individual stars or star clusters.

‡ N. G. C. 221 and 224 may probably be counted as one system. The two approaching nebulae are the largest spirals in the sky.

§ We are limited to the region in which $(1-\frac{1}{3}\lambda r^2)$ is positive since light cannot cross the barrier.

The conservation of energy is satisfied in de Sitter's world; but from the practical standpoint it is abrogated in large scale problems such as that of the system of the spirals, since these are able to withdraw kinetic energy from a source not generally taken into account.

Equation (39·44) $$\frac{1}{\gamma}\left(\frac{h}{r^2}\frac{dr}{d\phi}\right)^2 + \frac{h^2}{r^2} - \frac{c^2}{\gamma} = -1$$

becomes on substituting for γ

$$\left(\frac{h}{r^2}\frac{dr}{d\phi}\right)^2 + \frac{h^2}{r^2} = c^2 - 1 - \tfrac{1}{3}\lambda h^2 + \tfrac{1}{3}\lambda r^2,$$

or writing $u = 1/r$ $$\left(\frac{du}{d\phi}\right)^2 + u^2 = \frac{c^2 - 1}{h^2} - \tfrac{1}{3}\lambda + \frac{\tfrac{1}{3}\lambda}{h^2 u^2}.$$

Whence, differentiating

$$\frac{d^2u}{d\phi^2} + u = -\frac{\tfrac{1}{3}\lambda}{h^2}u^{-3} \quad \text{.............................(70·3).}$$

The orbit is the same as that of a particle under a repulsive force varying directly as the distance. (This applies only to the form of the orbit, not to the velocity in the orbit.) For the motion of light the constant of areas h is infinite, and the tracks of light-rays are the solutions of

$$\frac{d^2u}{d\phi^2} + u = 0,$$

i.e. straight lines. Determination of distance by parallax-measurements rests on the assumption that light is propagated in straight lines, and hence the method is exact in this system of coordinates. In so far as the distances of celestial objects are determined by parallaxes or parallactic motions, the coordinate r will agree with their accepted distances. This result may be contrasted with the solution for the field of a particle in § 38 where the coordinate r has no immediate observational significance. Radial distances determined by direct operations with measuring-rods correspond to $R\chi$, not r.

The spectroscopic radial velocity is not exactly equivalent to dr/dt, but the divergence is unimportant. A pulse of light emitted by an atom situated at $r = R\sin\chi$ at time t will reach the observer at the origin at time t', where by (67·5)

$$t' = t + \log\tan\left(\tfrac{1}{4}\pi + \tfrac{1}{2}\chi\right),$$

so that for the time-interval between two pulses

$$\begin{aligned} dt' &= dt + \sec\chi\, d\chi \\ &= \left(1 + \sec\chi\frac{d\chi}{dt}\right)\frac{dt}{ds}ds \\ &= \left(\sec\chi + \sec^2\chi\frac{d\chi}{dt}\right)ds, \qquad \text{by (67·33)} \end{aligned}$$

neglecting the square of the velocity of the atom. If dt_0' is the time for a similar atom at rest at the origin,

$$\frac{dt'}{dt_0'} = \sec\chi + \sec^2\chi\frac{d\chi}{dt}$$

$$= \sec\chi + \sec^3\chi\frac{1}{R}\frac{dr}{dt} \quad \text{.................. (70·4).}$$

The first term represents the general shift to the red dependent on position and not on velocity. Assuming that it has been allowed for, the remaining part of the shift corresponds to a velocity of $\sec^3\chi\frac{dr}{dt}$ instead of $\frac{dr}{dt}$. The correction is scarcely of practical importance.

The acceleration $\frac{1}{3}\lambda r$ found in (70·22), if continued for the time $R\chi$ taken by the light from the object to reach the origin, would cause a change of velocity of the order $\frac{1}{3}\lambda r^2$ or r^2/R^2. The Doppler effect of this velocity would be roughly the same as the shift to the red caused by the slowing down of atomic vibrations. We may thus regard the red shift for distant objects at rest as *an anticipation* of the motion of recession which will have been attained before we receive the light. If de Sitter's interpretation of the red shift in the spiral nebulae is correct, we need not regard the deduced large motions of recession as entirely fallacious; it is true that the nebulae had not these motions when they emitted the light which is now examined, but they have acquired them by now. Even the standing still of time on the horizon becomes intelligible from this point of view; we are supposed to be observing a system which has *now* the velocity of light, having acquired it during the infinite time which has elapsed since the observed light was emitted.

The following paradox is sometimes found puzzling. Take coordinates for an observer A at rest at the origin, and let B be at rest at the time t at a considerable distance from the origin. The vibrations of an atom at B are slower (as measured in the time t) than those of an atom at A, and since the coordinate-system is static this difference will be detected experimentally by *any* observer who measures the frequency of the light he receives. Accordingly B must detect the difference, and conclude that the light from A is displaced towards the violet relatively to his standard atom. This is absurd since, if we choose B as origin, the light from A should be displaced towards the red. The fallacy lies in ignoring what has happened during the long time of propagation from A to B or B to A; during this time the two observers have ceased to be in relative rest, so that compensating Doppler effects are superposed.

To obtain a clearer geometrical idea of de Sitter's world, we consider only one dimension of space, neglecting the coordinates θ and ϕ. Then by (67·31)

$$-ds^2 = R^2(d\omega^2 + \sin^2\omega\, d\zeta^2) = R^2(d\chi^2 - \cos^2\chi\, dt^2)$$

$$= dx^2 + dy^2 + dz^2,$$

where
$$x = R \sin \omega \cos \zeta = R \cos \chi \sin it,$$
$$y = R \sin \omega \sin \zeta = R \sin \chi,$$
$$z = R \cos \omega \quad = R \cos \chi \cos it,$$
and
$$x^2 + y^2 + z^2 = R^2.$$

It will be seen that real values of χ and t correspond to imaginary values of ω and ζ, and accordingly for real events x is imaginary and y and z are real. Introducing a real coordinate $\xi = -ix$, real space-time will be represented by the hyperboloid of one sheet with its axis along the axis of ξ,

$$y^2 + z^2 - \xi^2 = R^2,$$

the geometry being of the Galilean type

$$ds^2 = d\xi^2 - dy^2 - dz^2.$$

We have
$$r = R \sin \chi = y,$$
$$\tanh t = -i \tan it = -ix/z = \xi/z,$$

so that the space-partitions are made by planes perpendicular to the axis of y, and the time-partitions by planes through the axis of y cutting the hyperboloid into lunes.

The light-tracks, $ds = 0$, are the generators of the hyperboloid. The tracks of undisturbed particles are (non-Euclidean) geodesics on the hyperboloid; and, except for $y = 0$, the space-partitions will not be geodesics, so that particles do not remain at rest.

The coordinate-frame (r, t) of a single observer does not cover the whole world. The range from $t = -\infty$ to $t = +\infty$ corresponds to values of ξ/z between ± 1. The whole experience of any one observer of infinite longevity is comprised within a 90° lune. Changing the origin we can have another observer whose experience covers a different lune. The two observers cannot communicate the non-overlapping parts of their experience, since there are no light-tracks (generators) taking the necessary course.

A further question has been raised, Is de Sitter's world really empty? In formula (70·1) there is a singularity at $r = \sqrt{(3/\lambda)}$ similar to the singularity at $r = 2m$ in the solution for a particle of matter. Must we not suppose that the former singularity also indicates matter—a "mass-horizon" or ring of peripheral matter necessary in order to distend the empty region within. If so, it would seem that de Sitter's world cannot exist without large quantities of matter any more than Einstein's; he has merely swept the dust away into unobserved corners.

A singularity of ds^2 does not necessarily indicate material particles, for we can introduce or remove such singularities by making transformations of coordinates. It is impossible to know whether to blame the world-structure or the inappropriateness of the coordinate-system. In a finite region we avoid this difficulty by choosing a coordinate-system initially appropriate—how this is done is very little understood—and permitting only transformations which have no singularity in the region. But we can scarcely apply this to a consideration of the whole finite world since all the ordinary analytical transformations (even a change of origin) introduce a singularity somewhere. If de Sitter's form for an empty world is right it is impossible to find any coordinate-system which represents the whole of real space-time regularly. This is no doubt inconvenient for the mathematician, but I do not see that the objection has any other consequences

The whole of de Sitter's world can be reached by a process of continuation; that is to say the finite experience of an observer A extends over a certain lune; he must then hand over the description to B whose experience is partly overlapping and partly new; and so on by overlapping lunes The equation $G_{\mu\nu} = \lambda g_{\mu\nu}$ rests on the considerations of § 66, and simply by continuation of this equation from point to point we arrive at de Sitter's complete world without encountering any barrier or mass-horizon.

A possible indication that there is no real mass in de Sitter's world is afforded by a calculation of the gravitational flux (63·4). By (63·6) this is

$$4\pi r^2 \left(-\delta\gamma' - \frac{2}{r}\delta\gamma\right) dt,$$

since dt can no longer be replaced by ds. On substituting for γ it is found that the flux vanishes for all values of r. It is true that as we approach the boundary dt/ds becomes very great, but the complete absence of flux right up to the boundary seems inconsistent with the existence of a genuine mass-horizon.

I believe then that the mass-horizon is merely an illusion of the observer at the origin, and that it continually recedes as we move towards it.

71. Properties of Einstein's cylindrical world.

Einstein does not regard the relation (69·5)

$$M = \tfrac{1}{2}\pi R = \tfrac{1}{2}\pi\lambda^{-\frac{1}{2}} \quad \text{.........................(71·1)}$$

as merely referring to the limiting case when the amount of matter in the world happens to be sufficient to make the form cylindrical. He considers it to be a necessary relation between λ and M; so that the constant λ occurring in the law of gravitation is a function of the total mass of matter in the world, and the volume of space is conditioned by the amount of matter contained in it

The question at once arises, By what mechanism can the value of λ be adjusted to correspond with M? The creation of a new stellar system in a distant part of the world would have to propagate to us, not merely a gravitational field, but a modification of the law of gravitation itself. We cannot trace the propagation of any such influence, and the dependence of λ upon distant masses looks like sheer action at a distance.

But the suggestion is perhaps more plausible if we look at the inverse relation, viz. M as a function of λ. If we can imagine the gradual destruction of matter in the world (e.g. by coalescence of positive and negative electrons), we see by (71·1) that the radius of space gradually contracts; but it is not clear what is the fixed standard of length by which R is supposed to be measured. The natural standard of length in a theoretical discussion is the radius R itself. Choosing it as unit, we have $M = \frac{1}{2}\pi$, whatever the number of elementary particles in the world. Thus with this unit the mass of a particle must be inversely proportional to the number of particles. Now the gravitational mass is the radius of a sphere which has some intimate relation to the structure of the particle; and we must conclude that as the destruction of particles proceeds, this sphere must swell up as though some pressure were being relaxed. We might try to represent this pressure by the gravitational flux (§ 63) which proceeds from every particle; but I doubt whether that leads to a satisfactory solution. However that may be, the idea that the particles each endeavour to monopolise all space, and restrain one another by a mutual pressure, seems to be the simplest interpretation of (71·1) if it is to be accepted.

We do not know whether the actual (or electrical) radius of the particle would swell in the same proportion—by a rough guess I should anticipate that it would depend on the square root of the above ratio. But this radius, on which the scale of ordinary material standards depends, has nothing to do with equation (71·1), and if we suppose that it remains constant, the argument of § 66 need not be affected.

In favour of Einstein's hypothesis is the fact that among the constants of nature there is one which is a very large pure number; this is typified by the ratio of the radius of an electron to its gravitational mass $= 3 \cdot 10^{42}$. It is difficult to account for the occurrence of a pure number (of order greatly different from unity) in the scheme of things; but this difficulty would be removed if we could connect it with the number of particles in the world—a number presumably decided by pure accident*. There is an attractiveness in the idea that the total number of the particles may play a part in determining the constants of the laws of nature; we can more readily admit that the laws of the actual world are specialised by the accidental circumstance of a particular number of particles occurring in it, than that they are specialised by the same number occurring as a mysterious ratio in the fine-grained structure of the continuum.

In Einstein's world one direction is uncurved and this gives a kind of absolute time. Our critic who has been waiting ever since § 1 with his blank label "true time" will no doubt seize this opportunity of affixing it. More-

* The square of $3 \cdot 10^{42}$ might well be of the same order as the total number of positive and negative electrons. The corresponding radius is 10^{14} parsecs. But the result is considerably altered if we take the proton instead of the electron as the more fundamental structure.

over absolute velocity is to some extent restored, for there is by hypothesis a frame of reference with respect to which material bodies on the average have only small velocities. Matter is essential to the existence of a space-time frame according to Einstein's view; and it is inevitable that the space-time frame should become to some extent materialised, thereby losing some of the valuable elusiveness of a purely aetherial frame. It has been suggested that since the amount of matter necessary for Einstein's world greatly exceeds that known to astronomers, most of it is spread uniformly through space and is undetectable by its uniformity. This is dangerously like restoring a crudely material aether—regulated, however, by the strict injunction that it must on no account perform any useful function lest it upset the principle of relativity. We may leave aside this suggestion, which creates unnecessary difficulties. I think that the matter contemplated in Einstein's theory is ordinary stellar matter. Owing to the irregularity of distribution of stars, the actual form of space is not at all a smooth sphere, and the formulae are only intended to give an approximation to the general shape.

The Lorentz transformation continues to hold for a limited region. Since the advent of the general theory, it has been recognised that the special theory only applies to particular regions where the $g_{\mu\nu}$ can be treated as constants, so that it scarcely suffers by the fact that it cannot be applied to the whole domain of spherical space. Moreover the special principle is now brought into line with the general principle. The transformations of the theory of relativity relate to the differential equations of physics, and our tendency to choose simple illustrations in which these equations are integrable over the whole of space-time (as simplified in the mathematical example) is responsible for much misconception on this point.

The remaining features of Einstein's world require little comment. His spherical space is commonplace compared with de Sitter's. Each observer's coordinate-system covers the whole world, so that the fields of their finite experience coincide. There is no scattering force to cause divergent motions. Light performs the finite journey round the world in a finite time. There is no passive "horizon," and in particular no mass-horizon, real or fictitious. Einstein's world offers no explanation of the red shift of the spectra of distant objects; and to the astronomer this must appear a drawback. For this and other reasons I should be inclined to discard Einstein's view in favour of de Sitter's, if it were not for the fact that the former appears to offer a distant hope of accounting for the occurrence of a very large pure number as one of the constants of nature.

72. The problem of the homogeneous sphere.

For comparison with the results for naturally curved space, we consider a problem in which the curvature is due to the presence of ordinary matter.

The problem of determining ds^2 at points within a sphere of fluid of uniform density has been treated by Schwarzschild, Nordström and de Donder. Schwarzschild's solution* is

$$ds^2 = -e^\lambda dr^2 - r^2 d\theta^2 - r^2 \sin^2\theta\, d\phi^2 + e^\nu dt^2,$$

where

$$\left.\begin{aligned} e^\lambda &= 1/(1 - \alpha r^2) \\ e^\nu &= \tfrac{1}{4}(3\sqrt{(1-\alpha a^2)} - \sqrt{(1-\alpha r^2)})^2 \end{aligned}\right\} \quad\text{..............(72·1)},$$

and a and α are constants.

The formulae (46·9), which apply to this form of ds, become on raising one suffix

$$\left.\begin{aligned} -8\pi T_1^1 &= e^{-\lambda}(\nu'/r - (e^\lambda - 1)/r^2) \\ -8\pi T_2^2 &= e^{-\lambda}(\tfrac{1}{2}\nu'' - \tfrac{1}{4}\lambda'\nu' + \tfrac{1}{4}\nu'^2 + \tfrac{1}{2}(\nu' - \lambda')/r) \\ -8\pi T_3^3 &= -8\pi T_2^2 \\ -8\pi T_4^4 &= e^{-\lambda}(-\lambda'/r - (e^\lambda - 1)/r^2) \end{aligned}\right\} \quad\text{......(72·2)}.$$

We find from (72·1) that

$$(e^\lambda - 1)/r^2 = \tfrac{1}{2}\lambda'/r;\quad \tfrac{1}{2}\nu'' - \tfrac{1}{4}\lambda'\nu' + \tfrac{1}{4}\nu'^2 = \tfrac{1}{2}\nu'/r.$$

Hence

$$T_1^1 = T_2^2 = T_3^3 = \frac{1}{8\pi} e^{-\lambda}(\tfrac{1}{2}\lambda' - \nu')/r \quad\text{..............(72·31)},$$

$$T_4^4 = \frac{1}{8\pi} e^{-\lambda} \,.\, \tfrac{3}{2}\lambda'/r = 3\alpha/8\pi \quad\text{..................(72·32)}.$$

Referred to the coordinate-system (r, θ, ϕ), T_4^4 represents the density and T_1^1, T_2^2, T_3^3 the stress-system. Hence Schwarzschild's solution gives uniform density and isotropic hydrostatic pressure at every point.

On further working out (72·31), we find that the pressure is

$$p = -T_1^1 = \frac{\alpha}{8\pi} \frac{\{\tfrac{3}{2}(1-\alpha r^2)^{\frac{1}{2}} - \tfrac{3}{2}(1-\alpha a^2)^{\frac{1}{2}}\}}{\{\tfrac{3}{2}(1-\alpha a^2)^{\frac{1}{2}} - \tfrac{1}{2}(1-\alpha r^2)^{\frac{1}{2}}\}} \quad\text{.........(72·4)}.$$

We see that the pressure vanishes at $r = a$, and would become negative if we attempted to continue the solution beyond $r = a$. Hence the sphere $r = a$ gives the boundary of the fluid. If it is desired to continue the solution outside the sphere, another form of ds^2 must be taken corresponding to the equations for empty space.

Unless $a > \sqrt{(8/9\alpha)}$ the pressure will everywhere be finite. This condition sets an upper limit to the possible size of a fluid sphere of given density. The limit exists because the presence of dense matter increases the curvature of space, and makes the total volume of space smaller. Clearly the volume of the material sphere cannot be larger than the volume of space.

* Schwarzschild's solution is of considerable interest, but I do not think that he solved exactly the problem which he intended to solve, viz. that of an incompressible fluid. For that reason I do not give the arguments which led to the solution, but content myself with discussing what distribution of matter his solution represents. A full account is given by de Donder, *La Gravifique Einsteinienne*, p. 169 (Gauthier-Villars, 1921). The original gravitational equations are used, the natural curvature of space being considered negligible compared with that superposed by the material sphere.

For spheres which are not unduly large (e.g. not much larger than the stars) this solution corresponds approximately to the problem of the equilibrium of an incompressible fluid. The necessary conditions are satisfied, viz.

(1) The density is uniform.

(2) The pressure is zero at the surface.

(3) The stress-system is an isotropic hydrostatic pressure, and therefore satisfies the conditions of a perfect fluid.

(4) The pressure is nowhere infinite, negative, or imaginary.

Further equation (72·4) determines the pressure at any distance from the centre.

But the problem is only solved approximately, and the material here discussed is not strictly incompressible nor is it a perfect fluid. The values of T_1^1, T_2^2, T_3^3, T_4^4 refer to the particular coordinates used; these are arbitrary and do not correspond to natural measure. So long as the sphere is small, the difference does not amount to much, but for large spheres the solution ceases to correspond to a problem of any physical importance since it does not refer to natural measure. It is unfortunate that the solution breaks down for large spheres, because the existence of a limit to the size of the sphere is one of the most interesting objects of the research.

Clearly we need a solution in which the density referred to natural measure is constant throughout; i.e. T constant, instead of T_4^4 constant. The condition for a perfect fluid also needs modification. (But it would be of considerable interest to find the solution for a solid capable of supporting non-isotropic stress, if the problem of the fluid proves too difficult.) So far as I know, no progress has been made with the exact solution of this problem. It would throw interesting light on the manner in which the radius of space contracts as the size of the sphere continually increases.

If it is assumed that Schwarzschild's result

$$a < \sqrt{(8/9\alpha)}$$

is correct as regards order of magnitude, the radius of the greatest possible mass of water would be 370 million kilometres. The radius of the star Betelgeuse is something like half of this; but its density is much too small to lead to any interesting applications of the foregoing result.

Admitting Einstein's modification of the law of gravitation, with λ depending on the total amount of matter in the world, the size of the greatest sphere is easily determined. By (69·4) $R^2 = 1/4\pi\rho_0$, from which R (for water) is very nearly 300 million kilometres.

CHAPTER VI

ELECTRICITY

73. The electromagnetic equations.

In the classical theory the electromagnetic field is described by a scalar potential Φ and a vector potential (F, G, H). The electric force (X, Y, Z) and the magnetic force (α, β, γ) are derived from these according to the equations

$$\left.\begin{aligned} X &= -\frac{\partial \Phi}{\partial x} - \frac{\partial F}{\partial t} \\ \alpha &= \frac{\partial H}{\partial y} - \frac{\partial G}{\partial z} \end{aligned}\right\} \qquad \text{.........................(73·1)}$$

The classical theory does not consider any possible interaction between the gravitational and electromagnetic fields. Accordingly these definitions, together with Maxwell's equations, are intended to refer to the case in which no field of force is acting, i.e. to Galilean coordinates. We take a special system of Galilean coordinates and set

$$\kappa^\mu = (F, G, H, \Phi) \qquad \text{.........................(73·21)}$$

for that system. Having decided to make κ^μ a contravariant vector we can find its components in any other system of coordinates, Galilean or otherwise, by the usual transformation law; but, of course, we cannot tell without investigation what would be the physical interpretation of those components. In particular we must not assume without proof that the components of κ^μ in another Galilean system would agree with the new F, G, H, Φ determined experimentally for that system. At the present stage, we have defined κ^μ in all systems of coordinates, but the equation (73·21) connecting it with experimental quantities is only known to hold for one particular Galilean system.

Lowering the suffix with Galilean $g_{\mu\nu}$, we have

$$\kappa_\mu = (-F, -G, -H, \Phi) \qquad \text{.........................(73·22).}$$

Let the tensor

$$F_{\mu\nu} \equiv \kappa_{\mu\nu} - \kappa_{\nu\mu} = \frac{\partial \kappa_\mu}{\partial x_\nu} - \frac{\partial \kappa_\nu}{\partial x_\mu} \qquad \text{.........................(73·3)}$$

as in (32·2).

Then by (73·1)

$$F_{14} = \frac{\partial \kappa_1}{\partial x_4} - \frac{\partial \kappa_4}{\partial x_1} = \frac{\partial (-F)}{\partial t} - \frac{\partial \Phi}{\partial x} = X,$$

$$F_{23} = \frac{\partial \kappa_2}{\partial x_3} - \frac{\partial \kappa_3}{\partial x_2} = \frac{\partial (-G)}{\partial z} - \frac{\partial (-H)}{\partial y} = \alpha.$$

Accordingly the electric and magnetic forces together form the curl of the electromagnetic potential. The complete scheme for $F_{\mu\nu}$ is

$$F_{\mu\nu} = \begin{array}{cccc} 0 & -\gamma & \beta & -X \\ \gamma & 0 & -\alpha & -Y \\ -\beta & \alpha & 0 & -Z \\ X & Y & Z & 0 \end{array} \qquad \begin{array}{l} \xrightarrow{\ \mu\ } \\ \downarrow \\ \nu \end{array} \quad \ldots\ldots\ldots\ldots\ldots\ldots\ldots (73\cdot41).$$

Using Galilean values of $g^{\mu\nu}$ to raise the two suffixes,

$$F^{\mu\nu} = \begin{array}{cccc} 0 & -\gamma & \beta & X \\ \gamma & 0 & -\alpha & Y \\ -\beta & \alpha & 0 & Z \\ -X & -Y & -Z & 0 \end{array} \quad \ldots\ldots\ldots\ldots\ldots\ldots\ldots (73\cdot42).$$

Let ρ be the density of electric charge and $\sigma_x, \sigma_y, \sigma_z$ the density of electric current. We set

$$J^{\mu} = (\sigma_x, \sigma_y, \sigma_z, \rho) \quad \ldots\ldots\ldots\ldots\ldots\ldots\ldots\ldots (73\cdot5).$$

Here again we must not assume that the components of J^{μ} will be recognised experimentally as electric charge and current-density except in the original system of coordinates.

The universally accepted laws of the electromagnetic field are those given by Maxwell. Maxwell's equations are

$$\frac{\partial Z}{\partial y} - \frac{\partial Y}{\partial z} = -\frac{\partial \alpha}{\partial t}, \quad \frac{\partial X}{\partial z} - \frac{\partial Z}{\partial x} = -\frac{\partial \beta}{\partial t}, \quad \frac{\partial Y}{\partial x} - \frac{\partial X}{\partial y} = -\frac{\partial \gamma}{\partial t} \quad \ldots (73\cdot61),$$

$$\frac{\partial \gamma}{\partial y} - \frac{\partial \beta}{\partial z} = \frac{\partial X}{\partial t} + \sigma_x, \quad \frac{\partial \alpha}{\partial z} - \frac{\partial \gamma}{\partial x} = \frac{\partial Y}{\partial t} + \sigma_y, \quad \frac{\partial \beta}{\partial x} - \frac{\partial \alpha}{\partial y} = \frac{\partial Z}{\partial t} + \sigma_z \quad \ldots\ldots (73\cdot62),$$

$$\frac{\partial X}{\partial x} + \frac{\partial Y}{\partial y} + \frac{\partial Z}{\partial z} = \rho \quad \ldots\ldots\ldots\ldots\ldots\ldots\ldots\ldots (73\cdot63),$$

$$\frac{\partial \alpha}{\partial x} + \frac{\partial \beta}{\partial y} + \frac{\partial \gamma}{\partial z} = 0 \quad \ldots\ldots\ldots\ldots\ldots\ldots\ldots\ldots (73\cdot64).$$

The Heaviside-Lorentz unit of charge is used so that the factor 4π does not appear. The velocity of light is as usual taken to be unity. Specific inductive capacity and magnetic permeability are merely devices employed in obtaining macroscopic equations, and do not occur in the exact theory.

It will be seen by reference to (73·41) and (73·42) that Maxwell's equations are equivalent to

$$\frac{\partial F_{\mu\nu}}{\partial x_{\sigma}} + \frac{\partial F_{\nu\sigma}}{\partial x_{\mu}} + \frac{\partial F_{\sigma\mu}}{\partial x_{\nu}} = 0 \quad \ldots\ldots\ldots\ldots\ldots\ldots\ldots (73\cdot71),$$

$$\frac{\partial F^{\mu\nu}}{\partial x_{\nu}} = J^{\mu} \ldots\ldots\ldots\ldots\ldots\ldots\ldots\ldots\ldots (73\cdot72).$$

The first comprises the four equations (73·61) and (73·64); and the second comprises (73·62) and (73·63).

On substituting $F_{\mu\nu} = \partial\kappa_\mu/\partial x_\nu - \partial\kappa_\nu/\partial x_\mu$ in (73·71) it will be seen that the equation is satisfied identically. Also (73·72) is the simplified form for Galilean coordinates of $(F^{\mu\nu})_\nu = J^\mu$. Hence Maxwell's laws reduce to the simple form

$$F_{\mu\nu} = \frac{\partial\kappa_\mu}{\partial x_\nu} - \frac{\partial\kappa_\nu}{\partial x_\mu} \quad \text{.......................(73·73)},$$

$$F^{\mu\nu}_{\nu} = J^\mu \quad \text{...............................(73·74)},$$

which are *tensor equations*.

By (51·52) the second equation becomes

$$\frac{\partial\mathfrak{F}^{\mu\nu}}{\partial x_\nu} = \mathfrak{J}^\mu \quad \text{..............................(73·75)}.$$

Owing to the antisymmetry of $\mathfrak{F}^{\mu\nu}$, $\partial^2\mathfrak{F}^{\mu\nu}/\partial x_\mu \partial x_\nu$ vanishes, the terms in the summation cancelling in pairs. Hence

$$\frac{\partial^2\mathfrak{F}^{\mu\nu}}{\partial x_\mu \partial x_\nu} = \frac{\partial\mathfrak{J}^\mu}{\partial x_\mu} = 0 \quad \text{.....................(73·76)},$$

whence, by (51·12), $$(J^\mu)_\mu = 0 \quad \text{..............................(73·77)}.$$

The divergence of the charge-and-current vector vanishes.

For our original coordinates (73·77) becomes

$$\frac{\partial\sigma_x}{\partial x} + \frac{\partial\sigma_y}{\partial y} + \frac{\partial\sigma_z}{\partial z} + \frac{\partial\rho}{\partial t} = 0 \quad \text{....................(73·78)}.$$

If the current is produced by the motion of the charge with velocity (u, v, w), we have $\sigma_x, \sigma_y, \sigma_z = \rho u, \rho v, \rho w$, so that

$$\frac{\partial(\rho u)}{\partial x} + \frac{\partial(\rho v)}{\partial y} + \frac{\partial(\rho w)}{\partial z} + \frac{\partial\rho}{\partial t} = 0,$$

which is the usual equation of continuity (cf. (53·71)), showing that electric charge is conserved

It may be noted that even in non-Galilean coordinates the charge-and-current vector satisfies the strict law of conservation

$$\frac{\partial\mathfrak{J}^\mu}{\partial x_\mu} = 0.$$

This may be contrasted with the material energy and momentum which, it will be remembered, do not in the general case satisfy

$$\frac{\partial\mathfrak{T}^\nu_\mu}{\partial x_\nu} = 0,$$

so that it becomes necessary to supplement them by the pseudo-energy-tensor t^ν_μ (§ 59) in order to maintain the formal law. Both $T^{\mu\nu}$ and J^μ have the property which in the relativity theory we recognise as the natural generalisation of conservation, viz. $T^{\mu\nu}_\nu = 0$, $J^\mu_\mu = 0$.

If the charge is moving with velocity

$$\frac{dx}{dt}, \frac{dy}{dt}, \frac{dz}{dt},$$

we have
$$J^\mu = \rho\frac{dx}{dt},\ \rho\frac{dy}{dt},\ \rho\frac{dz}{dt},\ \rho$$
$$= \rho\frac{ds}{dt}\left(\frac{dx}{ds},\ \frac{dy}{ds},\ \frac{dz}{ds},\ \frac{dt}{ds}\right) \quad\text{.................(73·81).}$$

The bracket constitutes a contravariant vector; consequently $\rho ds/dt$ is an invariant. Now ds/dt represents the FitzGerald contraction, so that a volume which would be measured as unity by an observer moving with the charge will be measured as ds/dt by an observer at rest in the coordinates chosen. The invariant $\rho ds/dt$ is the amount of charge in this volume, i.e. unit proper-volume.

We write
$$\rho_0 = \rho\frac{ds}{dt},$$
so that ρ_0 is the proper-density of the charge. If A^μ is the velocity-vector dx_μ/ds of the charge, then (73·81) becomes
$$J^\mu = \rho_0 A^\mu \quad\text{.............................(73·82).}$$

Charge, unlike mass, is not altered by motion relative to the observer. This follows from the foregoing result that the amount of charge in an absolutely defined volume (unit proper-volume) is an invariant. The reason for this difference of behaviour of charge and mass will be understood by reference to (53·2) where the FitzGerald factor ds/dt occurs squared.

For the observer S using our original system of Galilean coordinates, the quantities κ_μ, $F_{\mu\nu}$ and J^μ represent the electromagnetic potential, force, and current, according to definition. For another observer S' with different velocity, we have corresponding quantities κ_μ', $F'_{\mu\nu}$, J'^μ, obtained by the transformation-laws; but we have not yet shown that these are the quantities which S' will measure when he makes experimental determinations of potential, force, and current relative to his moving apparatus Now if S' recognises certain measured quantities as potential, force, and current it must be because they play the same part in the world relative to him, as κ_μ, $F_{\mu\nu}$ and J^μ play in the world relative to S To play the same part means to have the same properties, or fulfil the same relations or equations. But κ_μ', $F'_{\mu\nu}$ and J'^μ fulfil the same equations in S''s coordinates as κ_μ, $F_{\mu\nu}$ and J^μ do in S's coordinates, *because the fundamental equations* (73·73), (73·74) *and* (73·77) *are tensor equations holding in all systems of coordinates* The fact that Maxwell's equations are tensor equations, enables us to make the identification of κ_μ, $F_{\mu\nu}$, J^μ with the experimental potential, force, and current in all systems of Galilean coordinates and not merely in the system initially chosen.

In one sense our proof is not yet complete. There are other equations obeyed by the electromagnetic variables which have not yet been discussed. In particular there is the equation which prescribes the motion of a particle carrying a charge in the electromagnetic field. We shall show in § 76 that this also is of the tensor form, so that the accented variables continue to play the same part in S''s experience which the unaccented variables play in S's experience. But even as it stands our proof is sufficient to show that *if* there exists for S' a potential, force, and current precisely analogous to the potential, force, and current of S, these must be expressed by κ_μ', $F'_{\mu\nu}$, J_μ', because other quantities would not satisfy the equations already obtained. The proviso must clearly be fulfilled unless the special principle of relativity is violated.

When an observer uses non-Galilean coordinates, he will as usual treat them as though they were Galilean and attribute all discrepancies to the effects of the field of force which is introduced. κ_μ, $F_{\mu\nu}$ and J^μ will be identified with the potential, force, and current, just as though the coordinates were Galilean. These quantities will no longer accurately obey Maxwell's original form of the equations, but will conform to our generalised tensor equations (73·73) and (73·74). The replacement of (73·72) by the more general form (73·74) extends the classical equations to the case in which a gravitational field of force is acting in addition to the electromagnetic field.

74. Electromagnetic waves.

(*a*) *Propagation of electromagnetic potential.*

It is well known that the electromagnetic potentials F, G, H, Φ are not determinate. They are concerned in actual phenomena only through their curl—the electromagnetic force. The curl is unaltered, if we replace

$$-F,\ -G,\ -H,\ \Phi \quad \text{by} \quad -F+\frac{\partial V}{\partial x},\ \ -G+\frac{\partial V}{\partial y},\ \ -H+\frac{\partial V}{\partial z},\ \ \Phi+\frac{\partial V}{\partial t},$$

where V is an arbitrary function of the coordinates. The latter expression gives the same field of electromagnetic force and may thus equally well be adopted for the electromagnetic potentials.

It is usual to avoid this arbitrariness by selecting from the possible values the set which satisfies

$$\frac{\partial F}{\partial x}+\frac{\partial G}{\partial y}+\frac{\partial H}{\partial z}+\frac{\partial \Phi}{\partial t}=0.$$

Similarly in general coordinates we remove the arbitrariness of κ_μ by imposing the condition

$$(\kappa^\mu)_\mu = 0 \qquad \text{.............................(74·1).}$$

When the boundary-condition at infinity is added, the value of κ_μ becomes completely determinate.

By (73·74) and (73·3)

$$\begin{aligned} J_\mu = (F_\mu{}^\alpha)_\alpha = (g^{\alpha\beta} F_{\mu\beta})_\alpha &= g^{\alpha\beta}(F_{\mu\beta})_\alpha \\ &= g^{\alpha\beta}(\kappa_{\mu\beta\alpha}-\kappa_{\beta\mu\alpha}) \qquad \text{........................(74·2)} \\ &= g^{\alpha\beta}(\kappa_{\mu\beta\alpha}-\kappa_{\beta\alpha\mu}+B^\epsilon_{\beta\alpha\mu}\kappa_\epsilon) \qquad \text{by (34·3)} \\ &= g^{\alpha\beta}(\kappa_\mu)_{\beta\alpha}-(\kappa^\alpha_\alpha)_\mu+G^\epsilon_\mu\kappa_\epsilon. \end{aligned}$$

The operator $g^{\alpha\beta}(\dots)_{\beta\alpha}$ has been previously denoted by $\Box$. Also, by (74·1) $\kappa^\alpha_\alpha=0$. Hence

$$\Box\kappa_\mu = J_\mu - G^\epsilon_\mu \kappa_\epsilon \qquad \text{.....................(74·31).}$$

In empty space this becomes

$$\Box \kappa_\mu = 0 \quad \text{.........................(74·32)},$$

showing that κ_μ is propagated with the fundamental velocity.

If the law of gravitation $G_{\mu\nu} = \lambda g_{\mu\nu}$ for curved space-time is adopted, the equation in empty space becomes

$$(\Box + \lambda)\, \kappa_\mu = 0 \quad \text{.........................(74·33)}.$$

(b) *Propagation of electromagnetic force.*

To determine a corresponding law of propagation of $F_{\mu\nu}$ we naturally try to take the curl of (74·31); but care is necessary since the order of the operations curl and $\Box$ is not interchangeable.

By (74·2)

$$J_{\mu\nu} = g^{\alpha\beta}(\kappa_{\mu\beta\alpha\nu} - \kappa_{\beta\mu\alpha\nu})$$

$$= g^{\alpha\beta}(\kappa_{\mu\beta\nu\alpha} - \kappa_{\beta\mu\nu\alpha}) - g^{\alpha\beta}(B^{\epsilon}_{\mu\nu\alpha}\kappa_{\epsilon\beta} + B^{\epsilon}_{\beta\nu\alpha}\kappa_{\mu\epsilon} - B^{\epsilon}_{\beta\nu\alpha}\kappa_{\epsilon\mu} - B^{\epsilon}_{\mu\nu\alpha}\kappa_{\beta\epsilon})$$

by (34·8)

$$= g^{\alpha\beta}(\kappa_{\mu\beta\nu} - \kappa_{\beta\mu\nu})_\alpha - g^{\alpha\beta}(B^{\epsilon}_{\mu\nu\alpha}F_{\epsilon\beta} - B^{\epsilon}_{\beta\nu\alpha}F_{\epsilon\mu})$$

$$= g^{\alpha\beta}(\kappa_{\mu\nu\beta} - \kappa_{\beta\mu\nu} + B^{\epsilon}_{\mu\beta\nu}\kappa_\epsilon)_\alpha - B_{\mu\nu\alpha\epsilon}F^{\epsilon\alpha} - G^{\epsilon}_{\nu}F_{\epsilon\mu}.$$

Hence

$$J_{\mu\nu} - J_{\nu\mu} = g^{\alpha\beta}(\kappa_{\mu\nu\beta} - \kappa_{\nu\mu\beta} - B^{\epsilon}_{\beta\mu\nu}\kappa_\epsilon + B^{\epsilon}_{\mu\beta\nu}\kappa_\epsilon - B^{\epsilon}_{\nu\beta\mu}\kappa_\epsilon)_\alpha$$
$$- (B_{\mu\nu\alpha\epsilon} - B_{\nu\mu\alpha\epsilon})F^{\epsilon\alpha} - G^{\epsilon}_{\nu}F_{\epsilon\mu} + G^{\epsilon}_{\mu}F_{\epsilon\nu}.$$

But by the cyclic relation (34·6)

$$B^{\epsilon}_{\beta\mu\nu} + B^{\epsilon}_{\mu\nu\beta} + B^{\epsilon}_{\nu\beta\mu} = 0.$$

Also by the antisymmetric properties

$$(B_{\mu\nu\alpha\epsilon} - B_{\nu\mu\alpha\epsilon})F^{\epsilon\alpha} = 2B_{\mu\nu\alpha\epsilon}F^{\epsilon\alpha}.$$

Hence the result reduces to

$$J_{\mu\nu} - J_{\nu\mu} = g^{\alpha\beta}(\kappa_{\mu\nu} - \kappa_{\nu\mu})_{\beta\alpha} - G^{\epsilon}_{\nu}F_{\epsilon\mu} + G^{\epsilon}_{\mu}F_{\epsilon\nu} - 2B_{\mu\nu\alpha\epsilon}F^{\epsilon\alpha},$$

so that $$\Box F_{\mu\nu} = J_{\mu\nu} - J_{\nu\mu} - G^{\epsilon}_{\mu}F_{\epsilon\nu} + G^{\epsilon}_{\nu}F_{\epsilon\mu} + 2B_{\mu\nu\alpha\epsilon}F^{\epsilon\alpha} \quad \text{.........(74·41)}.$$

In empty space this becomes

$$\Box F_{\mu\nu} = 2B_{\mu\nu\alpha\epsilon}F^{\epsilon\alpha} \quad \text{.........................(74·42)}$$

for an infinite world. For a curved world undisturbed by attracting matter, in which $G^{\epsilon}_{\mu} = \lambda g^{\epsilon}_{\mu}$, $B_{\mu\nu\alpha\epsilon} = \frac{1}{3}\lambda(g_{\mu\nu}g_{\alpha\epsilon} - g_{\mu\alpha}g_{\nu\epsilon})$, the result is

$$(\Box + \tfrac{4}{3}\lambda)\, F_{\mu\nu} = 0 \quad \text{.........................(74·43)}$$

It need not surprise us that the velocity of propagation of electromagnetic potential and of electromagnetic force is not the same (cf. (74·33) and (74·43)). The former is not physically important since it involves the arbitrary convention $\kappa^{\alpha}_{\alpha} = 0$.

But the result (74·42) is, I think, unexpected. It shows that the equations of propagation of electromagnetic force involve the Riemann-Christoffel tensor; and therefore this is not one of the phenomena for which the ordinary Galilean equations can be immediately generalised by the principle of equivalence.

This naturally makes us uneasy as to whether we have done right in adopting the invariant equations of propagation of light ($ds = 0$, $\delta \int ds = 0$) as true in all circumstances; but the investigation which follows is reassuring.

(c) *Propagation of a wave-front.*

The conception of a "ray" of light in physical optics is by no means elementary. Unless the wave-front is of infinite extent, the ray is an abstraction, and to appreciate its meaning a full discussion of the phenomena of interference fringes is necessary. We do not wish to enter on such a general discussion here; and accordingly we shall not attempt to obtain the formulae for the tracks of rays of light for the case of general coordinates *ab initio*. Our course will be to reduce the general formulae to such a form, that the subsequent work will follow the ordinary treatment given in works on physical optics.

The fundamental equation treated in the usual theory of electromagnetic waves is

$$\left(\frac{\partial^2}{\partial t^2} - \frac{\partial^2}{\partial x^2} - \frac{\partial^2}{\partial y^2} - \frac{\partial^2}{\partial z^2}\right) \kappa_\mu = 0 \quad \ldots\ldots\ldots\ldots \quad (74\cdot51),$$

which is the form taken by $\Box \kappa_\mu = 0$ in Galilean coordinates. When the region of space-time is not flat we cannot immediately simplify $\Box \kappa_\mu$ in this way; but we can make a considerable simplification by adopting natural coordinates at the point considered. In that case the 3-index symbols (but not their derivatives) vanish, and

$$\begin{aligned} \Box \kappa_\mu &= g^{\alpha\beta} (\kappa_\mu)_{\alpha\beta} \\ &= g^{\alpha\beta} \left(\frac{\partial^2 \kappa_\mu}{\partial x_\alpha \partial x_\beta} - \frac{\partial}{\partial x_\alpha} \{\mu\beta, \epsilon\} \,.\, \kappa_\epsilon\right). \end{aligned}$$

Hence the law of propagation $\Box \kappa_\mu = 0$ becomes in natural coordinates

$$\left(\frac{\partial^2}{\partial t^2} - \frac{\partial^2}{\partial x^2} - \frac{\partial^2}{\partial y^2} - \frac{\partial^2}{\partial z^2}\right) \kappa_\mu = g^{\alpha\beta} \frac{\partial}{\partial x_\alpha} \{\mu\beta, \epsilon\} \,.\, \kappa_\epsilon \quad \ldots\ldots\ldots (74\cdot52).$$

At first sight this does not look very promising for a justification of the principle of equivalence. We cannot make all the derivatives $\partial \{\mu\beta, \epsilon\}/\partial x_\alpha$ vanish by any choice of coordinates, since these determine the Riemann-Christoffel tensor. It looks as though the law of propagation in curved space-time involves the Riemann-Christoffel tensor, and consequently differs from the law in flat space-time. But the inner multiplication by $g^{\alpha\beta}$ saves the situation. It is possible to choose coordinates such that $g^{\alpha\beta} \partial \{\mu\beta, \epsilon\}/\partial x_\alpha$ vanishes for all the sixteen possible combinations of μ and ϵ*. For these coordinates (74·52) reduces to (74·51), and the usual solution for flat space-time will apply at the point considered.

* According to (36·55) it is possible by a transformation to increase $\partial \{\mu\beta, \epsilon\}/\partial x_\alpha$ by an arbitrary quantity $a^\epsilon_{\mu\beta\alpha}$, symmetrical in μ, β and α. The sixteen quantities $g^{\alpha\beta} a^\epsilon_{\mu\beta\alpha}$ ($\mu, \epsilon = 1, 2, 3, 4$) will not have to fulfil any conditions of symmetry, and may be chosen independently of one another. Hence we can make the right-hand side of (74·52) vanish by an appropriate transformation.

A solution of (74·51), giving plane waves, is

$$\kappa_\mu = A_\mu \exp \frac{2\pi i}{\lambda}(lx + my + nz - ct) \quad \text{.........(74·53).}$$

Here A_μ is a constant vector; l, m, n are direction cosines so that $l^2 + m^2 + n^2 = 1$. Substituting in (74·51) we find that it will be satisfied if $c^2 = 1$ and the first and second derivatives of l, m, n, c vanish. According to the usual discussion of this equation (l, m, n) is the direction of the ray and c the velocity of propagation along the ray.

The vanishing of first and second derivatives of (l, m, n) shows that the direction of the ray is stationary at the point considered. (The light-oscillations correspond to $F_{\mu\nu}$ (not κ_μ) and the direction of the ray would not necessarily agree with (l, m, n) if the first derivatives did not vanish; consequently the stationary property depends on the vanishing of second derivatives as well.) Further the velocity c along the ray is unity.

It follows that in any kind of space-time the ray is a geodesic, and the velocity is such as to satisfy the equation $ds = 0$. Stated in this form, the result deduced for a very special system of coordinates must hold for all coordinate-systems since it is expressed invariantly. The expression for the potential (74·53) is, of course, only valid for the special coordinate-system.

We have thus arrived at a justification of the law for the track of a light-pulse (§ 47 (4)) which has been adopted in our previous work.

(*d*) *Solution of the equation* $\Box \kappa^\mu = J^\mu$.

We assume that space-time is flat to the order of approximation required, and accordingly adopt Galilean coordinates. The equation becomes

$$\frac{\partial^2 \kappa^\mu}{\partial t^2} - \nabla^2 \kappa^\mu = J^\mu,$$

of which the solution (well known in the theory of sound) is

$$\{\kappa^\mu\}_{x, y, z, t} = \frac{1}{4\pi} \iiint \{J^\mu\}_{\xi, \eta, \zeta, t-r} \cdot \frac{d\xi\, d\eta\, d\zeta}{r} \quad \text{.........(74·61),}$$

where r is the distance between (x, y, z) and (ξ, η, ζ).

The contributions to κ^μ of each element of charge or current are simply additive; accordingly we shall consider a single element of charge de moving with velocity A^μ, and determine the part of κ^μ corresponding to it. By (73·81) the equation becomes

$$\kappa^\mu = \frac{1}{4\pi} \frac{ds}{dt} A^\mu \iiint \rho \frac{d\xi\, d\eta\, d\zeta}{r} \quad \text{..................(74·62),}$$

where all quantities on the right are taken for the time $t - r$.

For an infinitesimal element we may take ρ constant and insert limits of integration, but these limits must be taken for the time $t - r$, and this introduces an important factor representing a kind of Doppler effect. If the element of charge is bounded by two planes perpendicular to the direction of r, the limits of integration are from the front plane at time $t - r$ to the rear plane at time $t-r-dr$. If v_r is the component velocity in the direction of r, the front plane has had time to advance a distance $v_r dr$. Consequently the instantaneous thickness of the element of charge is less than the distance between the limits of integration in the ratio $1-v_r$; and the integration is over a volume $(1-v_r)^{-1}$ times the instantaneous volume of the element of charge. Hence

$$\iiint \rho \, d\xi \, d\eta \, d\zeta = \frac{de}{1-v_r}.$$

Writing as usual β for the FitzGerald factor dt/ds, (74·62) becomes

$$\kappa^\mu = \left\{\frac{A^\mu de}{4\pi r \beta (1-v_r)}\right\}_{t-r} = \left\{\frac{de\,(u, v, w, 1)}{4\pi r\,(1-v_r)}\right\}_{t-r} \quad \text{.........(74·71).}$$

In most applications the motion of the charge can be regarded as uniform during the time of propagation of the potential through the distance r. In that case

$$\{r(1-v_r)\}_{t-r} = \{r\}_t,$$

the present distance being less than the antedated distance by $v_r r$. The result then becomes

$$\kappa^\mu = \left\{\frac{A^\mu de}{4\pi r \beta}\right\}_t = \left\{\frac{de\,(u, v, w, 1)}{4\pi r}\right\}_t \quad \text{..............(74·72).}$$

It will be seen that the scalar potential Φ of a charge is unaltered by uniform motion, and must be reckoned for the present position of the charge, *not from the antedated position.*

The equation (74·71) can be written in the pseudo-tensor form

$$\kappa^\mu = \left\{\frac{A^\mu de}{4\pi A^\nu R_\nu}\right\}_{R^\alpha R_\alpha = 0} \quad \text{....................(74·8),}$$

where R^μ is the pseudo-vector representing the displacement from the charge (ξ, η, ζ, τ) to the point (x, y, z, t) where κ^μ is reckoned. The condition $R^\alpha R_\alpha = 0$ gives

$$-(x-\xi)^2 - (y-\eta)^2 - (z-\zeta)^2 + (t-\tau)^2 = 0,$$

so that

$$\tau = t - r.$$

Also

$$\begin{aligned} A^\nu R_\nu &= -\beta u (x-\xi) - \beta v (y-\eta) - \beta w (z-\zeta) + \beta (t-\tau) \\ &= -\beta v_r r + \beta r \\ &= r\beta (1-v_r). \end{aligned}$$

A *finite* displacement R^μ is not a vector in the general theory. We call it a pseudo-vector because it behaves as a vector for Galilean coordinates and Lorentz transformations. Thus the equation (74·8) does not admit of application to coordinates other than Galilean.

75. The Lorentz transformation of electromagnetic force.

The Lorentz transformation for an observer S' moving relatively to S with a velocity u along the x-axis is

$$x_1' = q(x_1 - ux_4), \quad x_2' = x_2, \quad x_3' = x_3, \quad x_4' = q(x_4 - ux_1) \quad \text{...(75·1),}$$

where

$$q = (1-u^2)^{-\frac{1}{2}}$$

We use q instead of β in order to avoid confusion with the component β of magnetic force.

We have

$$\frac{\partial x_1'}{\partial x_1} = \frac{\partial x_4'}{\partial x_4} = q, \quad \frac{\partial x_1'}{\partial x_4} = \frac{\partial x_4'}{\partial x_1} = -qu, \quad \frac{\partial x_2'}{\partial x_2} = \frac{\partial x_3'}{\partial x_3} = 1 \quad \text{......(75·2)},$$

and all other derivatives vanish.

To calculate the electromagnetic force for S' in terms of the force for S, we apply the general formulae of transformation (23·21). Thus

$$\gamma' = F'^{12} = \frac{\partial x_1'}{\partial x_\alpha}\frac{\partial x_2'}{\partial x_\beta}F^{\alpha\beta}$$

$$= \frac{\partial x_1'}{\partial x_1}\frac{\partial x_2'}{\partial x_2}F^{12} + \frac{\partial x_1'}{\partial x_4}\frac{\partial x_2'}{\partial x_2}F^{42}$$

$$= q\gamma - quY.$$

Working out the other components similarly, the result is

$$\left.\begin{aligned} X' &= X, \quad Y' = q(Y - u\gamma), \quad Z' = q(Z + u\beta) \\ \alpha' &= \alpha, \quad \beta' = q(\beta + uZ), \quad \gamma' = q(\gamma - uY) \end{aligned}\right\} \quad \text{......(75·3)},$$

which are the formulae given by Lorentz.

The more general formulae when the velocity of the observer S' is (u, v, w) become very complicated. We shall only consider the approximate results when the square of the velocity is neglected. In that case $q = 1$, and the formulae (75·3) can be completed by symmetry, viz.

$$\left.\begin{aligned} X' &= X - w\beta + v\gamma \\ \alpha' &= \alpha + wY - vZ \end{aligned}\right\} \quad \text{........................(75·4)}.$$

76. Mechanical effects of the electromagnetic field.

According to the elementary laws, a piece of matter carrying electric charge of density ρ experiences in an electrostatic field a mechanical force

$$\rho X, \quad \rho Y, \quad \rho Z$$

per unit volume. Moving charges constituting electric currents of amount $(\sigma_x, \sigma_y, \sigma_z)$ per unit volume are acted on by a magnetic field, so that a mechanical force

$$\gamma\sigma_y - \beta\sigma_z, \quad \alpha\sigma_z - \gamma\sigma_x, \quad \beta\sigma_x - \alpha\sigma_y$$

per unit volume is experienced.

Hence if (P, Q, R) is the total mechanical force per unit volume

$$\left.\begin{aligned} P &= \rho X + \gamma\sigma_y - \beta\sigma_z \\ Q &= \rho Y + \alpha\sigma_z - \gamma\sigma_x \\ R &= \rho Z + \beta\sigma_x - \alpha\sigma_y \end{aligned}\right\} \quad \text{....................(76·1)}.$$

The rate at which the mechanical force does work is

$$S = \sigma_x X + \sigma_y Y + \sigma_z Z.$$

The magnetic part of the force does no work since it acts at right angles to the current of charged particles.

By (73·41) and (73·5) we find that these expressions are equivalent to

$$(P, Q, R, -S) = F_{\mu\nu} J^\nu.$$

We denote the vector $F_{\mu\nu} J^\nu$ by h_μ. Raising the suffix with Galilean $g_{\mu\nu}$, we have

$$(P, Q, R, S) = -h^\mu = -F^\mu{}_\nu J^\nu \quad \text{.................(76·2).}$$

The mechanical force will change the momentum and energy of the material system; consequently the material energy-tensor taken alone will no longer be conserved. In order to preserve the law of conservation of momentum and energy, we must recognise that the electric field contains an electromagnetic momentum and energy whose changes are equal and opposite to those of the material system*. The whole energy-tensor will then consist of two parts, M^ν_μ due to the matter and E^ν_μ due to the electromagnetic field.

We keep the notation T^ν_μ for the whole energy-tensor—the thing which is always conserved, and is therefore to be identified with $G^\nu_\mu - \frac{1}{2} g^\nu_\mu G$. Thus

$$T^\nu_\mu = M^\nu_\mu + E^\nu_\mu \quad \text{..........................(76·3).}$$

Since P, Q, R, S measure the rate of increase of momentum and energy of the material system, they may be equated to $\partial M^{\mu\nu}/\partial x_\nu$ as in (53·82). Thus

$$\frac{\partial M^{\mu\nu}}{\partial x_\nu} = -h^\mu.$$

The equal and opposite change of the momentum and energy of the electromagnetic field is accordingly given by

$$\frac{\partial E^{\mu\nu}}{\partial x_\nu} = +h^\mu.$$

These equations apply to Galilean or to natural coordinates. We pass over to general coordinates by substituting covariant derivatives, so as to obtain the tensor equations

$$M^{\mu\nu}_\nu = -h^\mu = -E^{\mu\nu}_\nu \quad \text{........................(76·4),}$$

which are independent of the coordinates used. This satisfies

$$T^{\mu\nu}_\nu = (M^{\mu\nu} + E^{\mu\nu})_\nu = 0.$$

Consider a charge moving with velocity (u, v, w). We have by (75·4)

$$\begin{aligned} \rho X' &= \rho X - (\rho w)\beta + (\rho v)\gamma \\ &= \rho X - \sigma_z \beta + \sigma_y \gamma \\ &= P. \end{aligned}$$

* Notwithstanding the warning conveyed by the fate of potential energy (§ 59) we are again running into danger by generalising energy so as to conform to an assigned law. I am not sure that the danger is negligible. But we are on stronger ground now, because we know that there is a world-tensor which satisfies the assigned law $T^{\mu\nu}_\nu = 0$, whereas the potential energy was introduced to satisfy $\partial \mathfrak{S}^\nu_\mu / \partial x_\nu = 0$, and it was only a speculative possibility (now found to be untenable) that there existed a tensor with that property.

The square of the velocity has been neglected, and to this order of approximation $\rho' = \rho$. Thus to the first order in the velocities, the mechanical force on a moving charge is $(\rho' X', \rho' Y', \rho' Z')$, just as the mechanical force on a charge at rest is $(\rho X, \rho Y, \rho Z)$. We obtain the force on the moving charge either by applying the formula (76·1) in the original coordinates, or by transforming to new coordinates in which the charge is at rest so that $\sigma_x, \sigma_y, \sigma_z = 0$. The equivalence of the two calculations is in accordance with the principle of relativity for uniform motion.

If the square of the velocity is not neglected, no such simple relation exists. The mechanical force (mass × acceleration) will not be exactly the same in the accented and unaccented systems of coordinates, since the mass and acceleration are altered by terms involving the square of the velocity. In fact we could not expect any accurate relation between the mechanical force (P, Q, R) and the electric force (X, Y, Z) in different systems of coordinates; the former is part of a vector, and the latter part of a tensor of the second rank.

Perhaps it might have been expected that with the advent of the electron theory of matter it would become unnecessary to retain a separate material energy-tensor $M^{\mu\nu}$, and that the whole energy and momentum could be included in the energy-tensor of the electromagnetic field. But we cannot dispense with $M^{\mu\nu}$. The fact is that an electron must not be regarded as a purely electromagnetic phenomenon, that is to say, something enters into its constitution which is not comprised in Maxwell's theory of the electromagnetic field. In order to prevent the electronic charge from dispersing under its own repulsion, non-Maxwellian "binding forces" are necessary, and it is the energy, stress and momentum of these binding forces which constitute the material energy-tensor $M^{\mu\nu}$.

77. The electromagnetic energy-tensor.

To determine explicitly the value of E_μ^ν we have to rely on the relation found in the preceding section

$$E_{\mu\nu}^{\nu} = h_\mu = F_{\mu\nu} J^\nu = F_{\mu\nu} F_\sigma^{\nu\sigma} \quad \text{.................. (77·1)}.$$

The solution of this differential equation is

$$E_\mu^\nu = -F^{\nu\alpha} F_{\mu\alpha} + \tfrac{1}{4} g_\mu^\nu F^{\alpha\beta} F_{\alpha\beta} \quad \text{.................. (77·2)}.$$

To verify this we take the divergence, remembering that covariant differentiation obeys the usual distributive law and that g_μ^ν is a constant.

$$E_{\mu\nu}^{\nu} = -F_\nu^{\nu\alpha} F_{\mu\alpha} - F^{\nu\alpha} F_{\mu\alpha\nu} + \tfrac{1}{4} g_\mu^\nu (F_\nu^{\alpha\beta} F_{\alpha\beta} + F^{\alpha\beta} F_{\alpha\beta\nu})$$

$$= -F_\nu^{\nu\alpha} F_{\mu\alpha} - F^{\nu\alpha} F_{\mu\alpha\nu} + \tfrac{1}{2} g_\mu^\nu F^{\alpha\beta} F_{\alpha\beta\nu} \qquad \text{by (26·3)}$$

$$= -F_\nu^{\nu\alpha} F_{\mu\alpha} - \tfrac{1}{2} F^{\beta\alpha} F_{\mu\alpha\beta} - \tfrac{1}{2} F^{\alpha\beta} F_{\mu\beta\alpha} + \tfrac{1}{2} F^{\alpha\beta} F_{\alpha\beta\mu}$$

by changes of dummy suffixes,

$$= F_\nu^{\alpha\nu} F_{\mu\alpha} + \tfrac{1}{2} F^{\alpha\beta} (F_{\mu\alpha\beta} + F_{\beta\mu\alpha} + F_{\alpha\beta\mu})$$

by the antisymmetry of $F^{\mu\nu}$

It is easily verified that

$$F_{\mu\alpha\beta} + F_{\beta\mu\alpha} + F_{\alpha\beta\mu} = \frac{\partial F_{\mu\alpha}}{\partial x_\beta} + \frac{\partial F_{\beta\mu}}{\partial x_\alpha} + \frac{\partial F_{\alpha\beta}}{\partial x_\mu} = 0$$

by (30·3) and (73·71); the terms containing the 3-index symbols mutually cancel.

Hence $$E^\nu_{\mu\nu} = F^{\alpha\nu}_{\nu} F_{\mu\alpha} = J^\alpha F_{\mu\alpha},$$

agreeing with (77·1).

It is of interest to work out the components of the energy-tensor (77·2) in Galilean coordinates by (73·41) and (73·42). We have

$$F^{\alpha\beta}F_{\alpha\beta} = 2(\alpha^2 + \beta^2 + \gamma^2 - X^2 - Y^2 - Z^2) \quad \text{.........(77·3)},$$

$$E^1_1 = \tfrac{1}{2}(\alpha^2 - \beta^2 - \gamma^2) + \tfrac{1}{2}(X^2 - Y^2 - Z^2) \quad \text{.........(77·41)},$$

$$E^2_1 = \alpha\beta + XY \quad \text{.........(77·42)},$$

$$E^4_1 = \beta Z - \gamma Y \quad \text{.........(77·43)},$$

$$E^4_4 = \tfrac{1}{2}(\alpha^2 + \beta^2 + \gamma^2) + \tfrac{1}{2}(X^2 + Y^2 + Z^2) \quad \text{.........(77·44)}.$$

The last gives the energy or mass of the electromagnetic field, the third expression gives the momentum; the first two give the stresses in the field. In all cases these formulae agree with those of the classical theory.

Momentum, being rate of flow of mass, is also the rate of flow of energy. In the latter aspect it is often called Poynting's vector. It is seen from (77·43) that the momentum is the vector-product of the electric and magnetic forces —to use the terminology of the elementary vector theory.

From E^ν_μ we can form a scalar E by contraction, just as T is formed from T^ν_μ. The invariant density T will be made up of the two parts E and M, the former arising from the electromagnetic field and the latter from the matter or non-Maxwellian stresses involved in the electron. It turns out, however, that E is identically zero, so that the electromagnetic field contributes nothing to the invariant density. The invariant density must be attributed entirely to the non-Maxwellian binding stresses. Contracting (77·2)

$$E = -F^{\mu\alpha}F_{\mu\alpha} + \tfrac{1}{4}g^\mu_\mu F^{\alpha\beta}F_{\alpha\beta} = 0 \quad \text{.........(77·5)},$$

since $g^\mu_\mu = 4$.

The question of the origin of the inertia of matter presents a very curious paradox. We have to distinguish—

the invariant mass m arising from the invariant density T, and
the relative mass M arising from the coordinate density T^{44}.

As we have seen, the former cannot be attributed to the electromagnetic field. But it is generally believed that the latter—which is the ordinary mass as understood in physics—arises solely from the electromagnetic fields of the electrons, the inertia of matter being simply the energy of the electromagnetic fields contained in it. It is probable that this view, which arose in consequence of J. J. Thomson's researches*, is correct; so that ordinary or relative mass

* *Phil. Mag.* vol. 11 (1881), p. 229.

may be regarded as entirely electromagnetic, whilst invariant mass is entirely non-electromagnetic.

How then does it happen that for an electron at rest, invariant mass and relative mass are equal, and indeed synonymous?

Probably the distinction of Maxwellian and non-Maxwellian stresses as tensors of different natures is artificial—like the distinction of gravitational and inertial fields—and the real remedy is to remodel the electromagnetic equations so as to comprehend both in an indissoluble connection. But so long as we are ignorant of the laws obeyed by the non-Maxwellian stresses, it is scarcely possible to avoid making the separation. From the present point of view we have to explain the paradox as follows—

Taking an electron at rest, the relative mass is determined solely by the component E^{44}, but the stress-components of $E^{\mu\nu}$ make a contribution to E which exactly cancels that of E^{44}, so that $E=0$. These stresses are balanced by non-Maxwellian stresses $M^{11}, \ldots M^{33}$; the balancing being not necessarily exact in each element of volume, but exact for the region round the electron taken as a whole. Thus the term which cancels E^{44} is itself cancelled, and E^{44} becomes reinstated. The final result is that the integral of T is equal to the integral of E^{44} for the electron at rest.

It is usually assumed that the non-Maxwellian stresses are confined to the interior, or the close proximity, of the electrons, and do not wander about in the detached way that the Maxwellian stresses do, e.g. in light-waves. I shall adopt this view in order not to deviate too widely from other writers, although I do not see any particular reason for believing it to be true*.

If then all non-Maxwellian stresses are closely bound to the electrons, it follows that in regions containing no matter E_μ^ν is the entire energy-tensor. Then (54·3) becomes

$$G_\mu^\nu - \tfrac{1}{2} g_\mu^\nu G = -8\pi E_\mu^\nu \quad \text{......................(77·6)}.$$

Contracting, $$G = 8\pi E = 0,$$

and the equation simplifies to

$$G_{\mu\nu} = -8\pi E_{\mu\nu} \quad \text{......................(77·7)}$$

for regions containing electromagnetic fields but no matter. We may notice that the Gaussian curvature of space-time is zero even when electromagnetic energy is present provided there are no electrons in the region.

Since for electromagnetic energy the invariant mass, m, is zero, and the relative mass, M, is finite, the equation (12·3)

$$M = m\, dt/ds$$

shows that ds/dt is zero. Accordingly free electromagnetic energy must always have the velocity of light.

* We may evade the difficulty by extending the definition of electrons or matter to include all regions where Maxwell's equations are inadequate (e.g. regions containing quanta).

78. The gravitational field of an electron.

This problem differs from that of the gravitational field of a particle (§ 38) in that the electric field spreads through all space, and consequently the energy-tensor is not confined to a point or small sphere at the origin.

For the most general symmetrical field we take as before

$$g_{11} = -e^{\lambda}, \quad g_{22} = -r^2, \quad g_{33} = -r^2 \sin^2\theta, \quad g_{44} = e^{\nu} \quad \text{......(78·1).}$$

Since the electric field is static, we shall have

$$F, G, H = \kappa_1, \kappa_2, \kappa_3 = 0,$$

and κ_4 will be a function of r only. Hence the only surviving components of $F_{\mu\nu}$ are

$$F_{41} = -F_{14} = \kappa_4' \quad \text{..........................(78·2),}$$

the accent denoting differentiation with respect to r. Then

$$F^{41} = g^{44}g^{11}F_{41} = -e^{-(\lambda+\nu)}\kappa_4',$$

and $$\mathfrak{F}^{41} = F^{41}\sqrt{-g} = -e^{-\frac{1}{2}(\lambda+\nu)}r^2 \sin\theta \,.\, \kappa_4'.$$

Hence by (73·75) the condition for no electric charge and current (except at the singularity at the origin) is

$$\frac{\partial \mathfrak{F}^{41}}{\partial x_1} = -\sin\theta \frac{\partial}{\partial r}\left(e^{-\frac{1}{2}(\lambda+\nu)}r^2\kappa_4'\right) = 0 \quad \text{..............(78·3),}$$

so that $$\kappa_4' = \frac{\epsilon}{r^2}e^{\frac{1}{2}(\lambda+\nu)} \quad \text{..........................(78·4),}$$

where ϵ is a constant of integration.

Substituting in (77·2) we find

$$E_1^1 = -E_2^2 = -E_3^3 = E_4^4 = \tfrac{1}{2}e^{-\lambda-\nu}\kappa_4'^2$$
$$= \frac{1}{2}\frac{\epsilon^2}{r^4} \quad \text{....................(78·5)}$$

By (77·7) we have to substitute $-8\pi E_{\mu\nu}$ for zero on the right-hand side of (38·61–38·64). The first and fourth equations give as before $\lambda' = -\nu'$; and the second equation now becomes

$$e^{\nu}(1 + r\nu') - 1 = -8\pi g_{22}E_2^2$$
$$= -4\pi\epsilon^2/r^2.$$

Hence writing $e^{\nu} = \gamma$, $$\gamma + r\gamma' = 1 - 4\pi\epsilon^2/r^2,$$

so that $$r\gamma = r + 4\pi\epsilon^2/r - 2m,$$

where $2m$ is a constant of integration.

Hence the gravitational field due to an electron is given by

$$ds^2 = -\gamma^{-1}dr^2 - r^2d\theta^2 - r^2\sin^2\theta d\phi^2 + \gamma dt^2,$$

with $$\gamma = 1 - \frac{2m}{r} + \frac{4\pi\epsilon^2}{r^2} \quad \text{....................(78·6).}$$

This result appears to have been first given by Nordström. I have here followed the solution as given by G. B. Jeffery*.

* *Proc. Roy. Soc.* vol. 99 A, p. 123.

The effect of the term $4\pi\epsilon^2/r^2$ is that the effective mass decreases as r decreases. This is what we should naturally expect because the mass or energy is spread throughout space. We cannot put the constant m equal to zero, because that would leave a *repulsive* force on an uncharged particle varying as the inverse cube of the distance; by (55·8) the approximate Newtonian potential is $m/r - 2\pi\epsilon^2/r^2$.

The constant m can be identified with the mass and $4\pi\epsilon$ with the electric charge of the particle. The known experimental values for the negative electron are

$$m = 7 \,.\, 10^{-56} \text{ cm.},$$

$$a = \frac{2\pi\epsilon^2}{m} = 1{\cdot}5 \,.\, 10^{-13} \text{ cm.}$$

The quantity a is usually considered to be of the order of magnitude of the radius of the electron, so that at all points outside the electron m/r is of order 10^{-40} or smaller. Since $\lambda + \nu = 0$, (78·4) becomes

$$F_{41} = \kappa_4{}' = \frac{\epsilon}{r^2},$$

which justifies our identification of $4\pi\epsilon$ with the electric charge.

This example shows how very slight is the gravitational effect of the electronic energy. We can discuss most electromagnetic problems without taking account of the non-Euclidean character which an electromagnetic field necessarily imparts to space-time, the deviations from Euclidean geometry being usually so small as to be negligible in the cases we have to consider.

When r is diminished the value of γ given by (78·6) decreases to a minimum for $r = 2a$, and then increases continually becoming infinite at $r = 0$. There is no singularity in the electromagnetic and gravitational fields except at $r = 0$. It is thus possible to have an electron which is strictly a point-singularity, but nevertheless has a finite mass and charge.

The solution for the gravitational field of an uncharged particle is quite different in this respect. There is a singularity at $r = 2m$, so that the particle must have a finite perimeter not less than $4\pi m$. Moreover this singularity is caused by γ vanishing, whereas for the point-electron the singularity is due to γ becoming infinite.

This demonstration that a point-electron may have exactly the properties which electrons are observed to have is a useful corrective to the general belief that the radius of an electron is known with *certainty*. But on the whole, I think that it is more likely that an electron is a structure of finite size; our solution will then only be valid until we enter the substance of the electron, so that the question of a singularity at the origin does not arise.

Assuming that we do not encounter the substance of the electron outside the sphere $r = a$, the total energy of the electromagnetic field beyond this radius would be equal to the mass of the electron determined by observation.

For this reason a is usually taken as the radius of the electron. If it is admitted that the electromagnetic field continues undisturbed within this limit, an excess of energy accumulates, and it is therefore necessary to suppose that there exists negative energy in the inner portion, or that the effect of the singularity is equivalent to a negative energy. The conception of negative energy is not very welcome according to the usual outlook.

Another reason for believing that the charge of an electron is distributed through a volume of radius roughly equal to a will be found in the investigation of § 80. Accordingly I am of opinion that the point-electron is no more than a mathematical curiosity, and that the solution (78·6) should be limited to values of r greater than a.

79. Electromagnetic action.

The invariant integral

$$A = \tfrac{1}{4}\int F^{\mu\nu} F_{\mu\nu} \sqrt{-g}\, d\tau \qquad \text{......................(79·1)}$$

is called the action of the electromagnetic field. In Galilean coordinates it becomes by (77·3)

$$\int dt \iiint \tfrac{1}{2}(\alpha^2 + \beta^2 + \gamma^2 - X^2 - Y^2 - Z^2)\, dx\, dy\, dz \qquad \text{.........(79·2).}$$

Regarding the magnetic energy as kinetic (T) and the electric energy as potential (V) this is of the form

$$\int (T - V)\, dt,$$

i.e. the time-integral of the Lagrangian function*. The derivation of the electromagnetic equations by the stationary variation of this integral has been investigated in the classical researches of Larmor†

We shall now show that the two most important electromagnetic tensors, viz. the energy-tensor $E^{\mu\nu}$ and the charge-and-current vector J^{μ}, are the Hamiltonian derivatives of the action, the formulae being

$$\frac{\mathfrak{h}}{\mathfrak{h} g_{\mu\nu}}(\tfrac{1}{4} F^{\mu\nu} F_{\mu\nu}) = \tfrac{1}{2} E^{\mu\nu} \qquad \text{.....................(79·31),}$$

$$\frac{\mathfrak{h}}{\mathfrak{h} \kappa_{\mu}}(\tfrac{1}{4} F^{\mu\nu} F_{\mu\nu}) = -J^{\mu} \qquad \text{.................(79·32).}$$

* In dynamics there are two integrals which have the stationary property under proper restrictions, viz. $\int T dt$ and $\int (T - V)\, dt$. The first of these is the action as originally defined. In the general theory the term has been applied to both integrals somewhat indiscriminately, since there is no clear indication of energy which must be reckoned as potential.

† *Aether and Matter*, Chapter VI.

First consider small variations $\delta g_{\mu\nu}$, the κ_μ remaining constant The $F_{\mu\nu}$ (but not the $F^{\mu\nu}$) will accordingly remain unvaried. We have then

$$\begin{aligned}\delta(F^{\mu\nu}F_{\mu\nu}\sqrt{-g}) &= F^{\mu\nu}F_{\mu\nu}\,\delta(\sqrt{-g}) + F_{\alpha\beta}F_{\mu\nu}\sqrt{-g}\,.\,\delta(g^{\mu\alpha}g^{\nu\beta})\\ &= F^{\sigma\tau}F_{\sigma\tau}\sqrt{-g}\,.\,\frac{1}{2}\frac{\delta g}{g} + F_{\alpha\beta}F_{\mu\nu}\sqrt{-g}\,(g^{\mu\alpha}\delta g^{\nu\beta} + g^{\nu\beta}\delta g^{\mu\alpha})\\ &= \sqrt{-g}\,\{-\tfrac{1}{2}F^{\sigma\tau}F_{\sigma\tau}g_{\nu\beta}\delta g^{\nu\beta} + 2F_{\alpha\beta}F_{\mu\nu}g^{\mu\alpha}\delta g^{\nu\beta}\}\\ &= 2\sqrt{-g}\,.\,\delta g^{\nu\beta}\,\{-\tfrac{1}{4}g_{\nu\beta}F^{\sigma\tau}F_{\sigma\tau} + F^{\mu}{}_{\beta}F_{\mu\nu}\}\\ &= -2E_{\nu\beta}\sqrt{-g}\,.\,\delta g^{\nu\beta} \qquad \text{by (77 2)}\\ &= \quad 2E^{\nu\beta}\sqrt{-g}\,.\,\delta g_{\nu\beta} \qquad \text{by (35 2)}\end{aligned}$$

From this (79·31) follows immediately.

Next consider variations $\delta\kappa_\mu$, the $g_{\mu\nu}$ remaining constant. We have

$$\begin{aligned}\delta(F^{\mu\nu}F_{\mu\nu}\sqrt{-g}) &= 2F^{\mu\nu}\sqrt{-g}\,.\,\delta F_{\mu\nu}\\ &= 2F^{\mu\nu}\sqrt{-g}\left(\frac{\partial(\delta\kappa_\mu)}{\partial x_\nu} - \frac{\partial(\delta\kappa_\nu)}{\partial x_\mu}\right)\\ &= 4F^{\mu\nu}\sqrt{-g}\,.\,\frac{\partial(\delta\kappa_\mu)}{\partial x_\nu}\end{aligned}$$

owing to the antisymmetry of $F^{\mu\nu}$

$$= -4\frac{\partial}{\partial x_\nu}(F^{\mu\nu}\sqrt{-g})\,\delta\kappa_\mu + 4\frac{\partial}{\partial x_\nu}(F^{\mu\nu}\sqrt{-g}\,.\,\delta\kappa_\mu).$$

The second term can be omitted since it is a complete differential, and yields a surface-integral over the boundary where the variations have to vanish. Hence

$$\begin{aligned}\delta\int F^{\mu\nu}F_{\mu\nu}\sqrt{-g}\,d\tau &= -4\int\frac{\partial}{\partial x_\nu}(F^{\mu\nu}\sqrt{-g})\,.\,\delta\kappa_\mu\,d\tau\\ &= -4\int J^\mu\delta\kappa_\mu\,.\,\sqrt{-g}\,d\tau\end{aligned}$$

by (73·75). This demonstrates (79·32).

In a region free from electrons

$$T^{\mu\nu} - E^{\mu\nu} = 0.$$

Hence by (60·43) and (79·31)

$$\frac{\mathfrak{h}}{\mathfrak{h}g_{\mu\nu}}(G - 4\pi F^{\mu\nu}F_{\mu\nu}) = 0 \quad \text{......................(79 4).}$$

In the mechanical theory, neglecting electromagnetic fields, we found that the action G was stationary in regions containing no matter. We now see that when electromagnetic fields are included, the quantity which is stationary is $G - 4\pi F^{\mu\nu}F_{\mu\nu}$. Moreover it is stationary for variations $\delta\kappa_\mu$ as well as $\delta g_{\mu\nu}$, since when there are no electrons present J^μ must be zero.

The quantity $G - 4\pi F^{\mu\nu}F_{\mu\nu}$ thus appears to be highly significant from the physical point of view, in the discrimination between matter (electrons) and electromagnetic fields. But this significance fails to appear in the analytical expression. Analytically the combination of the two invariants G and $F^{\mu\nu}F_{\mu\nu}$ —the one a spur, and the other a square of a length—appears to be quite nonsensical. We can only regard the present form of the expression as a stepping-stone to something simpler. It will appear later that $G - 4\pi F^{\mu\nu}F_{\mu\nu}$ is perhaps not the exact expression for the significant physical quantity, it may be an approximation to a form which is analytically simpler, in which the gravitational and electromagnetic variables appear in a more intelligible combination.

Whereas material and gravitational actions are two aspects of the same thing, electromagnetic action stands entirely apart. There is no gravitational action associated with an electromagnetic field, owing to the identity $E = 0$. Thus any material or gravitational action is additional to electromagnetic action—if "addition" is appropriate in connection with quantities which are apparently of dissimilar nature.

80. Explanation of the mechanical force.

Why does a charged particle move when it is placed in an electromagnetic field? We may be tempted to reply that the reason is obvious; there is an electric force lying in wait, and it is the nature of a force to make bodies move. But this is a confusion of terminology; electric force is not a force in the mechanical sense of the term; it has nothing to do with pushing and pulling. Electric force describes a world-condition essentially different from that described by a mechanical force or stress-system; and the discussion in § 76 was based on empirical laws without theoretical explanation.

If we wish for a representation of the state of the aether in terms of mechanical forces, we must employ the stress-system (77·41, 77·42). In fact the pulling and pushing property is described by the tensor $E_{\mu\nu}$ not by $F_{\mu\nu}$. Our problem is to explain why a somewhat arbitrary combination of the electromagnetic variables $F_{\mu\nu}$ should have the properties of a mechanical stress-system.

To reduce the problem to its simplest form we consider an isolated electron. In an electromagnetic field its world-line does not follow a geodesic, but deviates according to laws which have been determined experimentally. It is worth noticing that the behaviour of an isolated electron has been directly determined by experiment, this being one of the few cases in which microscopic laws have been found immediately and not inferred hypothetically from macroscopic experiments. We want to know what the electron is trying to accomplish by deviating from the geodesic—what condition of existence is fulfilled, which makes the four-dimensional structure of an accelerated electron a possible one, whereas a similar structure ranged along a geodesic track would be an impossible one.

The law which has to be explained is*

$$-m\left\{\frac{d^2x_\mu}{ds^2}+\{\alpha\beta,\mu\}\frac{dx_\alpha}{ds}\frac{dx_\beta}{ds}\right\}=h^\mu=F^\mu{}_\nu J^\nu \quad\text{...........(80·1)},$$

which is the tensor equation corresponding to the law of elementary electrostatics

$$m\frac{d^2x}{dt^2}=Xe.$$

Let A^μ be the velocity-vector of the electron ($A^\mu = dx_\mu/ds$), and ρ_0 the proper-density of the charge, then by (73·82)

$$J^\mu=\rho_0 A^\mu \quad\text{........................(80·21)},$$

and

$$\frac{d^2x_\mu}{ds^2}+\{\alpha\beta,\mu\}\frac{dx_\alpha}{ds}\frac{dx_\beta}{ds}=A^\nu(A^\mu)_\nu \quad\text{. ....(80·22)},$$

as in (33·4).

Considering the verification of (80·1) by experiment we remark that X or $F_{\mu\nu}$ refers to the applied external field, no attention being paid to the possible disturbance of this field caused by the accelerated electron itself. To distinguish this we denote the external field by $F'_{\mu\nu}$. The equation to be explained accordingly becomes

$$mA^\nu(A^\mu)_\nu=-F'^\mu{}_\nu(\rho_0 A^\nu),$$

or, lowering the suffix μ,

$$mA^\nu A_{\mu\nu}=-F'_{\mu\nu}eA^\nu \quad\text{........................(80·3)}.$$

We have replaced the *density* ρ_0 by the *quantity* e for the reason explained in the footnote.

Consider now the field due to the electron itself in its own neighbourhood. This is determined by (74·41)

$$\Box F_{\mu\nu}=J_{\mu\nu}-J_{\nu\mu}-G^\epsilon_\mu F_{\epsilon\nu}+G^\epsilon_\nu F_{\epsilon\mu}+2B_{\mu\nu\alpha\epsilon}F^{\epsilon\alpha}.$$

The discussion of § 78 shows that we may safely neglect the gravitational field caused by the energy of the electron or of the external field. Hence approximately

$$\Box F_{\mu\nu}=J_{\mu\nu}-J_{\nu\mu}.$$

The solution is as in (74·72)

$$F_{\mu\nu}=\int\frac{de\,(A_{\mu\nu}-A_{\nu\mu})}{4\pi\beta r}$$

$$=\frac{1}{4\pi\beta}(A_{\mu\nu}-A_{\nu\mu})\int\frac{de}{r} \quad\text{....................(80·4)},$$

if all parts of the electron have the same velocity A^μ. This result is obtained primarily for Galilean coordinates, but it is a tensor equation applying to all coordinate-systems provided that $\int de/\beta r$ is treated as an invariant and calculated in natural measure. We shall reckon it in proper-measure and accordingly drop the factor β.

* In this and a succeeding equation I have a *quantity* on the left-hand side and a *density* on the right-hand side. I trust to the reader to amend this mentally. It would, I think, only make the equations more confusing if I attempted to indicate the amendment symbolically.

Now suppose that the electron moves in such a way that its own field on the average just neutralises the applied external field $F'_{\mu\nu}$ in the region occupied by the electron. The value of $F_{\mu\nu}$ averaged for all the elements of charge constituting the electron is given by

$$eF_{\mu\nu} = \frac{1}{4\pi}(A_{\mu\nu} - A_{\nu\mu}) \iint \frac{de_1 de_2}{r_{12}}$$
$$= \frac{1}{4\pi}(A_{\mu\nu} - A_{\nu\mu}) \frac{e^2}{a},$$

where $1/a$ is an average value of $1/r_{12}$ for every pair of points in the electron. We may leave indeterminate the exact weighting of the pairs of points in taking the average, merely noting that a will be a length comparable with the radius of the sphere throughout which the charge (or the greater part of it) is spread.

If this value of $F_{\mu\nu}$ is equal and opposite to $F'_{\mu\nu}$, we have

$$-eA^\nu F'_{\mu\nu} = \frac{1}{4\pi} A^\nu (A_{\mu\nu} - A_{\nu\mu}) \frac{e^2}{a}$$
$$= A^\nu A_{\mu\nu} \cdot \frac{e^2}{4\pi a} \quad \text{..................} \quad (80\cdot5),$$

because $$A^\nu A_{\nu\mu} = A_\nu (A^\nu)_\mu = \tfrac{1}{2}(A_\nu A^\nu)_\mu = \tfrac{1}{2}(1)_\mu = 0,$$
the square of the length of a velocity-vector being necessarily unity.

The result (80·5) will agree with (80·3) if the mass of the electron is

$$m = \frac{e^2}{4\pi a} \quad \text{..........................} \quad (80\cdot6).$$

The observed law of motion of the electron thus corresponds to the condition that it can be under no resultant electromagnetic field. We must not imagine that a resultant electromagnetic force has anything of a tugging nature that can deflect an electron. It never gets the chance of doing anything to the electron, because if the resultant field existed the electron could not exist—it would be an impossible structure.

The interest of this discussion is that it has led us to one of the conditions for the existence of an electron, which turns out to be of a simple character—viz. that on the average the electromagnetic force throughout the electron must be zero*. This condition is clearly fulfilled for a symmetrical electron at rest in no field of force; and the same condition applied generally leads to the law of motion (80·1).

For the existence of an electron, non-Maxwellian stresses are necessary, and we are not yet in a position to state the laws of these additional stresses. The existence of an electron contradicts the electromagnetic laws with which we have to work at present, so that from the present standpoint an electron at rest in no external field of force is a *miracle*. Our calculation shows that an

* The exact region of zero force is not determined. The essential point is that on some critical surface or volume the field has to be symmetrical enough to give no resultant.

electron in an external field of force having the acceleration given by (80·1) is *precisely the same miracle.* That is as far as the explanation goes.

The electromagnetic field within the electron will vanish on the average if it has sufficient symmetry. There appears to be an analogy between this and the condition which we found in § 56 to be necessary for the existence of a particle, viz. that its gravitational field should have symmetrical properties. There is further an analogy in the condition determining the acceleration in the two cases. An uncharged undisturbed body takes such a course that relative to it there is no resultant gravitational field; similarly an electron takes such a course that relative to it there is no resultant electromagnetic field. We have given a definite reason for the gravitational symmetry of a particle, viz. because in practical measurement it is itself the standard of symmetry; I presume that there is an analogous explanation of the electrical symmetry of an electron, but it has not yet been formulated. The following argument (which should be compared with §§ 64, 66) will show where the difficulty occurs.

The analogue of the interval is the flux $F_{\mu\nu}dS^{\mu\nu}$. As the interval between two adjacent points is the fundamental invariant of mechanics, so the flux through a small surface is the fundamental invariant of electromagnetism. Two electrical systems will be alike observationally if, and only if, all corresponding fluxes are equal. Equality of flux can thus be tested absolutely; and different fluxes can be measured (according to a conventional code) by apparatus constituted with electrical material. From the flux we can pass by mathematical processes to the charge-and-current vector, and this enables us to make the second contact between mathematical theory and the actual world, viz. the identification of electricity. We should now complete the cycle by showing that with electricity so defined apparatus can be constructed which will measure the original flux. Here, however, the analogy breaks down, at least temporarily. The use of electricity for measuring electromagnetic fluxes requires discontinuity, but this discontinuity is obtained in practice by complicated conditions such as insulation, constant contact differences of potential, etc. We do not seem able to reduce the theory of electrical measurement to direct dependence on an innate discontinuity of electrical charge in the same way that geometrical measurement depends on the discontinuity of matter. For this reason the last chain of the cycle is incomplete, and it does not seem permissible to deduce that the discontinuous unit of electric charge must become the standard of electrical symmetry in the same way that the discontinuous unit of matter (turned in different orientations) becomes the standard of geometrical symmetry.

According to (80·6) the mass of the electron is $e^2/4\pi a$, where a is a length comparable with the radius of the electron. This is in conformity with the usual view as to the size of an electron, and is opposed to the point-electron suggested in § 78 as an alternative. But the mass here considered is a purely electromagnetic constant, which only enters into equations in which electromagnetic forces are concerned When the right-hand side of (80·1) vanishes, the electron describes a geodesic just as an uncharged particle would; but m is now merely a constant multiplier which can be removed. We have still to find the connection between this electromagnetic mass

$$m_e = e^2/4\pi a \quad \text{.................. (80·71)}$$

and the gravitational (i.e. gravitation-producing) mass m_g, given by

$$m_g ds = \frac{1}{8\pi}\int G\sqrt{-g}\,d\tau \quad \text{.................(80·72)}$$

Since we believe that all negative electrons are precisely alike, m_g/m_e will be a constant for the negative electron, similarly it will be a constant for the positive electron. But positive and negative electrons are structures of very different kinds, and it does not follow that m_g/m_e is the same for both. As a matter of fact there is no experimental evidence which suggests that the ratio is the same for both Any gravitational field perceptible to observation is caused by practically equal numbers of positive and negative electrons, so that no opportunity of distinguishing their contributions occurs If, however, we admit that the principle of conservation of energy is universally valid in cases where the positive and negative electrons are separated to an extent never yet realised experimentally, it is possible to prove that m_g/m_e is the same for both kinds.

From the equation (80·1) we deduce the value of the electromagnetic energy-tensor as in §§ 76, 77, only, $E^{\mu\nu}$ will not be expressed in the same units as the whole energy-tensor $G_\mu^\nu - \frac{1}{2}g_\mu^\nu G$, since the mass appearing in (80·1) is m_e instead of m_g. In consequence, the law for empty space (77·6) must be written

$$G_\mu^\nu - \tfrac{1}{2}g_\mu^\nu G = -8\pi\frac{m_g}{m_e}\left(-F^{\nu\alpha}F_{\mu\alpha} + \tfrac{1}{4}g_\mu^\nu F^{\alpha\beta}F_{\alpha\beta}\right) \quad \text{......(80·8)}$$

We can establish this equation firstly by considering the motion of a positive electron and secondly by considering a negative electron Evidently we shall obtain inconsistent equations in the two cases unless m_g/m_e for the positive electron is the same as for the negative electron. Unless this condition is fulfilled, we should violate the law of conservation of energy and momentum by first converting kinetic energy of a negative electron into free electromagnetic energy and then reconverting the free energy into kinetic energy of a positive electron

Accordingly m_g/m_e is a constant of nature and it may be absorbed in equation (80·8) by properly choosing the unit of $F_{\mu\nu}$.

81. Electromagnetic volume.

If $a_{\mu\nu}$ is any tensor, the determinant $|a_{\mu\nu}|$ is transformed according to the law

$$|a_{\mu\nu}| = J^2\,|a'_{\mu\nu}|$$

by (48·8), whence it follows as in (49·3) that

$$\int \sqrt{(|a_{\mu\nu}|)}\, d\tau \qquad (81 \cdot 1)$$

for any four-dimensional region is an invariant.

We have already considered the case $a_{\mu\nu} = g_{\mu\nu}$, and it is natural now to consider the case $a_{\mu\nu} = F_{\mu\nu}$. Since the tensor $g_{\mu\nu}$ defines the metric of space-time, and the corresponding invariant is the metrical volume (natural volume) of the region, it seems appropriate to call the invariant

$$V_e = \int \sqrt{(|F_{\mu\nu}|)}\, d\tau \qquad (81 \cdot 2)$$

the electromagnetic volume of the region. The resemblance to metrical volume is purely analytical.

Since $|F_{\mu\nu}|$ is a skew-symmetric determinant of even order, it is a perfect square, and (81·2) is rational. It easily reduces to

$$V_e = \int (F_{23}F_{14} + F_{31}F_{24} + F_{12}F_{34})\, d\tau \qquad (81 \cdot 31).$$

In Galilean coordinates this becomes

$$V_e = \int (\alpha X + \beta Y + \gamma Z)\, d\tau \qquad (81 \cdot 32).$$

It is somewhat curious that the scalar-product of the electric and magnetic forces is of so little importance in the classical theory, for (81·32) would seem to be the most fundamental invariant of the field. Apart from the fact that it vanishes for electromagnetic waves propagated in the absence of any bound electric field (i.e. remote from electrons), this invariant seems to have no significant properties. Perhaps it may turn out to have greater importance when the study of electron-structure is more advanced.

From (81·31) we have

$$V_e = \int \Sigma \left(\frac{\partial \kappa_1}{\partial x_4} \frac{\partial \kappa_2}{\partial x_3} - \frac{\partial \kappa_1}{\partial x_3} \frac{\partial \kappa_2}{\partial x_4} \right) d\tau$$

the summation being for all permutations of the suffixes

$$= \int \Sigma \left\{ \frac{\partial}{\partial x_4} \left(\kappa_1 \frac{\partial \kappa_2}{\partial x_3} \right) - \frac{\partial}{\partial x_3} \left(\kappa_1 \frac{\partial \kappa_2}{\partial x_4} \right) \right\} d\tau.$$

Hence V_e reduces to a surface-integral over the boundary of the region, and it is useless to consider its variations by the Hamiltonian method. The electromagnetic volume of a region is of the nature of a flux through its three-dimensional boundary.

82. Macroscopic equations.

For macroscopic treatment the distribution and motion of the electrons are averaged, and the equivalent continuous distribution is described by two new quantities

the electric displacement, P, Q, R,
the magnetic induction, a, b, c,

in addition to

the electric force, X, Y, Z,
the magnetic force, α, β, γ

These are grouped cross-wise to form the two principal electromagnetic tensors

$$F_{\mu\nu} = \begin{matrix} 0 & -c & b & -X, \\ c & 0 & -a & -Y \\ -b & a & 0 & -Z \\ X & Y & Z & 0 \end{matrix} \qquad H^{\mu\nu} = \begin{matrix} 0 & -\gamma & \beta & P \\ \gamma & 0 & -\alpha & Q \\ -\beta & \alpha & 0 & R \\ -P & -Q & -R & 0 \end{matrix} \quad (82\cdot1).$$

$H^{\mu\nu}$ now plays the part previously taken by $F^{\mu\nu}$, but it is no longer derived from $F_{\mu\nu}$ by a mere raising of suffixes. The relation between the two tensors is given by the constitutive equations of the material; in simple cases it is specified by two constants, the specific inductive capacity κ and the permeability μ.

Equations (73·73) and (73·74) are replaced by

$$\left.\begin{aligned} F_{\mu\nu} &= \frac{\partial\kappa_\mu}{\partial x_\nu} - \frac{\partial\kappa_\nu}{\partial x_\mu} \\ H^{\mu\nu}_\nu &= J^\mu \end{aligned}\right\} \qquad (82\cdot2)$$

These represent the usual equations of the classical theory. It should be noticed that $\partial H/\partial y - \partial G/\partial z$ is now a, not α

In the simple case the constitutive equations are

$$(P, Q, R) = K(X, Y, Z); \quad (a, b, c) = \mu(\alpha, \beta, \gamma) \quad \ldots\ldots (82\cdot3),$$

so that

$$H^{11}, H^{12} \ldots H^{33} = \frac{1}{\mu}(F^{11}, F^{12} \ldots F^{33}), \quad H^{14}, H^{24}, H^{34} = K(F^{14}, F^{24}, F^{34}).$$

These simplified equations are not of tensor form, and refer only to coordinates with respect to which the material is at rest For general coordinates the constitutive equations must be of the form

$$H^{\mu\nu} = p^{\mu\alpha} p^{\nu\beta} F_{\alpha\beta},$$

where $p^{\mu\nu}$ is a tensor

The law of conservation of electric charge can be deduced from $H^{\mu\nu}_\nu = J^\mu$ just as in (73·76).

The macroscopic method is introduced for practical purposes rather than as a contribution to the theory, and there seems to be no advantage in developing it further here The chief theoretical interest lies in the suggestion of a possible generalisation of Maxwell's theory by admitting that the covariant and contravariant electromagnetic tensors may in certain circumstances be independent tensors, e g inside the electron This is the basis of a theory of matter developed by G. Mie.

CHAPTER VII

WORLD GEOMETRY

PART I WEYL'S THEORY

83. Natural geometry and world geometry.

Graphical representation is a device commonly employed in dealing with all kinds of physical quantities. It is most often used when we wish to set before ourselves a mass of information in such a way that the eye can take it in at a glance, but this is not the only use. We do not always draw the graphs on a sheet of paper, the method is also serviceable when the representation is in a conceptual mathematical space of any number of dimensions and possibly non-Euclidean geometry. One great advantage is that when the graphical representation has been made, an extensive geometrical nomenclature becomes available for description—straight line, gradient, curvature, etc.—and a self-explanatory nomenclature is a considerable aid in discussing an abstruse subject.

It is therefore reasonable to seek enlightenment by giving a graphical representation to all the physical quantities with which we have to deal. In this way physics becomes geometrised. But graphical representation does not assume any hypothesis as to the ultimate nature of the quantities represented. The possibility of exhibiting the whole world of physics in a unified geometrical representation is a test not of the nature of the world but of the ingenuity of the mathematician.

There is no special rule for representing physical quantities such as electric force, potential, temperature, etc.; we may draw the isotherms as straight lines, ellipses, spheres, according to convenience of illustration. But there are certain physical quantities (i e results of operations and calculations) which have a natural graphical representation, we habitually think of them graphically, and are almost unconscious that there is anything conventional in the way we represent them. For example, measured distances and directions are instinctively conceived by us graphically; and the space in which we represent them is for us *actual space*. These quantities are not in their intrinsic nature dissimilar from other physical quantities which are not habitually represented geometrically. If we eliminated the human element (or should we not say, the pre-human element?) in natural knowledge the device of graphical representation of the results of measures or estimates of distance would appear just as artificial as the graphical representation of thermometer readings. We cannot predict that a superhuman intelligence would conceive of distance in the way we conceive it; he would perhaps admit that our device of mentally plotting the results of a survey in a three-dimensional space is ingenious and scientifically helpful, but it would not occur to him that this space was more *actual* than the *pv* space of an indicator-diagram.

In our previous work we have studied this unsophisticated graphical representation of certain physical quantities, under the name Natural Geometry; we have slightly extended the idea by the addition of a fourth dimension to include time; and we have found that not only the quantities ordinarily regarded as geometrical but also mechanical quantities, such as force, density, energy, are fully represented in this natural geometry. For example the energy-tensor was found to be made up of the Gaussian curvatures of sections of actual space-time (65 72). But the electromagnetic quantities introduced in the preceding chapter have not as yet been graphically represented; the vector κ_μ was supposed to exist *in* actual space, not to be the measure of any property *of* actual space. Thus up to the present the geometrisation of physics is not complete.

Two possible ways of generalising our geometrical outlook are open. It may be that the Riemannian geometry assigned to actual space is not exact; and that the true geometry is of a broader kind leaving room for the vector κ_μ to play a fundamental part and so receive geometrical recognition as one of the determining characters of actual space. For reasons which will appear in the course of this chapter, I do not think that this is the correct solution. The alternative is to give all our variables, including κ_μ, a suitable graphical representation in some new conceptual space—not actual space. With sufficient ingenuity it ought to be possible to accomplish this, for no hypothesis is implied as to the nature of the quantities so represented. This generalised graphical scheme may or may not be helpful to the progress of our knowledge; we attempt it in the hope that it will render the interconnection of electromagnetic and gravitational phenomena more intelligible. I think it will be found that this hope is not disappointed.

In *Space, Time and Gravitation*, Chapter XI, Weyl's non-Riemannian geometry has been regarded throughout as expressing an amended and exact Natural Geometry. That was the original intention of his theory*. For the present we shall continue to develop it on this understanding. But we shall ultimately come to the second alternative, as Weyl himself has done, and realise that his non-Riemannian geometry is not to be applied to *actual* space-time, it refers to a graphical representation of that relation-structure which is the basis of all physics, and both electromagnetic and metrical variables appear in it as interrelated. Having arrived at this standpoint we pass naturally to the more general geometry of relation-structure developed in Part II of this chapter.

* The original paper (*Berlin. Sitzungsberichte*, 30 May 1918) is rather obscure on this point. It states the mathematical development of the corrected Riemannian geometry—"the physical application is obvious." But it is explicitly stated that the absence of an electromagnetic field is the necessary condition for Einstein's theory to be valid—an opinion which, I think, is no longer held.

We have then to distinguish between Natural Geometry, which is the single *true* geometry in the sense understood by the physicist, and World Geometry, which is the pure geometry applicable to a conceptual graphical representation of all the quantities concerned in physics We may perhaps go so far as to say that the World Geometry is intended to be closely descriptive of the fundamental relation-structure which underlies the various manifestations of space, time, matter and electromagnetism; that statement, however, is rather vague when we come to analyse it. Since the graphical representation is in any case conventional we cannot say that one method rather than another is right. Thus the two geometries discussed in Parts I and II of this chapter are not to be regarded as contradictory. My reason for introducing the second treatment is that I find it to be more illuminating and far-reaching, not that I reject the first representation as inadmissible.

In the following account of Weyl's theory I have not adhered to the author's order of development, but have adapted it to the point of view here taken up, which sometimes differs (though not, I believe, fundamentally) from that which he adopts It may be somewhat unfair to present a theory from the wrong end—as its author might consider, but I trust that my treatment has not unduly obscured the brilliance of what is unquestionably the greatest advance in the relativity theory after Einstein's work.

84. Non-integrability of length.

We have found in § 33 that the change δA_μ of a vector taken by parallel displacement round a small circuit is

$$\begin{aligned}\delta A_\mu &= \tfrac{1}{2}(A_{\mu\nu\sigma} - A_{\mu\sigma\nu})\, dS^{\nu\sigma} \\ &= \tfrac{1}{2} B^{\epsilon}_{\mu\nu\sigma} A_\epsilon dS^{\nu\sigma} \\ &= \tfrac{1}{2} B_{\mu\nu\sigma\epsilon} A^\epsilon dS^{\nu\sigma} \quad \text{.........................(84·1)}\end{aligned}$$

Hence
$$A^\mu \delta A_\mu = \tfrac{1}{2} B_{\mu\nu\sigma\epsilon} A^\mu A^\epsilon dS^{\nu\sigma} = 0,$$

since $B_{\mu\nu\sigma\epsilon}$ is antisymmetrical in μ and ϵ.

Hence by (26·4) δA_μ is perpendicular to A_μ, and the *length* of the vector A_μ is unaltered by its parallel displacement round the circuit. It is only the direction which changes.

We endeavoured to explain how this change of direction can occur in a curved world by the example of a ship sailing on a curved ocean (§ 33). Having convinced ourselves that there is no logical impossibility in the result that the direction changes, we cannot very well see anything self-contradictory in the length changing also. It is true that we have just given a mathematical proof that the length does not change; but that only means that a change of length is excluded by conditions which have been introduced, perhaps inadvertently, in the postulates of Riemannian geometry. We can construct a geometry in which the change of length occurs, without landing ourselves in a contradiction.

In the more general geometry, we have in place of (84·1)

$$\delta A_\mu = \tfrac{1}{2} {}^*B_{\mu\nu\sigma\epsilon} A^\epsilon dS^{\nu\sigma} \quad \text{..................(84·21)},$$

where $*B_{\mu\nu\sigma\epsilon}$ is a more general tensor which is *not* antisymmetrical in μ and ϵ. It will be antisymmetrical in ν and σ since a symmetrical part would be meaningless in (84·21), and disappear owing to the antisymmetry of $dS^{\nu\sigma}$. Writing

$$R_{\mu\nu\sigma\epsilon} = \tfrac{1}{2}(*B_{\mu\nu\sigma\epsilon} - *B_{\epsilon\nu\sigma\mu}), \quad F_{\mu\nu\sigma\epsilon} = \tfrac{1}{2}(*B_{\mu\nu\sigma\epsilon} + *B_{\epsilon\nu\sigma\mu}),$$

$$\delta A_\mu = \tfrac{1}{2}(R_{\mu\nu\sigma\epsilon} + F_{\mu\nu\sigma\epsilon}) A^\epsilon dS^{\nu\sigma} \quad \text{.................(84·22)},$$

where R is antisymmetrical, and F symmetrical, in μ and ϵ

Then the change of length l is given by

$$\delta(l^2) = 2A^\mu \delta A_\mu = F_{\mu\nu\sigma\epsilon} A^\mu A^\epsilon dS^{\nu\sigma} \quad \text{..............(84·3)},$$

which does not vanish.

To obtain Weyl's geometry we must impose two restrictions on $F_{\mu\nu\sigma\epsilon}$:

(*a*) $F_{\mu\nu\sigma\epsilon}$ is of the special form $g_{\mu\epsilon} F_{\nu\sigma}$,

(*b*) $F_{\nu\sigma}$ is the curl of a vector.

The second restriction is logically necessary. We have expressed the change of a vector taken round a circuit by a formula involving a surface bounded by the circuit. We may choose different surfaces, all bounded by the same circuit, and these have to give the same result for δA_μ. It is easily seen, as in Stokes's theorem, that these results will only be consistent if the co-factor of $dS^{\nu\sigma}$ is a curl.

The first restriction is not imperatively demanded, and we shall discard it in Part II of this chapter. It has the following effect. Equation (84·3) becomes

$$\delta(l^2) = F_{\nu\sigma} \cdot g_{\mu\epsilon} A^\mu A^\epsilon . dS^{\nu\sigma}$$

$$= F_{\nu\sigma} l^2 dS^{\nu\sigma},$$

so that

$$\frac{\delta l}{l} = \tfrac{1}{2} F_{\nu\sigma} dS^{\nu\sigma} \quad \text{..............................(84·4)}.$$

The change of length is proportional to the original length and is independent of the direction of the vector; whereas in the more general formula (84·3) the change of length depends on the direction.

One result of the restriction is that zero-length is still zero-length after parallel displacement round a circuit. If we have identified zero-length at one point of the world we can transfer it without ambiguity to every other point and so identify zero-length everywhere. Finite lengths cannot be transferred without ambiguity; a route of parallel displacement must be specified.

Zero-length is of great importance in optical phenomena, because in Einstein's geometry any element of the track of a light-pulse is a vector of zero-length; so that if there were no definite zero-length a pulse of light would not know what track it ought to take. It is because Weyl's theory makes no attempt to re-interpret this part of Einstein's theory that an absolute zero-length is required, and the restriction (*a*) is therefore imposed.

Another result of the restriction is that lengths at the same point but in different orientations become comparable without ambiguity The ambiguity is limited to the comparison of lengths at different places

85. Transformation of gauge-systems.

According to the foregoing section it is not possible to compare lengths (except zero-length) at different places, because the result of the comparison will depend on the route taken in bringing the two lengths into juxtaposition.

In Riemannian geometry we have taken for granted this possibility of comparing lengths. The interval at any point has been assigned a definite value, which implies comparison with a standard; it did not occur to us to question how this comparison at a distance could be made. We have now to define the geometry of the continuum in a way which recognises this difficulty.

We suppose that a definite but arbitrary *gauge-system* has been adopted; that is to say, at every point of space-time a standard of interval-length has been set up, and every interval is expressed in terms of the standard at the point where it is. This avoids the ambiguity involved in transferring intervals from one point to another to compare with a single standard.

Take a displacement at P (coordinates, x_μ) and transfer it by parallel displacement to an infinitely near point P' (coordinates, $x_\mu + dx_\mu$). Let its initial length measured by the gauge at P be l, and its final length measured by the gauge at P' be $l + dl$. We may express the change of length by the formula

$$d(\log l) = \kappa_\mu dx_\mu \quad \text{.............................(85·1)},$$

where κ_μ represents some vector-field. If we alter the gauge-system we shall, of course, obtain different values of l, and therefore of κ_μ

It is not necessary to specify the route of transfer for the small distance P to P'. The difference in the results obtained by taking different routes is by (84·4) proportional to the area enclosed by the routes, and is thus of the second order in dx_μ. As PP' is taken infinitely small this ambiguity becomes negligible compared with the first-order expression $\kappa_\mu dx_\mu$.

Our system of reference can now be varied in two ways—by change of coordinates and by change of gauge-system. The behaviour of $g_{\mu\nu}$ and κ_μ for transformation of coordinates has been fully studied; we have to examine how they will be transformed by a transformation of gauge.

A new gauge-system will be obtained by altering the length of the standard at each point in the ratio λ, where λ is an arbitrary function of the coordinates. If the standard is decreased in the ratio λ, the length of a displacement will be increased in the ratio λ. If accents refer to the new system

$$ds' = \lambda ds \quad \text{..............................(85·2)}.$$

The components dx_μ of a displacement will not be changed, since we are not altering the coordinate-system, thus

$$dx_\mu' = dx_\mu \quad \text{..............................(85·3)}.$$

Hence $\quad g'_{\mu\nu} dx_\mu' dx_\nu' = ds'^2 = \lambda^2 ds^2 = \lambda^2 g_{\mu\nu} dx_\mu dx_\nu = \lambda^2 g_{\mu\nu} dx_\mu' dx_\nu',$

so that $\quad g'_{\mu\nu} = \lambda^2 g_{\mu\nu} \quad \text{..............................(85·41)}.$

It follows at once that $$g' = \lambda^8 g \quad \text{.................} \quad (85\cdot42),$$

$$g'^{\mu\nu} = \lambda^{-2} g^{\mu\nu} \quad \text{.................} \quad (85\cdot43),$$

$$\sqrt{-g'} \, . \, d\tau' = \lambda^4 \sqrt{-g} \, d\tau \quad \text{.................} \quad (85\cdot44).$$

Again, by (85·1) $$\kappa_\mu' dx_\mu = d(\log l') = d\{\log(\lambda l)\}$$
$$= d(\log l) + d(\log \lambda)$$
$$= \kappa_\mu dx_\mu + \frac{\partial(\log \lambda)}{\partial x_\mu} dx_\mu.$$

Or, writing $$\phi = \log \lambda \quad \text{.................} \quad (85\cdot51),$$

then $$\kappa_\mu' = \kappa_\mu + \frac{\partial \phi}{\partial x_\mu} \quad \text{.................} \quad (85\cdot52).$$

The curl of κ_μ has an important property; if

$$F_{\mu\nu} = \frac{\partial \kappa_\mu}{\partial x_\nu} - \frac{\partial \kappa_\nu}{\partial x_\mu},$$

we see by (85·52) that $$F'_{\mu\nu} = F_{\mu\nu} \quad \text{.................} \quad (85\cdot6),$$

so that $F_{\mu\nu}$ is independent of the gauge-system. This is only true of the covariant tensor; if we raise one or both suffixes the function λ is introduced by (85·43).

It will be seen that the geometry of the continuum now involves 14 functions which vary from point to point, viz. ten $g_{\mu\nu}$ and four κ_μ. These may be subjected to transformations, viz. the transformations of gauge discussed above, and the transformations of coordinates discussed in Chapter II. Such transformations will not alter any intrinsic properties of the world; but any changes in the $g_{\mu\nu}$ and κ_μ other than gauge or coordinate transformations will alter the intrinsic state of the world and may reasonably be expected to change its physical manifestations.

The question then arises, How will the change manifest itself physically if we alter the κ_μ? All the phenomena of mechanics have been traced to the $g_{\mu\nu}$, so that presumably the change is not shown in mechanics, or at least the primary effect is not mechanical. We are left with the domain of electromagnetism which is not expressible in terms of $g_{\mu\nu}$ alone; and the suggestion arises that an alteration of κ_μ may appear physically as an alteration of the electromagnetic field.

We have seen that the electromagnetic field is described by a vector already called κ_μ, and it is an obvious step to identify this with the κ_μ introduced in Weyl's geometry. According to observation the physical condition of the world is not completely defined by the $g_{\mu\nu}$ and an additional vector must be specified; according to theoretical geometry the nature of a continuum is not completely indicated by the $g_{\mu\nu}$ and an additional vector must be specified. The conclusion is irresistible that the two vectors are to be identified.

Moreover according to (85·52) we can change κ_μ to $\kappa_\mu + \partial\phi/\partial x_\mu$ by a change of gauge without altering the intrinsic state of the world. It was explained at the beginning of § 74 that we can make the same change of the electromagnetic potential without altering the resulting electromagnetic field.

We accordingly accept this identification The κ_μ and $F_{\mu\nu}$ of the present geometrical theory will be the electromagnetic potential and force of Chapter VI. It will be best to suspend the convention $\kappa^\mu_\mu = 0$ (74 1) for the present, since that would commit us prematurely to a particular gauge-system.

It must be borne in mind that by this identification the electromagnetic force becomes expressed in some natural unit whose relation to the C.G.S. system is at present unknown For example the constant of proportionality in (77·7) may be altered. $F_{\mu\nu}$ is not altered by any change of gauge-system (85 6) so that its value is a pure number. The question then arises, How many volts per centimetre correspond to $F_{\mu\nu} = 1$ in any given coordinate-system? The problem is a difficult one, but we shall give a rough and rather dubious estimate in § 102.

I do not think that our subsequent discussion will add anything material to the present argument in favour of the electromagnetic interpretation of κ_μ. The case rests entirely on the apparently significant fact, that on removing an artificial restriction in Riemannian geometry, we have just the right number of variables at our disposal which are necessary for a physical description of the world.

86. Gauge-invariance.

It will be useful to discover tensors and invariants which, besides possessing their characteristic properties with regard to transformations of coordinates, are unaltered by any transformation of gauge-system. These will be called *in-tensors* and *in-invariants*.

There are other tensors or invariants which merely become multiplied by a power of λ when the gauge is altered. These will be called *co-tensors* and *co-invariants*.

Change of gauge is a generalisation of change of unit in physical equations, the unit being no longer a constant but an arbitrary function of position. We have only one unit to consider—the unit of interval. Coordinates are merely identification-numbers and have no reference to our unit, so that a displacement dx_μ is an in-vector. It should be noticed that if we change the unit-mesh of a rectangular coordinate-system from one mile to one kilometre, we make a change of coordinates not a change of gauge The distinction is more obvious when coordinates other than Cartesian are used. The most confusing case is that of Galilean coordinates, for then the special values of the $g_{\mu\nu}$ fix the length of side of unit mesh as equal to the unit of interval; and it is not easy to keep in mind that the *displacement* between two corners of the mesh is the number 1, whilst the *interval* between them is 1 kilometre.

According to (85 6) the electromagnetic force $F_{\mu\nu}$ is an in-tensor. $F^{\mu\nu}$ is only a co-tensor, and $F_{\mu\nu}F^{\mu\nu}$ a co-invariant.

Transforming the 3-index symbol $[\mu\nu, \sigma]$ by an alteration of gauge we have by (85·41)

$$[\mu\nu, \sigma]' = \frac{1}{2}\left(\frac{\partial(\lambda^2 g_{\mu\sigma})}{\partial x_\nu} + \frac{\partial(\lambda^2 g_{\nu\sigma})}{\partial x_\mu} - \frac{\partial(\lambda^2 g_{\mu\nu})}{\partial x_\sigma}\right)$$

$$= \lambda^2 [\mu\nu, \sigma] + \tfrac{1}{2} g_{\mu\sigma}\frac{\partial\lambda^2}{\partial x_\nu} + \tfrac{1}{2} g_{\nu\sigma}\frac{\partial\lambda^2}{\partial x_\mu} - \tfrac{1}{2} g_{\mu\nu}\frac{\partial\lambda^2}{\partial x_\sigma}$$

$$= \lambda^2 [\mu\nu, \sigma] + \lambda^2 (g_{\mu\sigma}\phi_\nu + g_{\nu\sigma}\phi_\mu - g_{\mu\nu}\phi_\sigma)$$

by (85·51) We have written $\phi_\mu \equiv \dfrac{\partial\phi}{\partial x_\mu}$.

Multiply through by $g'^{\sigma\alpha} = \lambda^{-2} g^{\sigma\alpha}$; we obtain

$$\{\mu\nu, \alpha\}' = \{\mu\nu, \alpha\} + g^\alpha_\mu \phi_\nu + g^\alpha_\nu \phi_\mu - g_{\mu\nu}\phi^\alpha \quad \text{.........(86·1)}$$

Let
$$^*\{\mu\nu, \alpha\} \equiv \{\mu\nu, \alpha\} - g^\alpha_\mu \kappa_\nu - g^\alpha_\nu \kappa_\mu + g_{\mu\nu}\kappa^\alpha \quad \text{.........(86·2).}$$

Then by (86·1) and (85·52)

$$^*\{\mu\nu, \alpha\}' = {}^*\{\mu\nu, \alpha\} \quad \text{.................(86·3).}$$

The "generalised 3-index symbol" $^*\{\mu\nu, \alpha\}$ has the "in-" property, being unaltered by any gauge-transformation. It is, of course, not a tensor.

We shall generally indicate by a star (*) quantities generalised from corresponding expressions in Riemannian geometry in order to be independent of (or covariant with) the gauge-system. The following illustrates the general method of procedure.

Let A^ν_μ be a symmetrical in-tensor, its divergence (51·31) becomes on gauge-transformation

$$A'^\nu_{\mu\nu} = \frac{1}{\lambda^4\sqrt{-g}}\frac{\partial}{\partial x_\nu}(A^\nu_\mu \lambda^4 \sqrt{-g}) - \tfrac{1}{2}(\lambda^{-2}A^{\alpha\beta})\frac{\partial}{\partial x_\mu}(\lambda^2 g_{\alpha\beta})$$

$$= \frac{1}{\sqrt{-g}}\frac{\partial}{\partial x_\nu}(A^\nu_\mu\sqrt{-g}) - \tfrac{1}{2}A^{\alpha\beta}\frac{\partial g_{\alpha\beta}}{\partial x_\mu} + A^\nu_\mu \cdot \frac{1}{\lambda^4}\frac{\partial\lambda^4}{\partial x_\nu} - \tfrac{1}{2}A^{\alpha\beta}g_{\alpha\beta}\cdot\frac{1}{\lambda^2}\frac{\partial\lambda^2}{\partial x_\mu}$$

$$= A^\nu_{\mu\nu} + 4A^\nu_\mu\phi_\nu - A\phi_\mu.$$

Hence by (85·52) the quantity

$$^*A^\nu_{\mu\nu} \equiv A^\nu_{\mu\nu} - 4A^\nu_\mu\kappa_\nu + A\kappa_\mu \quad \text{...................(86·4)}$$

is unaltered by any gauge-transformation, and is accordingly an in-vector.

This operation may be called in-covariant differentiation, and the result is the in-divergence.

The result is modified if $A^{\mu\nu}$ is the in-tensor, so that A^ν_μ is a co-tensor. The different associated tensors are not equally fundamental in Weyl's geometry, since only one of them can be an in-tensor.

Unless expressly stated a final suffix will indicate ordinary covariant (not in-covariant) differentiation.

87. The generalised Riemann-Christoffel tensor.

Corresponding to (34·4) we write

$$*B^{\epsilon}_{\mu\nu\sigma} = -\frac{\partial}{\partial x_\sigma} *\{\mu\nu, \epsilon\} + *\{\mu\sigma, \alpha\} *\{\alpha\nu, \epsilon\} + \frac{\partial}{\partial x_\nu} *\{\mu\sigma, \epsilon\} - *\{\mu\nu, \alpha\} *\{\alpha\sigma, \epsilon\} \quad \text{......(87·1)}.$$

This will be an in-tensor since the starred symbols are all independent of the gauge; and it will be evident when we reach (87·4) that the generalisation has not destroyed the ordinary tensor properties.

We consider the first two terms, the complete expression can then be obtained at any stage by interchanging ν and σ and subtracting. The additional terms introduced by the stars are by (86·2)

$$-\frac{\partial}{\partial x_\sigma}(-g^{\epsilon}_{\mu}\kappa_\nu - g^{\epsilon}_{\nu}\kappa_\mu + g_{\mu\nu}\kappa^{\epsilon}) + (-g^{\alpha}_{\mu}\kappa_\sigma - g^{\alpha}_{\sigma}\kappa_\mu + g_{\mu\sigma}\kappa^{\alpha})\{\alpha\nu, \epsilon\}$$

$$+(-g^{\epsilon}_{\alpha}\kappa_\nu - g^{\epsilon}_{\nu}\kappa_\alpha + g_{\alpha\nu}\kappa^{\epsilon})\{\mu\sigma, \alpha\} + (-g^{\alpha}_{\mu}\kappa_\sigma - g^{\alpha}_{\sigma}\kappa_\mu + g_{\mu\sigma}\kappa^{\alpha})(-g^{\epsilon}_{\alpha}\kappa_\nu - g^{\epsilon}_{\nu}\kappa_\alpha + g_{\alpha\nu}\kappa^{\epsilon})$$

$$= g^{\epsilon}_{\mu}\frac{\partial \kappa_\nu}{\partial x_\sigma} + g^{\epsilon}_{\nu}\frac{\partial \kappa_\mu}{\partial x_\sigma} - g_{\mu\nu}\frac{\partial \kappa^{\epsilon}}{\partial x_\sigma} - \frac{\partial g_{\mu\nu}}{\partial x_\sigma}\kappa^{\epsilon} - \kappa_\sigma\{\mu\nu, \epsilon\} - \kappa_\mu\{\sigma\nu, \epsilon\} + g_{\mu\sigma}\{\alpha\nu, \epsilon\}\kappa^{\alpha}$$

$$-\kappa_\nu\{\mu\sigma, \epsilon\} - g^{\epsilon}_{\nu}\{\mu\sigma, \alpha\}\kappa_\alpha + \kappa^{\epsilon}[\mu\sigma, \nu] + g^{\epsilon}_{\mu}\kappa_\sigma\kappa_\nu + g^{\epsilon}_{\nu}\kappa_\sigma\kappa_\mu - g_{\mu\nu}\kappa_\sigma\kappa^{\epsilon}$$

$$+g^{\epsilon}_{\sigma}\kappa_\mu\kappa_\nu + g^{\epsilon}_{\nu}\kappa_\mu\kappa_\sigma - g_{\sigma\nu}\kappa_\mu\kappa^{\epsilon} - g_{\mu\sigma}\kappa^{\epsilon}\kappa_\nu - g_{\mu\sigma}g^{\epsilon}_{\nu}\kappa^{\alpha}\kappa_\alpha + g_{\mu\sigma}\kappa_\nu\kappa^{\epsilon} \quad \text{...(87·2)},$$

which is equivalent to

$$g^{\epsilon}_{\mu}\frac{\partial \kappa_\nu}{\partial x_\sigma} + g^{\epsilon}_{\nu}(\kappa_\mu)_\sigma - g_{\mu\nu}(\kappa^{\epsilon})_\sigma + g^{\epsilon}_{\nu}\kappa_\mu\kappa_\sigma - g^{\epsilon}_{\nu}g_{\mu\sigma}\kappa_\alpha\kappa^{\alpha} + g_{\mu\sigma}\kappa_\nu\kappa^{\epsilon}. \quad \text{...(87·3)}.$$

[To follow this reduction let the terms in (87·2) be numbered in order from 1 to 19. It will be found that the following terms or pairs of terms are symmetrical in ν and σ, and therefore disappear when the expression is completed, viz. 5 and 8, 6, 11, 12 and 14, 13 and 17, 16. Further 4 and 10 together give $-[\nu\sigma, \mu]\kappa^{\epsilon}$, which is rejected for the same reason. We combine 2 and 9 to give $g^{\epsilon}_{\nu}(\kappa_\mu)_\sigma$. We exchange 7 for its counterpart $-g_{\mu\nu}\{\alpha\sigma, \epsilon\}\kappa^{\alpha}$ in the remaining half of the expression, and combine it with 3 to give $-g_{\mu\nu}(\kappa^{\epsilon})_\sigma$.]

Hence interchanging ν and σ, and subtracting, the complete expression is

$$*B^{\epsilon}_{\mu\nu\sigma} = B^{\epsilon}_{\mu\nu\sigma} + g^{\epsilon}_{\mu}\left(\frac{\partial \kappa_\nu}{\partial x_\sigma} - \frac{\partial \kappa_\sigma}{\partial x_\nu}\right) + (g^{\epsilon}_{\nu}\kappa_{\mu\sigma} - g^{\epsilon}_{\sigma}\kappa_{\mu\nu}) + (g_{\mu\sigma}\kappa^{\epsilon}_{\nu} - g_{\mu\nu}\kappa^{\epsilon}_{\sigma})$$

$$+(g^{\epsilon}_{\nu}\kappa_\mu\kappa_\sigma - g^{\epsilon}_{\sigma}\kappa_\mu\kappa_\nu) + (g^{\epsilon}_{\sigma}g_{\mu\nu} - g^{\epsilon}_{\nu}g_{\mu\sigma})\kappa_\alpha\kappa^{\alpha} + (g_{\mu\sigma}\kappa_\nu - g_{\mu\nu}\kappa_\sigma)\kappa^{\epsilon} \quad \text{...(87·4)}.$$

Next set $\epsilon = \sigma$. We obtain the contracted in-tensor

$$*G_{\mu\nu} = G_{\mu\nu} - F_{\mu\nu} + (\kappa_{\mu\nu} - 4\kappa_{\mu\nu}) + (\kappa_{\mu\nu} - g_{\mu\nu}\kappa^{\alpha}_{\alpha}) + (\kappa_\mu\kappa_\nu - 4\kappa_\mu\kappa_\nu)$$

$$+ (4g_{\mu\nu} - g_{\mu\nu})\kappa_\alpha\kappa^{\alpha} + (\kappa_\mu\kappa_\nu - g_{\mu\nu}\kappa_\alpha\kappa^{\alpha})$$

$$= G_{\mu\nu} - 2F_{\mu\nu} - (\kappa_{\mu\nu} + \kappa_{\nu\mu}) - g_{\mu\nu}\kappa^{\alpha}_{\alpha} - 2\kappa_\mu\kappa_\nu + 2g_{\mu\nu}\kappa_\alpha\kappa^{\alpha} \quad \text{......(87·5)}\dagger.$$

† The unit of κ_μ is arbitrary; and in the generalised theory in Part II the κ_μ there employed corresponds to twice the κ_μ of these formulae. This must be borne in mind in comparing, for example, (87·5) and (94·3).

Finally multiply by $g^{\mu\nu}$. We obtain the co-invariant

$$*G = G - 6\kappa^{\alpha}_{\alpha} + 6\kappa_{\alpha}\kappa^{\alpha} \quad \text{.........................(87·6).}$$

The multiplication by $g^{\mu\nu}$ reintroduces the unit of gauge, so that $*G$ becomes multiplied by λ^{-2} when the gauge is transformed.

If the suffix ϵ is lowered in (87·4) the only part of $*B_{\mu\nu\sigma\epsilon}$ which is symmetrical in μ and ϵ is $g_{\mu\epsilon}(\partial\kappa_{\nu}/\partial x_{\sigma} - \partial\kappa_{\sigma}/\partial x_{\nu}) = g_{\mu\epsilon}F_{\nu\sigma}$, which agrees with the condition (a) of Weyl's geometry (§ 84).

88. The in-invariants of a region.

There are no functions of the $g_{\mu\nu}$ and κ_{μ} at a point which are in-invariants; but functions which are in-invariant-densities may be found as follows—

Since $\sqrt{-g}$ becomes multiplied by λ^{4} on gauge-transformation we must combine it with co-invariants which become multiplied by λ^{-4}. The following are easily seen to be in-invariant-densities·

$$(*G)^2\sqrt{-g}; \quad *G_{\mu\nu}*G^{\mu\nu}\sqrt{-g}; \quad *B^{\epsilon}_{\mu\nu\sigma}*B^{\mu\nu\sigma}_{\epsilon}\sqrt{-g} \quad \text{......(88·1),}$$

$$F_{\mu\nu}F^{\mu\nu}\sqrt{-g} \quad \text{..............................(88·2).}$$

We can also form in-invariant-densities from the fundamental tensor of the sixth rank. Let $*(*B_{\mu\nu\sigma\rho})_{\alpha\beta}$ be the second co-covariant derivative of the co-tensor $*B_{\mu\nu\sigma\rho}$; the spur formed by raising three suffixes and contracting will vary as λ^{-4} and give an in-invariant-density on multiplication by $\sqrt{-g}$. There are three different spurs, according to the pairing of the suffixes, but I believe that there are relations between them so that they give only one independent expression. The simplest of them is

$$g^{\mu\nu}g^{\sigma\rho}g^{\alpha\beta}*(*B_{\mu\nu\sigma\rho})_{\alpha\beta}\sqrt{-g} = *\Box *G \,.\, \sqrt{-g} \quad \text{...........(88·3).}$$

If $\mathfrak{A}$ stands for any in-invariant-density,

$$\int \mathfrak{A}\, d\tau$$

taken over a four-dimensional region is a pure number independent of coordinate-system and gauge-system. Such a number denotes a property of the region which is absolute in the widest sense of the word; and it seems likely that one or more of these numerical invariants of the region must stand in a simple relation to all the physical quantities which measure the more general properties of the world. The simplest operation which we can perform on a regional invariant appears to be that of Hamiltonian differentiation, and a particular importance will therefore be attached to the tensors $\mathfrak{h}A/\mathfrak{h}g_{\mu\nu}$, $\mathfrak{h}A/\mathfrak{h}\kappa_{\mu}$.

It has been pointed out by Weyl that it is only in a four-dimensional world that a simple set of regional in-invariants of this kind exists. In an odd number of dimensions there are none; in two dimensions there is one, $*G\sqrt{-g}$; in six or eight dimensions the in-invariants are all very complex involving derivatives of at least the fourth order or else obviously artificial. This may give some sort of reason for the four dimensions of the world The argument appears to be that a world with an odd number of dimensions could contain nothing absolute, which would be unthinkable.

These conclusions are somewhat modified by the existence of a particularly simple regional in-invariant, which seems to have been generally overlooked because it is not of the type which investigators have generally studied. The quantity

$$\int \sqrt{\{-|{}^*G_{\mu\nu}|\}}\, d\tau \quad \text{.........................} \quad (88\cdot4)$$

is an invariant by (81 1) and it contains nothing which depends on the gauge It is not *more* irrational than the other in-invariants since these contain $\sqrt{-g}$. We shall find later that it is closely analogous to the metrical volume and the electromagnetic volume (§ 81) of the region It will be called the *generalised volume* This in-invariant would still exist if the world had an odd number of dimensions

It may be remarked that $F^{\mu\nu}\sqrt{-g}$, or $\mathfrak{F}^{\mu\nu}$, is an in-tensor-density. Thus the factor $\sqrt{-g}$ should always be associated with the contravariant tensor, if the formulae are to have their full physical significance. The electromagnetic action-density should be written

$$F_{\mu\nu}\mathfrak{F}^{\mu\nu},$$

and the energy-density

$$-F_{\mu\alpha}\mathfrak{F}^{\nu\alpha} + \tfrac{1}{4}g_\mu^\nu F_{\alpha\beta}\mathfrak{F}^{\alpha\beta}.$$

The field is thus characterised by an *intensity* $F_{\mu\nu}$ or a *quantity* of density $\mathfrak{F}^{\mu\nu}$; both descriptions are then independent of the gauge-system used.

89. The natural gauge.

For the most part the laws of mechanics investigated in Chapters III—V have been expressed by tensor equations but not in-tensor equations Hence they can only hold when a particular gauge-system is used, and will cease to be true if a transformation of gauge-system is made The gauge-system for which our previous work is valid (if it is valid) is called the *natural gauge*; it stands in somewhat the same position with respect to a general gauge as Galilean coordinates stand with respect to general coordinates.

Just as we have generalised the equations of physics originally found for Galilean coordinates, so we could generalise the equations for the natural gauge by substituting the corresponding in-tensor equations applicable to any gauge. But before doing so, we stop to ask whether anything would be gained by this generalisation. There is not much object in generalising the Galilean formulae, so long as Galilean coordinates are available; we required the general formulae because we discovered that there are regions of the world where no Galilean coordinates exist Similarly we shall only need the in-tensor equations of mechanics if there are regions where no natural gauge exists, that is to say, if no gauge-system can be found for which

Einstein's formulae are accurately true. It was, I think, the original idea of Weyl's theory that electromagnetic fields were such regions, where accordingly in-tensor equations would be essential.

There is in any case a significant difference between Einstein's generalisation of Galilean geometry and Weyl's generalisation of Riemannian geometry. We have proved directly that the condition which renders Galilean coordinates impossible *must* manifest itself to us as a gravitational field of force. That is the meaning of a field of force according to the definition of force. But we cannot prove that the break-down of the natural gauge would manifest itself as an electromagnetic field; we have merely speculated that the world-condition measured by the vector κ_μ which appears in the in-tensor equations may be the origin of electrical manifestations *in addition to* causing the failure of Riemannian geometry.

Accepting the original view of Weyl's theory, the ambiguity in the comparison of lengths at a distance has hitherto only shown itself in practical experiments by the electromagnetic phenomena supposed to be dependent on it but not (so far as we can see) immediately implied by it. This is not surprising when we attempt to estimate the order of magnitude of the ambiguity. Taking formula (84.4), $dl/l = \frac{1}{2}F_{\nu\sigma}dS^{\nu\sigma}$, we might perhaps expect that dl/l would be comparable with unity, if the electromagnetic force $F_{\nu\sigma}$ were comparable with that at the surface of an electron, $4 \,.\, 10^{18}$ volts per cm., and the side of the circuit were comparable with the radius of curvature of space. Thus for ordinary experiments dl/l would be far below the limits of experimental detection. Accordingly we can have a gauge-system specified by the transfer of material standards which is for all practical purposes unambiguous, and yet contains that minute theoretical ambiguity which is only of practical consequence on account of its side-manifestation as the cause of electrical phenomena. The gauge-system employed in practice is the natural gauge-system to which our previous mechanical formulae apply—or rather, since the practical gauge-system is slightly ambiguous and the theoretical formulae are presumably exact, the natural gauge is an exact gauge with which all practical gauges agree to an approximation sufficient for all observable mechanical and metrical phenomena.

According to Weyl the natural gauge is determined by the condition

$$^*G = 4\lambda \quad \text{.................... (89.1)},$$

where λ is a constant everywhere.

This attempt to reconcile a theoretical ambiguity of our system of measurement with its well-known practical efficiency seems to be tenable, though perhaps a little overstrained. But an alternative view is possible. This states that—

Comparison of lengths at different places is an unambiguous procedure having nothing to do with parallel displacement of a vector.

The practical operation of transferring a measuring-scale from one place to another is not to be confounded with the transfer by parallel displacement of the vector representing the displacement between its two extremities. If this is correct Einstein's Riemannian geometry, in which each interval has a unique length, must be accepted as exact; the ambiguity of transfer by parallel displacement does not affect his work. No attempt is to be made to apply Weyl's geometry as a Natural Geometry; it refers to a different subject of discussion.

Prof. Weyl himself has come to prefer the second alternative. He draws a useful distinction between magnitudes which are determined by *persistence* (*Beharrung*) and by *adjustment* (*Einstellung*); and concludes that the dimensions of material objects are determined by adjustment. The size of an electron is determined by adjustment in proportion to the radius of curvature of the world, and not by persistence of anything in its past history. This is the view taken in § 66, and we have seen that it has great value in affording an explanation of Einstein's law of gravitation.

The generalised theory of Part II leads almost inevitably to the second alternative. The first form of the theory has died rather from inanition than by direct disproof; it ceases to offer temptation when the problem is approached from a broader point of view. It now seems an unnecessary speculation to introduce small ambiguities of length-comparisons too small to be practically detected, merely to afford the satisfaction of geometrising the vector κ_μ which has more important manifestations.

The new view entirely alters the status of Weyl's theory. Indeed it is no longer a hypothesis, but a graphical representation of the facts, and its value lies in the insight suggested by this graphical representation. We need not now hesitate for a moment over the identification of the electromagnetic potential with the geometrical vector κ_μ; the geometrical vector is the potential because that is the way in which we choose to represent the potential graphically. We take a conceptual space obeying Weyl's geometry and represent in it the gravitational potential by the $g_{\mu\nu}$ for that space and the electromagnetic potential by the κ_μ for that space. We find that all other quantities concerned in physics are now represented by more or less simple geometrical magnitudes in that space, and the whole picture enables us to grasp in a comprehensive way the relations of physical quantities, and more particularly those reactions in which both electromagnetic and mechanical variables are involved. Parallel displacement of a vector in this space is a definite operation, and may in certain cases have an immediate physical interpretation; thus when an uncharged particle moves freely in a geodesic its velocity-vector is carried along by parallel displacement (33·4); but when a material measuring-rod is moved the operation is not one of parallel displacement, and must be described in different geometrical terms, which have reference to the natural gauging-equation (89·1).

When in Part II we substitute a conceptual space with still more general geometry, we shall not need to regard it as in opposition to the present discussion. We may learn more from a different graphical picture of what is going on; but we shall not have to abandon anything which we can perceive clearly in the first picture.

We consider now the gauging-equation $*G = 4\lambda$ assumed by Weyl. It is probably the one which most naturally suggests itself. Suppose that we have adopted initially some other gauge in which $*G$ is not constant. $*G$ is a co-invariant such that when the measure of interval is changed in the ratio μ, $*G$ changes in the ratio μ^{-2}. Hence we can obtain a new gauge in which $*G$ becomes constant by transforming the measure of the interval in the ratio $*G^{-\frac{1}{2}}$.

By (87·6) the gauging-equation is equivalent to

$$G - 6\kappa^a_a + 6\kappa_a\kappa^a = 4\lambda \quad \text{.....................(89·2)}.$$

But by (54·72) the proper-density of matter is

$$\rho_0 = \frac{1}{8\pi}(G - 4\lambda)$$

$$= \frac{3}{4\pi}(\kappa^a_a - \kappa_a\kappa^a) \quad \text{..........................(89·3)}$$

For empty space, or for space containing free electromagnetic fields without electrons, $\rho_0 = 0$, so that

$$\kappa^a_a = \kappa_a\kappa^a \quad \text{...............................(89·4)},$$

except within an electron. This condition should replace the equation $\kappa^a_a = 0$ which was formerly introduced in order to make the electromagnetic potential determinate (74·1).

We cannot conceive of any kind of measurement with clocks, scales, moving particles or light-waves being made *inside* an electron, so that any gauge employed in such a region must be purely theoretical having no significance in terms of practical measurement. For the sake of continuity we define the natural gauge in this region by the same equation $*G = 4\lambda$; it is as suitable as any other. Inside the electron κ^a_a will not be equal to $\kappa_a\kappa^a$ and the difference will determine the mass of the electron in accordance with (89·3). But it will be understood that this application of (89·3) is merely conventional; although it appears to refer to experimental quantities, the conditions are such that it ceases to be possible for the experiments to be made by any conceivable device.

90. Weyl's action-principle.

Weyl adopts an action-density

$$A\sqrt{-g} = (*G^2 - \alpha F_{\mu\nu}F^{\mu\nu})\sqrt{-g} \quad \text{.............(90·1)},$$

the constant α being a pure number. He makes the hypothesis that it obeys the principle of stationary action for all variations $\delta g_{\mu\nu}$, $\delta\kappa_\mu$ which vanish at the boundary of the region considered. Accordingly

$$\frac{\mathfrak{h}A}{\mathfrak{h}g_{\mu\nu}} = 0, \quad \frac{\mathfrak{h}A}{\mathfrak{h}\kappa_\mu} = 0 \quad \text{.....................(90·2).}$$

Weyl himself states that his action-principle is probably not realised in nature exactly in this form. But the procedure is instructive as showing the kind of unifying principle which is aimed at according to one school of thought.

The variation of ${}^*G^2\sqrt{-g}$ is

$$2\,{}^*G\,\delta({}^*G\sqrt{-g}) - {}^*G^2\,\delta(\sqrt{-g}),$$

which in the natural gauge becomes by (89·1)

$$8\lambda\,\delta({}^*G\sqrt{-g}) - 16\lambda^2\,\delta(\sqrt{-g})$$

Hence by (87·6)

$$\frac{1}{8\lambda}\,\delta(A\sqrt{-g}) = \delta\{(G - 6\kappa^\alpha_\alpha + 6\kappa_\alpha\kappa^\alpha - 2\lambda - \beta F_{\mu\nu}F^{\mu\nu})\sqrt{-g}\}$$

$$\text{..... (90·3),}$$

where $\beta = \alpha/8\lambda$.

The term $\kappa^\alpha_\alpha\sqrt{-g}$ can be dropped, because by (51·11)

$$\kappa^\alpha_\alpha\sqrt{-g} = \frac{\partial}{\partial x_\alpha}(\kappa^\alpha\sqrt{-g}).$$

This can be integrated, and yields a surface-integral over the boundary of the region considered. Its Hamiltonian derivatives accordingly vanish.

Again

$$\begin{aligned}\delta(\kappa_\alpha\kappa^\alpha\sqrt{-g}) &= \kappa_\alpha\kappa_\beta\,\delta(g^{\alpha\beta}\sqrt{-g}) + g^{\alpha\beta}\sqrt{-g}\,(\kappa_\alpha\delta\kappa_\beta + \kappa_\beta\delta\kappa_\alpha)\\ &= \kappa_\alpha\kappa_\beta\sqrt{-g}\,(\delta g^{\alpha\beta} + \tfrac{1}{2}g^{\alpha\beta}g^{\mu\nu}\delta g_{\mu\nu}) + 2g^{\alpha\beta}\sqrt{-g}\,\kappa_\beta\delta\kappa_\alpha\\ &= \kappa_\alpha\kappa_\beta\sqrt{-g}\,(-g^{\mu\alpha}g^{\nu\beta} + \tfrac{1}{2}g^{\alpha\beta}g^{\mu\nu})\,\delta g_{\mu\nu} + 2\kappa^\alpha\sqrt{-g}\,\delta\kappa_\alpha\\ &= \sqrt{-g}\,(-\kappa^\mu\kappa^\nu + \tfrac{1}{2}g^{\mu\nu}\kappa_\alpha\kappa^\alpha)\,\delta g_{\mu\nu} + 2\kappa^\alpha\sqrt{-g}\,\delta\kappa_\alpha.\end{aligned}$$

Hence

$$\frac{\mathfrak{h}}{\mathfrak{h}g_{\mu\nu}}(\kappa_\alpha\kappa^\alpha) = (-\kappa^\mu\kappa^\nu + \tfrac{1}{2}g^{\mu\nu}\kappa_\alpha\kappa^\alpha) \quad \text{...........(90·41),}$$

$$\frac{\mathfrak{h}}{\mathfrak{h}\kappa_\alpha}(\kappa_\alpha\kappa^\alpha) = 2\kappa^\alpha \quad \text{..............................(90·42).}$$

Hamiltonian derivatives of the other terms in (90·3) have already been found in (60·43), (79·31) and (79·32). Collecting these results we have

$$\begin{aligned}\frac{1}{8\lambda}\frac{\mathfrak{h}A}{\mathfrak{h}g_{\mu\nu}} &= -(G^{\mu\nu} - \tfrac{1}{2}g^{\mu\nu}G) - 6(\kappa^\mu\kappa^\nu - \tfrac{1}{2}g^{\mu\nu}\kappa_\alpha\kappa^\alpha) - \lambda g^{\mu\nu} - 2\beta E^{\mu\nu}\\ &= 8\pi T^{\mu\nu} - 2\beta E^{\mu\nu} - 6(\kappa^\mu\kappa^\nu - \tfrac{1}{2}g^{\mu\nu}\kappa_\alpha\kappa^\alpha) \quad \text{.............(90·51)}\end{aligned}$$

by (54·71), and

$$\frac{1}{8\lambda}\frac{\mathfrak{h}A}{\mathfrak{h}\kappa_\mu} = 12\kappa^\mu + 4\beta J^\mu \quad \text{.......................(90·52).}$$

If the hypothesis (90·2) is correct, these must vanish. The vanishing of (90·51) shows that the whole energy-tensor consists of the electromagnetic energy-tensor together with another term, which must presumably be identified with the material energy-tensor attributable to the binding forces of the electrons*. The constant $2\beta/8\pi$ correlates the natural gravitational and electromagnetic units. The material energy-tensor, being the difference between the whole tensor and the electromagnetic part, is accordingly

$$M^{\mu\nu} = \frac{3}{4\pi}(\kappa^\mu\kappa^\nu - \tfrac{1}{4}g^{\mu\nu}\kappa_\alpha\kappa^\alpha) \quad\text{..............(90·61).}$$

Hence, multiplying by $g_{\mu\nu}$,

$$\rho_0 = M = -\frac{3}{4\pi}\kappa_\alpha\kappa^\alpha \quad\text{..................(90·62)}$$

The vanishing of (90·52) gives the remarkable equation

$$\kappa^\mu = -\tfrac{1}{3}\beta J^\mu \quad\text{.........................(90·71).}$$

And since $J^\mu_\mu = 0$ (73·77), we must have

$$\kappa^\mu_\mu = 0 \quad\text{...........................(90·72),}$$

agreeing with the original limitation of κ_μ in (74·1).

We see that the formula for ρ_0 (90·62) agrees with that previously found (89·3) having regard to the limitation $\kappa^\mu_\mu = 0$.

The result (90·62) becomes by (90·71)

$$\rho_0 = -\frac{\beta^2}{12\pi}J_\mu J^\mu.$$

This shows that matter cannot be constituted without electric charge and current. But since the density of matter is always positive, the electric charge-and-current inside an electron must be a *space-like* vector, the square of its length being negative. It would seem to follow that the electron cannot be built up of elementary electrostatic charges but resolves itself into something more akin to magnetic charges.

It will be noticed that the result (90·72) is inconsistent with the formula $\kappa_\alpha\kappa^\alpha = \kappa^\alpha_\alpha$ which we have found for empty space (89·4). The explanation is afforded by (90·71) which requires that a charge-and-current vector must exist wherever κ_μ exists, so that no space is really empty. On Weyl's hypothesis $\kappa^\alpha_\alpha = 0$ is the condition which holds in all circumstances; whilst the additional condition $\kappa^\alpha_\alpha = \kappa_\alpha\kappa^\alpha$ holding in empty space reduces to the condition expressed by $J^\alpha = 0$. It is supposed that outside what is ordinarily considered to be the boundary of the electron there is a small charge and current $\frac{3}{\beta}\kappa^\alpha$ extending as far as the electromagnetic potential extends.

For an isolated electron at rest in Galilean coordinates $\kappa_4 = e/r$, so that $\kappa_\alpha\kappa^\alpha = e^2/r^2$. On integrating throughout infinite space the result is apparently

* I doubt if this is the right interpretation. See the end of § 100.

infinite; but taking account of the finite radius of space, the result is of order e^2R. By (90·62) this represents the part of the (negative) mass of the electron† which is not concentrated within the nucleus. The actual mass was found in § 80 to be of order e^2/a where a is the radius of the nucleus. The two masses e^2R and e^2/a are not immediately comparable since they are expressed in different units, the connection being made by Weyl's constant β whose value is left undecided. But since they differ in dimensions of length, they would presumably become comparable if the natural unit of length were adopted, viz. the radius of the world, in that case e^2/a is at least 10^{38} times e^2R, so that the portion of the mass outside the nucleus is quite insignificant.

The action-principle here followed out is obviously speculative. Whether the results are such as to encourage belief in this or some similar law, or whether they tend to dispose of it by something like a *reductio ad absurdum*, I will leave to the judgment of the reader. There are, however, two points which seem to call for special notice—

(1) When we compare the forms of the two principal energy-tensors

$$T_\mu^\nu = -\frac{1}{8\pi}\{G_\mu^\nu - \tfrac{1}{2}g_\mu^\nu(G-2\lambda)\},$$

$$E_\mu^\nu = -F_{\mu\sigma}F^{\nu\sigma} + \tfrac{1}{4}g_\mu^\nu F_{\alpha\beta}F^{\alpha\beta},$$

it is rather a mystery how the second can be contained in the first, since they seem to be anything but homologous. The connection is simplified by observing that the difference between them occurs in $\mathfrak{h}A/\mathfrak{h}g_{\mu\nu}$ (90·51) accompanied only by a term which would presumably be insensible except inside the electrons.

But the connection though reduced to simpler terms is not in any way explained by Weyl's action-principle. It is obvious that his action as it stands has no deep significance; it is a mere stringing together of two in-invariants of different forms. To subtract $F_{\mu\nu}F^{\mu\nu}$ from ${}^*G^2$ is a fantastic procedure which has no more theoretical justification than subtracting E_μ^ν from T_μ^ν. At the most we can only regard the assumed form of action A as a step towards some more natural combination of electromagnetic and gravitational variables.

(2) For the first term of the action, ${}^*G^2\sqrt{-g}$ was chosen instead of the simpler ${}^*G\sqrt{-g}$, *because the latter is not an in-invariant-density* and cannot be regarded as a measure of any absolute property of the region. It is interesting to trace how this improvement leads to the appearance of the term $\delta(-2\lambda\sqrt{-g})$ in (90·3), so that the cosmical curvature-term in the expression for the energy-tensor now appears quite naturally and inevitably. We may contrast this with the variation of $G\sqrt{-g}$ worked out in § 60, where no such term appears. In attributing more fundamental importance to the in-invariant ${}^*G^2\sqrt{-g}$ than to the co-invariant ${}^*G\sqrt{-g}$, Weyl's theory makes an undoubted advance towards the truth.

† This must not be confused with mass of the energy of the electromagnetic field. The present discussion relates to *invariant mass* to which the field contributes nothing

PART II. GENERALISED THEORY

91. Parallel displacement.

Let an infinitesimal displacement A^μ at the point P (coordinates, x_μ) be carried by parallel displacement to a point P' (coordinates, $x_\mu + dx_\mu$) infinitely near to P. The most general possible continuous formula for the change of A^μ is of the form

$$dA^\mu = -\Gamma^\mu_{\nu\alpha} A^\alpha dx_\nu \quad \text{..................(91·1)},$$

where $\Gamma^\mu_{\nu\alpha}$, which is not assumed to be a tensor, represents 64 arbitrary coefficients. Both A^α and dx_ν are infinitesimals, so that there is no need to insert any terms of higher order.

We are going to build the theory afresh starting from this notion of infinitesimal parallel displacement; and by so doing we arrive at a generalisation even wider than that of Weyl. Our fundamental axiom is that parallel displacement has some significance in regard to the ultimate structure of the world—it does not much matter what significance. The idea is that out of the whole group of displacements radiating from P', we can select one $A^\mu + dA^\mu$ which has some kind of *equivalence* to the displacement A^μ at P. We do not define the nature of this equivalence, except that it shall have reference to the part played by A^μ in the relation-structure which underlies the world of physics. Notice that—

(1) This equivalence is only supposed to exist in the limit when P and P' are infinitely near together. For more distant points equivalence can in general only be approximate, and gradually becomes indeterminate as the distance is increased. It can be made determinate by specifying a particular route of connection, in which case the equivalence is traced step by step along the route.

(2) The equivalence is not supposed to exist between any world-relations other than displacements. Hitherto we have applied parallel displacement to any tensor, but in this theory we only use it for displacements.

(3) It is not assumed that there is any complete observational test of equivalence. This is rather a difficult point which will be better appreciated later. The idea is that the scheme of equivalence need not be determinate observationally, and may have permissible transformations, just as the scheme of coordinate-reckoning is not determinate observationally and is subject to transformations.

Let PP_1 represent the displacement $A^\mu = \delta x_\mu$ which on parallel displacement to P' becomes $P'P_1'$; then by (91·1) the difference of coordinates of P_1' and P_1 is

$$A^\mu + dA^\mu = \delta x_\mu - \Gamma^\mu_{\nu\alpha} \delta x_\alpha dx_\nu,$$

so that the coordinates of P_1' relative to P are

$$dx_\mu + \delta x_\mu - \Gamma^\mu_{\nu\alpha} \delta x_\alpha dx_\nu \quad \text{........................(91·2)}.$$

Interchanging the two displacements, i.e. displacing PP' along PP_1, we shall not arrive at the same point P_1' unless

$$\Gamma^{\mu}_{\nu\alpha} = \Gamma^{\mu}_{\alpha\nu} \quad \text{..........................(91·3).}$$

When (91·3) is satisfied we have the parallelogram law, that if a displacement AB is equivalent to CD, then AC is equivalent to BD.

This is the necessary condition for what is called *affine geometry*. It is adopted by Weyl and other writers; but J. A. Schouten in a purely geometrical investigation has dispensed with it. I shall adopt it here.

All questions of the fundamental axioms of a science are difficult. In general we have to start somewhat above the fundamental plane and develop the theory backwards towards fundamentals as well as forwards to results. I shall defer until § 98 the examination of how far the axiom of parallel displacement and the condition of affine geometry are essential in translating the properties of a relation-structure into mathematical expression; and I proceed at once to develop the consequences of the specification here introduced.

By the symmetry condition the number of independent $\Gamma^{\mu}_{\nu\alpha}$ is reduced to 40, variable from point to point of space. They are descriptive of the relation-structure of the world, and should contain all that is relevant to physics. Our immediate problem is to show how the more familiar variables of physics can be extracted from this crude material.

92. Displacement round an infinitesimal circuit.

Let a displacement A^{μ} be carried by parallel displacement round a small circuit C. The condition for parallel displacement is by (91·1)

$$\frac{\partial A^{\mu}}{\partial x_{\nu}} = -\Gamma^{\mu}_{\nu\alpha} A^{\alpha} \quad \text{..........................(92·1).}$$

Hence the difference of the initial and final values is

$$\begin{aligned}\delta A^{\mu} &= \int_C \frac{\partial A^{\mu}}{\partial x_{\nu}} dx_{\nu} \\ &= -\int_C \Gamma^{\mu}_{\nu\alpha} A^{\alpha} dx_{\nu} \\ &= \frac{1}{2}\iint \left\{\frac{\partial}{\partial x_{\sigma}}(\Gamma^{\mu}_{\nu\alpha} A^{\alpha}) - \frac{\partial}{\partial x_{\nu}}(\Gamma^{\mu}_{\sigma\alpha} A^{\alpha})\right\} dS^{\nu\sigma}\end{aligned}$$

by Stokes's theorem (32·3).

The integrand is equal to

$$\begin{aligned}&A^{\alpha}\left(\frac{\partial}{\partial x_{\sigma}}\Gamma^{\mu}_{\nu\alpha} - \frac{\partial}{\partial x_{\nu}}\Gamma^{\mu}_{\sigma\alpha}\right) + \Gamma^{\mu}_{\nu\alpha}\frac{\partial A^{\alpha}}{\partial x_{\sigma}} - \Gamma^{\mu}_{\sigma\alpha}\frac{\partial A^{\alpha}}{\partial x_{\nu}} \\ &= A^{\epsilon}\left(\frac{\partial}{\partial x_{\sigma}}\Gamma^{\mu}_{\nu\epsilon} - \frac{\partial}{\partial x_{\nu}}\Gamma^{\mu}_{\sigma\epsilon}\right) - \Gamma^{\mu}_{\nu\alpha}\Gamma^{\alpha}_{\sigma\epsilon}A^{\epsilon} + \Gamma^{\mu}_{\sigma\alpha}\Gamma^{\alpha}_{\nu\epsilon}A^{\epsilon} \quad \text{by (92·1)} \\ &= -{}^{*}B^{\mu}_{\epsilon\nu\sigma}A^{\epsilon},\end{aligned}$$

where

$$ {}^{*}B^{\mu}_{\epsilon\nu\sigma} = -\frac{\partial}{\partial x_{\sigma}}\Gamma^{\mu}_{\nu\epsilon} + \frac{\partial}{\partial x_{\nu}}\Gamma^{\mu}_{\sigma\epsilon} + \Gamma^{\mu}_{\nu\alpha}\Gamma^{\alpha}_{\sigma\epsilon} - \Gamma^{\mu}_{\sigma\alpha}\Gamma^{\alpha}_{\nu\epsilon} \quad \text{........(92·2)}$$

Hence $$\delta A^\mu = -\frac{1}{2}\iint {}^*B^\mu_{\epsilon\nu\sigma} A^\epsilon dS^{\nu\sigma} \quad \text{......(92·31).}$$

As in § 33 the formula applies only to infinitesimal circuits In evaluating the integrand we assumed that A^α satisfies the condition of parallel displacement (92·1) not only on the boundary but at all points within the circuit. No single value of A^α can satisfy this, since if it holds for one circuit of displacement it will not hold for a second. But the discrepancies are of order proportional to $dS^{\nu\sigma}$, and another factor $dS^{\nu\sigma}$ occurs in the integration; hence (92·31) is true when the square of the area of the circuit can be neglected.

Writing $\Sigma^{\nu\sigma} = \iint dS^{\nu\sigma}$ for a small circuit, (92·31) approaches the limit

$$\delta A^\mu = -\tfrac{1}{2} {}^*B^\mu_{\epsilon\nu\sigma} A^\epsilon \Sigma^{\nu\sigma} \quad \text{......(92·32),}$$

which shows that ${}^*B^\mu_{\epsilon\nu\sigma}$ is a tensor†. Moreover it is an in-tensor, since we have not yet introduced any gauge. In fact all quantities introduced at present must have the "in-" property, for we have not begun to discuss the conception of length.

We can form an in-tensor of the second rank by contraction. With the more familiar arrangement of suffixes,

$$ {}^*B^\epsilon_{\mu\nu\sigma} = -\frac{\partial}{\partial x_\sigma}\Gamma^\epsilon_{\nu\mu} + \frac{\partial}{\partial x_\nu}\Gamma^\epsilon_{\sigma\mu} + \Gamma^\alpha_{\sigma\mu}\Gamma^\epsilon_{\nu\alpha} - \Gamma^\alpha_{\nu\mu}\Gamma^\epsilon_{\sigma\alpha} \quad \text{......(92·41),}$$

$$ {}^*G_{\mu\nu} = -\frac{\partial}{\partial x_\alpha}\Gamma^\alpha_{\nu\mu} + \frac{\partial}{\partial x_\nu}\Gamma^\alpha_{\alpha\mu} + \Gamma^\alpha_{\beta\mu}\Gamma^\beta_{\nu\alpha} - \Gamma^\alpha_{\nu\mu}\Gamma^\beta_{\beta\alpha} \quad \text{..... (92·42).}$$

Another contracted in-tensor is obtained by setting $\epsilon = \mu$, viz.

$$ -2F_{\nu\sigma} = -\frac{\partial}{\partial x_\sigma}\Gamma^\alpha_{\nu\alpha} + \frac{\partial}{\partial x_\nu}\Gamma^\alpha_{\sigma\alpha} \quad \text{......(92·43).}$$

We shall write $$\Gamma_\nu \equiv \Gamma^\alpha_{\nu\alpha} \quad \text{......(92·5).}$$

Then $$2F_{\nu\sigma} = \frac{\partial \Gamma_\nu}{\partial x_\sigma} - \frac{\partial \Gamma_\sigma}{\partial x_\nu} \quad \text{......(92·55).}$$

It will be seen from (92·42) that‡

$$ {}^*G_{\mu\nu} - {}^*G_{\nu\mu} = \frac{\partial \Gamma_\mu}{\partial x_\nu} - \frac{\partial \Gamma_\nu}{\partial x_\mu} = 2F_{\mu\nu} \quad \text{......(92·6),}$$

so that $F_{\mu\nu}$ is the antisymmetrical part of ${}^*G_{\mu\nu}$. Thus the second mode of contraction of ${}^*B^\epsilon_{\mu\nu\sigma}$ does not add anything not obtainable by the first mode, and we need not give $F_{\mu\nu}$ separate consideration

According to this mode of development the in-tensors ${}^*B^\epsilon_{\mu\nu\sigma}$ and ${}^*G_{\mu\nu}$ are the most fundamental measures of the intrinsic structure of the world. They

† Another independent proof that ${}^*B^\mu_{\epsilon\nu\sigma}$ is a tensor is obtained in equation (94·1); so that if the reader is uneasy about the rigour of the preceding analysis, he may regard it as merely suggesting consideration of the expression (92·2) and use the alternative proof that it is a tensor

‡ Here for the first time we make use of the symmetrical property of $\Gamma^\alpha_{\mu\nu}$. If $\Gamma^\alpha_{\mu\nu} \neq \Gamma^\alpha_{\nu\mu}$ the analysis at this point becomes highly complicated.

take precedence of the $g_{\mu\nu}$, which are only found at a later stage in our theory. Notice that we are not yet in a position to raise or lower a suffix, or to define an invariant such as $*G$, because we have no $g_{\mu\nu}$. If we wish at this stage to form an invariant of a four-dimensional region we must take its "generalised volume"

$$\iiiint \sqrt{\{-|*G_{\mu\nu}|\}}\, d\tau,$$

which is accordingly more elementary than the other regional invariants enumerated in § 88.

It may be asked whether there is any other way of obtaining tensors, besides the consideration of parallel displacement round a closed circuit I think not, because unless our succession of displacements takes us back to the starting-point, we are left with initial and final displacements at a distance, between which no comparability exists

The equation (92·55) does not prove immediately that $F_{\mu\nu}$ is the curl of a vector, because, notwithstanding the notation, Γ_μ is not usually a vector. But since $F_{\mu\nu}$ is a tensor

$$\begin{aligned}2F'_{\alpha\beta} &= 2F_{\mu\nu}\frac{\partial x_\mu}{\partial x_\alpha'}\frac{\partial x_\nu}{\partial x_\beta'}\\ &= \frac{\partial \Gamma_\mu}{\partial x_\nu}\frac{\partial x_\nu}{\partial x_\beta'}\frac{\partial x_\mu}{\partial x_\alpha'} - \frac{\partial \Gamma_\nu}{\partial x_\mu}\frac{\partial x_\mu}{\partial x_\alpha'}\frac{\partial x_\nu}{\partial x_\beta'}\\ &= \frac{\partial}{\partial x_\beta'}\left(\Gamma_\mu\frac{\partial x_\mu}{\partial x_\alpha'}\right) - \frac{\partial}{\partial x_\alpha'}\left(\Gamma_\nu\frac{\partial x_\nu}{\partial x_\beta'}\right).\end{aligned}$$

Now by (23·12) $\Gamma_\mu \partial x_\mu/\partial x_\alpha'$ is a vector. Let us denote it by $2\kappa_\alpha'$. Then

$$F'_{\alpha\beta} = \frac{\partial \kappa_\alpha'}{\partial x_\beta'} - \frac{\partial \kappa_\beta'}{\partial x_\alpha'}.$$

Thus $F'_{\alpha\beta}$ is actually the curl of a vector κ_α', though that vector is not necessarily equal to Γ_α' in all systems of coordinates. The general solution of

$$\frac{1}{2}\left(\frac{\partial \Gamma_\alpha'}{\partial x_\beta'} - \frac{\partial \Gamma_\beta'}{\partial x_\alpha'}\right) = \frac{\partial \kappa_\alpha'}{\partial x_\beta'} - \frac{\partial \kappa_\beta'}{\partial x_\alpha'}$$

is

$$\Gamma_\alpha' = 2\kappa_\alpha' + \frac{\partial \Omega}{\partial x_\alpha'} \quad \text{.....................}(92\cdot7),$$

and since Ω need not be an invariant, Γ_α' is not a vector.

93. Introduction of a metric.

Up to this point the interval ds between two points has not appeared in our theory. It will be remembered that the interval is the length of the corresponding displacement, and we have to consider how a length (an invariant) is to be assigned to a displacement dx_μ (a contravariant in-vector). In this section we shall assign it by the convention

$$ds^2 = g_{\mu\nu}dx_\mu dx_\nu \quad \text{.....................}(93\cdot11).$$

Here $g_{\mu\nu}$ must be a tensor, in order that the interval may be an invariant, but the tensor is chosen by us arbitrarily.

The adoption of a particular tensor $g_{\mu\nu}$ is equivalent to assigning a particular gauge-system—a system by which a unique measure is assigned to the interval between every two points. In Weyl's theory, a gauge-system is partly physical and partly conventional; lengths in different directions but at the same point are supposed to be compared by experimental (optical) methods; but lengths at different points are not supposed to be comparable by physical methods (transfer of clocks and rods) and the unit of length at each point is laid down by a convention. I think that this hybrid definition of length is undesirable, and that length should be treated as a purely conventional or else a purely physical conception. In the present section we treat it as a purely conventional invariant whose properties we wish to discuss, so that length as here defined is not anything which has to be consistent with ordinary physical tests. Later on we shall consider how $g_{\mu\nu}$ must be chosen in order that conventional length may obey the recognised physical tests and thereby become physical length; but at present the tensor $g_{\mu\nu}$ is unrestricted.

Without any loss of generality, we may take $g_{\mu\nu}$ to be a symmetrical tensor, since any antisymmetrical part would drop out on multiplication by $dx_\mu dx_\nu$ and would be meaningless in (93·11).

Let l be the length of a displacement A^μ, so that

$$l^2 = g_{\mu\nu} A^\mu A^\nu \quad \text{.......................... (93·12).}$$

Move A^μ by parallel displacement through dx_σ, then

$$d(l^2) = \left(\frac{\partial g_{\mu\nu}}{\partial x_\sigma} A^\mu A^\nu + g_{\mu\nu} A^\nu \frac{\partial A^\mu}{\partial x_\sigma} + g_{\mu\nu} A^\mu \frac{\partial A^\nu}{\partial x_\sigma}\right) dx_\sigma$$

$$= \left(\frac{\partial g_{\mu\nu}}{\partial x_\sigma} A^\mu A^\nu - g_{\mu\nu} A^\nu \Gamma^\mu_{\sigma\alpha} A^\alpha - g_{\mu\nu} A^\mu \Gamma^\nu_{\sigma\alpha} A^\alpha\right) dx_\sigma \quad \text{by (91·1)}$$

$$= \left(\frac{\partial g_{\mu\nu}}{\partial x_\sigma} - g_{\alpha\nu} \Gamma^\alpha_{\sigma\mu} - g_{\mu\alpha} \Gamma^\alpha_{\sigma\nu}\right) A^\mu A^\nu dx_\sigma$$

by interchanging dummy suffixes.

In conformity with the usual rule for lowering suffixes, we write

$$\Gamma_{\sigma\mu,\nu} = g_{\alpha\nu} \Gamma^\alpha_{\sigma\mu},$$

so that

$$d(l^2) = \left(\frac{\partial g_{\mu\nu}}{\partial x_\sigma} - \Gamma_{\sigma\mu,\nu} - \Gamma_{\sigma\nu,\mu}\right) A^\mu A^\nu (dx)^\sigma \quad \text{............(93·2).}$$

But $d(l^2)$, the difference of two invariants, is an invariant. Hence the quantity in the bracket is a covariant tensor of the third rank which is evidently symmetrical in μ and ν. We denote it by $2K_{\mu\nu,\sigma}$. Thus

$$2K_{\mu\nu,\sigma} = \frac{\partial g_{\mu\nu}}{\partial x_\sigma} - \Gamma_{\sigma\mu,\nu} - \Gamma_{\sigma\nu,\mu} \quad \text{............... (93·3).}$$

Similarly

$$2K_{\mu\sigma,\nu} = \frac{\partial g_{\mu\sigma}}{\partial x_\nu} - \Gamma_{\nu\mu,\sigma} - \Gamma_{\nu\sigma,\mu},$$

$$2K_{\nu\sigma,\mu} = \frac{\partial g_{\nu\sigma}}{\partial x_\mu} - \Gamma_{\mu\nu,\sigma} - \Gamma_{\mu\sigma,\nu}.$$

Adding these and subtracting (93·3) we have

$$K_{\mu\sigma,\nu}+K_{\nu\sigma,\mu}-K_{\mu\nu,\sigma}=\frac{1}{2}\left(\frac{\partial g_{\mu\sigma}}{\partial x_\nu}+\frac{\partial g_{\nu\sigma}}{\partial x_\mu}-\frac{\partial g_{\mu\nu}}{\partial x_\sigma}\right)-\Gamma_{\mu\nu,\sigma} \quad \text{...(93·4).}$$

Let $$S_{\mu\nu,\sigma}=K_{\mu\nu,\sigma}-K_{\mu\sigma,\nu}-K_{\nu\sigma,\mu} \quad \text{...(93·5).}$$

Then (93·4) becomes $\Gamma_{\mu\nu,\sigma}=[\mu\nu,\sigma]+S_{\mu\nu,\sigma}$,

so that, raising the suffix, $$\Gamma^\sigma_{\mu\nu}=\{\mu\nu,\sigma\}+S^\sigma_{\mu\nu} \quad \text{...(93·6).}$$

If $K_{\mu\nu,\sigma}$ has the particular form $g_{\mu\nu}\kappa_\sigma$,

$$S^\sigma_{\mu\nu}=g_{\mu\nu}\kappa^\sigma-g^\sigma_\mu\kappa_\nu-g^\sigma_\nu\kappa_\mu,$$

so that (93·6) reduces to (86·2) with $\Gamma^\sigma_{\mu\nu}={}^*\{\mu\nu,\sigma\}$.

Thus Weyl's geometry is a particular case of our general geometry of parallel displacement. His restriction $K_{\mu\nu,\sigma}=g_{\mu\nu}\kappa_\sigma$ is equivalent to that already explained in § 84.

94. Evaluation of the fundamental in-tensors.

In (92·41) ${}^*B^\epsilon_{\mu\nu\sigma}$ is expressed in terms of the non-tensor quantities $\Gamma^\sigma_{\mu\nu}$. By means of (93·6) it can now be expressed in terms of tensors $g_{\mu\nu}$ and $S^\sigma_{\mu\nu}$. Making the substitution the result is

$$\begin{aligned}{}^*B^\epsilon_{\mu\nu\sigma}=&-\frac{\partial}{\partial x_\sigma}\{\mu\nu,\epsilon\}+\frac{\partial}{\partial x_\nu}\{\mu\sigma,\epsilon\}+\{\mu\sigma,\alpha\}\{\nu\alpha,\epsilon\}-\{\mu\nu,\alpha\}\{\sigma\alpha,\epsilon\}\\&-\frac{\partial}{\partial x_\sigma}S^\epsilon_{\mu\nu}+\frac{\partial}{\partial x_\nu}S^\epsilon_{\mu\sigma}+S^\alpha_{\mu\sigma}\{\nu\alpha,\epsilon\}+S^\epsilon_{\nu\alpha}\{\mu\sigma,\alpha\}-S^\alpha_{\mu\nu}\{\sigma\alpha,\epsilon\}-S^\epsilon_{\sigma\alpha}\{\mu\nu,\alpha\}\\&+S^\alpha_{\mu\sigma}S^\epsilon_{\nu\alpha}-S^\alpha_{\mu\nu}S^\epsilon_{\sigma\alpha}.\end{aligned}$$

The first four terms give the ordinary Riemann-Christoffel tensor (34·4). The next six terms reduce to

$$-(S^\epsilon_{\mu\nu})_\sigma+(S^\epsilon_{\mu\sigma})_\nu,$$

where the final suffix represents ordinary covariant differentiation (not in-covariant differentiation), viz. by (30·4),

$$(S^\epsilon_{\mu\nu})_\sigma=\frac{\partial}{\partial x_\sigma}S^\epsilon_{\mu\nu}-\{\mu\sigma,\alpha\}S^\epsilon_{\alpha\nu}-\{\nu\sigma,\alpha\}S^\epsilon_{\mu\alpha}+\{\alpha\sigma,\epsilon\}S^\alpha_{\mu\nu}.$$

Hence $${}^*B^\epsilon_{\mu\nu\sigma}=B^\epsilon_{\mu\nu\sigma}-(S^\epsilon_{\mu\nu})_\sigma+(S^\epsilon_{\mu\sigma})_\nu+S^\alpha_{\mu\sigma}S^\epsilon_{\nu\alpha}-S^\alpha_{\mu\nu}S^\epsilon_{\sigma\alpha} \quad \text{...(94·1).}$$

This form makes its tensor-property obvious, whereas the form (92·41) made its "in-" property obvious.

We next contract by setting $\epsilon=\sigma$ and write

$$S^\alpha_{\mu\alpha}=2\kappa_\mu \quad \text{...(94·2),}$$

obtaining $${}^*G_{\mu\nu}=G_{\mu\nu}-(S^\alpha_{\mu\nu})_\alpha+2\kappa_{\mu\nu}+S^\alpha_{\mu\beta}S^\beta_{\nu\alpha}-2\kappa_\alpha S^\alpha_{\mu\nu} \quad \text{...(94·3).}$$

Again, multiplying by $g^{\mu\nu}$,

$${}^*G=G+2\lambda^\alpha_\alpha+2\kappa^\alpha_\alpha+4\kappa_\alpha\lambda^\alpha+S^{\alpha\beta}_\gamma S^\gamma_{\alpha,\beta} \quad \text{...(94·4),}$$

where we have set $$S^\alpha_{\alpha,\mu}=-2\lambda_\mu \quad \text{...(94·5).}$$

The difference between (94·5) and (94·2) is that λ_μ is formed by equating the two symmetrical suffixes, and κ_μ by equating one of the symmetrical suffixes with the third suffix in the S-tensor. κ_μ and λ_μ are, of course, entirely different vectors.

The only term on the right of (94·3) which is not symmetrical in μ and ν is $2\kappa_{\mu\nu}$. We write

$$R_{\mu\nu} = G_{\mu\nu} + (\kappa_{\mu\nu} + \kappa_{\nu\mu}) - (S^{\alpha}_{\mu\nu})_{\alpha} - 2\kappa_{\alpha} S^{\alpha}_{\mu\nu} + S^{\alpha}_{\mu\beta} S^{\beta}_{\nu\alpha} \quad \text{......(94·61)},$$

$$F_{\mu\nu} = \kappa_{\mu\nu} - \kappa_{\nu\mu} \quad \text{......(94·62)},$$

so that

$$^{*}G_{\mu\nu} = R_{\mu\nu} + F_{\mu\nu} \quad \text{......(94·63)},$$

and $R_{\mu\nu}$ and $F_{\mu\nu}$ are respectively its symmetrical and antisymmetrical parts. Evidently $R_{\mu\nu}$ and $F_{\mu\nu}$ will both be in-tensors.

We can also set

$$^{*}B_{\mu\nu\sigma\epsilon} = R_{\mu\nu\sigma\epsilon} + F_{\mu\nu\sigma\epsilon},$$

where R is antisymmetrical and F is symmetrical in μ and ϵ. We find that

$$F_{\mu\nu\sigma\epsilon} = (\mathrm{K}_{\mu\epsilon,\,\nu})_{\sigma} - (\mathrm{K}_{\mu\epsilon,\,\sigma})_{\nu},$$

a result which is of interest in connection with the discussion of § 84. But $R_{\mu\nu\sigma\epsilon}$ and $F_{\mu\nu\sigma\epsilon}$ are not in-tensors, since the $g_{\mu\nu}$ are needed to lower the suffix ϵ.

By (92·5) and (93·6)

$$\Gamma_\mu = \Gamma^{\alpha}_{\mu\alpha} = \{\mu\alpha, \alpha\} + S^{\alpha}_{\mu\alpha}$$

$$= \frac{\partial}{\partial x_\mu} (\log \sqrt{-g}) + 2\kappa_\mu \quad \text{......(94·7)}.$$

By comparison with (92·7) we see that the indeterminate function Ω is $\log \sqrt{-g}$, which is not an invariant.

95. The natural gauge of the world.

We now introduce the natural gauge of the world. The tensor $g_{\mu\nu}$, which has hitherto been arbitrary, must be chosen so that the lengths of displacements agree with the lengths determined by measurements made with material and optical appliances. Any apparatus used to measure the world is itself part of the world, so that the natural gauge represents the world as self-gauging. This can only mean that the tensor $g_{\mu\nu}$ which defines the natural gauge is not extraneous, but is a tensor already contained in the world-geometry. Only one such tensor of the second rank has been found, viz. $^{*}G_{\mu\nu}$. Hence natural length is given by

$$l^2 = {}^{*}G_{\mu\nu} A^\mu A^\nu.$$

The antisymmetrical part drops out, giving

$$l^2 = R_{\mu\nu} A^\mu A^\nu.$$

Accordingly by (93·12) we must take

$$\lambda g_{\mu\nu} = R_{\mu\nu} \quad \text{......(95·1)},$$

introducing a universal constant λ, in order to remain free to use the centimetre instead of the natural unit of length whose ratio to familiar standards is unknown.

The manner in which the tensor $R_{\mu\nu}$ is transferred *via* material structure to the measurements made with material structure, has been discussed in

§ 66. We have to replace the tensor $G_{\mu\nu}$ used in that section by its more general form $R_{\mu\nu}$, since $G_{\mu\nu}$ is not an in-tensor and has no definite value until *after* the gauging-equation (95·1) has been laid down. The gist of the argument is as follows—

First adopt any arbitrary conventional gauge which has no relation to physical measures. Let the displacement A^μ represent the radius in a given direction of some specified unit of material structure—e.g. an average electron, an average oxygen atom, a drop of water containing 10^{20} molecules at temperature of maximum density. A^μ is determined by laws which are in the main unknown to us. But just as we can often determine the results of unknown physical laws by the method of dimensions, after surveying the physical constants which can enter into the results, so we can determine the condition satisfied by A^μ by surveying the world-tensors at our disposal. This method indicates that the condition is

$$R_{\mu\nu}A^\mu A^\nu = \text{constant} \qquad \text{(95·11)}.$$

If now we begin to make measures of the world, using the radius of such a material structure as unit, we are thereby adopting a gauge-system in which the length l of the radius is unity, i.e.

$$1 = l^2 = g_{\mu\nu}A^\mu A^\nu \qquad \text{(95·12)}.$$

By comparing (95·11) and (95·12) it follows that $g_{\mu\nu}$ must be a constant multiple of $R_{\mu\nu}$; accordingly we obtain (95·1)*.

Besides making comparisons with material units, we can also compare the lengths of displacements by optical devices. We must show that these comparisons will also fit into the gauge-system (95·1). The light-pulse diverging from a point of space-time occupies a unique conical locus. This locus exists independently of gauge and coordinate systems, and there must therefore be an in-tensor equation defining it. The only in-tensor equation giving a cone of the second degree is

$$R_{\mu\nu}dx_\mu dx_\nu = 0 \qquad \text{(95·21)}.$$

Comparing this with Einstein's formula for the light-cone

$$ds^2 = g_{\mu\nu}dx_\mu dx_\nu = 0 \qquad \text{(95·22)}.$$

We see that again

$$R_{\mu\nu} = \lambda g_{\mu\nu} \qquad \text{(95·23)}.$$

Note however that the optical comparison is less stringent than the material comparison; because (95·21) and (95·22) would be consistent if λ were a function of position, whereas the material comparisons require that it shall be a universal constant. That is why Weyl's theory of gauge-transformation occupies a position intermediate between pure mathematics and physics. He admits the physical comparison of length by optical methods, so that his gauge-transformations are limited to those which do not infringe (95·23), but

* Note that the isotropy of the material unit or of the electron is not necessarily a symmetry of form but an independence of orientation. Thus a metre-rule has the required isotropy because it has (conventionally) the same length however it is orientated.

he does not recognise physical comparison of length by material transfer, and consequently he takes λ to be a function fixed by arbitrary convention and not necessarily a constant. There is thus both a physical and a conventional element in his "length."

A hybrid gauge, even if illogical, may be useful in some problems, particularly if we are describing the electromagnetic field without reference to matter, or preparatory to the introduction of matter. Even without matter the electromagnetic field is self-gauging to the extent of (95·23), λ being a function of position, so that we can gauge our tensors to this extent without tackling the problem of matter. Many of Weyl's in-tensors and in-invariants are not invariant for the unlimited gauge-transformations of the generalised theory, but they become determinate if optical gauging alone is employed; whereas the ordinary invariant or tensor is only determinate in virtue of relations to material standards. In particular $\mathfrak{F}^{\mu\nu}$ is not a complete in-tensor-density, but it has a self-contained absolute meaning, because it measures the electromagnetic field and at the same time electromagnetic fields (light-waves) suffice to gauge it. It may be contrasted with $F^{\mu\nu}$ which can only be gauged by material standards; $F^{\mu\nu}$ has an absolute meaning, but the meaning is not self-contained. For this reason problems will arise for which Weyl's more limited gauge-transformations are specially appropriate; and we regard the generalised theory as supplementing without superseding his theory.

Adopting the natural gauge of the world, we describe its condition by two tensors $g_{\mu\nu}$ and $K^{\sigma}_{\mu\nu}$. If the latter vanishes we recognise nothing but $g_{\mu\nu}$, i.e. pure metric. Now metric is the one characteristic of space. I refer, of course, to the conception of space in physics and in everyday life—the mathematician can attribute to his space whatever properties he wishes. If $K^{\sigma}_{\mu\nu}$ does not vanish, then there is something else present not recognised as a property of pure space; it must therefore be attributed to a "thing*." Thus if there is no "thing" present, i.e. if space is quite empty, $K^{\sigma}_{\mu\nu}=0$, and by (94·61) $R_{\mu\nu}$ reduces to $G_{\mu\nu}$. In empty space the gauging-equation becomes accordingly

$$G_{\mu\nu}=\lambda g_{\mu\nu} \quad \text{.............................(95·3)},$$

which is the law of gravitation (37·4). The gauging-equation is an *alias* of the law of gravitation.

We see by (66·2) that the natural unit of length ($\lambda = 1$) is $1/\sqrt{3}$ times the radius of curvature of the world in any direction in empty space. We do not know its value, but it must obviously be very large.

One reservation must be made with regard to the definition of empty space by the condition $K^{\sigma}_{\mu\nu}=0$. It is possible that we do not recognise $K^{\sigma}_{\mu\nu}$ by any physical experiment, but only certain combinations of its components. In that case definite values of $K^{\sigma}_{\mu\nu}$ would not be recognised as constituting a

* An electromagnetic field is a "thing"; a gravitational field is not, Einstein's theory having shown that it is nothing more than the manifestation of the metric.

"thing," if the recognisable combinations of its components vanished; just as finite values of κ_μ do not constitute an electromagnetic field, if the curl vanishes. This does not affect the validity of (95·3), because any breach of this equation is capable of being recognised by physical experiment, and therefore would be brought about by a combination of components of $K^\sigma_{\mu\nu}$ which had a physical significance.

96. The principle of identification.

In §§ 91–93 we have developed a pure geometry, which is intended to be descriptive of the relation-structure of the world. The relation-structure presents itself in our experience as a physical world consisting of *space, time* and *things*. The transition from the geometrical description to the physical description can only be made by identifying the tensors which measure physical quantities with tensors occurring in the pure geometry, and we must proceed by inquiring first what experimental properties the physical tensor possesses, and then seeking a geometrical tensor which possesses these properties *by virtue of mathematical identities*.

If we can do this completely, we shall have constructed out of the primitive relation-structure a world of entities which behave in the same way and obey the same laws as the quantities recognised in physical experiments. Physical theory can scarcely go further than this How the mind has cognisance of these quantities, and how it has woven them into its vivid picture of a perceptual world, is a problem of psychology rather than of physics.

The first step in our transition from mathematics to physics is the identification of the geometrical tensor $R_{\mu\nu}$ with the physical tensor $g_{\mu\nu}$ giving the metric of physical space and time. Since the metric is the only property of space and time recognised in physics, we may be said to have identified space and time in terms of relation-structure. We have next to identify "things," and the physical description of "things" falls under three heads.

(1) The energy-tensor T^ν_μ comprises the energy momentum and stress in unit volume. This has the property of conservation $(T^\nu_\mu)_\nu = 0$, which enables us to make the identification

$$-8\pi T^\nu_\mu = G^\nu_\mu - \tfrac{1}{2} g^\nu_\mu (G - 2\lambda) \quad \text{.....} \quad (96\cdot1),$$

satisfying the condition of conservation identically Here λ might be any constant, but if we add the usual convention that the zero-condition from which energy, momentum and stress are to be reckoned is that of empty space (not containing electromagnetic fields), we obtain the condition for empty space by equating (96·1) to zero, viz.

$$G_{\mu\nu} = \lambda g_{\mu\nu},$$

so that λ must be the same constant as in (95·3).

(2) The electromagnetic force-tensor $F_{\mu\nu}$ has the property that it fulfils the first half of Maxwell's equations

$$\frac{\partial F_{\mu\nu}}{\partial x_\sigma} + \frac{\partial F_{\nu\sigma}}{\partial x_\mu} + \frac{\partial F_{\sigma\mu}}{\partial x_\nu} = 0 \qquad \text{(96·2)}$$

This will be an identity if $F_{\mu\nu}$ is the curl of any covariant vector; we accordingly identify it with the in-tensor already called $F_{\mu\nu}$ in anticipation, which we have seen is the curl of a vector κ_μ (94·62).

(3) The electric charge-and-current vector J^μ has the property of conservation of electric charge, viz.

$$J^\mu_\mu = 0.$$

The divergence of J^μ will vanish identically if J^μ is itself the divergence of any antisymmetrical contravariant tensor. Accordingly we make the identification

$$J^\mu = F^{\mu\nu}_\nu \qquad \text{(96·3)},$$

a formula which satisfies the remaining half of Maxwell's equations.

The correctness of these identifications should be checked by examining whether the physical tensors thus defined have all the properties which experiment requires us to attribute to them. There is, however, only one further general physical law, which is not implicit in these definitions, viz. the law of mechanical force of an electromagnetic field. We can only show in an imperfect way that our tensors will conform to this law, because a complete proof would require more knowledge as to the structure of an electron; but the discussion of § 80 shows that the law follows in a very plausible way.

In identifying "things" we have not limited ourselves to in-tensors, because the "things" discussed in physics are in physical space and time and therefore presuppose the natural gauge-system. The laws of conservation and Maxwell's equations, which we have used for identifying "things," would not hold true in an arbitrary gauge-system.

No doubt alternative identifications would be conceivable. For example, $F_{\mu\nu}$ might be identified with the curl of λ_μ† instead of the curl of κ_μ. That would leave the fundamental in-tensor apparently doing nothing to justify its existence. We have chosen the most obvious identifications, and it seems reasonable to adhere to them, unless a crucial test can be devised which shows them to be untenable. In any case, with the material at our disposal the number of possible identifications is very limited.

97. The bifurcation of geometry and electrodynamics.

The fundamental in-tensor $^*G_{\mu\nu}$ breaks up into a symmetrical part $R_{\mu\nu}$ and an antisymmetrical part $F_{\mu\nu}$. The former is $\lambda g_{\mu\nu}$, or if the natural unit of length ($\lambda = 1$) is used, it is simply $g_{\mu\nu}$. We have then

$$^*G_{\mu\nu} = g_{\mu\nu} + F_{\mu\nu},$$

† The curl of λ_μ is not an in-tensor, but there is no obvious reason why an in-tensor should be required. If magnetic flux were measured in practice by comparison with that of a magneton transferred from point to point, as a length is measured by transfer of a scale, then an in-tensor would be needed. But that is not the actual procedure.

showing at once how the field or aether contains two characteristics, the gravitational potential (or the metric) and the electromagnetic force. These are connected in the most simple possible way in the tensor descriptive of underlying relation-structure; and we see in a general way the reason for this inevitable bifurcation into symmetrical and antisymmetrical—geometrical-mechanical and electromagnetic—characteristics.

Einstein approaches these two tensors from the physical side, having recognised their existence in observational phenomena. We here approach them from the deductive side endeavouring to show as completely as possible that they must exist for almost any kind of underlying structure. We confirm his assumption that the interval ds^2 is an absolute quantity, for it is our in-invariant $R_{\mu\nu} dx_\mu dx_\nu$; we further confirm the well-known property of $F_{\mu\nu}$ that it is the curl of a vector.

We not only justify the assumption that natural geometry is Riemannian geometry and not the ultra-Riemannian geometry of Weyl, but we can show a reason why the quadratic formula for the interval is necessary. The only simple absolute quantity relating to two points is

$$*G_{\mu\nu} dx_\mu dx_\nu.$$

To obtain another in-invariant we should have to proceed to an expression like

$$*B^\rho_{\mu\nu\sigma} * B^\sigma_{\lambda\tau\rho} dx_\mu dx_\nu dx_\lambda dx_\tau.$$

Although the latter quartic expression does theoretically express some absolute property associated with the two points, it can scarcely be expected that we shall come across it in physical exploration of the world so immediately as the former quadratic expression.

It is the new insight gained on these points which is the chief advantage of the generalised theory.

98. General relation-structure.

We proceed to examine more minutely the conceptions on which the fundamental axioms of parallel displacement and affine geometry depend.

The fundamental basis of all things must presumably have *structure* and *substance*. We cannot describe substance; we can only give a name to it. Any attempt to do more than give a name leads at once to an attribution of structure. But structure can be described to some extent, and when reduced to ultimate terms it appears to resolve itself into a complex of relations. And further these relations cannot be entirely devoid of comparability, for if nothing in the world is comparable with anything else, all parts of it are alike in their unlikeness, and there cannot be even the rudiments of a structure.

The axiom of parallel displacement is the expression of this comparability, and the comparability postulated seems to be almost the minimum conceivable. Only relations which are close together, i.e. interlocked in the relation-structure, are supposed to be comparable, and the conception of equivalence is applied only to one type of relation. This comparable relation is called displacement. By representing this relation graphically we obtain the idea of location in space; the reason why it is natural for us to represent this particular relation graphically does not fall within the scope of physics.

Thus our axiom of parallel displacement is the geometrical garb of a principle which may be called "the comparability of proximate relations."

There is a certain hiatus in the arguments of the relativity theory which has never been thoroughly explored. We refer all phenomena to a system of coordinates; but do not explain how a system of coordinates (a method of numbering events for identification) is to be found in the first instance. It may be asked, What does it matter how it is found, since the coordinate-system fortunately is entirely arbitrary in the relativity theory? But the arbitrariness of the coordinate-system is limited. We may apply any continuous transformation; but our theory does not contemplate a discontinuous transformation of coordinates, such as would correspond to a re-shuffling of the points of the continuum. There is something corresponding to an *order of enumeration* of the points which we desire to preserve, when we limit the changes of coordinates to continuous transformations.

It seems clear that this order which we feel it necessary to preserve must be a structural order of the points, i.e. an order determined by their mutual relations in the world-structure. Otherwise the tensors which represent structural features, and have therefore a possible physical significance, will become discontinuous with respect to the coordinate description of the world. So far as I know the only attempt to derive a coordinate order from a postulated structural relation is that of Robb*, this appears to be successful in the case of the "special" theory of relativity, but the investigation is very laborious. In the general theory it is difficult to discern any method of attacking the problem. It is by no means obvious that the interlocking of relations would necessarily be such as to determine an order reducible to the kind of order presumed in coordinate enumeration. I can throw no light on this question. It is necessary to admit that there is something of a jump from the recognition of a comparable relation called displacement to the assumption that the ordering of points by this relation is homologous with the ordering postulated when the displacement is represented graphically by a coordinate difference dx_μ.

The hiatus probably indicates something more than a temporary weakness of the rigorous deduction. It means that space and time are only approximate conceptions, which must ultimately give way to a more general conception of the ordering of events in nature not expressible in terms of a fourfold coordinate-system. It is in this direction that some physicists hope to find a solution of the contradictions of the quantum theory. It is a fallacy to think that the conception of location in space-time based on the observation of large-scale

* *The Absolute Relations of Time and Space* (Camb. Univ. Press). He uses the relation of "before and after."

phenomena can be applied unmodified to the happenings which involve only a small number of quanta. Assuming that this is the right solution it is useless to look for any means of introducing quantum phenomena into the later formulae of our theory; these phenomena have been excluded at the outset by the adoption of a coordinate frame of reference.

The relation of displacement between point-events and the relation of "equivalence" between displacements form parts of one idea, which are only separated for convenience of mathematical manipulation. That the relation of displacement between A and B amounts to such-and-such a quantity conveys no absolute meaning; but that the relation of displacement between A and B is "equivalent" to the relation of displacement between C and D is (or at any rate may be) an absolute assertion. Thus four points is the minimum number for which an assertion of absolute structural relation can be made. The ultimate elements of structure are thus four-point elements. By adopting the condition of affine geometry (91·3), I have limited the possible assertion with regard to a four-point element to the statement that the four points do, or do not, form a parallelogram. The defence of affine geometry thus rests on the not unplausible view that four-point elements are recognised to be differentiated from one another by a single character, viz. that they are or are not of a particular kind which is conventionally named *parallelogramical*. Then the analysis of the parallelogram property into a double equivalence of AB to CD and AC to BD, is merely a definition of what is meant by the equivalence of displacements.

I do not lay overmuch stress on this justification of affine geometry. It may well happen that four-point elements are differentiated by what might be called trapezoidal characters in which the pairs of sides are not commutable, so that we could distinguish an element $ABDC$ trapezoidal with respect to AB, CD from one trapezoidal with respect to AC, BD. I am quite prepared to believe that the affine condition may not always be fulfilled—giving rise to new phenomena not included in this theory. But it is probably best in aiming at the widest generality to make the generalisation in successive steps, and explore each step before ascending to the next.

In reference to the difficulties encountered in the most general description of relation-structure, the possibility may be borne in mind that in physics we have not to deal with individual relations but with statistical averages, and the simplifications adopted may have become possible because of the averaging.

99. The tensor $*B^{\epsilon}_{\mu\nu\sigma}$.

Besides furnishing the two tensors $g_{\mu\nu}$ and $F_{\mu\nu}$ of which Einstein has made good use, our investigation has dragged up from below a certain amount of apparently useless lumber. We have obtained the full tensor $*B^{\epsilon}_{\mu\nu\sigma}$ which has not been used except in the contracted form—that is to say certain components have been ignored entirely, and others have not been considered individually but as sums. Until the problem of electron-structure is more advanced it is premature to reject finally any material which could conceivably be relevant; although at present there is no special reason for anticipating that the full tensor will be helpful in constructing electrons.

Accordingly in the present state of knowledge the tensor $*B^{\epsilon}_{\mu\nu\sigma}$ cannot be considered to be a physical quantity; it *contains* a physical quantity $*G_{\mu\nu}$. Two states of the world which are described by different $*B^{\epsilon}_{\mu\nu\sigma}$ but the same $*G_{\mu\nu}$ are so far as we know identical states; just as two configurations of events described by different coordinates but the same intervals are identical configurations. If this is so, the $\Gamma^{\mu}_{\nu\alpha}$ must be capable of other transformations besides coordinate transformations without altering anything in the physical condition of the world.

Correspondingly the tensor $K^{\sigma}_{\mu\nu}$ can take any one of an infinite series of values without altering the physical state of the world. It would perhaps be possible to show that among these values is $g_{\mu\nu}\kappa^{\sigma}$, which gives Weyl's geometry, but I am not sure that it necessarily follows. It has been suggested that the occurrence of non-physical quantities in the present theory is a drawback, and that Weyl's geometry which contains precisely the observed number of "degrees of freedom" of the world has the advantage. For some purposes that may be so, but not for the problems which we are now considering. In order to discuss why the structure of the world is such that the observed phenomena appear, we must necessarily compare it with other structures of a more general type; that involves the consideration of "non-physical" quantities which exist in the hypothetical comparison-worlds, but are not of a physical nature because they do not exist in the actual world. If we refuse to consider any condition which is conceivable but not actual, we cannot account for the actual; we can only prescribe it dogmatically.

As an illustration of what is gained by the broader standpoint, we may consider the question why the field is described by exactly 14 potentials. Our former explanation attributed this to the occurrence of 14 variables in the most general type of geometry. We now see that this is fallacious and that a natural generalisation of Riemannian geometry admits 40 variables; and no doubt the number could be extended. The real reason for the 14 potentials is because, even admitting a geometry with 40 variables, the fundamental in-tensor of the second rank has 14 variables; and it is the in-tensor (a measure of the physical state of the world) not the world-geometry (an arbitrary graphical representation of it) which determines the phenomena.

The "lumber" which we have found can do no harm. If it does not affect the structure of electrons or quanta, then we cannot be aware of it because we are unprovided with appliances for detecting it; if it does affect their structure then it is just as well to have discovered it. The important thing is to keep it out of problems to which it is irrelevant, and this is easy since

$^*G_{\mu\nu}$ extracts the gold from the dross. It is quite unnecessary to specialise the possible relation-structure of the world in such a way that the useless variables have the fixed value zero; that loses sight of the interesting result that the world will go on just the same if they are not zero.

We see that two points of view may be taken—

(1) Only those things *exist* (in the physical meaning of the word) which could be detected by conceivable experiments.

(2) We are only aware of a selection of the things which *exist* (in an extended meaning of the word), the selection being determined by the nature of the apparatus available for exploring nature.

Both principles are valuable in their respective spheres. In the earlier part of this book the first has been specially useful in purging physics from metaphysical conceptions. But when we are inquiring why the structure of the world is such that just $g_{\mu\nu}$ and κ_μ appear and nothing else, we cannot ignore the fact that no structure of the world could make anything else appear if we had no cognizance of the appliances necessary for detecting it. Therefore there is no need to insert, and puzzle over the cause of, special limitations on the world-structure, intended to eliminate everything which physics is unable to determine. The world-structure is clearly not the place in which the limitations arise.

100. Dynamical consequences of the general properties of world-invariants.

We shall apply the method of § 61 to world-invariants containing the electromagnetic variables. Let $\mathfrak{K}$ be a scalar-density which is a function of $g_{\mu\nu}$, $F_{\mu\nu}$, κ_μ and their derivatives up to any order, so that for a given region

$\int \mathfrak{K} d\tau$ is an invariant.

It would have been possible to express $F_{\mu\nu}$ in terms of the derivatives of κ_μ; but in this investigation we keep it separate, because special attention will be directed to the case in which $\mathfrak{K}$ does not contain the κ_μ themselves but only their curl, so that it depends on $g_{\mu\nu}$ and $F_{\mu\nu}$ only.

By partial integration we obtain as in § 61

$$\delta \int \mathfrak{K} d\tau = \int (\mathfrak{P}^{\mu\nu} \delta g_{\mu\nu} - \mathfrak{H}^{\mu\nu} \delta F_{\mu\nu} + \mathfrak{Q}^\mu \delta \kappa_\mu) \, d\tau \text{ . } \quad \text{......(100·1)},$$

for variations which vanish at the boundary of the region. Here

$$P^{\mu\nu} = \frac{\mathfrak{h} K}{\mathfrak{h} g_{\mu\nu}}, \quad H^{\mu\nu} = -\frac{\mathfrak{h} K}{\mathfrak{h} F_{\mu\nu}}, \quad Q^\mu = \frac{\mathfrak{h} K}{\mathfrak{h} \kappa_\mu} \quad \text{.........(100·2)},$$

and $P^{\mu\nu}$ is a symmetrical tensor, $H^{\mu\nu}$ an antisymmetrical tensor.

We have

$$\mathfrak{H}^{\mu\nu} \delta F_{\mu\nu} = \mathfrak{H}^{\mu\nu} \left(\frac{\partial (\delta \kappa_\mu)}{\partial x_\nu} - \frac{\partial (\delta \kappa_\nu)}{\partial x_\mu} \right)$$

$$= 2 \mathfrak{H}^{\mu\nu} \frac{\partial (\delta \kappa_\mu)}{\partial x_\nu}$$

$$= - \frac{2 \partial \mathfrak{H}^{\mu\nu}}{\partial x_\nu} \delta \kappa_\mu$$

rejecting a complete differential,

$$= -2\mathfrak{H}_{\nu}^{\mu\nu}\delta\kappa_\mu \qquad \text{by } (51\cdot52).$$

Hence

$$\delta\int\mathfrak{K}d\tau = \int\{\mathfrak{P}^{\mu\nu}\delta g_{\mu\nu} + (2\mathfrak{H}_{\nu}^{\mu\nu} + \mathfrak{Q}^\mu)\,\delta\kappa_\mu\}\,d\tau \quad \text{.........}(100\cdot3).$$

Now suppose that the $\delta g_{\mu\nu}$ and $\delta\kappa_\mu$ arise solely from arbitrary variations δx_α of the coordinate-system in accordance with the laws of transformation of tensors and vectors. The invariant will not be affected, so that its variation vanishes By the same process as in obtaining (61·3) we find that the change of $\delta\kappa_\mu$, for a comparison of points having the same coordinates x_α in both the original and varied systems, is

$$-\delta\kappa_\mu = \kappa_\alpha\frac{\partial(\delta x_\alpha)}{\partial x_\mu} + \frac{\partial\kappa_\mu}{\partial x_\alpha}\delta x_\alpha.$$

Hence

$$-(\mathfrak{Q}^\mu + 2\mathfrak{H}_{\nu}^{\mu\nu})\,\delta\kappa_\mu = \left\{\frac{\partial\kappa_\mu}{\partial x_\alpha}(\mathfrak{Q}^\mu + 2\mathfrak{H}_{\nu}^{\mu\nu}) - \frac{\partial}{\partial x_\mu}\{\kappa_\alpha(\mathfrak{Q}^\mu + 2\mathfrak{H}_{\nu}^{\mu\nu})\}\right\}\delta x_\alpha$$

rejecting a complete differential. Since $\partial\mathfrak{H}_{\nu}^{\mu\nu}/\partial x_\mu \equiv 0$ (73·76), this becomes

$$\{F_{\mu\alpha}(\mathfrak{Q}^\mu + 2\mathfrak{H}_{\nu}^{\mu\nu}) - \kappa_\alpha\mathfrak{Q}_{\mu}^{\mu}\}.$$

Using the previous reduction for $\delta g_{\mu\nu}$ (61·4), our equation (100·3) reduces to

$$0 = \int\{2\mathfrak{P}_{\alpha\nu}^{\nu} - F_{\mu\alpha}(\mathfrak{Q}^\mu + 2\mathfrak{H}_{\nu}^{\mu\nu}) + \kappa_\alpha\mathfrak{Q}_{\mu}^{\mu}\}\,\delta x_\alpha d\tau \quad \text{.....}(100\cdot41)$$

for all arbitrary variations δx_α which vanish at the boundary of the region. Accordingly we must have identically

$$\mathfrak{P}_{\alpha\nu}^{\nu} = F_{\mu\alpha}\mathfrak{H}_{\nu}^{\mu\nu} + \tfrac{1}{2}F_{\mu\alpha}\mathfrak{Q}^\mu - \tfrac{1}{2}\kappa_\alpha\mathfrak{Q}_{\mu}^{\mu}$$

or, dividing by $\sqrt{-g}$, and changing dummy suffixes,

$$P_{\mu\nu}^{\nu} = -F_{\mu\nu}H_{\sigma}^{\nu\sigma} - \tfrac{1}{2}(F_{\mu\nu}Q^\nu + \kappa_\mu Q_{\nu}^{\nu}) \quad \text{...........}(100\cdot42).$$

First consider the case when $\mathfrak{K}$ is a function of $g_{\mu\nu}$ and $F_{\mu\nu}$ only, so that $Q^\mu = 0$. The equation

$$P_{\mu\nu}^{\nu} = -F_{\mu\nu}H_{\sigma}^{\nu\sigma} \quad \text{.......................}(100\cdot43)$$

at once suggests the equations of the mechanical force of an electromagnetic field

$$M_{\mu\nu}^{\nu} = -h_\mu = -F_{\mu\nu}J^\nu = -F_{\mu\nu}F_{\sigma}^{\nu\sigma}.$$

It has already become plain that anything recognised in physics as an energy-tensor must be of the nature of a Hamiltonian derivative of some invariant with respect to $g_{\mu\nu}$; and the property of conservation has been shown to depend on this fact. *We now see that the general theory of invariants also predicts the type of the reaction of any such derived tensor to the electromagnetic field*, viz. that its conservation is disturbed by a ponderomotive force of the type $F_{\mu\nu}H_{\sigma}^{\nu\sigma}$.

If we identify P^{ν}_{μ} with the material energy-tensor, $H^{\mu\nu}_{\nu}$ must be identified with the charge-and-current vector†, so that

$$J^{\mu} = H^{\mu\nu}_{\nu} \quad \text{.........................(100·44)},$$

which is the general equation given in (82 2). It follows without any further specialisation that electric charge must be conserved ($J^{\mu}_{\mu} = 0$).

The foregoing investigation shows that the antisymmetric part of the principal world-tensor will manifest itself in our experience by producing the effects of a force. This force will act on a certain stream-vector (in the manner that electromagnetic force acts on a charge and current); and further this stream-vector represents the flow of something permanently conserved The existence of electricity and the qualitative nature of electrical phenomena are thus predicted.

In considering the results of substituting a particular function for K, it has to be remembered that the equation (100·42) is an identity. We shall not obtain from it any fresh law connecting $g_{\mu\nu}$ and κ_{μ} The final result after making the substitutions will probably be quite puerile and unworthy of the powerful general method employed. The interest lies not in the identity itself but in the general process of which it is the result. We have seen reason to believe that the process of Hamiltonian differentiation is actually the process of creation of the perceptual world around us, so that in this investigation we are discovering the laws of physics by examining the mode in which the physical world is created. The identities expressing these laws may be trivial from the mathematical point of view when separated from the context; but the present mode of derivation gives the clue to their significance in our experience as fundamental laws of nature‡.

To agree with Maxwell's theory it is necessary to have $H^{\mu\nu} = F^{\mu\nu}$. Accordingly by (100 2) the invariant K should contain the term $-\frac{1}{2} F^{\mu\nu} F_{\mu\nu}$. The only natural way in which this can be combined linearly with other terms not containing $F_{\mu\nu}$ is in one of the invariants $\frac{1}{2} {}^*G_{\mu\nu} {}^*G^{\nu\mu}$ or $-\frac{1}{2} {}^*G_{\mu\nu} {}^*G^{\mu\nu}$. We take

$$\begin{aligned} K &= \tfrac{1}{2} {}^*G_{\mu\nu} {}^*G^{\nu\mu} \\ &= \tfrac{1}{2} (R_{\mu\nu} + F_{\mu\nu}) (R^{\nu\mu} + F^{\nu\mu}) \\ &= \tfrac{1}{2} (R_{\mu\nu} R^{\mu\nu} - F_{\mu\nu} F^{\mu\nu}) \quad \text{.....................(100 5)} \end{aligned}$$

by the antisymmetric properties of $F_{\mu\nu}$.

The quantity $R_{\mu\nu}$ can be expressed as a function of the variables in two ways, either by the gauging-equation

$$R_{\mu\nu} = \lambda g_{\mu\nu}$$

† This definition of electric charge through the mechanical effects experienced by charged bodies corresponds exactly to the definition employed in practice Our previous definition of it as $F^{\mu\nu}_{\nu}$ corresponded to a measure of the strength of the singularity in the electromagnetic field.

‡ The definitive development of the theory ends at this point. From here to the end of § 102 we discuss certain possibilities which may be on the track of further progress; but there is no certain guidance, and it may be suspected that the right clue is still lacking.

or by the general expressions (87·5) and (94·61). If the first form is adopted we obtain an identity, which, however, is clearly not the desired relation of energy.

If we adopt the more general expression some care is required. Presumably $\mathfrak{K}$ should be an in-invariant-density if it has the fundamental importance supposed. As written it is not formally in-invariant in our generalised theory though it is in Weyl's theory. We can make it in-invariant by writing $R_{\mu\nu}R^{\mu\nu}\sqrt{-g}$ in the form

$$g^{\mu\alpha}g^{\nu\beta}R_{\mu\nu}R_{\alpha\beta}\sqrt{-g},$$

where the $g^{\mu\nu}$ are to have the values for the natural gauge, but in the in-tensor $R_{\mu\nu}$ the general values for any gauge may be used. The general theory becomes highly complicated, and we shall content ourselves with the partially generalised expression in Weyl's theory, which will sufficiently illustrate the procedure. In this case $R_{\mu\nu}=\lambda g_{\mu\nu}$, but λ is a variable function of position. Accordingly $R_{\mu\nu}R^{\mu\nu}=4\lambda^2=\frac{1}{4}{}^*G^2$, so that

$$\mathfrak{K}=\tfrac{1}{8}({}^*G^2-4F_{\mu\nu}F^{\mu\nu})\sqrt{-g} \quad\text{..................}(100\cdot6)$$

Comparing with (90·1) we see that $\mathfrak{K}$ is equivalent to the action adopted by Weyl.

This appears to throw light on the meaning of the combination of ${}^*G^2$ with $F_{\mu\nu}F^{\mu\nu}$ which we have recognised in (90·1) as having an important significance. It is the degenerate form in Weyl's gauge of the natural combination ${}^*G_{\mu\nu}{}^*G^{\nu\mu}$. The alternation of the suffixes is primarily adopted as a trick to obtain the required sign, but is perhaps justifiable.

If this view of the origin of (90·1) is correct, the constant α must be equal to 4. Accordingly $\beta=1/2\lambda$, and by (90·51) the whole energy-tensor and the electromagnetic energy-tensor are reduced to the same units in the expressions

$$E^{\mu\nu}, \quad 8\pi\lambda T^{\mu\nu} \quad\text{..................}(100\cdot7)$$

The numerical results obtainable from this conclusion will be discussed in § 102.

In the discussion of § 90 it was assumed that $P^{\mu\nu}$ $(=\partial K/\partial g_{\mu\nu})$ vanished. I do not think there is any good reason for introducing an arbitrary action-principle of this kind, and it seems more likely that $P^{\mu\nu}$ will be a non-vanishing energy-tensor.

This seems to leave a superfluity of energy-tensors, because owing to the non-vanishing coefficient Q^{μ} we have the term $(\kappa^{\mu}\kappa^{\nu}-\frac{1}{2}g^{\mu\nu}\kappa_{\alpha}\kappa^{\alpha})$ in (90·51) which has to play some rôle. In § 90 this was supposed to be the material energy-tensor, but I am inclined to think that it has another interpretation. In order to liberate material energy we must relax the binding forces of the electrons, allowing them to expand. Suppose that we make a small virtual change of this kind. In addition to the material energy liberated by the process there will be another consequential change in the energy of the region. The electron furnishes the standard of length, so that all the gravitational energy will now have to be re-gauged. It seems likely that the function of the term $(\kappa^\mu \kappa^\nu - \frac{1}{2} g^{\mu\nu} \kappa_\alpha \kappa^\alpha)$ is to provide for this change. If so, nothing hinders us from identifying $P^{\mu\nu}$ with the true material energy-tensor.

101. The generalised volume.

Admitting that $^*G_{\mu\nu}$ is the building-material with which we have to construct the physical world, let us examine what are the simplest invariants that can be formed from it. The meaning of "simple" is ambiguous, and depends to some extent on our outlook. I take the order of simplicity to be the order in which the quantities appear in building the physical world from the material $^*G_{\mu\nu}$. Before introducing the process of gauging by which we obtain the $g_{\mu\nu}$, and later (by a rather intricate use of determinants) the $g^{\mu\nu}$, we can form in-invariants belonging respectively to a one-dimensional, a two-dimensional and a four-dimensional domain.

(1) For a line-element $(dx)^\mu$, the simplest in-invariant is

$$^*G_{\mu\nu}\,(dx)^\mu\,(dx)^\nu \quad \text{.........................(101·11)},$$

which appears physically as the square of the length.

(2) For a surface-element $dS^{\mu\nu}$, the simplest in-invariant is

$$^*G_{\mu\nu}dS^{\mu\nu} \quad \text{.................................(101·12)},$$

which appears physically as the flux of electromagnetic force. It may be remarked that this invariant, although formally pertaining to the surface-element, is actually a property of the bounding circuit only.

(3) For a volume-element $d\tau$, the simplest in-invariant is

$$V = \sqrt{(-\,|\,^*G_{\mu\nu}\,|)}\,d\tau \quad \text{....................(101·13)},$$

which has been called the generalised volume, but has not yet received a physical interpretation.

We shall first calculate $|\,^*G_{\mu\nu}\,|$ for Galilean coordinates. Since

$$^*G_{\mu\nu} = \lambda g_{\mu\nu} + F_{\mu\nu}$$

we have on inserting the Galilean values

$$|\,^*G_{\mu\nu}\,| = \begin{vmatrix} -\lambda & -\gamma & \beta & -X \\ \gamma & -\lambda & -\alpha & -Y \\ -\beta & \alpha & -\lambda & -Z \\ X & Y & Z & \lambda \end{vmatrix}$$

$$= -\{\lambda^4 + \lambda^2(\alpha^2 + \beta^2 + \gamma^2 - X^2 - Y^2 - Z^2) - (\alpha X + \beta Y + \gamma Z)^2\} \quad \text{......(101·2)}.$$

The relation of the absolute unit of electromagnetic force (which is here being used) to the practical unit is not yet known, but it seems likely that the fields used in laboratory experiments correspond to small values of $F_{\mu\nu}$†. If this is so we may neglect the fourth powers of $F_{\mu\nu}$ and obtain approximately

$$V = \sqrt{(-|{}^*G_{\mu\nu}|)}\,d\tau = \{\lambda^2 + \tfrac{1}{2}(\alpha^2 + \beta^2 + \gamma^2 - X^2 - Y^2 - Z^2)\}\,d\tau$$
$$= (\lambda^2 + \tfrac{1}{4}F_{\mu\nu}F^{\mu\nu})\,d\tau \quad \text{by (77·3).}$$

Since V is an invariant we can at once write down the result for any other coordinate-system, viz.

$$V = (\lambda^2 + \tfrac{1}{4}F_{\mu\nu}F^{\mu\nu})\sqrt{-g}\,d\tau \qquad \text{(101·31),}$$

or in the natural gauge $R_{\mu\nu} = \lambda g_{\mu\nu}$, this can be written

$$V = \tfrac{1}{4}(R_{\mu\nu}R^{\mu\nu} + F_{\mu\nu}F^{\mu\nu})\sqrt{-g}\,d\tau$$
$$= \tfrac{1}{4}{}^*G_{\mu\nu}{}^*G^{\mu\nu}\sqrt{-g}\,d\tau \qquad \text{(101·32)}$$

Thus if the generalised volume is the fundamental in-invariant from which the dynamical laws arise, we may expect that our approximate experimental laws will pertain to the invariant ${}^*G_{\mu\nu}{}^*G^{\mu\nu}\sqrt{-g}\,d\tau$, which is a close approximation to it except in very intense electromagnetic fields.

In (100·5) we took $K = {}^*G_{\mu\nu}{}^*G^{\nu\mu}$. The alternation of the suffixes seems to be essential if $\mathfrak{h}K/\mathfrak{h}g_{\mu\nu}$ is to represent the material energy (or to be zero according to Weyl's action-principle). If we do not alternate the suffixes the Hamiltonian derivative contains the whole energy-tensor plus the electromagnetic energy-tensor, whereas we must naturally attach more significance to the difference of these two tensors. It may, however, be noted that

$${}^*G_{\mu\nu}{}^*G^{\nu\mu} = {}^*G_{\mu\nu}{}^*G^{\mu\nu} - \kappa_{\mu\nu}\frac{\mathfrak{h}}{\mathfrak{h}\kappa_{\mu\nu}}({}^*G_{\mu\nu}{}^*G^{\mu\nu}) \qquad \text{(101·33)}$$

(variations of κ_μ being ignored except in so far as they affect $F_{\mu\nu}$). It would seem therefore that the invariant K previously discussed arises from V by the process of ignoration of the coordinates κ_μ. Equation (101·33) represents exactly the usual procedure for obtaining the modified Lagrangian function in dynamics.

If this view is correct, that the invariants which give the ordinary equations adopted in physics are really approximations to more accurate expressions based on the generalised volume, it becomes possible to predict the second-order terms which are needed to complete the equations currently used. It will sufficiently illustrate this if we consider the corrections to Maxwell's equations suggested by this method.

Whereas in (79·32) we found that J^μ was the Hamiltonian derivative of $\tfrac{1}{4}F^{\mu\nu}F_{\mu\nu}.\sqrt{-g}\,d\tau$, we now suppose that it is more exactly the Hamiltonian derivative of $\sqrt{(-|{}^*G_{\mu\nu}|)}\,d\tau$ with respect to κ_μ‡. We use Galilean (or natural) coordinates, and it is convenient to use the notation of § 82 in which (a, b, c) takes the place of (α, β, γ).

Let

$$\Delta = -|{}^*G_{\mu\nu}| = \lambda^4 + \lambda^2(a^2 + b^2 + c^2 - X^2 - Y^2 - Z^2) - S^2,$$

† This is doubtful, since the calculations in the next section do not bear it out.

‡ We consider only the variations of κ_μ as affecting $F_{\mu\nu}$.

where
$$S = aX + bY + cZ.$$

Then $$\delta(\sqrt{\Delta}) = \frac{1}{\sqrt{\Delta}}\lambda^2\left\{\left(a - \frac{SX}{\lambda^2}\right)\delta a + \ldots - \left(X + \frac{Sa}{\lambda^2}\right)\delta X - \ldots\right\}.$$

Take a permeability and specific inductive capacity given by

$$\mu = \frac{1}{K} = \frac{\sqrt{\Delta}}{\lambda^2} \quad \text{.......................(101·41)},$$

so that
$$\alpha = \lambda^2 a/\sqrt{\Delta}, \quad P = \lambda^2 X/\sqrt{\Delta},$$

and let
$$S' = S/\sqrt{\Delta} = (\alpha X + \beta Y + \gamma Z)/\lambda^2 \quad \text{..............(101·42)}.$$

Then

$$\delta(\sqrt{\Delta}) = (\alpha - XS')\,\delta\left(\frac{\partial H}{\partial y} - \frac{\partial G}{\partial z}\right) + .$$

$$- (P + aS')\,\delta\left(-\frac{\partial F}{\partial t} - \frac{\partial \Phi}{\partial x}\right) - \ldots$$

$$= \left\{-\frac{\partial}{\partial t}(P + aS') - \frac{\partial}{\partial z}(\beta - YS') + \frac{\partial}{\partial y}(\gamma - ZS')\right\}\delta F + \ldots$$

$$+ \left\{\frac{\partial}{\partial x}(P + aS') + \frac{\partial}{\partial y}(Q + bS') + \frac{\partial}{\partial z}(R + cS')\right\}\delta(-\Phi),$$

rejecting a complete differential. Equating the coefficients to the charge-and-current vector $(\sigma_x, \sigma_y, \sigma_z, \rho)$ we have

$$\sigma_x + \frac{\partial}{\partial t}(P + aS') = \frac{\partial}{\partial y}(\gamma - ZS') - \frac{\partial}{\partial z}(\beta - YS'),$$

$$\rho = \frac{\partial}{\partial x}(P + aS') + \frac{\partial}{\partial y}(Q + bS') + \frac{\partial}{\partial z}(R + cS').$$

These reduce to the classical form

$$\left.\begin{aligned} \frac{\partial \gamma}{\partial y} - \frac{\partial \beta}{\partial z} &= \frac{\partial P}{\partial t} + \sigma' \\ \frac{\partial P}{\partial x} + \frac{\partial Q}{\partial y} + \frac{\partial R}{\partial z} &= \rho' \end{aligned}\right\} \quad \text{.....................(101·5)},$$

provided that

$$\left.\begin{aligned} \sigma_x' &= \sigma_x + \frac{\partial(aS')}{\partial t} + \frac{\partial(ZS')}{\partial y} - \frac{\partial(YS')}{\partial z} \\ \rho' &= \rho - \frac{\partial(aS')}{\partial x} - \frac{\partial(bS')}{\partial y} - \frac{\partial(cS')}{\partial z} \end{aligned}\right\} \quad \text{............(101·6)}$$

These at once reduce to

$$\left.\begin{aligned} \sigma_x' &= \sigma_x + a\frac{\partial S'}{\partial t} + Z\frac{\partial S'}{\partial y} - Y\frac{\partial S'}{\partial z} \\ \rho' &= \rho - a\frac{\partial S'}{\partial x} - b\frac{\partial S'}{\partial y} - c\frac{\partial S'}{\partial z} \end{aligned}\right\} \quad \text{..............(101·7)}$$

The effect of the second-order terms is thus to make the aether appear to have a specific inductive capacity and permeability given by (101·41) and also to introduce a spurious charge and current given by (101·7).

This revision makes no difference whatever to the propagation of light. Since $\sqrt{(\mu K)}$ is always unity, the velocity of propagation is unaltered, and no spurious charge or current is produced because S' vanishes when the magnetic and electric forces are at right angles.

It would be interesting if all electric charges could be produced in this way by the second-order terms of the pure field equations, so that there would be no need to introduce the extraneous charge and current $(\sigma_x, \sigma_y, \sigma_z, \rho)$. I think, however, that this is scarcely possible. The total spurious charge in a three-dimensional region is equal to

$$\iiint(\rho' - \rho)\, dx\, dy\, dz = -\iint B_n S' dS \quad \text{by (101·6)},$$

where B_n is the normal magnetic induction across the boundary. This requires that $B_n S'$ in the field of an electron falls off only as the inverse square. It is scarcely likely that the electron has the distant magnetic effects that are implied.

It is readily verified that the spurious charge is conserved independently of the true charge.

It has seemed worth while to show in some detail the kind of amendment to Maxwell's laws which may result from further progress of theory. Perhaps the chief interest lies in the way in which the propagation of electromagnetic waves is preserved entirely unchanged. But the present proposals are not intended to be definitive.

102. Numerical values.

Our electromagnetic quantities have been expressed in terms of some absolute unit whose relation to the C.G.S. system has hitherto been unknown. It seems probable that we are now in a position to make this unit more definite because we have found expressions believed to be physically significant in which the whole energy-tensor and electromagnetic energy-tensor occur in unforced combination. Thus according to (100·6) Weyl's constant α in § 90 is 4, so that $\beta = 1/2\lambda$. Accordingly in (90·51) we have the combination

$$8\pi T^{\mu\nu} - \frac{1}{\lambda} E^{\mu\nu},$$

which can scarcely be significant unless it represents the difference of the two tensors reduced to a common unit. It appears therefore that in an electromagnetic field we must have

$$E^{\mu\nu} = 8\pi\lambda T^{\mu\nu} = -\lambda \{G^{\mu\nu} - \tfrac{1}{2} g^{\mu\nu} (G - 2\lambda)\},$$

where $E^{\mu\nu}$ is expressed in terms of the natural unit involved in $F_{\mu\nu}$. The underlying hypothesis is that in $^*G_{\mu\nu}$ the metrical and electrical variables occur in their natural combination.

The constant λ, which determines the radius of curvature of the world, is unknown; but since our knowledge of the stellar universe extends nearly to 10^{25} cm., we shall adopt

$$\lambda = 10^{-50} \text{ cm.}^{-2}$$

It may be much smaller.

Consider an electrostatic field of 1500 volts per cm., or 5 electrostatic units. The density of the energy is $5^2/8\pi$ or practically 1 erg per cubic cm. The mass is obtained by dividing by the square of the velocity of light, viz. $1{\cdot}1 \,.\, 10^{-21}$ gm. We transform this into gravitational units by remembering that the sun's mass, $1{\cdot}99 \,.\, 10^{33}$ gm, is equivalent to $1{\cdot}47 \,.\, 10^{5}$ cm. Hence we find—

The gravitational mass-density T_4^4 of an electric field of 1500 volts per cm. is $8{\cdot}4 \,.\, 10^{-50}$ cm. per c.c.

According to the equation $E^{\mu\nu} = 8\pi\lambda T^{\mu\nu}$ we shall have

$$E_4^4 = 2{\cdot}1 \,.\, 10^{-98} \text{ cm.}^{-4}.$$

For an electrostatic field along the axis of x in Galilean coordinates we have

$$E_4^4 = \tfrac{1}{2} F_{14}^2,$$

so that

$$F_{14} = 2 \,.\, 10^{-49}$$

in terms of the centimetre. The centimetre is not directly concerned as a gauge since F_{14} is an in-tensor; but the coordinates have been taken as Galilean, and accordingly the centimetre is also the width of the unit mesh.

Hence an electric force of 1500 volts per cm is expressed in natural measure by the number $2 \,.\, 10^{-49}$ referred to a Galilean coordinate-system with a centimetre mesh.

Let us take two rods of length l at a distance δx_1 cm. apart and maintain them at a difference of potential $\delta\kappa_4$ for a time δx_4 (centimetres). Compare their lengths at the beginning and end of the experiment. If they are all the time subject to parallel displacement in space and time there should be a discrepancy δl between the two comparisons, given by (84·4)

$$\begin{aligned} \frac{\delta l}{l} &= \tfrac{1}{2} F_{\mu\nu} dS^{\mu\nu} \\ &= F_{41}\, \delta x_1\, \delta x_4 \\ &= \frac{\partial \kappa_4}{\partial x_1} \delta x_1\, \delta x_4 = \delta\kappa_4\, \delta x_4. \end{aligned}$$

For example if our rods are of metre-length and maintained for a year (1 light-year $= 10^{18}$ cm.) at a potential difference of $1\frac{1}{2}$ million volts, the discrepancy is

$$\begin{aligned} \delta l &= 10^2 \,.\, 2 \,.\, 10^{-49} \,.\, 10^3 \,.\, 10^{18} \text{ cm.} \\ &= 2 \,.\, 10^{-26} \text{ cm} \end{aligned}$$

We have already concluded that the length of a rod is not determined by parallel displacement; but it would clearly be impossible to detect the discrepancy experimentally if it were so determined.

The value of F_{14} depends on the unit mesh of the coordinate-system. If we take a mesh of width 10^{25} cm and therefore comparable with the assumed radius of the world the value must be multiplied by 10^{50} in accordance with the law of transformation of a covariant tensor. Hence referred to this natural mesh-system the natural unit of electric force is about 75 volts per cm. The result rests on our adopted radius of space, and the unit may well be less than

75 volts per cm. but can scarcely be larger. It is puzzling to find that the natural unit is of the size encountered in laboratory experiments; we should have expected it to be of the order of the intensity at the boundary of an electron. This difficulty raises some doubt as to whether we are quite on the right track.

The result may be put in another form which is less open to doubt. Imagine the whole spherical world filled with an electric field of about 75 volts per cm. for the time during which a ray of light travels round the world. The electromagnetic action is expressed by an invariant which is a pure number independent of gauge and coordinate systems; and the total amount of action for this case is of the order of magnitude of the number 1. The natural unit of action is evidently considerably larger than the quantum. With the radius of the world here used I find that it is 10^{115} quanta.

103. Conclusion.

We may now review the general physical results which have been established or rendered plausible in the course of our work. The numbers in brackets refer to the sections in which the points are discussed.

We offer no explanation of the occurrence of electrons or of quanta; but in other respects the theory appears to cover fairly adequately the phenomena of physics. The excluded domain forms a large part of modern physics, but it is one in which all explanation has apparently been baffled hitherto. The domain here surveyed covers a system of natural laws fairly complete in itself and detachable from the excluded phenomena, although at one point difficulties arise since it comes into close contact with the problem of the nature of the electron.

We have been engaged in *world-building*—the construction of a world which shall operate under the same laws as the natural world around us. The most fundamental part of the problem falls under two heads, the building-material and the process of building.

The building-material. There is little satisfaction to the builder in the mere assemblage of selected material already possessing the properties which will appear in the finished structure. Our desire is to achieve the purpose with unselected material. In the game of world-building we lose a point whenever we have to ask for extraordinary material specially prepared for the end in view. Considering the most general kind of relation-structure which we have been able to imagine—provided always that it is *a structure*—we have found that there will always exist as building-material an in-tensor $*G_{\mu\nu}$ consisting of symmetrical and antisymmetrical parts $R_{\mu\nu}$ and $F_{\mu\nu}$, the latter being the curl of a vector (97, 98). This is all that we shall require for the domain of physics not excluded above.

The process of building. Here from the nature of the case it is impossible to avoid trespassing for a moment beyond the bounds of physics. The world which we have to build from the crude material is the world of perception, and the process of building must depend on the nature of the percipient Many things may be built out of $*G_{\mu\nu}$, but they will only appear in the perceptual world if the percipient is interested in them We cannot exclude the consideration of what kind of things are likely to appeal to the percipient The building process of the mathematical theory must keep step with that process by which the mind of the percipient endows with vivid qualities certain selected structural properties of the world. We have found reason to believe that this creative action of the mind follows closely the mathematical process of Hamiltonian differentiation of an invariant (64).

In one sense deductive theory is the enemy of experimental physics The latter is always striving to settle by crucial tests the nature of the fundamental things; the former strives to minimise the successes obtained by showing how wide a nature of things is compatible with all experimental results. We have called on all the evidence available in an attempt to discover what is the exact invariant whose Hamiltonian differentiation provides the principal quantities recognised in physics It is of great importance to determine it, since on it depend the formulae for the law of gravitation, the mass, energy, and momentum and other important quantities It seems impossible to decide this question without appeal to a perhaps dubious principle of simplicity; and it has seemed a flaw in the argument that we have not been able to exclude more definitely the complex alternatives (62). But is it not rather an unhoped for success for the deductive theory that all the observed consequences follow without requiring an arbitrary selection of a particular invariant?

We have shown that the physical things created by Hamiltonian differentiation must in virtue of mathematical identities have certain properties. When the antisymmetric part $F_{\mu\nu}$ of the in-tensor is not taken into account, they have the property of conservation or permanence; and it is thus that mass, energy and momentum arise (61). When $F_{\mu\nu}$ is included, its modifying effect on these mechanical phenomena shows that it will manifest itself after the manner of electric and magnetic force acting respectively on the charge-component and current-components of a stream-vector (100). Thus the part played by $F_{\mu\nu}$ in the phenomena becomes assigned

All relations of space and time are comprised in the in-invariant $*G_{\mu\nu}dx_\mu dx_\nu$, which expresses an absolute relation (the *interval*) between two points with coordinate differences dx_μ (97) To understand why this expresses space and time, we have to examine the principles of measurement of space and time by material or optical apparatus (95) It is shown that the conventions of measurement introduce an isotropy and homogeneity into measured space which need not originally have any counterpart in the relation-structure which is being surveyed This isotropy and homogeneity is exactly expressed by Einstein's law of gravitation (66).

The transition from the spatio-temporal relation of interval to space and time as a framework of location is made by choosing a coordinate-frame such that the quadratic form $*G_{\mu\nu}dx_\mu dx_\nu$ breaks up into the sum of four squares (4). It is a property of the world, which we have had to leave unexplained, that the sign of one of these squares is opposite to that of the other three (9); the coordinate so distinguished is called time. Since the resolution into four squares can be made in many ways, the space-time frame is necessarily indeterminate, and the Lorentz transformation connecting the spaces and times of different observers is immediately obtained (5). This gives rise to the *special* theory of relativity. It is a further consequence that there will exist a definite speed which is absolute (6); and disturbances of the tensor $F_{\mu\nu}$ (electromagnetic waves) are propagated in vacuum with this speed (74). The resolution into four squares is usually only possible in an infinitesimal region so that a world-wide frame of space and time as strictly defined does not exist. Latitude is, however, given by the concession that a space-time frame may be used which does not fulfil the strict definition, observed discrepancies being then attributed to a field of force (16). Owing to this latitude the space-time frame becomes entirely indeterminate; any system of coordinates may be described as a frame of space and time, and no one system can be considered superior since all alike require a field of force to justify them. Hence arises the *general* theory of relativity.

The law of gravitation in continuous matter is most directly obtained from the identification of the energy-tensor of matter (54), and this gives again the law for empty space as a particular case. This mode of approach is closely connected with the previous deduction of the law in empty space from the isotropic properties introduced by the processes of measurement, since the components of the energy-tensor are identified with coefficients of the quadric of curvature (65). To deduce the field of a particle (38) or the motion of a particle in the field (56), we have to postulate symmetrical properties of the particle (or average particle); but these arise not from the particle itself but because it provides the standard of symmetry in measurement (66). It is then shown that the Newtonian attraction is accounted for (39), as well as the refinements introduced by Einstein in calculating the perihelion of Mercury (40) and the deflection of light (41).

It is possible to discuss mechanics without electrodynamics but scarcely possible to discuss electrodynamics without mechanics. Hence a certain difficulty arises in our treatment of electricity, because the natural linking of the two subjects is through the excluded domain of electron-structure. In practice electric and magnetic forces are defined through their mechanical effects on charges and currents, and these mechanical effects have been investigated in general terms (100) and with particular reference to the electron (80). One half of Maxwell's equations is satisfied because $F_{\mu\nu}$ is the curl of a vector (92), and the other half amounts to the identification of $F^{\mu\nu}_{\nu}$ with the charge-and-current vector (73). The electromagnetic energy-tensor as deduced is found to agree in Galilean coordinates with the classical formulae (77).

Since a field of force is relative to the frame of space-time which is used, potential energy can no longer be treated on the same footing with kinetic energy It is not represented by a tensor (59) and becomes reduced to an artificial expression appearing in a mathematical mode of treatment which is no longer regarded as the simplest. Although the importance of "action" is enhanced on account of its invariance, the principle of least action loses in status since it is incapable of sufficiently wide generalisation (60, 63).

In order that material bodies may be on a definite scale of size there must be a curvature of the world in empty space. Whereas the differential equations governing the form of the world are plainly indicated, the integrated form is not definitely known since it depends on the unknown density of distribution of matter. Two forms have been given (67), Einstein's involving a large quantity of matter and de Sitter's a small quantity (69); but whereas in the latter the quantity of matter is regarded as accidental, in the former it is fixed in accordance with a definite law (71). This law at present seems mysterious, but it is perhaps not out of keeping with natural anticipations of future developments of the theory. On the other hand the evidence of the spiral nebulae possibly favours de Sitter's form which dispenses with the mysterious law (70).

Can the theory of relativity ultimately be extended to account in the same manner for the phenomena of the excluded domain of physics, to which the laws of atomicity at present bar the entrance? On the one hand it would seem an idle exaggeration to claim that the magnificent conception of Einstein is necessarily the key to all the riddles of the universe; on the other hand we have no reason to think that all the consequences of this conception have become apparent in a few short years. It may be that the laws of atomicity arise only in the presentation of the world to us, according to some extension of the principles of identification and of measurement. But it is perhaps as likely that, after the relativity theory has cleared away to the utmost the superadded laws which arise solely in our mode of apprehension of the world about us, there will be left an external world developing under specialised laws of behaviour.

The physicist who explores nature conducts experiments He handles material structures, sends rays of light from point to point, marks coincidences, and performs mathematical operations on the numbers which he obtains His result is a physical quantity, which, he believes, stands for something in the condition of the world. In a sense this is true, for whatever is actually occurring in the outside world is only accessible to our knowledge in so far as it helps to determine the results of these experimental operations. But we must not suppose that a law obeyed by the physical quantity necessarily has its seat in the world-condition which that quantity "stands for"; its origin may be disclosed by unravelling the series of operations of which the physical quantity is the result Results of measurement are the subject-matter of physics, and the moral of the theory of relativity is that we can only comprehend what the physical quantities *stand for* if we first comprehend what they *are*.

BIBLIOGRAPHY

The following is the classical series of papers leading up to the present state of the theory.

B. RIEMANN Über die Hypothesen, welche der Geometrie zu Grunde liegen, *Abhandlungen d K Gesells. zu Göttingen*, 13, p 133 (Habilitationsschrift, 1854)

H. A. LORENTZ Versuch einer Theorie der elektrischen und optischen Erscheinungen in bewegten Körpern. (Leiden, 1895)

J. LARMOR Aether and Matter, Chap XI (Cambridge, 1900)

H. A. LORENTZ Electromagnetic phenomena in a system moving with any velocity smaller than that of light, *Proc Amsterdam Acad*, 6, p 809 (1904).

A. EINSTEIN Zur Electrodynamik bewegter Körpern, *Ann d Physik*, 17, p 891 (1905).

H MINKOWSKI Raum und Zeit (Lecture at Cologne, 21 September, 1908.)

A. EINSTEIN. Über den Einfluss der Schwerkraft auf die Ausbreitung des Lichtes, *Ann d. Physik*, 35, p 898 (1911).

A EINSTEIN Die Grundlage der allgemeinen Relativitätstheorie, *Ann. d. Physik*, 49, p 769 (1916).

A EINSTEIN Kosmologische Betrachtungen zur allgemeinen Relativitätstheorie, *Berlin Sitzungsberichte*, 1917, p 142

H. WEYL Gravitation und Elektrizität, *Berlin Sitzungsberichte*, 1918, p 465.

The pure differential geometry used in the theory is based on

M. M G RICCI and T LEVI-CIVITA Méthodes de calcul différentiel absolu et leurs applications, *Math Ann*, 54, p 125 (1901)

T. LEVI-CIVITA Nozione di parallelismo in una varietà qualunque, *Rend del Circ Mat di Palermo*, 42, p 173 (1917).

A useful review of the subject is given by J. E Wright, Invariants of Quadratic Differential Forms (Camb Math. Tracts, No 9) Reference may also be made to J. Knoblauch, Differentialgeometrie (Teubner, Leipzig). W Blaschke, Vorlesungen über Differentialgeometrie (Springer, Berlin), promises a comprehensive treatment with special reference to Einstein's applications; but only the first volume has yet appeared

From the very numerous papers and books on the Theory of Relativity, I select the following as most likely to be helpful on particular points, or as of importance in the historic development. Where possible the subject-matter is indicated by references to the sections in this book chiefly concerned.

E CUNNINGHAM Relativity and the Electron Theory (Longmans, 1921). (Particularly full treatment of experimental foundations of the theory.)

T. DE DONDER. La Gravifique Einsteinienne, *Ann. de l'Obs. Royal de Belgique*, 3rd Ser , 1, p 75 (1921).

(Recommended as an example of treatment differing widely from that here chosen, but with equivalent conclusions See especially his electromagnetic theory in Chap v)

J DROSTE The Field of *n* moving centres on Einstein's Theory, *Proc. Amsterdam Acad*, 19, p 447 (1916), § 44

A S EDDINGTON. A generalisation of Weyl's Theory of the Electromagnetic and Gravitational Fields, *Proc Roy. Soc*, A 99, p. 104 (1921) §§ 91—97.

A EINSTEIN Über Gravitationswellen, *Berlin Sitzungsberichte*, 1918, p 154 § 57.

L. P. EISENHART and O. VEBLEN. The Riemann Geometry and its Generalisation, *Proc. Nat. Acad. Sci.*, 8, p. 19 (1922). §§ 84, 91.

A. D. FOKKER. The Geodesic Precession; a consequence of Einstein's Theory of Gravitation, *Proc. Amsterdam Acad.*, 23, p. 729 (1921). § 44.

A. E. HARWARD. The Identical Relations in Einstein's Theory, *Phil. Mag.*, 44, p. 380 (1922). § 52.

G. HERGLOTZ. Über die Mechanik des deformierbaren Körpers vom Standpunkte der Relativitätstheorie, *Ann. d. Physik*, 36, p. 493 (1911). § 53.

H. HILBERT. Die Grundlagen der Physik, *Göttingen Nachrichten*, 1915, p. 395; 1917, p. 53. § 61.

G. B. JEFFERY. The Field of an Electron on Einstein's Theory of Gravitation, *Proc. Roy. Soc.*, A 99, p. 123 (1921). § 78.

E. KASNER. Finite representation of the Solar Gravitational Field in Flat Space of Six Dimensions, *Amer. Journ. Mathematics*, 43, p. 130 (1921). § 65.

F. KLEIN. Über die Integralform der Erhaltungssätze und die Theorie der räumlichgeschlossenen Welt, *Göttingen Nachrichten*, 1918, p. 394. §§ 67, 70.

J. LARMOR. Questions in physical indetermination, *C. R. du Congrès International, Strasbourg* (1920).

T. LEVI-CIVITA. Statica Einsteiniana, *Rend. dei Lincei*, 26 (1), p. 458 (1917).

—— ds^2 Einsteiniani in Campi Newtoniani, *Rend. dei Lincei*, 26 (2), p. 307; 27 (1), p. 3; 27 (2), p. 183, etc. (1917–19).

H. A. LORENTZ. On Einstein's Theory of Gravitation, *Proc. Amsterdam Acad.*, 19, p. 1341, 20, p. 2 (1916).

G. MIE. Grundlagen einer Theorie der Materie, *Ann. d. Physik*, 37, p. 511; 39, p. 1; 40, p. 1 (1912–13).

G. NORDSTRÖM. On the Energy of the Gravitational Field in Einstein's Theory, *Proc. Amsterdam Acad.*, 20, p. 1238 (1918). §§ 43, 59, 78.

—— Calculation of some special cases in Einstein's Theory of Gravitation, *Proc. Amsterdam Acad.*, 21, p. 68 (1918). § 72.

A. A. ROBB. A Theory of Time and Space (Cambridge, 1914). § 98.

J. A. SCHOUTEN. Die direkte Analysis zur neueren Relativitätstheorie, *Verhandelingen Amsterdam Acad.*, 12 (1919).

—— On the arising of a Precession-motion owing to the non-Euclidean linear element, *Proc. Amsterdam Acad.*, 21, p. 533 (1918). § 44.

K. SCHWARZSCHILD. Über das Gravitationsfeld eines Massenpunktes nach der Einsteinschen Theorie, *Berlin Sitzungsberichte*, 1916, p. 189. § 38.

—— Über das Gravitationsfeld einer Kugel aus incompressibler Flüssigkeit, *Berlin Sitzungsberichte*, 1916, p. 424. § 72.

W. DE SITTER. On Einstein's Theory of Gravitation and its Astronomical Consequences, *Monthly Notices, R.A.S.*, 76, p. 699; 77, p. 155; 78, p. 3 (1916–17). §§ 44, 67–70.

H. WEYL. Über die physikalischen Grundlagen der erweiterten Relativitätstheorie, *Phys. Zeits.*, 22, p. 473 (1921).

—— Feld und Materie, *Ann. d. Physik*, 65, p. 541 (1921).

—— Die Einzigartigkeit der Pythagoreischen Massbestimmung, *Math. Zeits.*, 12, p. 114 (1922). § 97.

On two of these papers received whilst this book was in the press I may specially comment. Harward's paper contains a direct proof of "the four identities" more elegant than my proof in § 52. The paper of Eisenhart and Veblen suggests that, instead of basing the geometry of a continuum on Levi-Civita's conception of parallel displacement, we should base it on a specification of continuous tracks in all directions. This leads to Weyl's geometry (*not* the generalisation of Chap. VII, Part II). This would seem to be the most logical mode of approach to Weyl's theory, revealing clearly that it is essentially an analysis of physical phenomena as related to a reference-frame consisting of the tracks of moving particles and light-pulses—two of the most universal methods of practical exploration. Einstein's theory on the other hand is an analysis of the phenomena as related to a metrical frame marked out by transport of material objects. In both theories the phenomena are studied in relation to certain experimental avenues of exploration; but the possible existence of such means of exploration, being (directly or indirectly) a fundamental postulate of these theories, cannot be further elucidated by them. It is here that the generalised theory of § 91 adds its contribution, showing that the most general type of relation-structure yet formulated will necessarily contain within itself both Einstein's metric and Weyl's track-framework.

INDEX

The numbers refer to pages

Absolute change 69, physical quantities 5 (footnote); properties of a region 205; rotation 99
Abstract geometry and natural geometry 37
Acceleration of light-pulse 91; of charged particle 189; determined by symmetrical condition 192
Action, material or gravitational 137; electromagnetic 187; Weyl's formula 209, 231; numerical values of 237
Action, principle of Stationary 139, 147
Addition of velocities 18, 21, 22
Adjustment and persistence 208
Aether 224
Affine geometry 214
Angle between two vectors 58
Antisymmetrical tensors 67; of fourth rank 107
Aspect, relation of 49
Associated tensors 56
Atom, time of vibration of 91; in de Sitter's world 157, 161
Atomicity 120 (footnote), 139, 146

$B^{\epsilon}_{\mu\nu\sigma}$ (Riemann-Christoffel tensor) 72, 226
Bifurcation of geometry and electrodynamics 223

Canonical coordinates 79
Centrifugal force 38
Charge, electric, conservation of 173; invariance of 174
Charge-and-current vector 172; general existence of 230
Christoffel's 3-index symbols 58; generalisation of 203
Clocks, transport of 15, 27
Comparability of proximate relations 225
Components, covariant and contravariant 57
Composition of velocities 21, 22
Condition of the world 3, 47
Configuration of events 10
Conservation, formal law of 134
Conservation of momentum and mass 30; of energy 32; of matter 33; of electric charge 173
Constitutive equations 34, 195
Continuity, equation of 117; in electric flow 173
Continuous matter, gravitation in 101, 119
Contracted derivative (divergence) 113; second derivative (□) 64
Contraction, FitzGerald 25
Contraction of tensors 53
Contravariant vectors 43, 44; tensors 52; derivatives 62
Coordinate-systems, rectangular 13; Galilean 38, canonical 79, natural 80; proper 80; statical 81; isotropic 93
Coordinates 9, general transformation of 34, 43; representation of displacement 49; difficulty in the introduction of 225
Covariant derivative of vector 60; of tensor 62, 65; of invariant 63, utility of 63; significance of 68
Covariant vector 43; tensor 52
Creation of the physical world 147, 230, 238
Curl 67
Current, electric 172
Curvature, Gaussian 82, of 4-dimensional manifold 149; radius of spherical 151; quadric of 152
Curvature of light-tracks 91
Cylindrical world 155

Deductive theory and experiment 105
Deflection of light 90
Density, Lorentz transformation of 33; definitions of proper- 121
Density, scalar- and tensor- 111; invariant- 205
Derivative, covariant 60, 62, 65; contravariant 62; significance of 68; in-covariant 203
de Sitter's spherical world 155, 161
Determinants, manipulation of 107
Differentiation, covariant, rules for 65. *See also* Derivative
Differentiation of summed expression 75
Dimensions, principle of 48, 54
Dimensions, world of 3+1 25; reason for four 206
Displacement 49
Displacement, parallel 70, 213
Displacement of spectral lines to red, in sun 91; in nebulae 157, 161
Distance *See* Length
Divergence of a tensor 113; of energy-tensor 115, 119; of Hamiltonian derivative of an invariant 141
Dummy suffixes 51
Dynamical velocity 120, 125
Dynamics of a particle 125

$E_{\mu\nu}$ (electromagnetic energy-tensor) 181
Eclipse results 91
Einstein's cylindrical world 155, 166
Einstein's law of gravitation 81; in continuous matter 101, 119; interpretation of 154; alternatives to 143; equivalent to the gauging-equation 221
Electric charge, conservation of 173; invariance of 174
Electromagnetic action 187; energy-tensor 182; force 171, potential 171, signals 28, volume 194, waves, propagation of 175
Electron, non-Maxwellian stresses in 183; gravitational field of 185; acceleration in electromagnetic field 189; size of 192, magnetic constitution of 211
Elements of inner planets 89
Elliptical space 157
Empty space 221
Energy, identified with mass 32
Energy, potential 135
Energy-tensor of matter 116, 141; of electromagnetic field 182; obtained by Hamiltonian differentiation 147, 229
Entropy 34
Equivalence, Principle of 41
Equivalence of displacements 213, 226
Experiment and deductive theory 105
Explanation of phenomena, ideal 106
Extension and location 9

$F_{\mu\nu}$ (electromagnetic force) 171, 219
Fields of force 37
Finiteness of space 156
FitzGerald contraction 25
Fizeau's experiment 21
Flat space-time 16; condition for 76
Flux 67; gravitational 144; electromagnetic 192, 232
Force, covariant and contravariant components 50; expressed by 3-index symbols 122
Force, electromagnetic 171, Lorentz transformation of 179; mechanical force due to 180, 189, 229
Foucault's pendulum 99
Four dimensions of world 206
Fraunhofer lines, displacement of 91
Fresnel's convection-coefficient 21
Fundamental theorem of mechanics 115
Fundamental velocity 19; tensors 55, 79; invariants 141

$G_{\mu\nu}$ (Einstein tensor) 81
Galilean coordinates 38
Gauge-system 200, 217
Gauging-equation 219
Gaussian curvature 82, 151
Generalisation of Weyl's theory 213
Generalised volume 206, 232
Geodesic, equations of 60; produced by parallel displacement 71
Geodesic curvature 91
Geometry, Riemannian 11; abstract and natural 37; world geometry 198; affine geometry 214
German letters, denoting tensor-densities 111
Graphical representation 196
Gravitation 38. *See also* Einstein's law
Gravitation, Newtonian constant of 128
Gravitational field of a particle 82, of an electron 185
Gravitational flux 144
Gravitational mass of sun 87; equality with inertial mass 130, 145
Group 47

$\mathfrak{H}$ (Hamiltonian operator) 139
h_μ (ponderomotive force) 181
Hamiltonian derivative 139; of fundamental invariants 141; of electromagnetic action 187; of general world-invariants 228; creative aspect of 147, 230, 238
Homogeneous sphere, problem of 168
Horizon of world 101, 157, 165
Hydrodynamics, equations of 117, 118
Hydrostatic pressure 121

Identification, Principle of 119, 222
Identities satisfied by $G_{\mu\nu}$ 95, 115
Ignoration of coordinates 233
Imaginary intervals 12
In- (prefix) 202
Incompressibility 112, 122
In-covariant derivative 203
Indicatrix 150
Inductive theory 105
Inertia, elementary treatment 29; electromagnetic origin of 183
Inertial frame, precession of 99
Inertial mass 128; equal to gravitational mass 130, 145
In-invariants 205, 232
Inner multiplication 53
Integrability of parallel displacement 73; of length and direction 198
Intensity and quantity 111
In-tensors 202; fundamental 215
Interval 10
Invariant 30; formation of 58
Invariant density (proper-density) 121
Invariant-density (scalar-density) 111
Invariant mass 30, 183
Isotropic coordinates 93

J_μ (charge-and-current vector) 172
Jacobian 108

Kepler's third law 89
Kinematical velocity 120, 125

Lagrange's equations 132
Lagrangian function 131, 233

Length, definition of 1, 217 ; measurement of 11 ; non-integrability of 198
Length of a vector 57
Light, velocity of 19, 23 ; deflection in gravitational field 90 ; propagation of 175
Light-pulse, equation of track 37 ; in curved world 163 ; in-invariant equation 220
Location and extension 9
Longitudinal mass 31
Lorentz transformation 17, 25 ; for electromagnetic force 179

$M_{\mu\nu}$ (material energy-tensor) 181
Macroscopic electromagnetic equations 194
Magnetic constitution of electron 211
Manufacture of physical quantities 1
Mass, invariant and relative 30, 183 ; gravitational and inertial 128, 130, 145 ; electromagnetic 193
Mass, variation with velocity 30 ; identified with energy 32, of electromagnetic field 183
Mass of the world, total 166
Mass-horizon of world 165
Mathematics contrasted with physics 1
Matter, conservation of 33 ; identification of 119, 146
Maxwell's equations 172 ; second order corrections to 234
Measure of interval 11
Measure-code 2, 48
Measurement, principle of 220, 238
Mechanical force of electromagnetic field 180, explanation of 189 ; general theory of 229
Mercury, perihelion of 89
Mesh-system 9
Metric, introduction of 216 ; sole character of space and time 221
Michelson-Morley experiment 19
Mixed tensors 52
Momentum, elementary treatment 29 , conservation of 118 , electromagnetic 183
Moon, motion of 95
Multiplication, inner and outer 53

Natural coordinates 80; gauge 206, 219; geometry 38, 196; measure 80
Nebulae, velocities of 162
Non-integrability of length and direction 198
Non-Maxwellian stresses 182, 184
Non-Riemannian geometry 197
Normal, 6-dimensional 151
Null-cone 22
Number of electrons in the world 167
Numerical value of quantum 237

Operators, $\square$ 64, $\natural$ 139
Orbits of planets 85
Order, coordinate agreeing with structural 225

Parallel displacement 70, 213
Parallelogram-law 214
Parallelogramical property 226
Particle, motion of 36; gravitational field of 82, 100; dynamics of 125, symmetry of 125, 155
Percipient, determines natural laws by selection 238
Perigee, advance of 99
Perihelion, advance of 88; in curved world 100
Permanence 115
Permeability, magnetic 195, 234
Perpendicularity of vectors 57
Persistence and adjustment 208
Physical quantities 1; definition of 3
Planetary orbits 85
Point-electron 186
Ponderomotive force. *See* Mechanical force
Postulates, list of 104
Potential, gravitational 59, 124; electromagnetic 171, 175, 201
Potential energy 135, 148
Poynting's vector 183
Precession of inertial frame 99
Pressure, hydrostatic 121, in homogeneous sphere 169
Principle of dimensions 48, 54, of equivalence 41, of identification 119, 222; of least action 139, 147, 209, of measurement 220, 238
Problem of two bodies 95, of rotating disc 112; of homogeneous sphere 168
Product, inner and outer 53
Propagation of gravitational waves 130; of electromagnetic waves 175
Propagation with unit velocity 64; solution of equation 178
Proper- (prefix) 34. *See* Invariant mass *and* Density
Proper-coordinates 80
Proper-time 87
Proper-volume 110
Pseudo-energy-tensor 135
Pseudo-vector 179

Quadratic formula for interval 10, justification of 224
Quadric of curvature 152
Quantity and intensity 111
Quantum, excluded from coordinate calculations 225, numerical value of 237
Quotient law 54

$R_{\mu\nu}$ (gauging-tensor) 219
Rapidity 22
Recession of spiral nebulae 157, 161
Rectangular coordinates and time 13
Red-shift of spectral lines in sun 91; in nebulae 157, 161
Relation-structure 224
Relativity of physical quantities 5
Retardation of moving clocks 16, 26
Retarded potential 179
Riemann-Christoffel tensor 72; vanishing of 73, 76; importance of 79; generalisation of 204, 215

Riemannian geometry 11
Rotating axes, quadratic form for 35
Rotating disc 112
Rotation, absolute 99

Scalar 52
Scalar-density 111
Self-perpendicular vector 57
Simultaneity at different places 27
de Sitter's spherical world 155, 161
Space, a network of intervals 158
Spacelike intervals 22
Special theory of relativity 16
Spectral lines, displacement in sun 91, in nebulae 157, 161
Sphere, problem of homogeneous 168
Spherical curvature, radius of 151
Spherical world 155, 161
Spiral nebulae, velocities of 162
Spur 58
Static coordinates 81
Stationary action, principle of 139, 147, 209
Stokes's theorem 67; application of 214
Stress-system 117, gravitational field due to 104, electromagnetic 183, non-Maxwellian 184
Structure, represented by relations 224
Substitution-operator 51, 55
Suffixes, raising and lowering of 56
Summation convention 50
Sun, gravitational mass of 87
Surface-element 66; in-invariant pertaining to 232
Symmetry, a relative attribute 155; of a particle 125, 155; of an electron 192

$T_{\mu\nu}$ (energy-tensor) 102, 116
Temperature 34
Tensor 51
Tensor-density 111
Tensor equations 49
Things 221
Three-index symbol 58; contracted 74; generalised 203, 218
Time, definition of 14; convention in reckoning 15, 29, immediate consciousness of 23; extended meaning 39
Timelike intervals 22
Track of moving particle and light-pulse 36
Transformation of coordinates, Lorentz 17, general 34, 43
Transport of clocks 15, 27
Two bodies, problem of 95

Uniform vector-field 73, mesh-system 77
Unit, change of 48; of action 237

Vector 43; mathematical notion of 44; physical notion of 47
Velocity, fundamental 19
Velocity of light 19, in moving matter 21, in sun's gravitational field 93
Velocity-vector 71
Volume, physical and geometrical 110, electromagnetic 194, generalised 206, 232
Volume-element 109

Wave-equation, solution of 178
Waves, gravitational 130; electromagnetic 175
Weyl's theory 198; modified view of 208
World, shape of 155; mass of 160, 166
World geometry 198
World-invariants, dynamical properties of 228
World-line 125

Zero-length of light tracks 199

Printed in February 2023
by Rotomail Italia S.p.A., Vignate (MI) - Italy